TORTS

By

STEVEN R. FINZ

Director
Advance College of Continuing Legal Education
The Sea Ranch, California

THE PROFESSOR SERIES

Published by

emanuel®

Torts, 1st Edition (1982, 2000)
Emanuel Publishing Corp. • 1328 Boston Post Road • Larchmont, NY 10538

By EMANUEL PUBLISHING CORP.
1328 BOSTON POST ROAD
LARCHMONT, NY 10538

ISBN 1-56542-178-7

AUTHOR'S NOTE

This is not a book of canned briefs. Many of the Examples used in this outline are based on the decisions in actual cases. When this is so, the cases are cited.

Frequently, however, I have changed the facts to illustrate better the point which I was making.

The Examples used by me are not intended to be, and should not be used as, a substitute for reading the cases cited. The student should study all the cases and form his/her own judgments about them.

Steven R. Finz

TABLE OF CONTENTS

CHAPTER 3

AFFIRMATIVE DEFENSES TO INTENTIONAL TORTS

CHAPTER 4

NEGLIGENCE

CHAPTER 5

AFFIRMATIVE DEFENSES

CHAPTER 6

STRICT LIABILITY

CHAPTER 7

PROXIMATE CAUSE

CHAPTER 8

DAMAGE

CHAPTER 9

VICARIOUS LIABILITY

CHAPTER 10

NUISANCE

CHAPTER 11

MISREPRESENTATION

CHAPTER 12

INTERFERENCE WITH BUSINESS ADVANTAGE

CHAPTER 13

PRODUCTS LIABILITY

CHAPTER 14

DEFAMATION

CHAPTER 15

TORTS RELATED TO DEFAMATION

CHAPTER 16

INVASION OF PRIVACY

CHAPTER 17

MISUSE OF JUDICIAL PROCEDURE

CHAPTER 18

IMMUNITIES

CAPSULE SUMMARY

This Capsule Summary is intended for review at the end of the semester. Reading it is not a substitute for mastering the material in the main outline. The order of topics is occasionally somewhat different from that in the main outline; that's because this Capsule Summary is meant to be a separate outline for night-before-the exam review, not just be a summary of the main outline.

CHAPTER 1
INTRODUCTION AND ANALYSIS

I. DEFINITIONS

A. **Tort**: A tort is a violation of an obligation which one individual owes to another without regard to promises. [1]

B. **Statutory law**: Laws created by the legislature are called statutes. In recent years, statutory law has played an increasingly important role in shaping the law of torts. Since statutes usually vary from one state to another, however, this outline will not discuss statutes except in general terms. [2]

C. **Common law**: The body of rules derived from tradition and the judicial interpretation of statutes is known as the common law. [2-3]

II. TORT LIABILITY

A. **Three factors**: In most tort cases, it is necessary to consider three factors in deciding whether liability should attach: (1) basis of liability; (2) proximate causation and damage; and (3) the effect of affirmative defenses. [3]

1. **Basis of Liability**: Conduct may be liability-forming because of the defendant's fault or, under some circumstances, without regard to fault. [3]

   a. **Fault**: The fault requirement may be satisfied by intent, negligence, or aggravated negligence (*i.e.*, recklessness). [3]

   b. **Liability without fault (strict liability)**: In certain circumstances, tort law imposes liability without regard to defendant's fault or lack thereof. [4]

2. **Proximate cause and damage**: With only a few exceptions, tort liability is not imposed unless the plaintiff sustains actual damage and shows that the damage was proximately caused by defendant's conduct. [5]

3. **Affirmative defenses**: An affirmative defense is an argument which, although unrelated to the essential elements of the plaintiff's case, may prevent the defendant from being held liable to the plaintiff. [6]

B. **The "big picture"**: It is necessary to remember that all three factors must be considered in deciding whether liability should be imposed. [6]

CHAPTER 2

TORTS INVOLVING INTENT

I. GENERAL CONCEPT

A. Definition: In general, tortious intent is the desire (or knowledge to a substantial degree of certainty) that harm result from the defendant's volitional act. [7]

B. Distinguished from volition: Volition (*i.e.*, voluntariness) is the desire to perform a particular physical act or the desire to use muscles in a particular way. [7]

C. Distinguished from motive: Motive is the reason for desiring to bring about a particular consequence. [7]

D. Element of tort: The fact that a defendant had a tortious intent is not alone sufficient to result in liability. It is necessary that the intent be coupled with some act which results in a consequence for which the law of torts provides a remedy. [7]

E. Intentional invasions of person and property distinguished: "Intent" has a different meaning in each of the intentional torts. In general, however, the intent required in a tort based on intentional invasion of the person is a desire (or knowledge to a substantial certainty) that the plaintiff's right be invaded. On the other hand, the intent required in a tort based on intentional invasion of property is a desire (or knowledge to a substantial certainty) that the defendant's conduct affect the property involved. [8]

F. Liability of infants and insane persons: If a defendant has the requisite intent, liability will be imposed regardless of his age or state of mental health. [8]

II. BATTERY

A. General concept: Battery is an invasion of the right to be free of intentional and harmful or offensive physical touching. [8]

B. Essential elements: The essential elements of battery are (1) intent; and (2) harmful or offensive contact with plaintiff. [8]

1. **Intent**: In a battery case, intent is a desire (or knowledge to a substantial degree of certainty) that the defendant's act cause the plaintiff to experience harmful or offensive contact, or apprehension of such contact. [8]

2. **Harmful or offensive contact with plaintiff**: There is no liability for battery unless the defendant brings about a harmful or offensive contact with the plaintiff. [9-10]

   a. **Contact with plaintiff**: Contact with the plaintiff is a touching of the plaintiff's body or of an extension of the plaintiff's body. [9]

      i. **Causing contact**: A defendant may make contact with a plaintiff by setting a force in motion which results in a touching of the plaintiff. [9]

      ii. **Extension of plaintiff's body**: A defendant may make contact with a plaintiff by causing a touching of anything so closely associated with the plaintiff's body as to be regarded as an extension of it. [10]

   b. **Harmful (contact)**: A contact is harmful if it produces an injury to the body. [10]

   c. **Offensive (contact)**: A contact is offensive if it was not authorized by the plaintiff and would not have been authorized by the reasonable or ordinary person in the plaintiff's situation, or if the defendant was aware that it was not authorized by the plaintiff. [10]

III. ASSAULT

A. General concept: Assault is a violation of the right to be free of intentionally induced apprehension of harmful or offensive touching. [11]

B. Essential elements: The essential elements of assault are (1) intent; and (2) inducing the plaintiff's reasonable apprehension of an imminent harmful or offensive contact. [11]

1. **Intent**: In an assault case, intent is defined the same way as in a battery case. [11]

2. **Apprehension**: Apprehension refers to any anticipation of discomfort. [12-14]

   a. **Reasonable apprehension**: Plaintiff's apprehension is not sufficient to support an assault claim unless it would have been experienced by the reasonable or ordinary person in the plaintiff's position. [12]

      i. **Physical act**: Courts usually hold that unless the defendant performed some physical act, the plaintiff's apprehension was not reasonable. Thus, words alone, even as part of a telephone call, are not sufficient to result in assault liability. [12]

      ii. **Words may be relevant**: Although speech alone can not constitute an assault, the words used by a defendant may play a role in the plaintiff's interpretation of the defendant's physical act, and, therefore, in determining whether the plaintiff's apprehension was reasonable. [12]

      iii. **Apparent ability**: Unless the defendant appears to have the ability to make the threatened contact, plaintiff's apprehension probably will not be regarded as reasonable. [13]

      iv. **Known sensitivity**: If the defendant is aware that the plaintiff will become apprehensive as a result of the defendant's act, the plaintiff's apprehension can support an assault claim even if it is not "reasonable". [14]

3. **Imminent harmful or offensive contact**: Plaintiff's apprehension must be of a harmful or offensive contact with her body which appears imminent. [14]

CAPSULE SUMMARY

IV. FALSE IMPRISONMENT

A. General concept: False imprisonment is a confining of the plaintiff within fixed boundaries which results in a violation of the right to freedom of movement. [14]

B. Essential elements: The essential elements of false imprisonment are (1) intent; and (2) confinement of the plaintiff. In addition, some jurisdictions require the plaintiff to prove that the confinement was (3) unlawful. [15]

1. **Intent**: In a false imprisonment case, intent means the desire (or knowledge to a substantial degree of certainty) that the defendant's voluntary act result in a confinement of the plaintiff. [15]

2. **Confinement defined**: Confinement is an overcoming of the plaintiff's will to leave in a way which would overcome the reasonable person's will to leave. [15-16]

   a. **Must be involuntarily**: If the plaintiff remains voluntarily his will to leave has not been overcome and there is no confinement. [16]

   b. **Will to leave**: If the plaintiff does not wish to leave, there can be no confinement. [16]

   c. **Objective standard**: Generally, there has been no confinement unless the defendant's act would have overcome the will of the reasonable or ordinary person in the plaintiff's position, or the defendant was aware that the act would overcome the will of the plaintiff. [16]

3. **Unlawfulness**: All jurisdictions agree that if a confinement is lawful it will not support a claim for false imprisonment. Disagreement exists, however, as to whether the plaintiff or the defendant has the burden of proof. [17]

V. INTENTIONAL INFLICTION OF MENTAL HARM

A. **General concept**: Intentional infliction of mental harm is a violation of the right to be free of serious, intentional invasions of mental and emotional tranquility. [18]

B. **Essential elements**: The essential elements of intentional infliction of mental harm are (1) intent; (2) outrageous conduct; and (3) severe mental suffering. [18]

1. **Intent**: The intent requirement is satisfied if at the time of his conduct the defendant desired (or knew to a substantial degree of certainty) that the plaintiff experience mental suffering as a result. [18]

2. **Outrageous conduct**: For purposes of the tort of intentional infliction of emotional harm, conduct is outrageous if it exceeds all bounds normally tolerated by decent society and is "calculated" (*i.e.*, extremely likely) to cause severe mental suffering in the reasonable person or in a person with the plaintiff's known sensitivities. [18-19]

3. **Severe mental suffering**: Liability is not imposed unless the plaintiff experiences severe mental suffering. Some jurisdictions hold that mental suffering is not sufficiently severe unless it has a physical manifestation. [19-20]

VI. TRESPASS TO LAND

A. **General concept**: Trespass to land is a violation of the right to be free of unauthorized intentional entry on realty. [20]

B. **Essential elements**: The essential elements of trespass to land are (1) intent; (2) entry on plaintiff's realty; (3) which is unauthorized. [21]

1. **Intent**: Intent consists of a desire (or knowledge to a substantial degree of certainty) that the defendant's volitional act result in an entry onto the particular realty involved, regardless of whether defendant knows that the realty belongs to another. [21]

2. **Entry on plaintiff's realty**: There is no liability for trespass to land unless the defendant makes or causes a physical entry onto the realty. [22-26]

   a. **Tangible object**: No entry occurs unless some tangible object makes physical contact with the land. [22]

   b. **Remaining on the realty**: Remaining on realty after permission to do so has expired satisfies the requirement of an unauthorized entry, even if the original entry was authorized. [23]

   c. **Possession required**: The action for trespass to land may be brought by anyone in possession of the realty, regardless of whether such possession is lawful. [24-25]

   d. **Realty**: Real property is land or anything permanently attached to the land, and some of the air space above the land. [25]

   e. **Damage not required**: It is not necessary for a plaintiff to show that damage resulted from the defendant's entry. [26]

VII. TRESPASS TO CHATTEL AND CONVERSION

A. **General concept**: Trespass to chattel and conversion are both violations of the right to possess personal property (*i.e.*, chattels). [27]

B. **Trespass to chattel and conversion distinguished**: Trespass to chattel is an action for damage resulting from the defendant's act; conversion is an action to force a sale to defendant. Because the remedy of forced sale is extraordinary, it is generally understood that conversion is available only for a serious violation of the plaintiff's rights, while trespass to chattel is available for less serious invasions. [27]

C. **Essential elements**: The essential elements of trespass to chattel and conversion are (1) intent; (2) interference; (3) with plaintiff's chattel; and (4) damage. [27-33]

1. **Intent**: Intent in trespass to chattel or conversion cases is the desire (or knowledge to a substantial certainty) that the act affect the chattel involved. [27]

2. **Interference**: Interference means doing something with respect to the chattel which only the rightful possessor is entitled to do. The Restatement (2d) of Torts indicates that an interference is serious enough to be classified as a *conversion* if it amounts to an exercise of dominion and control, and is only a *trespass to chattel* if it amounts to a mere intermeddling. In practice, the difference between an exercise of dominion and control and a mere intermeddling is usually difficult to determine and is often the subject of controversy. [28-29]

3. **Right of possession**: The actions for trespass to chattel and conversion may only be brought by persons with a lawful right to present or future possession. [29]

4. **Chattel**: "Chattel" is any property other than real property. [30]

5. **Damage**: Damage is an essential element of both conversion and trespass-to-chattel torts and may be established by showing either damage to the chattel or interference with Plaintiff's right to possession. [30]

6. **Relative difference**: Although the essential elements of trespass to chattel and conversion are identical, there is a relative difference between the torts which is usually found by examining the elements of interference and damage. [31-32]

   a. **Motive**: If the defendant knew that the chattel involved belonged to another, the courts are more likely to view the interference as an exercise of dominion and control, and, therefore, a proper subject for a conversion claim. On the other hand, if the defendant was unaware that his conduct was affecting the chattel of another, the courts are more likely to view the interference as a mere intermeddling. [31]

   b. **Damage**: In deciding whether the defendant's interference was serious enough to amount to a conversion, courts may also consider the damage which resulted. The more severe the damage, the more likely the defendant's act is to be considered a conversion. [32]

   c. **Election of remedies**: A plaintiff cannot successfully maintain actions for both trespass to chattel and conversion, because it would be inconsistent to find that conversion of a chattel also damages a plaintiff when by definition the chattel becomes the property of the defendant. [33]

CHAPTER 3

AFFIRMATIVE DEFENSES TO INTENTIONAL TORTS

I. GENERAL CONCEPT

A. Affirmative defense: An affirmative defense is an argument raised by a defendant which is unrelated to the essential elements of the plaintiff's case, but which, if accepted, may protect the defendant from liability. [35]

B. Burden of proof: A defendant always has the burden of establishing the affirmative defense on which she wishes to rely. [35]

II. CONSENT

A. General concept: Since a tort is a violation of the plaintiff's rights, and since a person who has consented to an act cannot claim that it violates his rights, consent is an affirmative defense to all intentional torts. [36]

B. Definition: "Consent" means "willingness." [36]

1. **Express consent**: Express consent is willingness which is stated in words or a substitute for words. [36]

2. **Implied consent**: Implied consent is willingness which is not stated in words or a substitute for words but which will be gathered by the reasonable person observing the plaintiff's conduct. [36]

3. **Apparent consent**: Apparent consent is willingness which the reasonable person would gather from the circumstances. [36-37]

C. Mistake: Consent given because of a mistake in the mind of the plaintiff privileges the defendant, so long as the defendant is unaware of the plaintiff's mistake. [37]

D. Consent induced by fraud: Consent which is induced by fraud on the part of the defendant is said to be vitiated (*i.e.*, negated or undone) if the fraud relates to the act to which the consent referred. [37-38]

E. Consent to unlawful fights: Some jurisdictions have held that consent to an unlawful fight has no legal effect and that, therefore, one who consents is not prevented from asserting a battery claim against the other combatant. Other courts have continued to apply the general rule that one who consents to an act is prevented from suing for damages resulting from it. [38-39]

III. SELF DEFENSE

A. General concept: Self defense is a privilege to use force to protect oneself against a threatened attack. [39]

B. Essential elements: The essential elements of self-defense are (1) an attempt to prevent a tort against oneself; and (2) the use of reasonable force. [39]

1. **Attempt to prevent tort**: A person is privileged to use force in self defense when he is attempting to protect himself against a threatened contact or confinement. [39]

2. **Reasonable force**: Reasonable force is the force which would appear necessary to the reasonable person in the defendant's position. [39]

a. **Lethal force**: It is usually held that the use of lethal or deadly force (*i.e.*, force likely to result in death or serious bodily harm), is not reasonable unless the person using it is defending himself against force which reasonably appears to be lethal or deadly. [40]

b. **Retreat**: Some jurisdictions hold that it is never reasonable to use lethal or deadly force when there is a reasonable means of escape. [40]

C. **Application to intentional tort**: Since self defense is a privilege to use force, it may be raised as an affirmative defense against any tort action involving the intentional use of force against a person. This may include battery, assault, false imprisonment, and, under some circumstances, intentional infliction of mental suffering. [41]

IV. DEFENSE OF OTHERS

A. **General concept**: Defense of others is a privilege to protect other persons against threatened attack. [41]

B. **Essential elements**: The essential elements of defense of others are (1) attempt to protect another person against a threatened contact or confinement; and (2) use of reasonable force. [41

1. **Attempt to prevent tort**: A person is privileged to use force when she is attempting to protect another person against a threatened contact or confinement. [41]

2. **Reasonable force**: The definition of reasonable force is identical to that used in connection with self defense. In some jurisdictions a person acting in defense of another is privileged to use whatever force would appear necessary to the reasonable person in the position of the defender. In other jurisdictions, a person acting in defense of another is only privileged to use that amount of force which the person being defended would be privileged to use. [41]

C. **Application to intentional tort**: Since defense of another is a privilege to use force, it may be raised as an affirmative defense against any tort action involving the intentional use of force against a person. This may include battery, assault, false imprisonment, and, under some circumstances, intentional infliction of mental suffering. [42]

V. DEFENSE OF PROPERTY

A. **General concept**: Defense of property is a privilege to use reasonable force to protect one's own real or personal property against a threatened trespass. [42]

B. **Essential elements**: The essential elements of defense of property are (1) attempt to protect one's own property against a trespass; and (2) use of reasonable force. [42]

1. **Prevention of a trespass**: A defendant is privileged to use force to protect realty against intentional unauthorized entry or to protect personalty against intentional interference. [42]

2. **Reasonable force**: The definition of reasonable force as that term is used in connection with the privileges of self defense and defense of others applies to defense of property as well. [42-43]

a. **Lethal force**: Since no property is worth as much as the life of any human, lethal or deadly force is never reasonable in defense of property. [43]

b. **Escalation**: Since the value of property does not exceed the value of human life or safety, it is generally understood that only slight force is permitted to defend it. Since that use of force is privileged, however, any resistance which is offered to it may constitute a tort against which the property owner has a privilege to defend herself by using greater force. [43-44]

C. **Application to intentional tort**: Since defense of property is a privilege to use force, it may be raised as an affirmative defense against any tort involving the intentional use of force against a person. This may include battery, assault, false imprisonment, and, under some circumstances, intentional infliction of mental suffering. [44]

VI. RECAPTURE OF CHATTEL

A. **General concept**: In some cases, this privilege permits the use of force in attempting to recapture a chattel which has been wrongfully taken from the defendant. [44]

B. **Essential elements**: The essential elements of recapture of chattel are (1) wrongful dispossession of a chattel from the defendant; (2) prompt action to recover it; and (3) reasonable force. [44]

1. **Wrongful dispossession**: Wrongful dispossession occurs when the chattel is removed from the defendant's actual or constructive possession by one who has no right to do so. [44]
2. **Prompt action**: The privilege to use force only exists when the dispossession is discovered immediately, action begins immediately, and there is no substantial interruption or opportunity to cool down. [45]
3. **Reasonable force**: Since one recapturing a chattel is an aggressor rather than a defender, force is reasonable only if it would have been used by a reasonable person who was familiar with all the facts. Thus, a defendant who mistakenly uses force against someone other than the dispossessor or who uses force in the mistaken belief that he has been wrongfully dispossessed, or who mistakenly uses more force than is actually necessary, is not privileged. [45-46]

C. **Application to intentional tort**: Since recapture of chattel is a privilege to use force, it may be raised as an affirmative defense against any tort involving the intentional use of force against a person. This may include battery, assault, false imprisonment, and, under some circumstances, intentional infliction of mental suffering. [46]

VII. AUTHORITY OF LAW

A. **General concept**: Conduct which may otherwise be tortious may be privileged if performed under authority of law. [46]

B. **Essential elements**: The essential elements of the privilege to act under authority of law are (1) a legal mandate; and (2) reasonable conduct in carrying it out. [46-48]

1. **Legal mandate**: The source of legal authority may be a statute or an order of the court which the reasonable person acting under it would believe is valid. [46]
2. **Reasonable conduct**: Authority of law includes the privileges to use reasonable force against persons, to make reasonable entry onto real property, or to interfere reasonably with the chattel of another for the purpose of carrying out the mandate. [47-48]

C. **Application to intentional torts**: Since authority of law is a privilege to use force, it may be raised as a defense to any intentional tort involving the application of force against a person. These include battery, assault, false imprisonment, and, in some cases, intentional infliction of mental harm. Since it also is a privilege to enter realty or seize a chattel, it may be raised as a defense to any intentional tort involving entry onto realty or interference with a chattel. These include trespass to land, trespass to chattel, and conversion. [49]

VIII. NECESSITY

A. General concept: The privileges of necessity permit the violation of property rights for the purpose of protecting persons or property threatened by an emergency. [49]

B. Public and private necessity: There are actually two privileges based on necessity: public necessity and private necessity. [49]

1. **Public necessity a complete privilege**: Public necessity is a complete or absolute privilege. This means that a defendant who successfully asserts it is free from all liability for damage resulting from her act. [49]

2. **Private necessity a qualified privilege**: Private necessity is a qualified privilege: This means that a defendant who successfully asserts it has not committed a trespass, but may be liable for damage resulting from his act. [49]

C. Essential elements: The essential elements of the privilege of necessity are (1) an emergency; and (2) a reasonable invasion of property rights in response to it. [50-51]

1. **Emergency**: An emergency is a situation which threatens life or property and which requires immediate action. [50]

   a. **Public emergency**: A public emergency is a situation which threatens the lives or property of the general public and which requires immediate action. One who reasonably invades property rights to protect the public from a public emergency is privileged by public necessity. [50]

   b. **Private emergency**: A private emergency is a situation which threatens the life or property of defendant, or the lives or property of a limited group of people. One who reasonably invades property rights to protect himself, his property, or the lives and property of a limited group of people is privileged by private necessity. [50]

   c. **Emergency created by defendant**: Most jurisdictions agree that a person who creates an emergency is not privileged by necessity when acting in the face of that emergency. [51]

2. **Reasonable invasion**: In determining whether the invasion of a property right was reasonable, courts usually balance the value which was being protected against the value of the right which was invaded. [51]

IX. PRIVILEGE TO ENTER REALTY TO RECOVER CHATTEL

A. General concept: Under some circumstances, a person may be privileged to enter the realty of another for the purpose of retrieving a chattel. [52]

B. Essential elements: The essential elements of this privilege are (1) the presence of the defendant's chattel on the plaintiff's realty through no fault of the defendant; and (2) reasonable entry to retrieve it. [52-53]

1. **Importance of fault**: If the defendant's chattel is on the plaintiff's realty because of some fault by the defendant, there is no privilege to enter and retrieve it. If the defendant's chattel is on the plaintiff's realty as the result of some fault by the plaintiff, the defendant's privilege to enter and retrieve it is an absolute privilege. If the defendant's chattel is on the plaintiff's realty without any fault by the plaintiff, the defendant's privilege to enter and retrieve it is a qualified privilege, similar to the privilege of private necessity, and the defendant will be liable for any damage which results. [52]

2. **Reasonable entry to retrieve**: In deciding whether the entry was reasonable, courts usually balance the value of the chattel being retrieved against the value of the right invaded. [53]

CHAPTER 4
NEGLIGENCE

I. GENERAL CONCEPT

A. Distinguished from intent: While intent requires a volitional act performed with desire (or knowledge to a substantial degree of certainty) that harm result, negligence is based on unreasonable conduct in the face of a foreseeable risk that harm may result. [55]

B. Essential elements: The essential elements of negligence are (1) a duty of reasonable care; and (2) a breach of that duty. [55]

II. DUTY OF REASONABLE CARE

A. No negligence without duty: Unless the defendant owes the plaintiff a duty of reasonable care, his unreasonable conduct is not negligence as to the plaintiff. [55]

B. General rule: Ordinarily, a defendant owes a plaintiff a duty of reasonable care if a foreseeable risk to the plaintiff is created by defendant's conduct. [55]

1. **Foreseeable risk**: A foreseeable risk is a danger which would be anticipated by the reasonable person in the defendant's position. [55-57]

2. **Foreseeable plaintiff**: A defendant does not owe a duty of reasonable care to any specific plaintiff unless it is foreseeable that the defendant's conduct will endanger that particular plaintiff. [56-57]

   a. **Duty to rescuer**: Usually, it is foreseeable that a rescuer will come along and try to assist a person in peril. Thus, a defendant owes a duty of reasonable care to a person attempting to rescue one who is foreseeably imperiled by the defendant's conduct. [56]

   b. **Duty to one who observes injury to another**: The majority of jurisdictions hold that a defendant who negligently injures another owes a duty of reasonable care to observers who are in the foreseeable zone of physical danger. In a minority of jurisdictions, the duty is also owed to persons outside the zone of physical danger if they are closely related to the injured person, are nearby when the injury occurs, and perceive the injury with their own senses. In a smaller minority of jurisdictions, the duty is owed to any observers if it is foreseeable that they will experience mental suffering as a result of observing the injury inflicted by the defendant. [57]

3. **Risk created by defendant's conduct**: Ordinarily, a defendant does not owe a plaintiff a duty of reasonable care to protect against a risk unless that risk was created or increased by the defendant's conduct. A defendant may create a risk or increase an existing risk by: [58-61]

   a. promising aid in a way which induces the plaintiff's detrimental reliance.

   b. interfering with or discouraging other rescuers.

   c. causing plaintiff to ignore an existing risk.

   d. undertaking to move the plaintiff or otherwise change the plaintiff's position in a way which exposes the plaintiff to more danger than was initially present.

C. Duty based on relationship: Sometimes a duty of reasonable care results from the existence of a relationship between defendant and plaintiff or between defendant and a third party, and is imposed even though the defendant's conduct has not created a risk. [61-62]

D. Limited duty of landholder: In many jurisdictions, even though a landholder's conduct (or a condition of his land) creates a foreseeable risk to a person entering the land, the landholder's duty may be limited to that extent determined by the plaintiff's status on the land. [63]

1. **Trespassers**: If the plaintiff is a trespasser, defendant owes her no duty of reasonable care. For this purpose, a trespasser is one who enters without permission. [63]

   a. **Known trespassers**: If defendant knows of a trespasser's presence on the land, the defendant owes the same duty of care which she would owe to a licensee. [63-64]

   b. **Trespassing children**: If it is foreseeable that children will trespass and be injured, and if the plaintiff is a trespassing child who is too young to comprehend the dangers, the defendant owes the plaintiff the same duty of care which she would owe to an invitee, *infra*. [64]

2. **Licensees**: If the plaintiff is a licensee, the defendant owes a limited duty to give reasonable warning of known hidden dangers. For this purpose, a licensee is one who enters the land with the landholder's permission. [64]

   a. **Users of highway**: A user of the public highway who enters adjacent land for a purpose connected with his use of the highway is regarded as a licensee. [64]

   b. **Social guests**: Social guests are licensees, even if present in response to a social invitation. [65]

   c. **Public employee**: A public employee who enters premises on official business which does not confer an economic benefit on the landholder does so as a licensee, even if the entry is without the landholder's permission. [65]

3. **Invitees**: If the plaintiff is an invitee, the defendant owes him a duty to keep the premises reasonably safe. [65]

   a. **Economic benefit**: A plaintiff whose presence confers or is likely to confer an economic benefit on the landholder is an invitee. [65]

   b. **Public invitation**: A plaintiff who enters premises in response to an invitation issued to the general public is an invitee. [66]

4. **Status may change**: Since a person who enters the land of another may be welcome in one part of the realty at one time and unwelcome in another part of the realty at another time, his status on the realty may change as time passes or as she moves about. [67-68]

5. **Plaintiff's status relevant only in determining landholder's duty**: The plaintiff's status on land is not relevant in determining the duty owed to him by any person other than the landholder. [68]

E. Minority view: An important minority of jurisdictions has held that a landholder owes the plaintiff a duty of reasonable care regardless of the plaintiff's status on the land. Status is only relevant in determining what reasonable care is in that particular case. [69]

F. Natural and artificial conditions: The majority of jurisdictions holds that a landholder only owes a duty to protect against conditions of the realty if those conditions are artificial. A minority holds that a landholder may owe a duty to protect both against natural conditions of the land and artificial conditions. [69]

CAPSULE SUMMARY

III. BREACH

A. In general, the duty of reasonable care is breached when the defendant does something that the reasonable person would not have done, or fails to do something that the reasonable person would have done. [70]

1. **Balancing test**: Ordinarily, courts employ a balancing test to determine whether a particular act or omission was reasonable. If the advantages which a reasonable person would have expected from the act or omission outweigh the disadvantages, the act is reasonable. If the disadvantages outweigh the advantages, the act is unreasonable. [70]

2. **Specific allegation**: It is not possible to apply the balancing test unless the conduct alleged to be negligent is specifically identified. [71]

3. **Custom**: Although evidence of custom may be relevant for the purpose of determining how the ordinary person acts, it can not determine whether a particular act or omission is reasonable. [71]

B. **Characteristics of the reasonable person**: The "reasonable person" is a fiction, a hypothetical character which the law creates for judging conduct. [72-77]

1. **Knowledge and intelligence**: Ordinarily, the reasonable person is imagined to have ordinary knowledge and intelligence. [72]

   a. **Mental retardation**: In judging the conduct of a person who is mentally retarded, most jurisdictions do not use a standard based on the intelligence and knowledge of the ordinary person. [73]

   b. **Insanity**: In judging the conduct of a person who can be described as insane, courts generally make no allowance for insanity, applying the same standard which would be applied if the person were not insane. [73]

   c. **Sudden loss of sanity**: In judging conduct which results from sudden loss of sanity, courts usually hold that if the loss of sanity is unforeseeable, the conduct which results from it is not unreasonable. On the other hand, if the loss of sanity is foreseeable, the conduct which results from it may be unreasonable. [73]

2. **Physical attributes**: In judging the conduct of a person with physical disabilities, most courts visualize a reasonable person with the same physical attributes. [73]

3. **Children**: In judging the conduct of a child, most courts compare it to that of the reasonable person of the same age, experience, and intelligence as the child. If, however, the child is engaged in an adult activity, she is held to the same standard as an adult. For this purpose, an adult activity is one which traditionally is only performed by adults, or one which is unsafe unless performed by someone with the maturity of an adult. [74-75]

4. **Professionals**: If the defendant is a member of a profession, and it is alleged that she was negligent in the way she practiced that profession, the defendant's conduct is compared to that of the reasonable member of that profession. Negligence by a professional is called professional malpractice. [75-76]

   a. **Need for expert witness**: Since the plaintiff has the burden of establishing that the defendant failed to act like a reasonable member of his profession, and since a jury is not competent to decide how the reasonable member of a particular profession may act, a plaintiff must offer evidence as to what the reasonable member of the profession would have done. Since this is a matter of opinion, and since only an expert qualifies to testify to an opinion, it usually is necessary for the plaintiff to produce an expert witness who can testify as to what a reasonable member of the defendant's profession would have done. [75]

   b. **Conduct within understanding of layperson**: Expert testimony is not required if the ordinary layperson is competent to decide that the reasonable member of the defendant's profession would not have engaged in conduct like the defendant's. [76]

   c. **Informed consent**: In many jurisdictions, a physician who does not inform his patient of the risks connected with a certain treatment and the alternatives to that treatment, is presumed to be acting unreasonably. This presumption makes expert testimony in such a case unnecessary. [76-77]

C. **Proof of negligence**: The plaintiff in any tort case has the burden of proof. In a negligence case, this means that the plaintiff is required to offer evidence which would justify a jury's finding that the defendant failed to act reasonably. [77-78]

1. **Direct evidence**: Usually, a plaintiff attempts to meet the burden of proof by offering evidence of the defendant's conduct and asking the jury to decide that the conduct was unreasonable. [78]

2. **Circumstantial evidence**: Circumstantial evidence is proof of one fact from which another fact can be inferred. Sometimes the inference created by circumstantial evidence can assist a plaintiff in meeting his burden of proof. Under some circumstances, the mere fact that a particular accident occurred in a certain way is circumstantial evidence that the defendant did something unreasonable, even though there is no evidence as to what he did. This principle is identified by the term "*res ipsa loquitur.*" [78-80]

   a. **Essential elements**: The occurrence of an accident may be circumstantial evidence that the defendant acted unreasonably (*i.e., res ipsa loquitur*) if (1) the accident is of a kind which does not usually occur without negligence; and (2) the defendant is the only person who could have caused the accident. [79]

   b. **Not available when defendant's conduct known**: When defendant's conduct is known, *res ipsa loquitur* is not a substitute for argument about whether that conduct was unreasonable. In most jurisdictions, res ipsa loquitur may not be applied at all when defendant's conduct is known or even when specific allegations are made about what defendant did. [80]

3. **Violation of statute**: In some cases, the fact that a defendant violated a statute may help to establish negligence, without regard to whether that defendant's conduct was unreasonable. This is so only when the statute violated was designed (1) to protect a class of persons to which plaintiff belongs; and (2) to protect against a class of risks which includes the one which resulted in harm to the plaintiff. [80-85]

   a. **Excuse**: A statutory violation does not establish negligence if the violation was excused. Every jurisdiction recognizes that some statutes may not justifiably be violated under any circumstances. Violation of most statutes may be excused if the violation resulted from circumstances beyond the violator's control, or ignorance of the facts which made the statute applicable, or the existence of an emergency which made obeying the statute more dangerous than violating it. [83]

   b. **Effect of statutory violation**: If a statute is one which may not be justifiably violated under any circumstances, its violation results in an irrebuttable presumption of negligence. As to all other statutes, the majority of jurisdictions holds that the violation results in a presumption of negligence which may be rebutted by proof that the violation was excused. A minority of jurisdictions holds that the violation results in an inference of negligence sufficient to raise a jury question and is evidence which a jury may consider in deciding whether the defendant was negligent. [84]

   c. **Causation**: Even when the violation of statute helps to establish that the defendant was negligent, liability will not be imposed unless the violation is shown to be a cause of the harm sustained by the plaintiff. [85]

   d. **Effect of compliance**: Compliance with a statute does not of itself establish reasonable care or freedom from negligence. [85]

IV. AGGRAVATED NEGLIGENCE

A. General concept: Although qualitatively different from intent and negligence, aggravated negligence (also known as recklessness) is generally not viewed as a separate basis of liability, but rather as a variation on negligence. [85]

B. Definition: Aggravated negligence consists of the willful disregard of an obvious risk with a high probability of serious harm. [86]

C. Legal effect: Many jurisdictions permit punitive damages to be awarded against a defendant who is found guilty of aggravated negligence. [86]

CHAPTER 5

AFFIRMATIVE DEFENSES TO NEGLIGENCE

I. PLAINTIFF'S NEGLIGENCE

A. Concept: If it contributed to the plaintiff's injury, the plaintiff's failure to act reasonably may provide the defendant with either a complete or a partial affirmative defense. [87]

B. "All or nothing": Until recently, the majority of American jurisdictions applied the "all or nothing" rule of contributory negligence. Under the "all or nothing" rule, if the plaintiff's negligence contributed to the accident, the plaintiff receives nothing in compensation for his damage. [87-88]

1. **Question of fact:** Although courts sometimes decide as a matter of law that a defendant's conduct was negligent, courts in "all or nothing" jurisdictions are reluctant to find as a matter of law that a plaintiff's conduct was contributorily negligent. [87]

2. **Last clear chance:** In most "all or nothing" jurisdictions, when the plaintiff, because of her own negligence or inadvertence, is powerless to avoid injury, and when the defendant discovers or should discover the plaintiff's peril in time to avoid the injury by acting reasonably but fails to do so, the defendant is said to have had the "last clear chance" to avoid the accident, and the plaintiff's negligence is held to be irrelevant. [87-88]

C. Pure comparative negligence (or fault): In many jurisdictions, the "all or nothing" rule has been replaced by a system of pure comparative negligence in which the plaintiff's negligence does not prevent the plaintiff from collecting damages. Rather, those damages are diminished in proportion to the plaintiff's own fault. [88]

D. Modified comparative negligence: In some jurisdictions, the plaintiff's recovery is diminished in proportion to plaintiff's fault (as in "pure" comparative negligence systems), but if the plaintiff's fault is equal to (in some jurisdictions) or greater than (in some jurisdictions) the defendant's, the plaintiff is completely barred from recovery (as in "all or nothing" systems). [88-89]

II. ASSUMPTION OF THE RISK

A. General concept: A plaintiff who agrees in advance to relieve the defendant of liability for damage resulting from what would otherwise be negligent conduct, is prevented from recovering damages for harm resulting from that conduct. [89]

B. Express assumption: A plaintiff may expressly assume the risk by agreeing that the defendant will not be liable for harm resulting from the defendant's specified conduct. So long as the express agreement does not violate public policy, courts will enforce it by holding that the defendant is not liable. [89]

C. Implied assumption: A plaintiff may impliedly assume the risk by voluntarily encountering a known risk. [90-92]

1. **Circumstances interfering with free choice**: A plaintiff's encounter with a risk is not voluntary if there are circumstances which make it difficult for him to choose not to encounter it. [90]

2. **Rescue**: Courts usually hold that a plaintiff who knowingly encounters a risk while attempting to rescue an imperiled person is not acting voluntarily and, therefore, is not assuming the risk. [90-91]

   a. **"Fireman's rule."** Since persons who are engaged in an occupation which involves rescuing others voluntarily chose to pursue that occupation, most courts hold that, when performing a rescue, such persons voluntarily encounter, and therefore assume, the risks associated with the rescue. [91]

   b. **Reckless conduct**: Courts usually hold that a person who acts recklessly by undertaking a rescue which is obviously futile is voluntarily exposing herself to risks, and therefore assuming them, even though confronted by an emergency which imperils another. [91]

3. **Same risk**: The only risk which a plaintiff assumes is the risk of which she knows and which she voluntarily encounters. Thus, a plaintiff who voluntarily encounters a risk of which she knows, but is injured as the result of a different and unknown risk, does not assume the risk which leads to her injury. [91]

D. Availability as a defense: The majority of jurisdictions treats assumption of the risk as a complete affirmative defense which is separate from contributory / comparative negligence. In these jurisdictions, a plaintiff who has assumed the risk is completely barred from recovery. An important minority of jurisdictions has decided that assumption-of-the-risk should not be available as a separate and complete defense. These jurisdictions, all of which have adopted systems of pure comparative negligence, hold that conduct which would have supported an assumption of the risk defense may be regarded as comparative negligence and considered by the jury in determining the plaintiff's proportion of fault in bringing about the injury. [92-93]

CHAPTER 6
STRICT LIABILITY

I. GENERAL CONCEPT

A. Liability without fault: There are certain activities and situations to which the law of torts imposes liability without fault, or strict liability. [94]

B. Traditional development: Although strict liability serves as the basis of many torts, traditionally it has been applied to the keeping of animals, the storage of dangerous substances, and participation in extremely dangerous activities. [94]

II. ANIMALS

A. Wild animals: Ordinarily, liability for damage done by domestic animals is not imposed on their keepers without fault, while strict liability for damage done is imposed on one who keeps a wild animal. [95-96]

1. **Domestic animal defined**: A domestic animal is of a species which, because of its nature or its long association with humanity, can safely be kept by humans without special training or restraint. [95]

2. **Wild animal defined**: A wild animal is of a species which cannot safely be kept by humans without special training or restraint. [96]

B. **Domestic animals known to have dangerous propensities**: Most American jurisdictions impose strict liability for damage on the keeper of a domestic animal who knows of the animal's dangerous propensities. [96]

C. **Negligence variation**: Some jurisdictions hold that it is *prima facie* negligent for a person to keep a wild animal or a domestic animal which she knows to have a dangerous propensity. [97]

D. **Harm must relate to dangerous nature of the animal**: Strict liability is imposed only for injuries resulting from the animal's dangerous trait. [98]

E. **Statutory modification**: Many jurisdictions have enacted statutes modifying the common law regarding the liability of persons who keep wild or domestic animals. [98]

III. STORAGE OF SUBSTANCES

A. **General concept**: One who keeps a substance which, although harmless when confined, is likely to do great harm upon its escape, may be held strictly liable for damage resulting from its escape. [98]

B. **Essential elements**: The essential elements of this principle are (1) the use of realty in a non-natural manner; (2) to store a substance which is ordinarily harmless while stored; but (3) which is likely to do great harm upon its escape. [98-99]

C. **Nature of risk**: Since this theory imposes strict liability because of the danger that stored substances pose in the event of their escape, strict liability is imposed only for injuries which result from the escape of the stored substance. [100]

IV. EXCESSIVELY DANGEROUS ACTIVITIES

A. **General concept**: Some activities are so excessively dangerous that our society, through the courts and legislatures, has concluded that they should pay their own way. This is accomplished by imposing on persons engaging in those activities strict liability for damage resulting from them. [100]

B. **Ultra-hazardous activities**: The first Restatement of Torts indicated that persons engaging in ultra-hazardous activities should be held strictly liable for damage to persons or property which results from those activities. According to the Restatement, an activity is ultra-hazardous if (1) it necessarily involves a serious risk to persons or property which cannot be eliminated by the exercise of reasonable care; and (2) the activity is not a common one. [100-101]

C. **Abnormally dangerous activities**: The Restatement (2d) replaced the phrase "ultra-hazardous activity" with "abnormally dangerous activity," and stated that in deciding whether to impose strict liability, in addition to the factors listed by the first Restatement (set forth above), courts should consider the appropriateness of the activity to the location and the extent to which its dangerous attributes are outweighed by its value to the community. [102]

D. **Nature of risk**: Strict liability will be imposed only for damage which results from the excessively dangerous nature of the activity. [103-104]

V. AFFIRMATIVE DEFENSES

A. **Contributory / comparative fault**: The majority of jurisdictions holds that, since strict liability is not based on fault by the defendant, plaintiff's fault is not available as an affirmative defense in strict liability cases. A growing minority of jurisdictions, all of which have adopted pure comparative negligence, holds that the plaintiff's negligence can be asserted as a defense in a strict liability case. [104]

B. **Assumption of the risk**: The majority of jurisdictions permits assumption of the risk to be raised as a defense in a strict liability case. A minority of jurisdictions holds that assumption of the risk is subsumed into the concept of pure comparative negligence. In this minority, assumption of the risk is no longer a defense in strict liability cases, but comparative fault (*i.e.*, comparative negligence) is. [105]

CHAPTER 7
PROXIMATE CAUSE

I. GENERAL CONCEPT

A. **Requirement of proximate cause**: Any time a plaintiff seeks compensation for damage resulting from a tort, it is necessary for him to show that the defendant did something which could result in liability (*i.e.*, fault or a basis for imposing liability without fault). In addition, it is necessary to connect the defendant's liability-forming conduct to the harm sustained by plaintiff by showing that the defendant's conduct was a proximate cause of that harm. [107]

B. **One of the proximate causes**: It is not necessary to show that the defendant's conduct was the sole proximate cause of the plaintiff's harm. In most jurisdictions, if the plaintiff shows that the defendant's conduct was one of the proximate causes of the harm, the defendant may be held liable for the full extent of the harm. [107]

C. **Factual and legal cause**: In deciding whether a defendant's conduct was a proximate cause of the plaintiff's harm, it is first necessary to decide whether the defendant's conduct was a factual cause of that harm. If not, the causation question is resolved. If the defendant's conduct was a factual cause of the plaintiff's harm, it must then be determined whether it was a legal cause of that harm. If the defendant's conduct was both a factual and a legal cause of the plaintiff's injury, then it was a proximate cause of that injury. [108-116]

1. **Factual cause**: Conduct is a factual cause of harm if there is a cause-and-effect relationship between the conduct and the harm. Courts have developed several tests for determining whether this relationship exists. [109]

   a. **"But for"**: Conduct is a factual cause of injury if the injury would not have occurred without (*i.e.*, but for) the conduct. It is not necessary that the conduct in question be the sole factual cause of the plaintiff's injury. It is sufficient that it be something without which the plaintiff's injury would not have occurred. [110]

   b. **Substantial factor**: Conduct is a factual cause of injury if the conduct was a substantial factor in bringing about that injury. Conduct was a substantial factor in bringing about an injury if it contributed to the injury and was, alone, sufficient to bring about that injury. [111]

   c. **Alternate liability**: Where two or more defendants committed identical acts, either of which could have caused the plaintiff's injury, but it is impossible to determine which caused the injury, it may be presumed that both caused the injury. Each defendant may attempt to rebut the presumption of fault by proving that it was not she who caused the injury. [112]

2. **Legal cause**: After it has been determined that the defendant's conduct was a factual cause of the plaintiff's harm, it is necessary to determine whether the nature of that cause-and-effect relationship is such that liability should be imposed on the defendant. Although this is frequently a question of public policy, courts have developed several rules of law to justify or explain their determinations. [113]

   a. **Restatement view**: The Restatement (2d) states that a factual cause of harm is a legal cause of that harm unless there is some rule of law to the contrary. [115]

   b. **Direct consequence**: Some cases have held that conduct which is a factual cause of harm is a legal cause of that harm if the harm was a "direct consequence" of the conduct and was not brought about by the operation of new, independent, intervening causes. Harm is a "direct consequence" of conduct if, given the existing context of circumstances and conditions, the harm was a natural and inevitable result of that conduct. [115]

   c. **Foreseeability**: Some cases have held that a factual cause of harm is a legal cause of that harm if, with knowledge of the circumstances which existed at the time the defendant acted, the harm could have been foreseen by the reasonable person in the defendant's position. [116]

   d. **Not extraordinary in retrospect**: The Restatement (2d) suggests that conduct is not a legal cause of harm if, looking back from the harm to the negligent conduct, the harm appears to be a highly extraordinary consequence of the conduct. [117]

   e. **Retrospective analysis**: All legal cause theories require a retrospective analysis which accepts the circumstances and conditions which existed at the time of the defendant's conduct. Thus, in determining legal cause issues, it never is relevant to ask whether it was inevitable, or foreseeable, or extraordinary that the existing conditions would be the way they were. Instead, courts see these conditions as a "set stage" on which a defendant acts, and ask whether the result was inevitable, or foreseeable, or extraordinary given the stage setting. [117]

3. **Intervening causes**: In many cases, intervening causes must be considered in resolving legal cause issues. [118-125]

   a. **Definition**: An intervening cause is a factual cause (of the harm) which occurred after the defendant's conduct. It may be attributable to another defendant, to a person who is not a defendant, or even to a natural force. [120]

   b. **Concurring and superseding causes**: If an intervening cause of harm is found to be a concurring cause of that harm, the defendant's conduct may still be a proximate cause of the harm. If an intervening cause of harm is found to be a superseding cause of the harm, the defendant's conduct cannot be a proximate cause of the harm. Courts have developed several tests to determine whether an intervening cause is a concurring cause or a superseding cause. [121]

      i. **Dependent / independent intervention**: An intervention is a concurring cause of harm if its occurrence is dependent on the risk created by the defendant's conduct, and is a superseding cause of harm if its occurrence is not dependent on the risk created by the defendant's conduct. The occurrence of an intervention is dependent on the risk created by the defendant's conduct if the likelihood of that intervening occurrence is a foreseeable consequence of the conduct. [121]

      ii. **Foreseeable intervention**: An intervention is a concurring cause of harm if its occurrence would have been foreseeable to the reasonable person who knew of the circumstances and conditions which existed at the time the defendant acted, and is a superseding cause of harm if its occurrence would not have been foreseeable to the reasonable person who knew of those circumstances and conditions. [122]

iii. **Extraordinary intervention**: An intervention is a superseding cause of harm if in retrospect its occurrence appears to have been highly extraordinary, and is a concurring cause of harm if in retrospect its occurrence does not appear to have been highly extraordinary. [123]

iv. **Same type of harm**: Where the defendant's conduct creates a risk of a particular type of harm, an intervention which brings about that same type of harm is a concurring cause of that harm, unless the intervenor intentionally brought the harm about, in which case the intervention is a superseding cause of harm. [123]

v. **Normal intervention**: Even if it is not foreseeable or common, an intervention is a concurring cause of harm if it is within the range of normal responses to a situation created by defendant's conduct. An intervention is a superseding cause of harm if it is so outside the scope of what might be expected as to be regarded as an abnormal event. [124]

vi. **Negligent / criminal acts**: An intervention consisting of the negligent act of a third person is generally viewed as a concurring cause of harm because it is generally regarded as foreseeable that persons will be negligent. An intervention consisting of the criminal act of a third person is generally viewed as a superseding cause of harm because criminal acts are generally regarded as unforeseeable. [125]

4. **Particular types of damage**: There are certain kinds of damage which are not recoverable under certain theories. Some cases say that this is so because the harm complained of was not "damage"; other cases say that these kinds of damage are not proximately caused by the conduct involved. [126]

CHAPTER 8
DAMAGE

I. IN GENERAL

A. **Essential element of liability**: In most tort cases, there can be no recovery without proof of some actual damage. Sometimes, although a plaintiff has sustained harm, courts rule that there has been no "damage" as required by law. [128]

B. **"Damage" and "damages"**: "Damage" refers to the harm or injury which the plaintiff sustained. "Damages" refers to a sum of money awarded to the plaintiff as a remedy for the damage which she sustained. [128]

II. TYPES OF DAMAGES

A. **Nominal damages**: Nominal damages consist of a token sum of money which is awarded to a plaintiff who has made out a case but has failed to prove any actual damage. [128]

B. **Punitive or exemplary damages**: Punitive or exemplary damages may be awarded to the plaintiff to punish or to make an example of the defendant because the defendant's conduct was reprehensible or base. [128-130]

1. **Intentional tort**: Punitive damages are not available in intentional tort cases unless it can be shown that the defendant acted with malice. For this purpose, "malice" is defined as ill will or a desire to cause harm. [128-129]

2. **Aggravated negligence**: Punitive damages are available in negligence cases only if it can be shown that defendant's conduct amounted to aggravated negligence or reckless-

ness. Aggravated negligence or recklessness consists of the willful disregard of an obvious risk with a high probability of serious harm. [129]

3. **Strict liability**: A plaintiff who sues on a strict liability theory may recover punitive damages only if the defendant's conduct was reckless. [130]

4. **Plaintiff must make out a case**: Punitive damages may not be awarded unless it is found that the plaintiff is entitled at least to nominal or compensatory damages. [130]

5. **Relationship to compensatory damages**: Some jurisdictions hold that the amount of punitive damages must bear some rational relationship to the amount of compensatory damages awarded to the plaintiff. Other jurisdictions hold that no rational relationship is necessary at all. [130]

6. **Relationship to defendant's wealth**: Many jurisdictions admit evidence of the defendant's personal wealth in order to help the jury determine what award would be appropriate. [130]

7. **Functions of court and jury**: The court decides whether the proof could justify an award of punitive damages, and, if so, refers the question to a jury for determination. Punitive damages are never available as of right. [130]

8. **Minority view**: Since punitive damages are quasi-penal in nature, some courts hold that punitive damages may never be awarded in civil suits. [130]

C. **Compensatory damages**: Compensatory damages consist of a sum of money awarded to the plaintiff to compensate her for the damage (*i.e.*, harm) which she has sustained. [131]

1. **Functions of court and jury**: The amount of damages necessary to compensate a plaintiff for his damage is a question of fact. A court may conclude as a matter of law, however, that the jury's verdict is excessive or inadequate. A court which finds that a jury's verdict is excessive may enter judgment for a lower amount called a *remittitur.* A court which finds that a jury's verdict is inadequate may enter judgment for a higher amount called an *additur.* [131-132]

2. **Avoidable consequences**: A defendant who is liable for the plaintiff's damage is not liable for complications or consequences which the plaintiff could have avoided by acting reasonably after the injury occurred. [133]

3. **Collateral sources**: The majority of jurisdictions holds that compensation which a plaintiff receives from a collateral source (*i.e.*, not on behalf of a tortfeasor) is not relevant in measuring damages which the plaintiff is entitled to collect from the defendant. [133-134]

4. **Taking plaintiff as found**: It has been said that a defendant takes the plaintiff as she finds her. This means that a defendant is liable for the full extent of the injuries proximately caused by her conduct even though their severity may have resulted, in part, from an unusual pre-existing condition of the plaintiff. [134]

5. **Bodily injury**: Where appropriate, damages for injury to the plaintiff's body may be recovered under all theories of tort liability. [135]

6. **Mental suffering**: Damages for mental suffering may be available, depending on the circumstances and the theory of tort liability. [135]

   a. **Intentional tort**: Damages for mental suffering are available in intentional tort actions for interference with the person. These include battery, assault, and false imprisonment. In cases of intentional infliction of mental harm, however, some jurisdictions hold that mental suffering is not sufficiently severe to result in liability unless that suffering has a physical manifestation. [135]

   b. **Negligence and strict liability**: In claims based on negligence or strict liability, damages for mental suffering are available according to the following rules: [135]

i. **Resulting from bodily injury**: All jurisdictions agree that damages may be recovered for mental suffering which results from injury to the plaintiff's body. [135]

ii. **Physical manifestations**: If mental suffering is not the result of a physical injury to the plaintiff's body, a majority of jurisdictions holds that the plaintiff may recover damages for it if the mental suffering has a physical manifestation. [135]

iii. **Physical impact**: If mental suffering is not the result of a physical injury to the plaintiff's body, a small minority of jurisdictions holds that the plaintiff may recover damages for it only if the suffering resulted from some physical impact with plaintiff's body. [136]

iv. **Foreseeable mental suffering**: If mental suffering is not the result of a physical injury to the plaintiff's body, a small minority of jurisdictions holds that the plaintiff may recover damages for it if the mental suffering was a foreseeable result of the defendant's conduct. [136]

v. **Phobias**: In some jurisdictions, a phobia (*i.e.*, a chronic, abnormal fear of something) which a plaintiff develops as the result of a defendant's conduct, but not as the result of a physical injury, is a form of mental suffering for which the plaintiff may recover damages subject to the above principles. [137]

vi. **Observing harm to another**: If a plaintiff experiences mental suffering as the result of observing physical injury to another person, many jurisdictions continue to apply whichever of the above rules they have adopted. Other jurisdictions have developed special rules, however, which they apply either instead of the above rules or in combination with them. **Note**: Some cases have treated this as a question of whether the defendant owed the plaintiff a duty of reasonable care [see discussion above]. Other cases have treated this as a proximate cause problem. [138]

(1) **Zone of physical danger:** In the majority of jurisdictions, a person who injures another is liable for mental suffering experienced by observers only if they are in the zone of physical danger. [138]

(2) **Three part test:** In a minority of jurisdictions, a person who injures another is liable for mental suffering experienced by observers who are not in the zone of physical danger if they are closely related to the injured person, are nearby when the injury occurs, and perceive the injury with their own senses. [138]

(3) **Foreseeable mental suffering:** In a small minority of jurisdictions, a person who injures another is liable for the mental suffering of observers who are not in the zone of physical danger if it is foreseeable that they will experience mental suffering as a result of the injury inflicted by the defendant. [138]

7. **Death**: The death of an injured plaintiff may require consideration of two distinct concepts in tort law: the survival of personal injury actions, and the recovery of damages resulting from wrongful death. [139-144]

a. **Survival of personal injury actions**: Most jurisdictions regard the right to sue for personal injuries as inheritable property, so that a decedent's right to sue does not terminate, but survives (*i.e.*, outlives) the decedent and is inherited by the decedent's heirs and distributees, subject to any defenses which could have been raised against the decedent. [139-141]

b. **Wrongful death**: In causing the death of another person, a defendant may inflict serious economic injury on the decedent's dependents. These dependents may be entitled to sue for damages under a theory known as *wrongful death*, subject to any defenses which could have been raised against the decedent. In most jurisdictions, a wrongful death plaintiff is entitled to recover economic losses only. A few jurisdictions permit recovery of damages for grief. [142-144]

c. **Election and merger**: In most jurisdictions, survivors' personal injury actions and wrongful death actions are distinct causes of action which may coexist without limitation. According to statutes in some jurisdictions, an election must be made between actions, or the two actions merge into one. [144]

d. **Rights of creditors**: Creditors of the decedent are entitled to collect against the proceeds of the surviving personal injury action, but not against the proceeds of the wrongful death action. [144]

8. **Loss of consortium**: In many jurisdictions, if a defendant tortiously injures a plaintiff's spouse in a way which interferes with the plaintiff's right of consortium (*i.e.*, the society, services, and sexual attentions of his spouse), the plaintiff is entitled to recover damages to compensate for that loss. [145]

9. **Fetal injuries:** All jurisdictions agree that a child born with injuries which were inflicted prior to birth and which resulted from the defendant's conduct may recover damages for those injuries. A small minority permits a child to recover for injuries with which the child was born as the result of a tort committed against the child's parent(s) prior to the child's conception. [146]

10. **Wrongful life and wrongful birth:** If a defendant's conduct causes a child to be born who otherwise would not have been born, most jurisdictions hold that the child is not entitled to recover damages for his "wrongful life," and the parent is not entitled to recover for the "wrongful birth." A small minority permits recovery. [147-148]

11. **Property damage:** Damages to compensate a plaintiff for damage to his property consist of either the reasonable cost of repairing the damaged property, the reduction in the property's value resulting from the damage, or the total value of the property immediately prior to the damage, whichever is the least. [149]

12. **Commercial losses:** Lost profits or other financial losses which do not result from injury to the plaintiff's person or property are generally not items of damage for which a plaintiff can recover damages in actions founded on negligence or strict liability theories. [149

CHAPTER 9

VICARIOUS LIABILITY

I. IN GENERAL

A. **Concept**: In special situations, a relationship between a defendant and another person may make the defendant legally responsible for damage which proximately results from that other person's conduct. When this happens, the defendant is said to be "vicariously liable". Principles of vicarious liability may be applied to any type of liability-forming conduct. [150]

B. **No vicarious liability without tort**: Ordinarily, a defendant will not be vicariously liable unless the tortfeasor is herself liable. [150]

C. **Defenses**: A defendant on whom a plaintiff seeks to impose vicarious liability may raise any defense which the tortfeasor is entitled to raise. [151]

D. Not a defense: The fact that someone else is vicariously liable for a tort does not prevent the tortfeasor from being liable for it as well. For this reason, the vicarious liability of another is never a defense. [151]

E. Indemnity: All jurisdictions recognize that when one person has been held vicariously liable for a tort committed by another, he is entitled to indemnity (*i.e.*, repayment) from the one who actually committed the tort. [151]

II. RESPONDEAT SUPERIOR

A. General concept: Under the doctrine of *respondeat superior*, an employer is vicariously liable for certain acts and omissions of his employees. [152]

B. Essential elements: The essential elements of *respondeat superior* are (1) the tortfeasor was an employee of the defendant; and (2) when the tort was committed, the employee was acting within the scope of employment. [152]

1. **Employer**: In applying the doctrine of *respondeat superior*, an "employer" is anyone who hires or employs another to perform services. [152]

2. **Employee**: An employer is vicariously liable for torts committed by a person working for her only if that person is an employee as distinguished from an independent contractor. Courts take many factors into consideration in making this determination. [152]

   a. **Control of details**: If the worker has the right to control details of the work being performed, the worker is more likely to be considered an independent contractor. If the employer has the right to control details of the work being performed, the worker is more likely to be considered an employee. [152-153]

   b. **Negotiating with contractor**: Even in employing an independent contractor, an employer may determine some details of the work by negotiating for conditions in the contract between them. If, however, the contract is such that the employer has the right to add or change conditions after the work has begun, the worker is more likely to be classified as an employee. [153-154]

   c. **Furnishing tools**: A worker who furnishes his own tools is more likely to be regarded as an independent contractor than one for whom tools are furnished by the employer. [155]

   d. **Method of payment**: A worker who is paid by time unit (*e.g.*, hour, week, month, year) is more likely to be regarded as an employee than a worker who is paid for a result. [155]

3. **Scope of employment**: In deciding whether an employee was acting within the scope of employment, courts consider the factors of benefit and control. [155]

   a. **Benefit**: An employee was not acting within the scope of employment unless at the time the tort was committed, his conduct was intended to or likely to benefit the employer. [155]

      i. **Incidental needs of employee**: For the purpose of applying the doctrine of *respondeat superior*, an employer may be said to receive a benefit even when an employee stops working to satisfy a personal need, if the need is incidental to the employment and the employee cannot reasonably be expected to work without satisfying it. [156]

      ii. **Independent frolic**: An employee who acts for reasons which are purely personal and not in any way related to the employer's business is sometimes said to be on an "independent frolic," and not acting within the scope of employment. [156]

b. **Control**: An employee is not acting within the scope of employment unless, at the time the tort was committed, the employer had the right to control the employee's behavior. [157]

i. **Power to control not required**: So long as an employer has the right to control the employee's behavior, it is immaterial that the employer lacked the ability to exercise such control. [158]

ii. **Violation of employer's instructions**: So long as the employer has a right to exercise control over the employee's behavior, the employee may be acting within the scope of employment even when violating the employer's instructions or orders. [158]

III. INDEPENDENT CONTRACTORS

A. **In general**: While the doctrine of respondeat superior does not impose on the employer of an independent contractor vicarious liability for the torts of the contractor, there are some situations in which a person who employs an independent contractor may be held vicariously liable for the contractor's torts. [159]

B. **Particular risk**: If an independent contractor is employed to perform a job with which a particular risk is associated, the employer may be held vicariously liable for damage resulting from the contractor's unreasonable conduct in the face of that particular risk. [159]

C. **Non-delegable duty**: If a statute or administrative regulation creates a duty to provide specified safeguards for the protection of others, an employer who hires an independent contractor to provide those safeguards may be held vicariously liable for the contractor's negligence in doing so. In justifying this conclusion, courts sometimes say that the defendant had a "non-delegable duty." [159]

D. **Extremely dangerous activities**: A landholder who employs an independent contractor to work on the land at an activity for which strict liability is imposed, is vicariously liable for damages resulting from the independent contractor's activity. [160]

E. **Employer's negligence**: Sometimes, when the negligence of an independent contractor results in harm to a plaintiff, it is possible to show that the employer of that contractor was also negligent. In such a case, the essence of the plaintiff's claim is not that vicarious liability should be imposed on the employer, but rather that the employer's negligent conduct was, itself, a proximate cause of the plaintiff's harm. [160-161]

IV. ENTERPRISE LIABILITY

A. **General concept**: Members of a joint enterprise are vicariously liable for torts committed by other members of the joint enterprise acting within the scope of the enterprise. [161]

B. **Joint enterprise defined**: For the purpose of determining whether vicarious liability should be imposed, a joint enterprise is defined as an undertaking for profit by two or more persons who agree to share control over the undertaking. [161]

C. **Members of commercial chain usually not joint enterprisers**: Unless some special agreement exists between them, members of a chain of commercial distribution (*i.e.*, manufacturer, wholesaler, retailer) ordinarily are not involved in a joint enterprise. [162]

D. **Concert of action**: Even where persons have not agreed to a joint undertaking and have not agreed to share control, a court may find that they are engaged in a concert of action sufficient to make each vicariously liable for the other's torts if one of them aids, assists, or tacitly encourages the other(s) in accomplishing a commercial purpose. [162]

CHAPTER 10

NUISANCE

I. GENERAL CONCEPT

A. Characterization of right invaded: Unlike the names of other torts which tend to describe the defendant's conduct, the term "nuisance" describes the right which was invaded as a result of that conduct. [164]

B. Two separate torts: There are two separate areas of tort liability which are known by the term "nuisance": "public nuisance" and "private nuisance." A public nuisance is a liability-forming invasion of some right of the general public. A private nuisance is a liability-forming invasion of the plaintiff's right to use and enjoy real property. [164]

C. Liability-forming conduct: Any liability-forming conduct (*i.e.*, intent, negligence, or an activity for which strict liability is imposed) may be the basis of an action for nuisance if it results in the necessary invasion of right. [164-165]

1. **Intent**: A nuisance is based on intentional conduct if the defendant acted with a desire (or knowledge to a substantial certainty) that his conduct result in an invasion of a public right (public nuisance) or of the plaintiff's right to use and enjoy his realty (private nuisance). [164]

2. **Negligence**: A nuisance is based on negligence if the invasion of a public right (public nuisance) or of the plaintiff's right to use and enjoy realty (private nuisance) resulted from the defendant's failure to act reasonably in the face of a foreseeable risk. [165]

3. **Strict liability**: A nuisance may be based on strict liability if the invasion of a public right (public nuisance) or of the plaintiff's right to use and enjoy realty (private nuisance) results from the defendant's participation in an activity for which strict liability is imposed. [165]

D. Invasion of right: No invasion of right can be termed a nuisance unless it is substantial. For this purpose, an invasion of right is substantial if it would seriously inconvenience the ordinary person (*e.g.*, a person making ordinary use of land). [166]

II. PUBLIC NUISANCE

A. Definition: A public nuisance is an invasion of a right of the general public which results from conduct of the defendant. A right of the general public is a right which all members of the public are entitled to exercise, even though not all members of the general public actually do so. [167]

B. Criminal consequences: In most jurisdictions, criminal statutes written in general terms prohibit intentional or negligent invasions of public rights, characterizing such invasions as "nuisances" or "public nuisances." [167]

C. Public nuisance as a tort: Since damage to the public is likely to result from any invasion of a public right, conduct which constitutes a public nuisance may be a tort as well as a crime. [168]

D. Public is plaintiff: In a public nuisance tort action, the injured party is the general public. For this reason, the public is usually the plaintiff and is represented by the public attorney. [168]

E. Remedies: Remedies available to the public for a public nuisance include damages and injunction. [168]

F. **Action by private individual**: A private individual may maintain an action for public nuisance if a public nuisance existed which caused her to sustain damage different in kind from that sustained by the general public. No injunction is available in such an action. [168-169]

III. PRIVATE NUISANCE

A. **Definition**: A private nuisance is an interference with the plaintiff's right to use and enjoy realty which results from the defendant's conduct. [170]

B. **Possessory right**: The action for private nuisance is available only to plaintiffs who have a possessory right in the realty the use and enjoyment of which has been invaded. [172]

C. **Unreasonable invasion**: Courts frequently say that an invasion of the right to use and enjoy realty is a private nuisance only if that invasion is unreasonable. An invasion of the right to use and enjoy realty may be unreasonable if the gravity of the harm to the plaintiff's right outweighs the utility of the defendant's conduct. [173]

D. **Remedies**: A successful plaintiff in a private nuisance action may recover compensatory damages and, if damages are not sufficient, injunctive relief. [174]

E. **Affirmative defenses**: The affirmative defenses available in private nuisance actions depend on the theory of liability alleged by the plaintiff. If the plaintiff proceeds on an intent theory, the defendant may assert the defenses available in intentional tort cases. If the plaintiff proceeds on negligence or strict liability theories, the defendant may assert defenses available in those cases. [174-175]

CHAPTER 11
MISREPRESENTATION

I. GENERAL CONCEPT

A. **Two torts**: At common law, there are two different, but closely related, torts, both of which involve misrepresentation. These are intentional misrepresentation (also known as "fraud" or "deceit") and negligent misrepresentation. [177]

B. **Elements in common**: Intentional misrepresentation and negligent misrepresentation have the following elements in common: (1) a misrepresentation; (2) which induces the plaintiff's justified reliance; and (3) which reliance results in damage. [177-184]

1. **Misrepresentation**: A misrepresentation is a false assertion of material fact made with the intent to induce the plaintiff's reliance. [177]

   a. **False**: An assertion is false if it is not substantially true.

   b. **Assertion**: An assertion is a statement made either expressly or impliedly. An assertion is express if it is made in words or a substitute for words, and implied if it would be inferred or gathered by the reasonable person observing the defendant's conduct or the circumstances. [177]

      i. **Assertion implied by non-disclosure**: If a defendant is under a legal duty to disclose the existence of a particular fact, the failure to disclose that fact may be an assertion that the fact does not exist. [178]

      ii. **Partial disclosure**: A partial disclosure which was likely to mislead the reasonable person or which the seller knew would mislead the buyer might create an obligation to make full disclosure to avoid misunderstanding. [178]

iii. **Discovery of additional information**: If the seller made an assertion which was true when she made it, but learned, prior to the sale, that circumstances had changed, she may be under an affirmative obligation to advise the buyer of the change in circumstances. [179]

iv. **Active concealment**: A seller who has taken steps to actively conceal a fact from the purchaser is under an obligation to disclose that fact. [179]

v. **Facts material to the transaction**: Some jurisdictions hold that a seller is under an obligation to disclose any facts which go to the essence of the transaction and of which the reasonable buyer would expect disclosure. [180]

c. **Material**: An assertion is material if it is about something which would be important to the reasonable person in the position of the party to whom it was made. [180]

d. **Fact**: An assertion is of fact if it is capable of objective truth or falsity and if it does not contain an expression of doubt or equivocation. A statement which concerns a subjective matter or which equivocates or expresses doubt is an assertion of opinion rather than of fact. [180]

i. **Assertion that Defendant holds a particular opinion**: It is sometimes held that in expressing an opinion, a defendant is asserting as a fact that he actually holds that opinion. [181]

ii. **Falsity of assertion that defendant holds a particular opinion**: If the defendant actually did hold the opinion which he said he held, the assertion of fact was true, even if the opinion was incorrect. If he actually did not hold that opinion, his assertion was false. [182]

iii. **Assertion that defendant holds a particular opinion not usually material**: Even if a defendant's expression of opinion asserts as a fact that she holds that particular opinion, frequently that fact (*i.e.*, that the defendant actually holds a particular opinion) is not material. [182-183]

iv. **Expression of opinion may impliedly assert fact**: A seller who expresses an opinion about the thing sold may be impliedly asserting that she knows of facts which justify her opinion. If she does not know of such facts, the expression of opinion may imply a false statement of fact. [183-184]

e. **Intent to induce plaintiff's reliance**: Unless an assertion was made with the desire (or knowledge to a substantial certainty) that it induce the plaintiff's reliance, it was not a representation, and, therefore, even if false, could not be a misrepresentation. [184]

2. **Inducing plaintiff's justified reliance**: Unless the plaintiff actually relies on the defendant's statement and is justified in doing so, no liability for misrepresentation will be imposed. [185-187]

a. **Reliance**: A plaintiff relied on the representation if the plaintiff knew of the defendant's representation, believed it, and made it a significant factor in his decision. A plaintiff who conducted an independent investigation to ascertain whether the defendant's statement was true probably did not rely on the statement, but rather on the investigation. [185-187]

b. **Justified reliance**: Liability is not imposed unless the plaintiff's reliance was justified. A plaintiff's reliance is justified if the reasonable person in the plaintiff's position would have relied. Since the reasonable person is not usually influenced by a seller's predictions or opinions regarding the subject of the sale, a plaintiff is not ordinarily justified in relying on them. [187]

3. **Damage**: There are two accepted methods of calculating damage in a misrepresentation case: the "benefit of the bargain" approach and the "out of pocket" approach. [189-190]

   a. **Benefit of the bargain**: Under the majority rule, the plaintiff's damage consists of the difference between the value actually received and the value which the plaintiff would have received if things had been as the defendant represented them to be. [190]

   b. **Out of pocket**: Under a minority rule, plaintiff's damage consists of the difference between the price which the plaintiff paid and the value which she received. [190]

   c. **Rule of flexibility**: Some of the jurisdictions which generally apply the benefit-of-the-bargain approach have adopted a rule of flexibility which permits a plaintiff to elect the out-of-pocket approach when it is impossible to prove the extent of her benefit-of-the-bargain loss. [190]

C. **Liability without fault**: In exceptional cases, liability has been imposed without fault. Usually, however, these cases have involved statements which qualified as express warranties. [191]

D. **Fault**: In most cases, fault is an essential element of torts based on misrepresentation. The specific fault required differs from "fraud" or "deceit" (*i.e.*, intentional misrepresentation) or negligent misrepresentation. [191]

II. INTENTIONAL MISREPRESENTATION

A. **Intent sufficient fault**: All jurisdictions agree that intent to misrepresent is sufficient fault to result in liability for misrepresentation if all the other elements are satisfied. [192]

B. **Definition**: A defendant had the necessary "intent" to misrepresent if when he made the statement, he knew that the statement was false, or if he acted with a reckless disregard for the truth. [192]

III. NEGLIGENT MISREPRESENTATION

A. **Commercial losses resulting from negligence**: Liability is not usually imposed for commercial losses which result from negligence. For this reason, approximately half of the jurisdictions refuse to impose liability for negligent misrepresentation, except to award damages for resulting injury to the person or property of plaintiff. In other jurisdictions, however, liability may be imposed for commercial losses resulting from negligent misrepresentation. [193]

B. **Definition**: A defendant made a negligent misrepresentation if she owed the plaintiff a duty to act reasonably in ascertaining the truth of the representation she was making and breached that duty. [194]

1. **Duty of reasonable care**: Even though a defendant has acted unreasonably in ascertaining the truth of his representations, he is not negligent as to the plaintiff unless he owed the plaintiff a duty of reasonable care. [194-195]

   a. **Privity**: Most cases which permit recovery for negligent misrepresentation hold that no duty of reasonable care exists unless plaintiff and defendant are in privity. [194]

   b. **Close relationship**: Some cases have held that a defendant may owe a plaintiff a duty of reasonable care in ascertaining the truth of defendant's representations even if the parties are not in privity, so long as plaintiff and defendant are in a close relationship which is similar to privity. [195]

   c. **Foreseeable reliance**: Some jurisdictions hold that in a case of negligent misrepresentation a defendant owes a plaintiff a duty of acting reasonably in ascertaining the truth of the defendant's representations when it is foreseeable that the plaintiff will rely on those representations. [195]

2. **Breach**: When a duty of reasonable care exists, defendant breaches it by either performing an act which the reasonable person would not have performed or failing to perform an act which the reasonable person would have performed. [196]

CHAPTER 12

INTERFERENCE WITH BUSINESS ADVANTAGE

I. INTERFERENCE WITH PROSPECTIVE BUSINESS ADVANTAGE

A. **General concept**: This tort is committed by maliciously preventing the plaintiff from realizing a legitimate expectation of profit. [197]

B. **Essential elements**: The essential elements of interference with prospective business advantage are (1) malice; (2) interference with the plaintiff's prospective business advantage; and (3) damage. [197-200]

1. **Malice**: A defendant had sufficient malice to support an action for interference with prospective business advantage if his primary motive was to injure plaintiff rather than to make a profit, or, if driven by the profit motive, he acted in a way which was either unlawful or highly unethical. Exceptions to this requirement exist for the variations known as interference with contract, false marketing, and injurious falsehood. [197-199]

2. **Interference**: An interference occurs when the defendant's act results in a reduction in the value of an economic benefit which the plaintiff legitimately expected to derive. [199]

3. **Prospective business advantage**: A prospective business advantage is a legitimate expectation of financial gain. [199]

4. **Damage**: The majority of jurisdictions require proof of special damage. A small minority permits proof of general damage when circumstances make it impossible to show exactly how much was lost as the result of the defendant's conduct. [200]

II. INTERFERENCE WITH CONTRACT

A. **Special protection for contracts**: Interference with contract is a special form of interference with prospective advantage with essential elements which differ substantially from those of interference with prospective business advantage. [200-201]

B. **Essential elements**: The essential elements of interference with contract are (1) intent; (2) interference; (3) with plaintiff's valid and existing contract right. [201]

1. **Intent**: A defendant intends an interference with the plaintiff's contract right when she desires (or knows to a substantial degree of certainty) that her act interfere with a contract right belonging to plaintiff of which defendant is aware. [201]

2. **Interference**: An interference occurs when there is a reduction in the value of the plaintiff's contract right. [202]

3. **Plaintiff's contract right**: For liability to attach, the interference must be with an expectation which the plaintiff has of making a profit because of a contract to which the plaintiff is a party. [202-203]

   a. **Contracts terminable at will or unenforceable over objection**: Some jurisdictions hold that a contract which is terminable at will is nothing more than a prospective business advantage and therefore require malice before imposing liability for interfering with it. Other jurisdictions treat such a contract as any other contract, imposing liability on the basis of intent alone. [202-203]

4. **Damage**: The majority of jurisdictions presume that a contract right has a value and, therefore, do not require proof of special damage. [204]

III. AFFIRMATIVE DEFENSE OF JUSTIFICATION

A. **Essential elements**: The essential elements of the privilege of justification are (1) an attempt to protect a legitimate interest; and (2) use of reasonable means. [204-205]

1. **Legitimate interest**: For the purpose of this defense, legitimate interests include protection of one's own financial interest, of the interests of society, or of the interests of another person to whom the defendant owes a moral obligation. [204]

2. **Reasonable means**: The means which a defendant uses to protect a legitimate interest are reasonable if the advantages likely to result from his use of them outweigh the disadvantages likely to result, considering the rights of the parties involved and the needs of society. [205]

IV. FALSE MARKETING

A. **General concept**: The law of torts imposes liability on one who uses the trademark of another in a way which is likely to mislead the public. [205]

B. **Essential elements**: The essential elements of false marketing are (1) use of the plaintiff's mark; (2) in a way which is likely to mislead the public. [205-206]

1. **Plaintiff's mark**: A mark is any symbol, logo, phrase, or other communication which identifies a product or service with the plaintiff, regardless of whether the mark is registered. In order to qualify as a mark, the symbol must be fanciful rather than descriptive. [205]

2. **Likelihood that public will be misled or negative effect**: There is no liability unless the defendant's use of the plaintiff's mark is likely to mislead the public into believing that it is buying plaintiff's product or service, or unless the defendant's use of the plaintiff's mark is likely to have a negative effect on sales of the plaintiff's product or service. [206]

3. **Strict liability**: If a defendant uses a plaintiff's mark in a way which is likely to mislead the public, the defendant is realizing a profit which should actually be the plaintiff's. For this reason, liability is imposed regardless of fault. [207]

4. **Damages**: Damages usually consist of the profit which the defendant realized as a result of the confusion which led consumers to believe that the defendant's product was the plaintiff's. [207]

5. **Statutory modification**: Federal statutes prohibiting unfair competition may create causes of action similar to the common law action for false marketing. These statutes are not discussed in this outline. [208]

CHAPTER 13
PRODUCTS LIABILITY

I. GENERAL CONCEPT

A. **Definition**: The term "products liability" characterizes a fact pattern in which the plaintiff claims to have been damaged as the result of contact or other association with a product which was furnished or handled by the defendant. [209]

B. **Common products liability theories**: Liability may be imposed if the result was intended, or if the defendant's conduct was negligent (*i.e.*, if there was fault). Liability may also be imposed if the defendant breached a warranty, made a misrepresentation, or simply furnished a defective product (*i.e.*, strict liability). [209]

II. INTENT

A. General concept: A defendant who furnishes a product with the desire (or knowledge to a substantial certainty) that the plaintiff, or one similarly situated, be injured by it, may be committing an intentional tort. [209]

B. Unlikely theory: It is possible for injuries which result from a plaintiff's contact with the defendant's product to be the basis of claims for battery, assault, and intentional infliction of mental harm. In a commercial setting, however, it is unusual for a provider of products to market them with the intent that such products cause harm. For this reason, few products liability cases are brought on intentional tort theories. [211]

III. NEGLIGENCE

A. General concept: Negligence is a breach of the duty of reasonable care. Thus, one who acts unreasonably in furnishing or handling a product may be held liable for negligence to a person to whom she owed a duty of reasonable care and who is injured as a result of the breach of that duty. [211]

1. **Duty of reasonable care**: At one time, it was understood that a manufacturer of products did not owe a duty of reasonable care to anyone who was not in privity of contract with him. It is now understood that, in designing, fabricating, or otherwise handling products, a defendant owes the plaintiff a duty of reasonable care whenever it is foreseeable that the defendant's product will create a risk to that plaintiff. [211]

2. **Breach**: In general, the duty of reasonable care is breached when the defendant does something that the reasonable person would not have done or fails to do something that the reasonable person would have done. Ordinarily, courts determine whether a particular act or omission was reasonable by weighing the advantages foreseeably resulting from the act or omission against the disadvantages foreseeably resulting from it. [213-215]

   a. **Specific allegation**: It is not possible to apply the balancing test unless the conduct alleged to be negligent is specifically identified. [214]

   b. **Res Ipsa Loquitur**: The doctrine of *res ipsa loquitur* may be applied to products liability cases when the plaintiff's theory is negligence. [214]

   c. **Violation of statute**: In some cases, the fact that a defendant violated a statute may help to establish negligence, without regard to whether that defendant's conduct was unreasonable. [215]

IV. BREACH OF WARRANTY

A. Contract principles: The law of torts has borrowed the warranty concept for use in products liability claims. Since it is essentially based on contracts principles, it may result in the imposition of liability without fault. [215]

B. Warranty defined: A warranty is a promise regarding the quality or condition of a product. Like any other promise, a warranty may be express or implied. [216]

1. **Express warranty**: A warranty is express if it is stated in words or a substitute for words. [216]

2. **Implied warranty**: A warranty is implied if it would be gathered or inferred by the reasonable person observing the circumstances and the defendant's conduct. [216]

C. **Essential elements**: The essential elements of any claim for breach of warranty are (1) the existence of a warranty; (2) that it flowed from the defendant to the plaintiff; (3) that it was breached; and (4) that the breach was a proximate cause of the damage. [217]

D. **Breach of Express Warranty**: A defendant who has made an express warranty regarding a product is liable to any plaintiff to whom the warranty flows, for any damage which results proximately from a breach of the warranty. [217]

1. **Existence of warranty**: An express warranty exists when an assertion of fact is made which becomes part of the basis of the bargain. [217]

2. **Warranty must flow from defendant to plaintiff**: In a products liability case, an express warranty flows from any party who made it to any party who relied on it. [219]

3. **Breach**: An express warranty is breached if the product fails to conform to the promise which was made about it. [219]

E. **Breach of Implied Warranty of Merchantability**: When a product is sold with an implied warranty that it is merchantable, the seller is liable without fault for damage which results proximately from the product's failure to be fit for the use intended. [220]

1. **Existence of warranty**: UCC section 2-314 provides that in the absence of a valid disclaimer every sale by a merchant implies a warranty that the product sold is merchantable. [220]

a. **Disclaimer**: The UCC provides that in order for a writing to disclaim the implied warranty of merchantability, the disclaimer must appear in conspicuous print and must contain the word "merchantability", or a phrase such as "as is", "with all faults", or other language which in common understanding indicates that there are no implied warranties. [220]

b. **Definition of merchant**: Under the UCC, a "merchant" is a person in the business of buying and selling the kind of products involved, or who holds himself out to have special knowledge about products like the one involved, or who employs a person who has or holds himself out to have special knowledge about the product. [220]

c. **Definition of merchantable**: A product is merchantable if it is fit for ordinary use. [220]

2. **Warranty must flow from defendant to plaintiff**: [220-222]

a. **From whom the warranty flows**: The implied warranty of merchantability flows from all persons handling the finished product from the time it is manufactured, which includes the manufacturer, all wholesalers and middle-persons, and the retailer. Many jurisdictions hold that the implied warranty of merchantability does not flow from suppliers of component parts. [220]

b. **To whom the warranty flows**: UCC section 2-318 defines to whom an implied warranty flows, and was adopted in three alternative forms. Alternative A extends the protection of the warranty to all members of the purchaser's household who foreseeably will be affected by the product and who sustain personal injury. Alternative B extends the protection of the warranty to all natural persons who foreseeably will be affected by the product and who sustain personal injury. Alternative C extends the protection of the warranty to all natural and artificial persons who (which) foreseeably will be affected by the product and who (which) sustain personal injury or property damage. [221-222]

3. **Breach**: The implied warranty of merchantability is breached if the product is unfit for ordinary use. Ordinary use includes the kind of use which is common by the kind of person

who could reasonably be expected to come into contact with the product, even though such use was not intended by the manufacturer and even though such use may be improper or negligent. [223]

F. Implied Warranty of Fitness for Buyer's Particular Purpose: If a seller impliedly warrants that the product sold is fit for the particular purpose which the buyer had in mind when purchasing it, that seller is liable without fault for damage which results from the product's failure to be fit for that purpose. [225-226]

1. **Existence of warranty**: UCC section 2-315 provides that when a seller knows of a buyer's particular purpose in purchasing a product and knows that the buyer is relying on the seller's skill and judgment in furnishing a product to fit that purpose, the sale implies a warranty that the product is fit for the buyer's particular purpose. [225]

2. **Warranty must flow from defendant to plaintiff**: The warranty of fitness for the buyer's particular purpose flows from the seller who selected the product to members of the group specified by whichever alternative form of UCC section 2-318 is adopted by the particular jurisdiction. [226]

3. **Breach**: The implied warranty of fitness for buyer's particular purpose is breached if the product is unfit for the buyer's particular purpose. [226]

G. Exclusion or modification of warranties: Although the law provides for the existence and enforcement of warranties, parties are free to contract to exclude or modify these warranties. [227]

1. **Express warranty**: Under the UCC, words or conduct which tend to create an express warranty and words or conduct which tend to negate or exclude such a warranty shall be construed as consistent with each other wherever reasonable. The UCC further provides that negation or limitation is inoperative to the extent that such construction would be unreasonable. [227]

2. **Implied warranties**: Under the UCC, implied warranties may be excluded or modified by conspicuous writing in language which, in common understanding, makes it clear that there are no implied warranties. In addition, a written attempt to modify the implied warranty of merchantability must contain the word "merchantability." If, before entering into a contract for sale, the buyer has examined or refused to examine the goods, there is no implied warranty with respect to defects that an examination would have disclosed to a reasonable person. [228]

H. Limitation of remedy: The UCC provides that parties may agree to limit remedies or to provide for exclusive remedies for breach of warranty. [228]

1. **Not exclusive unless so specified**: Unless the agreement specifies that named remedies are the exclusive remedies, common law and UCC remedies continue to be available. [228]

2. **Remedy which fails of purpose**: Where circumstances make an exclusive or limited remedy fail of its essential purpose, all other remedies continue to be available. [229]

3. **Unconscionable limitation**: An agreement which limits or excludes consequential damages is enforceable unless it is unconscionable. Limitation of consequential damages for personal injury is *prima facie* unconscionable. [229]

V. MISREPRESENTATION

A. Common law: Since suppliers of products frequently make representations concerning those products, it may be possible for a plaintiff to proceed on a misrepresentation theory if she is injured because the statements are false. Ordinarily, a plaintiff proceeding on this theory is required to prove fault. [229]

B. **Restatement (2d) of Torts, section 402B**: Some jurisdictions have adopted the view expressed in section 402B of the Restatement (2d) of Torts. The essential elements of this theory are (1) the defendant is a professional seller; (2) who made a public misrepresentation; (3) which induced plaintiff's justified reliance; (4) resulting in damage. [230-232]

1. **Professional sellers**: The Restatement applies only to professional sellers of chattels. [230]
2. **Public misrepresentation**: The Restatement specifies that it applies where the misrepresentation is made in labeling, advertising, or otherwise to the public. [230-231]
3. **Plaintiff's justified reliance**: Under the Restatement, this requirement is identical to its counterpart in the common law. [231]
4. **Liability without regard to fault or privity**: Where applicable, the Restatement modifies the common law by eliminating the requirements of fault and privity. [231-232]

VI. STRICT PRODUCTS LIABILITY (STRICT LIABILITY IN TORT)

A. **General concept**: Under section 402A of the Restatement (2d) of Torts, a professional seller of a product may be held strictly liable for damage which results from a defect in the product which existed when it left the defendant's hands and which made the product unreasonably dangerous. [234-235]

B. **Essential elements**: Under the Restatement view as modified by judicial decisions, the following essential elements must be satisfied: (1) it was foreseeable that the plaintiff would be affected by the product; (2) the defendant was a professional seller or supplier; (3) the product was expected to and did in fact reach the consumer in a substantially unchanged condition after leaving the defendant's hands; (4) when the defendant placed the product in the stream of commerce, it was defective; and (5) the defect made the product unreasonably dangerous. [234-235]

1. **All members of chain of commercial distribution**: Strict products liability may be imposed on all sellers and suppliers of the finished product, including manufacturers, wholesalers, middlepersons, and retailers. Most jurisdictions have been unwilling to extend this liability to manufacturers of parts which went into the finished product. [236]
2. **Suppliers other than sellers**: Some jurisdictions have imposed strict products liability on lessors, professionals who furnish products as part of the professional services rendered, and other suppliers, although they are non-sellers. [236-237]
3. **Defective condition**: Courts have developed several tests and definitions to determine whether a product is in a defective condition. [240]
   a. **Consumer expectation**: Under this approach, a product is defective if its condition would defeat the reasonable expectations of the reasonable consumer. A product may defeat these expectations in the way it is packaged, labeled, marketed, or in the warnings and instructions which accompany it. [241]
   b. **Reasonable seller with knowledge**: Some cases have stated that a product is defective if a reasonable seller with knowledge of its condition would not have sold it. [243]
   c. **Design defects and manufacturing defects**: Some jurisdictions impose strict liability for damage resulting from a manufacturing defect, but not for damage resulting from a design defect. [244]
      i. **Design defect**: If the product is made the way it was designed to be made but still is defective it has a design defect. [244]
      ii. **Manufacturing defect**: If the product is defective because it was not made the way it was designed to be made, it has a manufacturing defect. [244]

4. **Unreasonably dangerous condition**: In many jurisdictions, the rules used to determine whether a product is "defective" may also be used to determine whether a product is "unreasonably dangerous." In other jurisdictions, different definitions are applied. [245]

   a. **Restatement view**: Restatement section 402A, comment (i), states that a product is unreasonably dangerous if it is dangerous "to an extent beyond that which would be contemplated by the ordinary consumer who purchases it, with the ordinary knowledge common to the community as to its characteristics." [245]

   b. **Balancing disadvantages against advantages**: If the condition of a product creates more foreseeable risk than foreseeable benefit, it is unreasonably dangerous. [245-246]

5. **Unavoidably unsafe products**: Products which are incapable of being made safe for their intended or ordinary use, but which are necessary or desirable, are not defective if accompanied by proper instructions and warnings. [244]

C. **Minority views**: Some cases have held that strict liability may be imposed if the product was defective, without regard to whether it was unreasonably dangerous. Some cases have held that strict liability may be imposed if the product was unreasonably dangerous without regard to whether it was defective. Some cases have held that strict liability may be imposed if the product was either defective or unreasonably dangerous. [248]

CHAPTER 14
DEFAMATION

I. GENERAL CONCEPTS

A. **Protection of reputation**: Defamation is the generic name given to libel and slander, torts which involve damage to the plaintiff's reputation. [249]

B. **Essential elements**: The essential elements of defamation are (1) a defamatory statement concerning plaintiff; (2) falsity; (3) fault; (4) publication; and (5) damage. [249]

1. **Defamatory**: A statement is defamatory if it tends to injure the plaintiff's reputation by holding the plaintiff up to shame, disgrace, or ridicule in the eyes of a substantial group of respectable people. [249-250]

   a. **Ambiguous statements**: If a statement is capable of having more than one meaning, courts usually hold that it means whatever the reasonable person hearing (or reading) it would think it means. [250-251]

   b. **Defamation by innuendo**: If a statement contains all the facts necessary to damage the plaintiff's reputation, it is said to be defamatory on its face. If the statement alone would not damage the plaintiff's reputation, but there exists a fact not mentioned in the statement which when taken with the statement would tend to damage the plaintiff's reputation, the statement is said to be defamatory by innuendo. [251]

2. **Statement**: A statement is any communication and need not be made in words. [252]

3. **Concerning plaintiff**: A statement is one concerning the plaintiff if the reasonable person with knowledge of the plaintiff or of the plaintiff's attributes would believe that the statement was about the plaintiff. [253]

   a. **Group to which plaintiff belongs**: If a defamatory statement is made about a group of persons to which the plaintiff belongs, it is a statement concerning the plaintiff if the group is small enough so that the reasonable person who knows that the plaintiff is a member of the group would believe that the statement is about the plaintiff. Courts frequently treat a defamatory statement about some members of a group as if it were made about all members of that group. [253-254]

b. **Living person only**: Most jurisdictions agree that only a living person can be defamed. [254]

4. **Falsity**: The United States Supreme Court has held that in a defamation action brought by a private person against a media defendant, or by a public person against anybody, the plaintiff is required to prove that the defamatory statement made by the defendant was false. So far, the Supreme Court has not clarified the Constitutional requirements in a defamation claim brought by a private person against a non-media defendant. [255]

   a. **Definition**: A statement is false if it is not substantially true. [255]

   b. **Meaning of statement**: If one of the statement's meanings is true, but the meaning which the reasonable person would give it is false, the statement is false. [255]

5. **Opinion**: The United States Supreme Court has stated that there is no such thing as a false opinion. For this reason, a statement of opinion cannot be false, and cannot result in liability for defamation. [256]

   a. **Definition**: An opinion is a statement which is not capable of objective truth or falsity. [256]

   b. **Expression of doubt not sufficient to make statement an opinion**: If the statement made about the plaintiff is capable of objective truth or falsity, it is an assertion of fact, even if expressions of doubt are annexed to it. [256-257]

   c. **Ambiguous statements**: In deciding whether an ambiguous statement is an expression of fact or of opinion it is necessary to determine which of its possible meanings the reasonable person hearing or reading it would understand it to have. [257]

   d. **Four-part test**: In deciding whether a statement is an expression of fact or of opinion, several Circuits of the U.S. Court of Appeals have recognized a four part test which considers the statement's precision, verifiability, literary context, and public context. [258]

   e. **Defamatory part of statement only**: In deciding whether the statement was false, it is necessary to consider only the defamatory part of the statement. [259]

6. **Fault**: The United States Supreme Court has held that in defamation actions brought by private persons against media defendants or by public officials or public figures against anybody, the Constitution requires a showing of fault. So far, the Supreme Court has not clarified the Constitutional requirements in defamation actions brought by private persons against non-media defendants. (See *supra*.) [260-264]

   a. **Public official**: The United States Supreme Court has defined a public official as an employee in the hierarchy of government who has or reasonably appears to have substantial control over the conduct of public affairs. [260]

   b. **Public figure**: The United States Supreme Court has said that an involuntary public figure is a person who, without necessarily seeking to do so, has achieved such pervasive fame and notoriety that she is known to the great mass of society. A voluntary public figure is a person who has injected himself into a public controversy for the purpose of influencing public opinion (*i.e.*, has "mounted the rostrum"). [260]

   c. **Private person**: A private person is a plaintiff who is neither a public official nor a public figure. [261]

   d. **Media defendant**: A media defendant is one who (which) is in the business of publishing or who (which) customarily publishes information. [261]

   e. **Kind of fault required**: If the plaintiff is a public person (*i.e.*, public official or public figure), she is required to show that the defendant acted with actual malice. If the plaintiff is a private person suing a media defendant, she is required to show that the defendant acted either with actual malice or negligently. [262]

i. **Actual malice**: A defendant acts with "actual malice" when she makes a false statement with knowledge that it is false, or while entertaining subjective doubts about its truth or falsity. [262]

ii. **Negligence**: A defendant has acted negligently when the reasonable person in defendant's situation would have known that the statements were false, or would have entertained doubts about their truth, or when the defendant fails to make the investigation which the reasonable person in his situation would have made. [263]

7. **Publication**: There is no liability for making a defamatory statement unless that statement is published. [264-269]

a. **Definition**: Publication means communication to at least one person other than plaintiff who understood the statement (although not necessarily in its defamatory sense). [264]

b. **Fault in publication**: Communication does not satisfy the requirement of publication unless the defendant intended to publish it [*i.e.*, desired (or knew to a substantial degree of certainty) that it be communicated to a third person], or unless the publication resulted from the defendant's negligence. [265]

c. **Repetition and republication**: One who repeats a defamatory statement which she heard from another may be liable for damage resulting from the publication. In addition, a person who publishes a defamatory statement to another when she knows or should know that the other will repeat it may also be held liable for damages resulting from the repetition. [266-267]

d. **Single publication rule**: A majority of jurisdictions in the United States holds that all copies of a single edition of a printed publication constitute a single publication. A minority of jurisdictions regards each copy as a separate publication. [267-268]

e. **Form of publication**: Defamatory statements which are published in written or printed form are classified as libel. Defamatory statements which are published in spoken form are classified as slander. [268]

8. **Damage**: The element of damage is satisfied if the plaintiff's reputation has been injured as a result of the defamatory statement published by the defendant. [269-272]

a. **Other damage**: Once the plaintiff establishes injury to her reputation, other damage which results proximately from the injury may also be recoverable. [269]

b. **Presumed damage**: In some defamation cases it has been traditional for courts to permit the plaintiff to rely on a presumption of damage. [269-271]

i. **Slander**: In cases of ordinary slander, the plaintiff may not rely on a presumption of damage. However, if the slander accuses plaintiff of a crime of moral turpitude, a loathsome disease, unchastity (in a female), or unfitness for plaintiff's occupation, it is called slander *per se*, and damage may be presumed. [270]

ii. **Libel**: If the defendant's statement is libelous on its face (sometimes called "libel *per se*"), the plaintiff may rely on a presumption of damage. If the statement is libelous by innuendo (sometimes called "libel *per quod*"), the rules which apply to slander should be applied to it. (*i.e.*, There is no presumption of damage unless the statement fits into one of the categories which would, if it were spoken, make it slander *per se*.) [271]

c. **Punitive damages**: As in any tort case, the plaintiff may recover punitive damages if she can show that the defendant was motivated by malice. [272]

d. **Constitutional requirements**: Although a private person may make out a defamation case without establishing actual malice, the United States Supreme Court has held that damage can not be presumed in the case of a private person who sues a non-media defendant, in the absence of a showing of actual malice. [272]

CHAPTER 15

TORTS RELATED TO DEFAMATION

I. INJURIOUS FALSEHOOD

A. **General concept**: Injurious falsehood, sometimes called business defamation, is a tort committed by injuring the plaintiff's business reputation. [274]

B. **Distinguished from defamation**: A statement is defamatory if it tends to injure the plaintiff's personal reputation. A statement which tends to damage the plaintiff's business reputation may be an injurious falsehood. [274]

C. **Essential elements**: The essential elements of injurious falsehood are substantially similar to the essential elements of defamation, and consist of (1) a disparaging statement concerning the plaintiff's business interest; (2) falsity; (3) fault; (4) publication; and (5) damage. [274]

1. **Disparaging statement concerning plaintiff's business interest**: A statement is disparaging if it would lead a substantial group of people not to do business with the plaintiff. [275]

2. **Falsity**: The Constitutional requirements which necessitate that the plaintiff prove falsity in a defamation action apply also to injurious falsehood claims. [275]

3. **Fault**: The few cases which have been decided by the United States Supreme Court indicate that the fault requirement in injurious falsehood claims is substantially the same as in defamation claims. [275]

4. **Publication**: The publication element of injurious falsehood is substantially identical to the publication element of defamation. [276]

5. **Damage**: Injurious falsehood differs from defamation in that there is no presumption of damage. The majority of jurisdictions requires proof of special damages to support an injurious falsehood claim. A growing minority of jurisdictions holds that where it is not possible for the plaintiff to prove special damage, the question of damages may be submitted to a jury. [276]

II. FALSE LIGHT

A. **General concept**: Casting the plaintiff in a false light in the public eye (*i.e.*, "false light") is committed by publishing false statements about the plaintiff which would embarrass the plaintiff and which would be offensive to the reasonable person in the plaintiff's situation. [276-277]

B. **Essential elements**: The essential elements of false light privacy are similar to those of defamation and are as follows: (1) embarrassing statement concerning plaintiff; (2) falsity; (3) fault; (4) publication; and (5) damage. [277-278]

1. **Embarrassing statement concerning plaintiff**: Although a statement is not defamatory unless it would hold the plaintiff up to shame, disgrace or ridicule, a statement is sufficiently embarrassing to be the subject of a false light claim if the reasonable person in the plaintiff's situation would be offended by its publication. [277]

2. **Concerning plaintiff**: As in defamation cases, a statement concerns the plaintiff if the reasonable person who knows the plaintiff would recognize him from the statement. [278]

3. **Falsity**: This requirement is substantially identical to its counterpart in a defamation action. Although the Supreme Court has not yet indicated whether the Constitution requires that the plaintiff prove falsity, it is clear that a true statement cannot be the basis of liability for this tort. It is likely that all Constitutional requirements which have been applied to defamation will also be applied to false light. [278]

4. **Fault**: Decisions of the Supreme Court indicate that in any false light privacy action against a media defendant, actual malice as defined in defamation cases is required. [278]

5. **Publication**: This requirement is substantially identical to its counterpart in defamation actions. [278]

6. **Damage**: Since false light is not based on damage to reputation, it is not necessary for the plaintiff to show that her reputation has suffered. Some proof of damage is required, although this may consist entirely of mental suffering by the plaintiff. [278]

III. INTENTIONAL INFLICTION OF MENTAL SUFFERING

A. Relationship to defamation: In an attempt to avoid the constitutional requirements in defamation cases, attempts have been made to assert claims for intentional infliction of mental suffering in cases involving the publication of insulting statements about the plaintiff. [278]

B. Constitutional requirements: The United States Supreme Court has stated that if the claim of mental suffering is based upon the publication of statements about the plaintiff which are alleged to hold the plaintiff up to shame, disgrace, or ridicule, the same Constitutional requirements which apply to defamation liability apply to liability for intentional infliction of the mental suffering. [279]

IV. AFFIRMATIVE DEFENSES

A. Neutral reportage: Many jurisdictions recognize a privilege which protects a media defendant who (which) neutrally reports on newsworthy events. [279]

B. Justification: A defendant's publication of defamatory statements may be privileged if the publication was a reasonable way to protect a legitimate interest. [280]

1. **Legitimate interest**: A legitimate interest is one's own financial interest, the interest of another person to whom a moral obligation is owed, or the interest of society. [280]

2. **Reasonable means**: The defendant's attempt to protect a legitimate interest must be by reasonable means. This means publication in a reasonable manner to persons who are in a position to help protect the interest involved. In addition, many jurisdictions require that the defendant have a reasonable belief in the truth of the statements published. [280-281]

C. Retraction: In some jurisdictions, statutory or common law rules provide that a defendant may mitigate damages resulting from the publication of defamatory statements by retracting those statements. Some jurisdictions provide that a defendant who does so is liable only for actual damage. [282]

CHAPTER 16
INVASION OF PRIVACY

I. BACKGROUND AND GENERAL CONCEPT

A. **Four torts**: It is generally recognized that there are four separate ways of committing a tort by invading privacy, each based on a different concept. One of these, casting the plaintiff in a false light in the public eye (*i.e.*, false light), has already been discussed as a variation on defamation, *supra*. [284]

B. **Personal right**: It is generally recognized that the right of privacy is personal and is not inherited by an individual's survivors following her death. [284]

C. **Damage**: In most cases, a plaintiff is not required to prove damage resulting from the invasion of her privacy. It is presumed that such an invasion results at least in mental suffering. [284]

II. APPROPRIATION OF PLAINTIFF'S IDENTITY

A. **General concept**: This tort is based on the principle that a plaintiff's identity is like an item of property, the commercial use of which she has a right to control. Unauthorized use of a plaintiff's identity by a defendant who does so for purposes of personal gain is a violation of this right. [284]

B. **Essential elements**: The essential elements of invasion of privacy by appropriation of identity are (1) unauthorized use; (2) of the plaintiff's identity; (3) for a commercial purpose. [285-287]

1. **Unauthorized use**: A defendant has made unauthorized use of the plaintiff's identity if she has used it without the permission of the plaintiff. [285]

2. **Plaintiff's identity**: Anything which serves to identify the plaintiff (*e.g.*, photograph, voice) may be the subject of liability. [285]

3. **Commercial purpose**: Most cases hold that the use of the plaintiff's identity is not tortious unless it does, or is likely to, enrich the defendant in some way. If the use of the plaintiff's identity is newsworthy, however, it does not lead to liability for appropriation, even if the defendant is in some way enriched by it. [286]

4. **Strict liability**: The plaintiff may recover without showing intent or negligence by the defendant. [287]

C. **Damage**: Although damage, at least in the form of mental suffering, is usually presumed in cases of invasion of privacy, a plaintiff seeking damages for appropriation of identity may also be entitled to whatever profit the defendant derived from the unauthorized use of the plaintiff's identity. [288]

D. **Right of publicity**: Although it is generally recognized that the right of privacy dies with the person to whom it belongs, a person who profits from the commercial use of his identity while alive may thus convert it to an inheritable property right (sometimes called the right of publicity). Invasion of this right may be the subject of action by his heirs subsequent to his death. [288-289]

III. INTRUSION INTO SECLUSION

A. **General concept**: This tort is based on the principle that every person has a private space in which she is entitled to be let alone, and that an unreasonable intrusion into that space is a violation of that right. [289]

B. **Essential elements**: The essential elements of this tort are (1) intentional; (2) intrusion; (3) into plaintiff's private space; (4) in an offensive manner. [289-291]

1. **Intent**: An intrusion is intended when the defendant desires (or knows) that his conduct result in an invasion of the plaintiff's private space. [289]

2. **Intrusion**: Intrusion consists of an entry into the plaintiff's private space, either physically or by electronic means. [290]

3. **Plaintiff's private space**: Since intrusion is an invasion of privacy, the incident must occur at a time when, and in a place where, the plaintiff is entitled to seclusion. [290]

4. **Offensive manner**: An intrusion is not tortious unless the method by which it is accomplished would be offensive to the reasonable person in the plaintiff's situation. [291]

IV. PUBLIC DISCLOSURE

A. **General concept**: This tort is committed by publicly revealing offensive secrets about the plaintiff. It is based on the belief that a person has a right to keep certain facts about himself from public knowledge. [292]

B. **Essential elements**: The essential elements of this invasion of privacy tort are (1) public disclosure; (2) of private facts about the plaintiff; (3) the disclosure of which would be offensive to the reasonable person in the plaintiff's situation. [292]

1. **Public disclosure**: The essence of this tort is that secret information about the plaintiff has been made public, against her wishes. In order for a disclosure to be sufficiently public, it must be made to the public in general, or to a large number of persons. [292]

2. **Private fact**: The information disclosed must be something which was not formerly known to the general public. The United States Supreme Court has held that no fact which is a matter of public record may be regarded as a private fact. [292-293]

3. **Offensive to reasonable person**: For liability to attach, the disclosure must be one which the reasonable person in the plaintiff's situation would find offensive. [293-294]

CHAPTER 17

MISUSE OF JUDICIAL PROCEDURE

I. GENERAL CONCEPT

A. **A group of torts**: This outline considers three torts based on misuse of judicial procedure. Two of these — malicious prosecution and malicious use of process — are so closely related that many jurisdictions and writers treat them as one. They involve the improper institution or continuation of a criminal or civil proceeding. The third — abuse of process — involves the use of a judicial proceeding for an improper purpose. [295]

B. **Nomenclature**: Since the plaintiff in an action for misuse of judicial procedure was probably a defendant in the proceding which was the basis of the lawsuit, care should be taken to understand that reference in this outline to parties as "plaintiff" or "defendant" is based on their status in a lawsuit brought on one of the three theories discussed in this section. [295]

II. MALICIOUS PROSECUTION

A. **General concept**: Malicious prosecution is a tort committed by improperly causing the plaintiff to be the subject of a criminal prosecution. [295]

B. Essential elements: The essential elements of malicious prosecution are (1) institution or continuation by defendant of a criminal proceeding against plaintiff; (2) termination of that proceeding in favor of plaintiff; (3) lack of probable cause; (4) malice; and (5) damage. [295]

1. **Institution or continuation of a criminal proceeding against plaintiff**: A proceeding is criminal if it can lead to the incarceration or execution of the person being prosecuted. "Institution" refers to the actual commencement of a criminal proceeding and ordinarily takes place when a warrant or indictment is issued or an arrest is made. Continuation of a criminal proceeding occurs when the defendant prevents it from terminating when it might or fails to terminate it when she should. [296-298]

2. **Termination in favor of plaintiff**: No action for malicious prosecution can be brought until the proceeding against the plaintiff which is the subject of that action has terminated. [298-301]

   a. **Dismissal without prejudice**: Since a proceeding may be reinstituted after being dismissed without prejudice, such a dismissal is not a termination sufficient to support a subsequent action for malicious prosecution. [298]

   b. **Appeals**: In the event of an appeal, termination is not final until the appellate process is complete. [298]

   c. **Discontinuance with leave to renew**: So long as the proceeding can be re-instituted, its termination is not final. [298]

   d. **On the merits**: A termination on the merits is an indication that the person prosecuted was not guilty. For this purpose, a termination is on the merits if it occurs after a trial has begun. [299]

   e. **Lack of evidence**: A dismissal for lack of evidence, even if it occurs prior to the commencement of trial, is an indication that the person prosecuted is innocent and satisfies the requirement of termination. [299]

   f. **Abandonment and failure to prosecute**: Abandonment of the prosecution and willful failure to prosecute, are both regarded as indications that the prosecutor realized that the person being prosecuted was not guilty, and are usually regarded as final terminations in favor of the person being prosecuted. [299]

   g. **Relitigation of plaintiff's guilt**: A defendant in a malicious prosecution action is permitted to prove by a preponderance of the evidence that the plaintiff really was guilty of the crime for which she was prosecuted. If the defendant is successful in doing so, the termination of the criminal proceeding does not satisfy the requirement of termination in favor of the plaintiff, and plaintiff's action for malicious prosecution should fail. [300]

3. **Lack of probable cause**: Liability for malicious prosecution cannot be imposed on a person who instituted a criminal proceeding against another if she had probable cause to believe that the person prosecuted was guilty of a crime. Probable cause is defined as a sincere and reasonable belief that a crime has been committed and that the person prosecuted is the one who committed it. [301]

   a. **Sincere belief**: A defendant has a sufficiently sincere belief if she is personally convinced that the person prosecuted has committed a crime. [301]

   b. **Reasonable belief**: A belief that the person being prosecuted is guilty is reasonable if it is supported by facts which would lead the reasonable person to so believe. [301]

   c. **Exception for public prosecutor**: A public prosecutor has sufficient probable cause to avoid liability if she has a reasonable, but not necessarily sincere, belief in the guilt of the person being prosecuted. [301]

d. **Conviction**: The fact that the Plaintiff was convicted establishes a presumption that there was probable cause for the prosecution. [301]

4. **Malice**: Malice specifically means a primary purpose other than to accomplish justice, and may be inferred from a lack of probable cause. [301-302]

5. **Damage**: Since it is almost inevitable that a person prosecuted for a crime will suffer damage as a result, many jurisdictions recognize a presumption of damage. [302-303]

III. MALICIOUS USE OF PROCESS

A. **General concept**: Malicious use of process is a tort committed by improperly causing the plaintiff to be the subject of a civil proceeding. [303]

B. **Essential elements**: The essential elements for malicious use of process are substantially identical to the essential elements of malicious prosecution, and are as follows: (1) institution or continuation of a civil proceeding against plaintiff; (2) termination in favor of plaintiff; (3) lack of probable cause for the proceeding; (4) malice; and (5) damage. [303-305]

1. **Institution or continuation of civil proceeding**: Ordinarily, a civil proceeding is instituted by either the filing or service of process. [304]

2. **Termination in favor of plaintiff**: It is necessary for the plaintiff to show that the proceeding which was instituted against him terminated in a way which establishes that he was not liable. Since this termination would have been based on a preponderance of the evidence, and since that is the same burden of proof which would be applied in the malicious use of process case, there can be no relitigation of the issue of plaintiff's liabilty. [304]

3. **Lack of probable cause**: This requirement is similar to its counterpart in malicious prosecution, except that it means a sincere and reasonable belief that the person being sued is liable. [305]

4. **Malice**: The requirement of malice is similar to its counterpart in malicious prosecution in that it means a primary purpose other than to do justice. [305]

5. **Damage**: Since the winner of a civil proceeding is usually awarded a judgment for statutory costs, a plaintiff suing for malicious use of process must prove damage in excess of the costs received in the proceeding. [305]

IV. ABUSE OF PROCESS

A. **General concept**: Abuse of process is a tort committed by using a legitimate process of the court for an illegitimate purpose. [306]

B. **Essential elements**: The essential elements of abuse of process are (1) use of legitimate process of the court (2) for an illegitimate purpose. [306-309]

1. **Illegitimate purpose**: Since abuse of process is based on the issuance of a process which the defendant was entitled to issue (*i.e.*, legitimate process of the court), liability will be imposed only if the defendant's purpose was illegitimate. In most cases, this illegitimate purpose involves an attempt at collateral coercion. [307]

2. **Termination in plaintiff's favor not required**: It is not necessary for the plaintiff to show that the proceeding which is the subject of her abuse of process claim terminated in her favor. [308-309]

CHAPTER 18
IMMUNITIES

I. GENERAL CONCEPT

A. **Definition**: Immunity is freedom from liability for conduct which would ordinarily be regarded as liability-forming. [310]

B. **Modern trend**: In recent years, most traditional rules of immunity have either been abolished or severely restricted and modified. [310]

II. GOVERNMENTAL IMMUNITY

A. **General concept**: Traditionally, governments are immune from tort liability to their subjects unless they grant their subjects permission to sue. In the United States, this rule of immunity has been softened by statutes which grant permission to sue the government on certain theories as long as certain conditions are met. [310]

B. **Federal immunity**: The Federal Torts Claims Act of 1946 waives the federal government's immunity in certain cases by stating that the government is liable "in the same manner and to the same extent as a private individual." This statutory authorization is subject to restrictions and qualifications. [310-311]

1. **State law applies**: Although actions against the United States must be brought in Federal courts, the FTCA provides that state rules of tort law should be applied. [310]
2. **No jury trials**: No claim against the United States brought under the FTCA may be tried before a jury. Instead, the judge sits as the trier of the facts as well as of the law. [310]
3. **Requirement of notice**: Under the FTCA, before a claim can be instituted against the United States, it is necessary that notice be given to the appropriate agency within two years after the claim arises. [311]
4. **No strict liability**: The United States Supreme Court has held that under the FTCA the federal government cannot be held liable under a strict liability theory. [311]
5. **War and postal service**: The FTCA does not waive the federal government's immunity from liability for damage resulting from military activities in wartime or from delivery of the mail. [311]
6. **Exercise of discretion**: The FTCA does not waive the federal government's immunity from liability for damage resulting from "discretionary functions or duties" of the government. [311]

C. **State immunity**: In the same way as the federal government, almost all of the state governments have enacted legislation granting blanket permission for tort claims to be made. [311-312]

D. **Municipal immunity**: Under common law, municipalities are immune from tort liability. Most states have enacted laws waiving this immunity, however. [312]

III. PUBLIC OFFICIALS

A. **General concept**: To assure that public officials will be free to carry out their duties without the inhibitions likely to result from fear of tort liability, they all enjoy some form of immunity. [312]

B. **Judicial officials**: So long as they are carrying out a judicial function, judges and other judicial officials are absolutely immune from tort liability. [312-313]

C. Legislators: So long as they are carrying out a legislative function, legislators are absolutely immune from tort liability. [313-314]

D. Executive immunity: In most jurisdictions, executive officials are immune from tort liability for discretionary acts but not for ministerial acts. A discretionary act is one which requires the official to exercise judgment. A ministerial act is one which does not. [314]

CHAPTER 1

INTRODUCTION AND ANALYSIS

I. GENERAL CONCEPT

A. Rights and duties: A right is a legal entitlement. A duty is a legal obligation. Thus, in effect, rights and duties are the counterparts of each other.

> **Example:** Mary is required by law to protect John. Since Mary has a legal obligation to protect John, she has a duty to do so. Since John is legally entitled to Mary's protection, he has a right to it. It may also be said that protection is a right which John has against Mary and a duty which Mary owes to John.

B. Constitutional law, criminal law, and civil law distinguished:

1. **Constitutional law:** Constitutional law is the study of the duties which society owes to its individual members, and of the rights which its individual members have against society.

2. **Criminal law:** Criminal law is the study of the duties which individual members of society owe to society, and the rights which society has against its individual members. A violation of an individual's duty to society (or of a right which society has against an individual) is called a crime.

3. **Civil law:** Civil law is the study of the duties which individual members of society owe to each other, and of the rights which individual members of society have against each other.

C. Contracts and torts distinguished: The law of contracts and the law of torts are branches of the civil law, because they both concern themselves with the duties which individual members of society owe to each other, and the rights which individual members of society have against each other.

1. **Contracts:** Sometimes individuals have rights against each other and owe duties to each other because of promises which have been made. These rights and duties are the subject of the law of contracts. A violation of one of these duties is called a breach of contract.

2. **Torts:** Some of the rights which individuals have against each other and duties which they owe each other exist without regard to whether promises were made. These rights and duties are the subject of the law of torts. ***If a right or duty exists without regard to whether a promise was made, its violation is called a tort.***

Example: Plaintiff gets into Defendant's taxi and asks Defendant to drive her to the airport, saying, "I will pay you ten dollars extra if you promise not to drive faster than 35 miles per hour." Defendant says, "I promise." While driving to the airport, Defendant drives 50 miles per hour, which is an unreasonable speed at that particular location. As a result, the taxi collides with a pole, causing Plaintiff to be injured. The state has a law which provides that no person shall drive at that particular location at a speed in excess of 40 miles per hour and that any person who does so is guilty of a misdemeanor.

Since the state law imposed on drivers a duty to society not to drive faster than 40 miles per hour, and since Defendant violated that duty, Defendant may be guilty of a crime. Since Defendant promised not to drive faster than 35 miles per hour and violated that promise, Defendant may have breached a contract with Plaintiff.

Since all drivers owe their passengers a duty to drive reasonably, and since Defendant violated that duty, Defendant may have committed a tort against Plaintiff. If Defendant is prosecuted for the crime of speeding, or if Plaintiff asserts a legal claim against Defendant for breach of contract and/or tort, the United States Constitution gives Defendant the right to a fair trial (*i.e.*, the Constitution imposes on society the duty of providing Defendant with a fair trial).

D. Statutory law and common law:

1. **Statutory law:** One of the branches of our government is the legislature, which has the power and the duty to create laws. Laws created by the legislature are called statutes. In recent years, statutory law has played an increasingly important role in shaping the law of torts. Since statutes usually vary from one state to another, however, this outline will not discuss statutes except in general terms.

2. **Common law:** Our legal system also recognizes rules of law which were not created by any legislature. Some of these rules are the result of traditions which are hundreds or thousands of years old. Others have resulted from judicial interpretations of statutes and of these traditions. This body of rules is known as the ***common law***. Until recently, the law of torts depended almost entirely on common law. Although statutes have begun to play a more important role than ever before in shaping the law of torts, ***the bulk of tort law continues to be common law***. As is traditional in studying tort law, this outline will concentrate on the common law rules.

Example: Defendant has a pet dog named Toby. Although Defendant is reasonably careful in the way he maintains Toby,

Toby bites Plaintiff, injuring him. Defendant had no reason to believe that Toby would bite anyone and did not intend it to happen. Plaintiff asserts a tort claim against Defendant for damage resulting from his injury.

According to common law, the keeper of a dog is not legally responsible for damage done by the dog unless that damage resulted from some fault of the keeper. Since Defendant maintained Toby in a reasonable manner and did not intend that Toby bite Plaintiff or have any reason to believe that Toby would do so, Plaintiff's injuries did not result from Defendant's fault. For this reason, in jurisdictions which apply the common law rule, Defendant will not be liable to Plaintiff for the damage. In some jurisdictions, a statute provides that the keeper of a dog is liable without regard to fault for damages done by his dog. In these jurisdictions, Defendant will be liable to Plaintiff even though the injury did not result from Defendant's fault.

E. Tort Liability: In most tort cases, it is necessary to consider three factors in deciding whether liability should attach. These are: (1) ***basis of liability***; (2) ***proximate causation and damage***; and (3) ***the effect of affirmative defenses***.

1. Basis of Liability: If defendant's conduct is such that liability may be based on it, it is referred to as liability-forming. The law of torts recognizes that conduct may be liability-forming because of the defendant's fault or, under some circumstances, without regard to fault.

a. Fault: In tort law, three different states of mind or kinds of behavior may satisfy the requirement of fault. These are ***intent***, ***negligence***, and ***recklessness or aggravated negligence***. Although all will subsequently be examined in detail, a brief description of each follows:

i. Intent: A defendant intends a particular consequence when she performs a voluntary act with the ***desire (or knowledge to a substantial degree of certainty) that the act produce that consequence*** (*infra*, p. 7).

Example: Defendant, the operator of a restaurant, knows that rat poison has gotten into the apple pie and that it will severely injure anyone who eats it. In spite of this knowledge, Defendant serves the pie to Plaintiff, a customer in the restaurant. Since Defendant served the pie to Plaintiff knowing that any person eating the pie would be injured, Defendant intended that Plaintiff would be injured.

ii. Negligence: A defendant is negligent when he ***acts unreasonably in the face of a foreseeable risk*** (*infra*, p. 55).

Example: Defendant, the operator of a restaurant, handles rat poison before preparing apple pie. Because Defendant does not wash his hands after touching the poison, some of it gets into the apple pie. Unaware of this fact, Defendant serves the apple pie to Plaintiff, who becomes ill as a result. Since people eat food, and since rat poison usually makes people who eat it sick, the risk that someone would become sick if the poison got into the food was foreseeable. Since it would only have taken a moment to wash his hands before preparing the food, and since doing so would have prevented a serious injury, the reasonable person probably would have washed after touching the poison and before preparing food. For these reasons, Defendant probably was negligent.

iii. Aggravated negligence (recklessness): A defendant is guilty of aggravated negligence (or recklessness) when she ***willfully disregards an obvious risk with a high probability of serious harm*** (*infra*, p. 86).

Example: Defendant, the operator of a restaurant, is aware that rat poison has somehow gotten into the apple pie. Defendant knows that 90 people out of 100 will be severely injured by eating the poison. Hoping that Plaintiff is among the ten in 100 who will not be injured by eating poison, Defendant serves the pie to Plaintiff, who becomes ill as a result. Since Defendant was aware of an obvious risk with a high probability of serious harm and wilfully disregarded that risk, she probably was guilty of recklessness or aggravated negligence.

b. Liability without fault (strict liability): In certain circumstances, tort law imposes liability without regard to whether the defendant was at fault (*i.e.*, strict liability, *infra*, p. 94).

Example: Defendant is blasting with dynamite while excavating the foundation for a building. Although Defendant does not intend any harm and is acting reasonably, shock waves from the blast cause damage to Plaintiff's house. Plaintiff asserts a claim against Defendant.

Since Defendant did not intend the harm and acted reasonably, Defendant was without fault. In most jurisdictions, however, strict liability is imposed for damage resulting from the use of explosives. If the accident occurred in such a jurisdiction, Defendant would be liable to Plaintiff even though without fault. *Spano v. Perini*, 250 N.E.2d 31 (N.Y. 1969).

2. **Proximate cause and damage:** With only a few exceptions, tort liability is not imposed unless the plaintiff sustains actual damage. In addition, it is necessary that the plaintiff's damage be ***proximately caused*** by whatever conduct furnishes the basis of liability.

   a. **Damage:** Not all harm is recognized as damage by the law of torts. It is necessary that the harm which the plaintiff sustained be the kind for which the law of torts recognizes a remedy (*infra*, p. 128).

   Example: Defendant is the manufacturer of a birth control device. As a result of Defendant's negligence, the device fails, causing the plaintiff to experience an unwanted pregnancy. Plaintiff asserts a claim against Defendant for damages resulting from her pregnancy and the birth of her child.

   Most jurisdictions will not permit the plaintiff to recover the expenses of her pregnancy and childbirth because they hold that pregnancy and childbirth are not harm. *McKernan v. Aasheim*, 687 P.2d 850 (Wash. 1984).

   b. **Proximate cause:** Unless there is a causal relationship between the defendant's liability-forming conduct and the plaintiff's damage, the defendant will not be financially responsible for the damage. Even where there is a causal relationship, however, the defendant will not be held responsible unless the relationship of cause to effect is ***sufficiently close*** to satisfy "a rough sense of justice combined with a rough sense of expediency." *Palsgraf v. Long Island R.R. Co.*, 162 N.E. 99 (N.Y. 1928) (*infra*, pp. 56 and 113).

   Example: Defendant operates his car in a negligent manner and collides with Explo's car, which explodes on impact, fracturing the skull of Explo who was driving it. Pedex, who was walking on the sidewalk, is struck by flying debris and bruised. The shock wave breaks a window in an apartment on the second floor of a building facing the street, causing Winnie, who is sitting by the window, to be cut by shattered glass. The sound of the explosion frightens Nurse, who is working in a hospital ten blocks away, causing her to drop Baby whom she is carrying and who sprains a wrist as a result. Nurse is so upset at seeing Baby injured, that she has a heart attack. All injured persons assert claims against Defendant.

   Since none of the injuries would have occurred without Defendant's negligence, Defendant's negligence was a contributing cause of all the injuries. A court probably would find that although it was a "proximate" cause of Explo's injury, it was not a "proximate" cause of Nurse's heart attack. Courts might disagree about whether it was a proximate cause of Pedex's bruise, Winnie's cut, and Baby's sprain. See Judge Andrews' dissent in *Palsgraf*, *supra*.

3. **Affirmative defenses:** An affirmative defense is ***an argument which, although unrelated to the essential elements of the plaintiff's case, might prevent the defendant from being liable to the plaintiff***. Ordinarily, the affirmative defenses which are available to a defendant depend on the plaintiff's theory of recovery (*i.e.*, basis of liability).

   Example: Plaintiff runs at Defendant waving a hatchet and slaps Defendant's face. Defendant strikes Plaintiff with a stick, intending to hurt her so that she will stop attacking him. Plaintiff is injured and asserts a claim against Defendant for battery, which is defined as intentional harmful or offensive contact with another. Defendant argues that he acted in self defense.

   The law recognizes a privilege called self-defense, which permits a person to use reasonable force to protect himself against an attack. Since Defendant was attempting to prevent Plaintiff from further attacking him, he was privileged to use reasonable force. If the force Defendant used was reasonable, he will not be liable for battery even though he intentionally made harmful contact with Plaintiff. *Edgar v. Emily*, 637 S.W.2d 412 (Mo. 1982).

4. **The "big picture":** It is necessary to remember that all three factors (basis of liability; proximate cause and damage; absence of affirmative defense) must be considered in deciding whether liability should be imposed. The fact that a defendant was negligent, for example, is not sufficient to result in liability unless that negligence was a proximate cause of damage. Even if it was, liability will still not be imposed if the defendant has an effective affirmative defense.

CHAPTER 2

TORTS INVOLVING INTENT

I. GENERAL CONCEPT

A. Definition: In general, tortious intent is the ***knowledge to a substantial degree of certainty that harm will result from the defendant's volitional act***.

B. Distinguished from volition: Volition (*i.e.*, voluntariness) is the desire to perform a particular physical act or to use muscles in a particular way. Without volition there can be no intent, but ***volition alone does not satisfy the requirement of intent***.

> **Example:** Defendant, the operator of a restaurant, voluntarily serves apple pie to Plaintiff. Although the pie contains rat poison, Defendant is not aware of this fact. Plaintiff becomes ill as a result of eating the poison in the pie, and asserts a claim against Defendant on an intentional tort theory.
>
> Since Defendant did not know that the pie contained poison, she did not intend that Plaintiff eat poison.

C. Distinguished from motive: Motive is the word used to characterize a person's reason for desiring to bring about a particular consequence. Although an evil motive may result in liability for punitive or exemplary damages, ***motive is generally irrelevant in determining whether intentional tort liability exists***.

> **Example:** Defendant puts syrup of ipecac in apple pie and serves it to Plaintiff. Defendant knows that syrup of ipecac is an emetic (*i.e.*, a substance which induces vomiting) and that Plaintiff would not be willing to eat the pie if he knew its contents. Defendant's purpose is to play a joke on Plaintiff. Plaintiff eats the pie and vomits. Subsequently, Plaintiff asserts a claim against Defendant on the ground that Defendant intended Plaintiff to vomit as a result of eating the syrup of ipecac. Defendant argues that his purpose was to play a joke.
>
> Since Defendant desired to induce Plaintiff to eat something which Defendant knew would make Plaintiff vomit, Defendant had the intent to make Plaintiff vomit, even though Defendant's motive was to play a joke.

D. Element of tort: The fact that a defendant had a tortious intent is not alone sufficient to result in liability. It is, of course, necessary that the intent be coupled with some act which results in a consequence for which the law of torts provides a remedy. In effect, then, ***intent only***

has meaning as an element of a specific intentional tort. But intent is a basis of liability in many tort cases, and there are seven torts which are generally known as the intentional torts.

E. Intentional invasions of person and property distinguished: Four of the seven intentional torts involve intentional invasions of the person: battery, assault, false imprisonment, and intentional infliction of mental suffering. Three involve intentional invasions of property rights: trespass to land, trespass to chattel, and conversion. "Intent" has a different specific meaning in each of the intentional torts. In general, however, the ***intent required in a tort based on intentional invasion of the person is a desire (or knowledge) that the plaintiff's right be invaded.*** On the other hand, the ***intent required in a tort based on intentional invasion of property right is a desire (or knowledge) that the defendant's conduct affect the property involved.***

F. Liability of infants and insane persons: If a defendant has the requisite intent, ***liability will be imposed regardless of that defendant's age or the state of defendant's mental health.***

> **Example:** Defendant, an insane person, brandishes a stick and says to Plaintiff, "If you come into this room, I will split your head open with this stick." Plaintiff enters the room, and Defendant strikes her in the head with the stick. Plaintiff subsequently asserts an intentional tort claim on the ground that Defendant intentionally made harmful contact with her. Defendant argues that she should not be liable because she is insane.
>
> Defendant's words make it clear that she desired (or knew) that her act inflict a harmful contact on Plaintiff. For this reason, Defendant intended the contact and will be held liable even though she is insane. *McGuire v. Almy*, 8 N.E.2d 760 (Mass. 1937).

II. BATTERY

A. General concept: Battery is an invasion of the right to be free of intentional, harmful or offensive physical contact.

B. Essential elements: The essential elements of ***"battery"*** are: (1) ***intentional***; and (2) ***harmful or offensive contact with plaintiff.***

1. **Intent:** In a battery case, intent may consist of any one of the following six states of mind:

   a. ***Desire*** that the defendant's volitional act result in ***harmful contact*** with the plaintiff.

b. ***Knowledge*** to a substantial degree of certainty that the defendant's volitional act will result in harmful contact with the plaintiff.

c. ***Desire*** that the defendant's volitional act result in ***offensive contact*** with the plaintiff.

d. ***Knowledge*** to a substantial degree of certainty that the defendant's volitional act will result in offensive contact with the plaintiff.

e. ***Desire*** that the defendant's volitional act ***cause*** the plaintiff to be apprehensive of imminent harmful or offensive contact.

Example: Defendant shoots a gun toward Plaintiff so that Plaintiff will be frightened but aims over plaintiff's head. The bullet strikes Plaintiff, injuring her. Plaintiff asserts a claim for battery. Defendant argues that she did not intend to strike Plaintiff with the bullet.

Since Defendant desired her act to make Plaintiff apprehensive, she had the intent required for battery liability. Because a harmful contact resulted, Defendant will be liable for battery.

f. ***Knowledge*** to a substantial degree of certainty that the defendant's volitional act will cause the plaintiff to be apprehensive of imminent harmful or offensive contact.

2. Harmful or offensive contact with plaintiff: Even if defendant acts with one of the states of mind described above, he is not liable for battery unless he actually brings about a harmful or offensive contact with the plaintiff.

a. Contact with plaintiff: Contact with the plaintiff is a ***touching of the plaintiff's body or of an extension of the plaintiff's body***. A defendant may be responsible for making contact with a plaintiff even though no part of the defendant's body touches a part of the plaintiff's body.

i. Causing contact: A defendant may make contact with a plaintiff by ***setting a force in motion which results in a touching of the plaintiff***.

Example: Defendant puts a substance in Plaintiff's food, knowing that Plaintiff would not be willing to eat it if she knew that the substance was there. Plaintiff eats the food and becomes ill as a result. Plaintiff asserts a battery claim against Defendant. Defendant argues that there was no contact with Plaintiff because he never physically touched her.

Since Defendant caused Plaintiff to ingest the substance involved, Defendant has made contact with Plaintiff. In this case, the contact (*i.e.*, between Plaintiff and the substance) occurred when Plaintiff ate the poisoned food. *Commonwealth v. Stratton*, 114 Mass. 303 (1873).

ii. **Extension of plaintiff's body:** A defendant may make contact with a plaintiff by causing a touching of ***something so closely associated with the plaintiff's body as to be regarded as an extension of it***.

Example: Plaintiff is waiting in line for a buffet lunch when Defendant rudely snatches a plate from Plaintiff's hand. Plaintiff subsequently asserts a claim for battery. Defendant argues that there was no contact because no part of Plaintiff's body was touched.

Since the plate was held in Plaintiff's hand, it probably would be regarded as an extension of Plaintiff's body. If so, Defendant made contact with Plaintiff when he touched the plate. *Fisher v. Carrousel Motor Hotel, Inc.*, 424 S.W.2d 627 (Tex. 1967).

b. **Harmful (contact):** A contact is ***harmful if it produces an injury to the body.***

c. **Offensive (contact):** A contact is offensive if it ***was not authorized by the plaintiff*** and ***would not have been authorized by the reasonable or ordinary person in the plaintiff's situation;*** or if the ***defendant is aware that it is not authorized by the plaintiff.***

Example 1: Defendant, seeking to attract Plaintiff's attention, taps her politely on the shoulder. Plaintiff, who is offended by the contact, asserts a claim for battery.

The ordinary person probably is willing to be tapped politely on the shoulder by one seeking to attract her attention. If this is so, Defendant's contact with Plaintiff was not "offensive" even though Plaintiff was offended by it.

Example 2: In the above (tap on the shoulder) Example, assume that when he tapped Plaintiff on the shoulder, Defendant was aware that Plaintiff was unwilling to be touched and would be offended by it.

Since Defendant knew of Plaintiff's sensitivity, the contact may be regarded as offensive even though the ordinary person would not have been offended by it.

III. ASSAULT

A. General concept: Assault is a violation of the right to be free of intentionally induced apprehension of harmful or offensive touching. It has been said that while battery is a touching of the body, assault is a touching of the mind. *Kline v. Kline*, 54 N.E. 9 (Ind. 1902).

B. Essential elements: The essential elements of ***"assault"*** are: (1) ***intent***, and (2) ***inducing the plaintiff's reasonable apprehension of an imminent harmful or offensive contact***.

1. **Intent:** In an assault case, ***intent is defined in the same way as it is defined in a battery case*** (*supra*, p. 8). This means that any one of the following six states of mind can satisfy the intent requirement:

   a. **Desire** that the defendant's volitional act result in ***harmful contact*** with the plaintiff.

   Example: Defendant shoots a gun toward Plaintiff, desiring to strike her with the bullet. The bullet misses Plaintiff, but when Plaintiff sees Defendant fire, she becomes apprehensive that the bullet will strike her. Plaintiff asserts an assault claim against Defendant.

   Since Defendant desired to make harmful contact with Plaintiff (*i.e.*, to strike her with the bullet), he had the intent necessary to support assault liability. Defendant will probably be liable for assault because of Plaintiff's resulting apprehension.

   b. **Knowledge to a substantial degree of certainty** that the defendant's volitional act will result in harmful contact with the plaintiff.

   c. **Desire** that the defendant's volitional act result in ***offensive contact*** with the plaintiff.

   d. **Knowledge to a substantial degree of certainty** that the defendant's volitional act will result in offensive contact with the plaintiff.

   e. **Desire** that the defendant's volitional act cause the plaintiff to be ***apprehensive of*** imminent harmful or offensive contact.

   f. **Knowledge to a substantial degree of certainty** that the defendant's volitional act will cause the plaintiff to be apprehensive of imminent harmful or offensive contact.

2. **Apprehension:** Although fear always includes apprehension, apprehension does not always involve fear. In general, ***apprehension refers to any anticipation of discomfort***.

   a. **Reasonable apprehension:** Generally, the plaintiff's apprehension is ***not sufficient*** to support an assault claim ***unless*** it is apprehension which ***would have been experienced by the reasonable or ordinary person in the plaintiff's position***.

      i. **Physical act:** Courts usually hold that unless the defendant has performed some ***physical act***, the plaintiff's apprehension is not reasonable. Thus, words alone, such as part of a telephone call, are not sufficient to result in assault liability.

   Example 1: Defendant comes to Plaintiff's home and threatens to beat him up. Plaintiff becomes apprehensive and subsequently asserts a claim for assault.

   Since Defendant did not perform any physical act, Plaintiff's apprehension may not be reasonable, and Plaintiff's assault claim may be dismissed. *Cucinotti v. Ortman*, 159 A.2d 216 (Pa. 1960).

   Example 2: Defendant comes to Plaintiff's home and threatens to beat him up, at the same time reaching for a blackjack which is stuck into his belt. Plaintiff becomes apprehensive and subsequently asserts a claim for assault.

   Since Defendant's act tended to indicate that he was preparing to strike Plaintiff with the blackjack, the ordinary person in Plaintiff's position probably would have become apprehensive as a result of Defendant's act. If so, Plaintiff's apprehension was reasonable, and Plaintiff may successfully maintain his assault claim. *Cucinotti v. Ortman*, *supra*.

      ii. **Words may be relevant:** Although speech alone does not constitute an assault, the words used by a defendant may play a role in the plaintiff's interpretation of the defendant's physical act, and, therefore, in determining whether the plaintiff's apprehension was reasonable.

   Example 1: During a conversation, Defendant reaches into her pocket. Plaintiff, who becomes apprehensive that Defendant will pull a knife and stab him, subsequently asserts an assault claim.

   Because the ordinary person in Plaintiff's position would not entertain such apprehension, Plaintiff's apprehension probably was not reasonable.

Example 2: During a heated conversation, Defendant reaches into her pocket and says, "I'll stab you for that." Plaintiff, who becomes apprehensive that Defendant will pull a knife and stab him, subsequently asserts an assault claim.

Since Defendant said that she would stab Plaintiff, the reasonable person in Plaintiff's position probably would have believed that Defendant was reaching for a knife with which to stab him. For this reason, it was probably reasonable for Plaintiff to become apprehensive as a result of Defendant's movement.

Note: If Plaintiff was assaulted, it was by Defendant's physical act of reaching into her pocket, not by Defendant's words. The words are relevant only in deciding whether it was reasonable for Plaintiff to become apprehensive when Defendant performed that physical act.

Example 3: During a conversation, Defendant holds a knife in her hand and says, "If I wasn't worried about going to jail, I wouldn't take such language from you." Plaintiff becomes apprehensive that Defendant will stab him and subsequently asserts an assault claim against Defendant.

Although Defendant's act (*i.e.*, holding the knife) might make the reasonable person in Plaintiff's position apprehensive that he would be stabbed, Defendant's words indicated that she would not stab Plaintiff. Since this probably would have prevented the ordinary person in Plaintiff's position from becoming apprehensive, Plaintiff's apprehension probably was not reasonable. *Tuberville v. Savage*, 86 Eng. Rep. 684 (Eng. 1669).

iii. **Apparent ability:** Unless the defendant appears to have the ability to make the threatened contact, plaintiff's apprehension probably will not be regarded as reasonable.

Example: Defendant reaches across a counter toward Plaintiff and says that he would like to love and pet her. Plaintiff becomes apprehensive that Defendant will touch her and subsequently asserts a claim for assault. Defendant argues that the counter was too wide and his arms too short for him to be able to reach Plaintiff.

If the reasonable person in Plaintiff's position would have realized that it was impossible for Defendant to reach and touch her, then Plaintiff's apprehension was not reasonable.

On the other hand, if the reasonable person in Plaintiff's position would not have realized that it was impossible for Defendant to touch her, then, even if it actually was impossible,

Plaintiff's apprehension was reasonable. *Western Union Telegraph Co. v. Hill*, 150 So. 709 (Ala. 1933).

iv. Known sensitivity: If the defendant is aware that the plaintiff will become apprehensive as a result of the defendant's act, the plaintiff's apprehension can support an assault claim even if it is not "reasonable".

Example: Defendant, who is aware that Plaintiff has a morbid fear of being bitten by a spider, places a realistic looking rubber spider in Plaintiff's desk drawer. When Plaintiff opens the drawer, she sees the rubber spider, believes that it is real, and becomes apprehensive that it will bite her. Plaintiff subsequently asserts a claim for assault against Defendant. Defendant argues that the ordinary person would not have become apprehensive under the circumstances.

Since Defendant was aware of Plaintiff's special sensitivity (*i.e.*, her morbid fear of being bitten by a spider) Plaintiff's apprehension may support the assault claim even if the reasonable person in Plaintiff's position would not have experienced it.

3. **Imminent harmful or offensive contact:** Plaintiff's apprehension must be of a harmful or offensive contact with her body which ***appears imminent***.

Example 1: Defendant loads a pistol and says to Plaintiff, "Next Thursday I'm going to kill you with this gun." Plaintiff becomes apprehensive and asserts a claim for assault.

Since the contact of which Plaintiff was apprehensive was not imminent (*i.e.*, to take place immediately), Plaintiff's apprehension will not support an assault claim.

Example 2: Defendant loads a pistol and points it at Plaintiff's mother while Plaintiff is watching. Plaintiff becomes apprehensive that Defendant will shoot her mother and subsequently asserts a claim for assault.

Since Plaintiff's apprehension was not of a contact with her own body, it will not support a claim for assault.

IV. FALSE IMPRISONMENT

A. General concept: False imprisonment is a violation of the right to freedom of movement. A restriction of movement is not imprisonment, however, unless the plaintiff has been confined within some boundaries.

B. Essential elements: The essential elements of ***"false imprisonment"*** are: (1) ***intent***; and (2) ***confinement of the plaintiff***. In addition, some jurisdictions require the plaintiff to prove that the confinement was (3) ***unlawful***.

1. Intent: In a false imprisonment case, intent means the ***desire (or knowledge to a substantial degree of certainty) that the defendant's voluntary act result in a confinement*** of the plaintiff.

Example: Defendant, a night watchman, sees Plaintiff enter a building which has only one door and no windows. Although Defendant observes the door continuously, he does not see Plaintiff leave. Defendant locks the door. Plaintiff, who is confined as a result, subsequently asserts a claim for false imprisonment. Defendant argues that he did not lock the door for the purpose of confining Plaintiff.

Since Defendant continuously observed the door and did not see Plaintiff leave, Defendant knew that Plaintiff was inside the building when he locked the door. Because intent may consist of knowledge to a substantial certainty that a confinement will result, Defendant had the necessary intent to support Plaintiff's claim for false imprisonment.

2. Confinement defined: Confinement is an ***overcoming of the plaintiff's will to leave in a way which would overcome the reasonable person's will to leave***.

a. Preventing plaintiff from leaving: Obviously, if the defendant's act does not actually prevent the plaintiff from leaving, the plaintiff's will to leave has not been overcome and there is no confinement.

Example 1: Plaintiff is in a room located on the third story of a building. With the intent to confine Plaintiff, Defendant locks all doors, but leaves a window unlocked. Plaintiff jumps out the window and is unhurt. Plaintiff subsequently asserts a claim for false imprisonment.

Since Defendant did not succeed in preventing Plaintiff from leaving, Plaintiff's will to leave has not been overcome, and Plaintiff has not been confined.

Example 2: Defendant refuses to allow Plaintiff to enter the street where Plaintiff lives because a race is being conducted there to which Plaintiff does not have a ticket. Plaintiff asserts a claim for false imprisonment.

Since Plaintiff was free to leave, Plaintiff's will to leave was not overcome by Defendant's act. Therefore, Plaintiff was not confined and cannot successfully maintain a false imprisonment claim. *Bird v. Jones*, 115 Eng. Rep. 668 (Q.B. 1845).

b. Must be involuntarily: If the plaintiff remains voluntarily, her will to leave has not been overcome and there is no confinement.

Example: Defendant suspects Plaintiff, an employee, of theft, and orders Plaintiff to come into Defendant's office for interrogation. He tells Plaintiff that she will be fired if she refuses. Plaintiff goes into the room for interrogation, and subsequently asserts a claim for false imprisonment.

All employed persons make a voluntary choice either to be where their employers tell them to be or to lose their jobs. In choosing to obey her employer's direction, Plaintiff made a voluntary choice to go into the room for interrogation rather than lose her job. Since this choice was voluntary, her will to leave was not overcome, and there was no confinement. *Hardy v. LaBelle's*, 661 P.2d 35 (Mont. 1983).

c. Will to leave: If the plaintiff does not wish to leave (*i.e.*, does not have the will to leave) there can be no confinement.

Example 1: Defendant police officer found Plaintiff intoxicated and unconscious. While Plaintiff remained unconscious, Defendant locked Plaintiff in the back of a police car. Defendant removed Plaintiff from the police car before Plaintiff regained consciousness. Plaintiff subsequently asserted a claim for false imprisonment.

Because an unconscious person has no will to leave (or to do anything else), Plaintiff's will was not overcome. Therefore, Plaintiff was not confined by Defendant. *Parvi v. City of Kingston*, 362 N.E.2d 960 (N.Y. 1977), *infra*, p. 61.

Example 2: Plaintiff was a student at Defendant's boarding school. When Plaintiff's mother came to take Plaintiff home for the Christmas holiday, Defendant refused to let Plaintiff leave because his tuition was in arrears. Plaintiff was unaware that his mother had come for him or that Defendant was preventing him from leaving and did not have any particular desire or intention to leave.

Since Plaintiff had no desire or intention to leave, he had no will to leave. Therefore, his will to leave was not overcome, and there was no confinement. *Herring v. Boyle*, 149 Eng. Rep. 1126 (Eng. 1834).

d. Objective standard: Even if the defendant's act does overcome the plaintiff's will to leave, ***there has been no confine-***

ment unless that act would have overcome the will of the reasonable or ordinary person in the plaintiff's position.

Example: Defendant shopkeeper suspects Plaintiff of shoplifting and seizes her purse, saying, "Come with me to the security office." Plaintiff goes without objection and remains until Defendant searches the purse and returns it. Plaintiff subsequently asserts a claim for false imprisonment. Defendant argues that there was no confinement because Plaintiff was free to leave at all times.

Had Plaintiff left, she would have been forced to do so without her purse. If the reasonable person in her position would not have left without her purse, then Defendant's seizure and retention of the purse may have resulted in a confinement of Plaintiff. If, on the other hand, the reasonable person in Plaintiff's position would have left without her purse, then Defendant's seizure and retention of the purse did not result in a confinement. *Ashland v. Wages*, 195 S.W.2d 312 (Ky. 1946).

3. **Unlawfulness:** All jurisdictions agree that ***if a confinement is lawful it will not support a claim for false imprisonment.*** In some jurisdictions the burden is on the plaintiff to prove the confinement unlawful. In some jurisdictions the burden is on the defendant to prove that the confinement was lawful. In some jurisdictions the defendant has the burden of proving that the confinement was lawful unless the defendant was acting under color of legal authority, in which case the plaintiff has the burden of proving the confinement unlawful.

Example: Plaintiff is sitting in a parked car while allowing her dog to run without a leash in violation of a local law. Ordinarily, persons violating that law are given citations ordering them to appear in court at a specified time. Defendant, a police officer, issues a citation to Plaintiff. In the course of doing so, Defendant demands to see Plaintiff's driver's license. Plaintiff offers to show other identification, but refuses to show her driver's license. Defendant says that if she does not show her driver's license he will arrest her. Plaintiff continues to refuse and Defendant places Plaintiff under arrest. Plaintiff subsequently asserts a claim for false imprisonment, arguing that since she was not driving, she was not obligated to show her driver's license and that her arrest and imprisonment were therefore unlawful.

In some jurisdictions, a plaintiff's action for false imprisonment will fail unless she establishes that her confinement was unlawful. In other jurisdictions, plaintiff is not generally required to establish that her confinement was unlawful, except when the defendant is a police officer who acted under color of legal authority. In still other jurisdictions, plaintiff is not required to prove that her confinement was unlawful, but if defendant can prove that it was lawful, the complaint will fail. *Enright v. Groves*, 560 P.2d 851 (Colo. Ct. App. 1977).

V. INTENTIONAL INFLICTION OF MENTAL HARM

A. General concept: Intentional infliction of mental harm is a violation of the right to be free of serious, intentional invasions of mental and emotional tranquility.

B. Essential elements: The essential elements of ***"intentional infliction of mental harm"*** are: (1) ***intent***; (2) ***outrageous conduct***; and (3) ***severe mental suffering***.

1. **Intent:** The intent requirement is satisfied if at the time of her conduct, the defendant ***desired (or knew to a substantial degree of certainty) that the plaintiff experience mental suffering as a result***.

   Example: Defendant beats up Plaintiff's father while Plaintiff is watching from an apartment window. As a result, Plaintiff experiences serious mental suffering. Plaintiff subsequently asserts a claim against Defendant for intentional infliction of mental harm. Defendant argues that he did not know that Plaintiff was watching.

   If Defendant did not know that Plaintiff was watching, he could not have desired (or known) that his act cause her to experience mental suffering. Since Defendant did not have the necessary intent, he is not liable to Plaintiff. *Taylor v. Vallelunga*, 339 P.2d 910 (Cal. 1959).

2. **Outrageous conduct:** For purposes of the tort of intentional infliction of mental harm, conduct is outrageous if it satisfies two requirements:

   a. **Bounds of a decent society:** The conduct must ***exceed all bounds normally tolerated by a decent society***.

   Example: While shopping in Defendant's grocery store, Plaintiff asks Defendant the price of an item. Defendant answers, "Find out for yourself. You stink to me." Plaintiff asserts a claim for intentional infliction of mental harm.

   Since our constitution protects freedom of speech, our society ordinarily tolerates insulting language. For this reason, Defendant's insult probably does not constitute outrageous conduct, and Plaintiff's claim probably will fail. *Slocum v. Food Fair Stores of Florida*, 100 So.2d 396 (Fla. 1958).

b. **Suffering almost inevitable:** It must be ***almost inevitable that the reasonable person in the plaintiff's situation or that a person with the plaintiff's known sensitivities would experience mental suffering*** as a result of the conduct.

Note: Many courts use the phrase "calculated to cause mental suffering" to mean that mental suffering is almost inevitable. In this context, "calculated" does not mean "planned" as it may in the ordinary sense of the word, but rather means "extremely likely" or "almost inevitable".

Example: Plaintiff returned to work after a heart transplant and many weeks of convalescence. His doctors advised him to avoid all strain and tension. Plaintiff's employer, anxious to replace plaintiff with a younger and healthier worker, began the systematic person of harassing plaintiff at every turn. In the presence of other workers, he called plaintiff "an old relic", "a weak link', "a has-been" and "a ticking time-bomb". The other workers began to taunt plaintiff with similar remarks. Plaintiff experienced severe mental and emotional suffering as a result and sued Defendant for intentional infliction of mental harm.

Ordinarily, insulting language is not regarded as outrageous conduct because society tolerates it and because it is not almost inevitable that it will result in severe mental suffering. In this case, however, Defendant was aware of Plaintiff's condition and the potential for mental suffering. Under these circumstances, such language probably does exceed the bounds normally tolerated by decent society, and mental suffering is almost inevitable. For these reasons, Defendant may be liable for intentional infliction of mental harm. *Clark v. Associated Retail Credit Men,* 105 F.2d 62 (D.C. Cir. 1938).

3. **Severe mental suffering:** All jurisdictions agree that liability will not be imposed unless the plaintiff experiences severe mental suffering; and that no recovery will be permitted ***for trivial harm*** such as embarrassment, humiliation, or discomfort. In addition, ***some jurisdictions hold that mental suffering is not sufficiently severe unless it has a physical manifestation***.

Example 1: Defendant manufactures a white bathing suit, knowing that when wet it becomes translucent. Plaintiff purchases the bathing suit and wears it while swimming at a public pool. After the suit becomes wet, Plaintiff realizes that it is translucent and experiences mild embarrassment until her daughter covers her with a towel. Plaintiff subsequently asserts a claim for intentional infliction of mental harm.

Since Plaintiff experienced nothing more than mild embarrassment, Defendant is probably not liable for intentional infliction of mental harm — Plaintiff's mental suffering was not sufficiently severe. *Holden v. Kayser-Roth*, N.E.2d 426 (Ill. 1968), *infra*, p. 210-211.

Example 2: Defendant, a business competitor of Plaintiff, warns Plaintiff that if Plaintiff continues to compete with Defendant, Defendant will have Plaintiff attacked and Plaintiff's business destroyed. As a result, Plaintiff experiences severe mental suffering and loses sleep. Plaintiff subsequently asserts a claim for intentional infliction of mental harm. Defendant argues that Plaintiff's suffering was not sufficiently severe because there were no physical manifestations.

In some jurisdictions, severe mental suffering can support a claim for intentional infliction of mental harm even without physical manifestations. In such jurisdictions, whether Plaintiff's mental suffering was sufficiently severe will be a question for the jury.

In other jurisdictions, mental suffering is not sufficiently severe to support a claim for intentional infliction of mental harm unless it has a physical manifestation. In such jurisdictions, it will be necessary for the court to determine whether loss of sleep is a physical manifestation of mental suffering. *State Rubbish Collectors v. Siliznoff*, 240 P.2d 282 (Cal. 1952).

VI. TRESPASS TO LAND

A. General concept: Trespass to land is a violation of the right to be free of unauthorized intentional entry on realty.

B. Background: When it was first conceived, the action of trespass to land was used primarily as a way for courts to determine the ownership of land. A plaintiff would allege that the defendant had made entry on the plaintiff's realty; the defendant would assert that the realty was his own; and the issue of who owned the land was thus placed before the court. In recent years, trespass to land has come to be recognized as an intentional tort. Although unintended entries onto realty may result in tort liability, such entries may not be trespasses, for trespass liability does not require proof of damage, and liability for any other kind of entry does.

C. Essential elements: The essential elements of trespass to land are: (1) ***intent***; (2) ***entry on plaintiff's realty***; and (3) ***entry that is unauthorized***.

1. Intent: In a trespass to land case, intent consists of a ***desire (or knowledge to a substantial degree of certainty) that the defendant's volitional act result in an entry onto the particular realty involved***.

Example 1: Defendant is flying an airplane when it suddenly runs out of fuel. As a result, Defendant loses control of the plane, and it crashes onto Plaintiff's realty. Plaintiff subsequently asserts a claim for trespass to land. Defendant argues that he did not have the requisite intent.

Since Defendant did not commit any volitional act with the desire (or knowledge) that it result in an entry on Plaintiff's realty, he lacked the requisite intent and cannot be liable for trespass to land.

Example 2: Defendant is flying an airplane when it suddenly runs out of fuel. Defendant manages to maintain control of the plane while looking for a place to crash land. Seeing a level field below, Defendant decides to crash land on it and does so. Plaintiff, who is the owner of the field, subsequently asserts a claim for trespass to land. Defendant argues that he did not have the requisite intent.

Because Defendant desired to land on the field and did so, Defendant had the requisite intent and could be liable to Plaintiff for trespass to land.

Note: Defendant may avoid liability by relying on the defense of private necessity, discussed below.

a. Intent to violate rights not required: Unlike torts involving intentional invasions of the person, ***trespass to land does not require a desire (or knowledge) that the defendant's act violate the rights of any person***.

Example: Defendant's uncle gives Defendant the key to his mountain cabin and says that Defendant may go there and use it any time. Subsequently, the uncle sells the cabin to Plaintiff without telling Defendant. Defendant thereafter goes to the cabin and lets himself in with the key. Plaintiff subsequently learns of Defendant's entry and asserts a claim against Defendant for trespass to land. Defendant argues that he did not have the requisite intent.

Since intent in a trespass to land case is desire (or knowledge) that an entry result from the defendant's volitional act, and since Defendant desired to enter the cabin, he had the intent required to result in liability for trespass to land.

b. **Not necessary to know that realty belongs to another:** A defendant has the requisite intent when he desires (or knows to a substantial degree of certainty) that an entry occur, whether or not he is aware that the realty involved belongs to another.

Example: After purchasing realty, Defendant hires a surveyor who tells her where the boundaries are. Defendant then walks on the realty, careful not to step over the boundaries. The surveyor was incorrect about the location of one of the boundaries, however. As a result, Defendant actually sets foot on land which belongs to her neighbor, Plaintiff. Plaintiff asserts a claim for trespass to land. Defendant argues that she lacked the necessary intent because she reasonably believed that the land on which she was walking was her own.

Since the intent required in a trespass to land case is the desire (or knowledge) that an entry occur on the realty involved, and since Defendant desired to walk where she did walk, she had the necessary intent to result in liability for trespass to land.

2. **Entry on plaintiff's realty:** There are other areas of tort liability based on interference with rights which a plaintiff has in realty; but trespass to land does not occur without an actual physical entry.

a. **Entry defined:** To enter realty is to go upon it.

i. **Causing entry:** A defendant may "enter" realty by ***causing something to go upon it***.

Example: Defendant, standing outside Plaintiff's land, fires a shotgun onto Plaintiff's land. Plaintiff asserts a claim for trespass to land. Defendant argues that he did not make an entry because he did not go upon Plaintiff's land. Since Defendant caused shot to go upon Plaintiff's land, Defendant did make the necessary entry and may be liable for trespass to land. *Herrin v. Sutherland*, 241 P. 328 (Mont. 1925).

ii. **Tangible object:** No entry occurs unless some ***tangible object*** makes physical contact with the land. Although most of the cases dealing with this issue have held that gases and microscopic particles are not sufficiently tangible to make entry onto realty, a few recent cases hold that they are.

Example 1: Defendant shines a beam of light into Plaintiff's bedroom window. Plaintiff asserts a claim for trespass to land. Defendant argues that he did not make entry since he did not cause any tangible thing to enter Plaintiff's realty.

Since light is not physical (*i.e.*, tangible) all jurisdictions agree that shining a light on Plaintiff's realty does not constitute an entry sufficient to lead to liability for trespass to land.

Example 2: Defendant operates a smelter which discharges microscopic particles of cadmium and other metals which settle onto Plaintiff's realty. Plaintiff asserts a claim for trespass to land. Defendant argues that he has not made entry because he has not caused any tangible thing to make contact with the realty.

The majority of jurisdictions hold that particulate matter (*i.e.*, particles so small that they are undetectable to the human senses) are not tangible and, therefore, cannot make "entry" on realty. In these jurisdictions, Defendant has not caused an entry, and Plaintiff's case will be dismissed.

A minority of jurisdictions, however, hold that particulate matter is tangible. In these jurisdictions, Defendant has caused entry and may be liable for trespass to land. *Bradley v. American Smelting & Refining Co.*, 709 P.2d 782 (Wash. 1985), *infra*, p. 171.

iii. Remaining on the realty: ***Remaining on realty*** after permission to do so has expired satisfies the requirement of an unauthorized entry, even if the original entry was authorized.

Example: Defendant has Plaintiff's permission to erect a snow fence on Plaintiff's realty and to keep it there throughout the winter. Defendant erects the fence, but fails to remove it when winter ends. Plaintiff asserts a claim for trespass to land. Defendant argues that he never made an unauthorized entry because when he erected the snow fence, he had Plaintiff's permission to do so.

Since Plaintiff gave Defendant permission to maintain the snow fence on Plaintiff's property only during the winter, Defendant's failure to remove it when winter ended satisfies the requirement of an unauthorized entry. For this purpose, the entry took place when Defendant's permission to maintain the snow fence expired. *Rogers v. Board of Road Commissioners*, 30 N.W.2d 358 (Mich. 1948).

b. **Possession required:** An action for trespass to land may be brought by anyone in possession of the realty. For this purpose, it is ***not necessary that the possession be lawful***.

   i. **Possession defined:** For this purpose, possession means custody and control.

Example: While visiting a friend, Plaintiff is sitting on the porch of her friend's house when Defendant enters the porch without Plaintiff's permission. Plaintiff asserts a claim for trespass to land. Defendant argues that Plaintiff is not entitled to bring such an action because Plaintiff was not in possession of the realty at the time of Defendant's entry.

Because Plaintiff was only a visitor on her friend's porch, the friend continued to have the right and power to permit or complain of entry by Defendant. Plaintiff thus lacked the control necessary to make her a possessor of the realty. For this reason, Plaintiff is not entitled to assert the trespass claim.

   ii. **Constructive possession:** The action for trespass to land may be brought by a plaintiff in constructive possession of the realty invaded. For this purpose, constructive possession is defined as former custody with an intent to return to custody and a continuing intent to exercise control.

Example: Plaintiff owns and occupies a house in the city. Plaintiff leaves the city on a business trip with the intention of returning to her house and continuing to exercise control over it. While Plaintiff is away, Defendant enters the house without Plaintiff's permission. Plaintiff subsequently asserts a claim for trespass to land. Defendant moves to dismiss the claim on the ground that at the time of Defendant's entry, Plaintiff was not in possession of the realty.

Since Plaintiff had been in custody, and intended to return to custody and to continue to exercise control, Plaintiff was in constructive possession at the time of Defendant's entry, and may maintain an action for trespass to land.

   iii. **Possession by agent:** A person may be "possessed" of realty for purposes of maintaining an action for trespass if it is possessed by a person whom she has designated to represent her on the realty.

Example: Plaintiff is the owner of an apartment building. Although Plaintiff never goes to the building, Plaintiff has hired Manager to act as caretaker and superintendent of the building. Defendant enters the building without permission from Plaintiff or Manager. Plaintiff asserts a claim for trespass to land. Defendant argues that Plaintiff was not in possession of the realty at the time of Defendant's entry.

Since Plaintiff designated Manager to serve as caretaker and building superintendent, Manager was Plaintiff's agent, and Plaintiff was in possession of the realty by an agent. For this reason, Plaintiff can maintain the action of trespass to land against Defendant.

iv. **Lawful possession not required:** Most jurisdictions agree that the action for trespass to land may be brought by any person in possession, even if that possession is not lawful, so long as the person against whom the action is brought does not have a right to possession which is superior to the plaintiff's.

Example: Oscar holds title to realty located in a forested area. Knowing that Oscar rarely visits the realty, Plaintiff moves onto it and builds a cabin. One day, Defendant enters the premises without permission from Plaintiff or Oscar. Friend then enters the premises with permission from Oscar but not from Plaintiff; and Oscar enters the premises without consulting with Plaintiff. Plaintiff asserts claims for trespass to land against Defendant, Friend, and Oscar, all of whom move to dismiss on the ground that Plaintiff did not have a lawful right to possess the realty involved.

Since Defendant had nobody's permission to enter, his right is inferior to that of Plaintiff who was already in possession. For this reason, Plaintiff can maintain the trespass action against Defendant.

Since Oscar is the owner, Friend, who entered with Oscar's permission, has a right which is superior to Plaintiff's. For this reason, Plaintiff cannot maintain a trespass action against Friend.

Since Oscar is the owner of the realty, and since he did not give Plaintiff permission to occupy it, Oscar's right is superior to Plaintiff's. For this reason, Plaintiff cannot maintain a trespass action against Oscar.

c. **Realty:** Since trespass to land is a violation of the right to undisturbed possession of realty, the plaintiff must show that the entry has been onto realty.

i. **Real property defined:** All property can be classified as either real or personal. Real property is ***land or anything permanently attached to the land***. All other property is personal.

Example: Defendant enters Plaintiff's land and cuts down a tree which is growing there. Then Defendant cuts the tree into firewood and carries it away. Plaintiff asserts a claim for trespass to land, demanding compensation for the value which the tree had while it was growing and for its value as firewood after it was cut. Defendant argues that the tree was not part of the realty.

Since realty is land or anything permanently attached to the land, the tree was realty while it was growing in the ground. For this reason, Defendant will be liable for the value which the tree had while it was growing. On the other hand, once the tree was cut, it was no longer attached to the land and, therefore, ceased to be realty. For this reason, Defendant will not be liable on a trespass-to-land theory for the value of the firewood which he cut.

ii. Air space: All jurisdictions agree that realty includes not only the land, but also ***some of the air above the land***. Jurisdictions have various views about how far up the realty extends. All agree, however, that there is some limit. Federal law prescribes an altitude called the "minimum safe altitude." Air space above the minimum safe altitude is not part of the realty. Air space below the minimum safe altitude may be part of the realty, depending on state law.

Example: Plaintiff sues Defendant airline for trespass, alleging that Defendant flew through the air above Plaintiff's land. Plaintiff is unable to show the altitude at which Defendant flew. Defendant moves to dismiss on the ground that Plaintiff has failed to show an entry onto Plaintiff's realty.

Flights above the minimum safe altitude are not in air space which is part of the realty, and even flights below the minimum safe altitude are not in air space which is part of the realty unless they are below a level fixed by the state. Plaintiff's inability to show the altitude at which Defendant flew is a failure to show that the flight was within air space which was part of Plaintiff's realty. For this reason, Plaintiff's claim should be dismissed. *City of Newark v. Eastern Airlines*, 159 F.Supp. 750 (D.N.J. 1958).

d. Damage not required: It is not necessary for a plaintiff to show that damage resulted from the defendant's entry. Some writers have explained this by saying that damage is presumed to result from every entry. This is not correct, however, since a presumption of damage is simply an aid to proving damage. The fact is that ***trespass to land*** is one of the few torts which ***can***

be committed without any damage at all. Liability is imposed for interference with the right to possession whether that interference results in damage or not.

VII. TRESPASS TO CHATTEL AND CONVERSION

A. General concept: Trespass to chattel and conversion are violations of the right to possess personal property (*i.e.*, chattels).

B. Historical background: Trespass to chattel and conversion are derived from early attempts to protect against intentional interference with the personal property of others. Trespass to chattel was a traditional tort action, in which the plaintiff sought to recover for damage sustained as the result of the defendant's interference with his personal property. Conversion was an action based on an implied contract theory, in which the plaintiff claimed that by interfering with the plaintiff's chattel the defendant had made it the defendant's (*i.e.*, converted it to his own) and now had an obligation to pay the value which the chattel had at the time of that conversion. For this reason, conversion is sometimes called an action for a forced sale.

C. Trespass to chattel and conversion distinguished: One real difference between trespass to chattel and conversion is the remedy available for each. Trespass to chattel is an action for damage resulting from the defendant's act; conversion is an action to force a sale. Because the remedy of forced sale is extraordinary, however, the courts are less willing to grant it. For this reason, it is generally understood that conversion is available only for a serious violation of the plaintiff's rights, while trespass to chattel is available for a less serious invasion. This is actually a difference in degree only, since, generally, both torts have the same essential elements.

D. Essential elements: The essential elements of trespass to chattel and conversion are: (1) intent; (2) interference; (3) impact on plaintiff's chattel; and (4) resulting damage.

1. **Intent:** As in trespass to land, intent in trespass-to-chattel or conversion cases is simply the ***desire (or knowledge to a substantial degree of certainty) that the act result in a certain outcome***. Though the defendant's motive may be innocent, he may still have the requisite intent.

   Example 1: Defendant, licensed to hunt wolves, sees Plaintiff's dog, which looks like a wolf. Believing it to be a wolf, Defendant shoots it. Plaintiff subsequently asserts a claim for trespass to chattel or conversion. Defendant argues that, because he believed the animal to be a wolf, he did not have the intent necessary for these torts.

Since the intent required is a desire (or knowledge) that the act involved result in a certain outcome, and since Defendant desired to shoot the animal in question, Defendant had the necessary intent, even though he was mistaken about the character of the animal he was shooting. *Ranson v. Kitner*, 31 Ill. App. 241 (1888).

Example 2: Thief steals Plaintiff's television and sells it to Second, the owner of a second hand store. Byer purchases the television from Second's store. Subsequently, Plaintiff asserts claims against Thief, Second and Byer. Second and Byer argue that they did not know that the television was stolen.

Intent is a desire (or knowledge) that the chattel be affected. Since Second desired to purchase the television from Thief and to sell it to Byer, Second had the necessary intent. Since Byer desired to purchase the television from Second, Byer had the necessary intent. For this reason, all could be held liable to Plaintiff.

2. **Interference:** For this purpose, interference means doing ***something with respect to the chattel which only the rightful possessor is entitled to do***.

   a. **Exercise of dominion and control:** The Restatement (2d) of Torts indicates that an ***interference may be serious enough to warrant a forced sale (i.e.***, to be classified as a conversion) if it amounts to an exercise of dominion and control.

   b. **Intermeddling:** The Restatement (2d) also indicates that an ***interference is not serious enough to warrant a forced sale (i.e.***, is ***only a trespass to chattel***) ***if it amounts to a mere intermeddling***.

   c. **Difference not clear:** In practice, the difference between an exercise of dominion and control and a mere intermeddling is usually difficult to determine and is often the subject of controversy.

   Example 1: Defendant and Plaintiff share a house until they have an argument and Plaintiff moves out. Defendant moves all of Plaintiff's furniture into a storage warehouse, arranges to have it available to Plaintiff on demand, and notifies Plaintiff where it is located. Plaintiff asserts alternative claims for trespass to chattel and conversion.

   Since Defendant arranged to have the furniture available to Plaintiff on demand and notified Plaintiff as to its location, it can be argued that Defendant's conduct amounted to a mere intermeddling, and that Plaintiff cannot successfully maintain a claim for conversion.

On the other hand, since Defendant moved the furniture to a location of his own choice, and made it necessary for Plaintiff to retrieve it from a different place than its original location, it can be argued that Defendant's conduct amounted to an exercise of dominion and control, and that Plaintiff, therefore, can maintain an action for conversion. *Zaslow v. Kroenert*, 176 P.2d 1 (Cal. 1946).

Example 2: Plaintiff went to Defendant's auto dealership to inquire about the purchase of a new car. Defendant asked Plaintiff for the keys to Plaintiff's car so that Defendant could evaluate it for a possible trade-in. When Plaintiff decided that he wanted to leave, Defendant pretended that he could not find Plaintiff's keys, forcing Plaintiff to remain and listen to Defendant's sales pitch. Plaintiff could have called his wife and asked her to bring him an extra key, but he did not do so. Plaintiff subsequently asserted alternative claims for trespass to chattel and conversion.

Since Defendant kept the keys for only a short time, and Plaintiff could have gotten an extra set of keys from his wife, it can be argued that Defendant's conduct amounted to no more than an intermeddling and that Plaintiff cannot maintain an action for conversion.

On the other hand, since Defendant deliberately kept Plaintiff's keys from him without any justification at all, knowing that Plaintiff could not take his car without the keys, it may be argued that Defendant's conduct amounted to an exercise of dominion and control, and that Plaintiff may successfully maintain an action for conversion. *Russell-Vaughn Ford, Inc. v. Rouse*, 206 So.2d 371 (Ala. 1968).

3. **Right of possession:** Unlike trespass to land, the actions for trespass to chattel and conversion ***may only be brought by persons with a lawful right to present or future possession*** (*supra*, p. 24).

Example: Owner goes on vacation, leaving his automobile behind. Plaintiff takes the automobile without Owner's permission and drives it to a supermarket where she parks it in the parking lot while shopping. Defendant steals the automobile. Plaintiff and Owner subsequently assert alternative claims against Defendant for trespass to chattel and conversion. Defendant moves to dismiss on the ground that Owner was not in possession and Plaintiff was not in lawful possession at the time of

Defendant's act.

Because the automobile belonged to Owner, Owner had a right to possess it. He may, therefore, assert the claims even though he was not in actual possession at the time of Defendant's conduct. On the other hand, since Plaintiff took the car without Owner's permission, she had no right to possess it. For this reason, she may not assert the claims against Defendant, and her case should be dismissed.

4. **Chattel:** ***"Chattel"*** is another name for personalty or personal property. Any property other than real property (*i.e.*, land and anything permanently attached to it) is classified as personalty, or personal property, or chattel.

    Example: Defendant enters Plaintiff's land and cuts down a tree which is growing there. Then Defendant cuts the tree into firewood and carries it away. Plaintiff asserts alternative claims for trespass-to-chattel and conversion. Defendant argues that the tree was not chattel since it was part of the realty at the time he cut it down.

    Since realty is land or anything permanently attached to the land, the tree was realty while it was growing in the ground. Once the tree was cut, however, it was no longer attached to the land and, therefore, ceased to be realty and became chattel (*supra*, p. 25).

5. **Damage:** Although damage is an essential element of both conversion and trespass-to-chattel torts, it is ***not necessary to show that the chattel was damaged, so long as the plaintiff can establish damage to herself***. Usually, this is established by showing an interference with Plaintiff's right to possession.

    Example: Defendant pulls the ears of Plaintiff's dog, but does not injure the dog. Plaintiff asserts alternative claims for trespass to chattel and conversion. Defendant argues that her conduct did not result in damage to Plaintiff's chattel or to Plaintiff's right to possess it.

    Since the dog was not injured, there has been no damage to Plaintiff's chattel. Because strangers frequently touch and fondle the pets of others, pulling the ears of a dog probably is not inconsistent with the rights of its owner. For this reason, there probably has been no damage to Plaintiff's right of possession. Therefore, Plaintiff probably will not be successful in maintaining an action for trespass to chattel or conversion. *Glidden v. Szybiak*, 63 A.2d 233 (N.H. 1949).

6. **Relative difference:** Although the essential elements of trespass to chattel and conversion are identical, there is a relative difference between the torts which is usually found by examining the elements of interference and damage.

   a. **Motive:** In deciding whether the interference amounts to a mere intermeddling or to an exercise of dominion and control, courts usually examine the defendant's ***motive.*** If the defendant knew that the chattel involved belonged to another and that her conduct was a violation of that other person's rights, the courts are more likely to view the interference as an exercise of dominion and control, and, therefore, a proper basis for a conversion claim. On the other hand, if the defendant was unaware that her conduct was affecting the chattel of another, the courts are more likely to view the interference as a mere intermeddling, and, therefore, not a proper basis for a conversion claim.

   Example 1: Defendant is leaving a restaurant when he picks up Plaintiff's umbrella, believing it to be his own. After carrying it for several blocks, Defendant realizes his mistake and attempts to return it. Plaintiff subsequently asserts alternative claims for trespass to chattel and conversion.

   Defendant had the requisite intent because he desired to take Plaintiff's umbrella. His conduct was an interference, because only Plaintiff had the right to carry off that umbrella. It resulted in damage, because the Plaintiff was denied the right to possess his chattel. Defendant has committed a trespass to chattel. If the interference was so serious as to constitute an exercise of dominion and control, his conduct amounts to a conversion as well. Since Defendant's act was the result of an innocent mistake, most courts would probably conclude that it was not serious enough to justify a forced sale, and, therefore, was not a conversion but only a trespass to chattel.

   Example 2: When leaving a restaurant, Defendant realizes that he has left his own umbrella at home. It's raining hard and when he sees Plaintiff's umbrella, Defendant takes it. After Defendant carries the umbrella for several blocks, the rain stops, and Defendant returns the umbrella. Plaintiff subsequently asserts alternative claims for trespass to chattel and conversion. Defendant argues that because he returned the umbrella soon after taking it, his conduct amounted to no more than a mere intermeddling, and that Plaintiff cannot maintain a claim for conversion.

   Although the quick return of the umbrella minimized Plaintiff's damages, the courts are likely to look to Defendant's motive in deciding whether his interference with Plaintiff's chattel was serious enough to warrant a forced sale. Since Defendant knew that the umbrella was not his own and that he was not entitled to take it, a court probably would find that the interference amounted to an exercise of dominion and control, and would permit Plaintiff to maintain the action for conversion.

b. Damage: In deciding whether the defendant's interference was serious enough to amount to a conversion, courts may also consider the damage which resulted. If the damage was ***severe***, the courts are more likely to view the defendant's interference as an exercise of dominion and control. If the damage was ***not severe***, the courts are more likely to view the defendant's interference as an intermeddling.

Example 1: Plaintiff is the owner of a prize buck goat known as Tommy, and usually charges a fee for use of Tommy as a breeding stud. While Plaintiff is away, Defendant takes his doe goat to Tommy's barn and breeds her to Tommy without Plaintiff's permission. Plaintiff subsequently asserts alternative claims for trespass to chattel and conversion.

Since Plaintiff has lost nothing more than the fee which he would have charged for the use of Tommy, and since Plaintiff can be made whole by recovering that fee from Defendant, a court probably would find that Defendant's conduct was a mere intermeddling, and, therefore, not serious enough to warrant a forced sale (*i.e.*, conversion).

Example 2: In the above Example, assume that Defendant's doe is carrying leptospirosis (*i.e.*, a sexually transmitted disease of goats), and that as a result of the breeding Tommy contracts the disease and dies.

Because Defendant's act resulted in total destruction of the chattel, a court probably would conclude that Defendant's interference amounted to an exercise of dominion and control and was sufficiently serious to warrant a forced sale (*i.e.*, conversion action).

Example 3: In the above Examples, assume that the features of Defendant's doe are not compatible with the features of Tommy, and that, for this reason, Plaintiff would not have authorized the breeding, even if the fee had been paid. Assume further that because of the incompatibility, the offspring which result from the breeding are of poor quality, and that this causes Tommy's reputation as a breeding buck to suffer.

Since Tommy's reputation as a breeding animal has been

damaged, Plaintiff may successfully argue that the only way for him to be made whole is to require Defendant to purchase Tommy for the value which Tommy had as a breeding buck prior to the breeding. If this argument is successful, a court probably will conclude that Defendant's interference amounted to an exercise of dominion and control, and, therefore, that Plaintiff can successfully maintain a conversion claim.

On the other hand, since Tommy is still as good a breeding buck as ever, Defendant may successfully argue that all it would take to make Plaintiff whole is an award of damages to compensate him for the injury to Tommy's reputation. If this argument is successful, a court probably will conclude that Defendant's interference amounted to a mere intermeddling, and that Plaintiff cannot successfully maintain a conversion claim.

c. **Election of remedies:** Since a conversion occurs when the defendant makes the plaintiff's chattel her own, a plaintiff who is successful in maintaining an action for conversion sells the chattel to the defendant when the judgment is satisfied. The sale takes effect at the time the interference occurred.

If the chattel became the defendant's at the time of the conversion, it would be inconsistent to find that the defendant's act with respect to that chattel damaged the plaintiff. For this reason, ***a plaintiff cannot successfully recover for both trespass to chattel and conversion.*** In those cases in which the defendant's interference is not serious enough to be a conversion, the plaintiff's only successful claim will be for trespass to chattel. When the defendant's interference is sufficiently serious to be a conversion, however, the plaintiff may choose to assert a trespass-to-chattel claim instead.

Example: Defendant shoots and kills Plaintiff's dog. Although the interference probably was serious enough to warrant a forced sale (*i.e.*, to constitute conversion), Plaintiff, who wishes to keep the body and have it stuffed and mounted, sues for trespass to chattel. Defendant argues that since the dog was destroyed, the interference amounted to a conversion and that after paying the judgment, Defendant should become the owner of the body.

Because the dog was destroyed by the defendant's act, the interference is sufficient to warrant a forced sale. This means that if Plaintiff chose to sue for conversion and won, Defendant would become the owner of the dog's remains upon payment of the judgment. Every interference which is serious enough to amount to a conversion, however, may also be regarded as a trespass to chattel. Because Plaintiff has the right to elect the remedy which he will pursue, and because Plaintiff wishes to keep the body, Plaintiff has correctly elected to pursue the lesser remedy of trespass to chattel.

CHAPTER 3

AFFIRMATIVE DEFENSES TO INTENTIONAL TORTS

I. GENERAL CONCEPTS

A. Affirmative defense: An affirmative defense is an ***argument raised by a defendant which may be unrelated to the essential elements of the plaintiff's case, but which, if accepted, will protect the defendant from liability.*** (*supra*, p. 6).

Example: Plaintiff raises a gun to shoot at Defendant. Before he can do so, Defendant slaps the gun from Plaintiff's hand. Plaintiff asserts a battery claim. Defendant argues that he is not liable because he was acting in self-defense (*i.e.*, a privilege to use reasonable force in protecting oneself against a tort, *infra*, p. 39).

Since a battery is an intentional harmful or offensive contact, and since Defendant deliberately slapped Plaintiff's hand without Plaintiff's permission, all the elements of a battery are satisfied. Defendant's argument that he is not liable because he was acting in self-defense is not related to any of these elements. It does not prevent Defendant's act from being intentional, or the contact with Plaintiff from being harmful or offensive. Nevertheless, if it is found that Defendant was acting in self-defense, he will not be liable. Self-defense may, therefore, be included in the class of affirmative defenses.

B. Burden of proof: A defendant always has the burden of establishing the affirmative defense on which she wishes to rely.

Note: Some outlines and study aids make the absence of affirmative defenses part of the definition of intentional torts. They may, for example, define battery as "intentional harmful or offensive contact with the plaintiff without consent or legal privilege." However, this distorts the concept that the burden of establishing an affirmative defense should be on the defendant. Since a definition which makes the absence of privilege an essential element of a tort might result in shifting to the plaintiff the burden of proving that there are no affirmative defenses, such definitions are incorrect and should be avoided.

C. Essential elements: Just as intentional torts are defined in terms of their essential elements, affirmative defenses should also be defined in terms of their essential elements.

II. CONSENT

A. General concept: Since a tort is a violation of the plaintiff's rights, and since a person who has consented to an act cannot claim that it violated his rights, consent is an affirmative defense to all intentional torts.

B. Definition: ***Consent*** simply means ***willingness***.

1. **Express consent:** Express consent is willingness which is ***stated in words or a substitute*** for words.

   Example: Defendant is a doctor who gives vaccinations on the deck of a ship to passengers before they disembark. Defendant asks Plaintiff, "Do you want a vaccination?" Plaintiff nods her head. Defendant vaccinates Plaintiff who subsequently sues for battery. Defendant asserts the affirmative defense of consent.

   Since a nod of the head is generally understood to be a substitute for the word "yes", Plaintiff gave express consent in response to Defendant's question, "Do you want a vaccination?" For this reason, Defendant will not be liable for battery.

2. **Implied consent:** Implied consent is willingness which is ***not stated*** in words or a substitute for words but which ***would be gathered by the reasonable person observing the plaintiff's conduct***.

   Example: Defendant is a doctor who gives vaccinations on the deck of a ship to passengers before they disembark. Plaintiff stands at the end of a long line of passengers waiting for vaccinations. When she reaches the front of the line, she rolls up her sleeve and holds out her arm. The doctor vaccinates her and Plaintiff subsequently sues for battery. Defendant asserts the affirmative defense of consent.

   Since it was obvious that Defendant was giving vaccinations, and since vaccinations are usually given to an exposed arm, Plaintiff's conduct of standing in line and then exposing her arm to Defendant probably would have led the reasonable person observing her to gather that she was willing to be vaccinated. For this reason, she probably has given implied consent to the vaccination. If so, Defendant is not liable for battery. *O'Brien v. Cunard S.S. Co.*, 28 N.E. 266 (Mass. 1891).

3. **Apparent consent:** Apparent consent is willingness which the ***reasonable person would gather from the circumstances***.

   Example 1: Plaintiff is brought into a hospital unconscious and bleeding. Defendant, a doctor, knows that if the bleeding is not stopped, Plaintiff will die. Defendant operates on Plaintiff to stop the bleeding. Plaintiff subsequently asserts a claim for battery. Defendant argues that he was privileged by Plaintiff's apparent consent.

Since Plaintiff was unconscious, it was impossible to ask Plaintiff whether he was willing to have the operation or to gather anything from his conduct. For this reason, Defendant had no choice but to determine from the circumstances whether or not Plaintiff was willing. Since most people in Plaintiff's position would have been willing to submit to an operation necessary to save their lives, it probably was reasonable for Defendant to believe that Plaintiff was willing. If so, Defendant was privileged by apparent consent.

Example 2: Plaintiff is brought into a hospital conscious but bleeding. Defendant, a doctor, realizes that Plaintiff will die if the bleeding is not stopped. Defendant begins to operate on Plaintiff to stop the bleeding, but Plaintiff says, "Do not touch me." Defendant hears Plaintiff, but continues with the operation. Plaintiff subsequently asserts a battery claim. Defendant argues that he was privileged by apparent consent.

Since Plaintiff clearly stated that he did not want to be touched, it probably was not reasonable for Defendant to gather from the circumstances that Plaintiff was willing to be touched. For this reason, Defendant probably is not privileged by apparent consent, and probably is liable for battery.

C. **Mistake:** Consent given because of a mistake in the mind of the plaintiff privileges the defendant, so long as the defendant is unaware of the plaintiff's mistake.

Example: Defendant, an insurance salesman, knocks on Plaintiff's door. Plaintiff, who was expecting a visit from a friend, believes that it is her friend who is knocking and shouts, "Come in." Defendant enters, and Plaintiff subsequently asserts a claim for trespass to land. Defendant argues that he was privileged by Plaintiff's consent.

Although Plaintiff was not actually willing to have Defendant enter, she expressed consent to his entry because she was mistaken about his identity. Since Defendant did not know and could not have known this, Defendant was privileged, and is not liable for trespass.

D. **Consent induced by fraud:** Consent which is ***induced by fraud*** on the part of the defendant is said to be ***vitiated (i.e.***, negated or undone) if the fraud relates to the nature of the act to which the consent referred.

Example 1: Defendant, a physician, induced Plaintiff, who was one of his patients, to have sexual intercourse with him by convincing her that he was using a medical procedure to take a sample of vaginal tissue. Plaintiff subsequently asserted a claim for battery against Defendant. Defendant argued that Plaintiff consented.

Since Defendant convinced Plaintiff that he was performing a medical procedure on her when in fact he was having sexual intercourse with her, he induced her consent by fraud. For this reason, the consent was vitiated and did not privilege Defendant. *People v. Minkowski*, 23 Cal. Rptr. 92 (Cal. 1962).

Example 2: Defendant induced Plaintiff to have sexual intercourse with him by convincing her that having sexual intercourse with him would help immunize her against certain diseases. Plaintiff subsequently asserted a battery claim against him. Defendant argued that he was privileged by consent.

Although Defendant misled Plaintiff about the reason for having intercourse, Plaintiff knew that she was having intercourse. Since Defendant's fraud did not relate to the nature of the act to which Plaintiff was consenting, consent was effective and Defendant was privileged by it.

E. **Consent to unlawful fights:** Although a person who consents to an act is usually prevented from suing for damages resulting from that act, a controversy has developed regarding consent to unlawful fights.

1. **Additional deterrent:** Some jurisdictions have held that consent to an unlawful fight has no legal effect and that, therefore, one who consents is not prevented from asserting a battery claim against the other combatant. Courts which have stated this rule have usually said that its purpose is to serve as an additional deterrent to unlawful fighting.

2. **Reward for violating law:** Other courts have continued to apply the general rule that one who consents to an act is prevented from suing for damages resulting from it. In applying this rule to unlawful fights, they have usually stated that to permit the lawsuit would be to give the plaintiff a reward for breaking the law.

Example: Plaintiff and Defendant fight in violation of a statute which prohibits fighting. During the course of the fight, Defendant strikes Plaintiff. Plaintiff subsequently asserts a battery claim against Defendant. Defendant argues that he was privileged by consent.

In some jurisdictions, it will be held that consent to an unlawful fight is ineffective. For this reason, Plaintiff will be able to maintain the action against Defendant even though he consented to the fight and to the blow which occurred as a natural part of it.

In other jurisdictions, Plaintiff will be prevented from maintaining the claim on the ground that his consent gave Defendant a privilege to strike Plaintiff. *Hart v. Geysel*, 294 P. 570 (Wash. 1930).

3. **Application to other unlawful conduct:** The cases relating to unlawful fighting led the persons who drafted the Restatement (2d) to suggest that consent to any unlawful act might be legally ineffective and that a person injured by an unlawful act might assert a claim for damages even though she consented to it. So far, very few cases have applied this principle.

III. SELF DEFENSE

A. General concept: Self defense is a privilege to use force to protect oneself against a threatened attack.

B. Essential elements: The essential elements of ***"self-defense"*** are: (1) ***an attempt to prevent a tort against oneself***; and (2) ***the use of reasonable force***.

1. **Attempt to prevent tort:** A person is privileged to use force in self defense when she is attempting to protect herself against a threatened contact or confinement.

2. **Reasonable force:** Reasonable force is the ***force which would appear necessary to the reasonable person in the defendant's position***.

   a. **Apparent necessity:** Force may be reasonable even if unnecessary so long as the ordinary person in the defendant's position would have believed that it was necessary.

   Example: During an argument with Defendant, Plaintiff, who has a reputation for shooting people, reaches into his pocket for a handkerchief. Defendant, believing that Plaintiff is going to pull a gun and shoot him, strikes Plaintiff. Plaintiff subsequently asserts a battery claim against Defendant. Defendant argues that he was acting in self-defense.

   Although Plaintiff was not actually reaching for a gun, his reputation may have made it reasonable for Defendant to believe that he was. If such belief was reasonable, Defendant's use of force in self-defense was privileged. *Keep v. Quallman*, 32 N.W. 233 (Wis. 1887).

b. Reasonableness: In determining whether conduct (*e.g.*, the use of a particular degree of force) is reasonable, courts generally ***balance*** the ***apparent disadvantage of the conduct against the apparent advantage***. If the disadvantage outweighs the advantage, the conduct (or force) is said to be unreasonable. If the advantage outweighs the disadvantage, the conduct (or force) is said to be reasonable.

Example: Plaintiff threatens to hit Defendant with a large feather pillow. In order to prevent him from doing so, Defendant shoots Plaintiff with a large caliber pistol. Plaintiff subsequently asserts a battery claim. Defendant argues that he was acting in self-defense.

The advantage of shooting Plaintiff with a large caliber pistol was that it prevented Plaintiff from striking Defendant with a feather pillow. The disadvantage was that death or serious injury was likely to result from the shooting. Since a feather pillow is not capable of doing any serious harm, the advantage of shooting Plaintiff was slight compared to the disadvantage. For this reason, the force used by Defendant probably was not reasonable.

i. Lethal force: Since nothing is as valuable as human life, the use of lethal or deadly force (*i.e.*, force likely to result in death or serious bodily harm), is ***not reasonable unless the person using it is defending himself against force which reasonably appears to be lethal or deadly.***

ii. Retreat: Some jurisdictions hold that it is never reasonable to use lethal or deadly force when there is a reasonable means of escape available.

Example: Defendant is a very fast runner. Plaintiff, a slow runner, waves a realistic-looking plastic toy knife at Defendant and threatens to stab him with it. Defendant could run away from Plaintiff without increasing his apparent danger, but instead draws his own knife and stabs Plaintiff. Plaintiff subsequently asserts a claim for battery against Defendant. Defendant argues that he was acting in self-defense.

If it was reasonable for Defendant to believe that the knife waved by Plaintiff was real and that Plaintiff was going to attack him with it, all jurisdictions would agree that Defendant was entitled to use whatever force was reasonable in the face of lethal force.

In some jurisdictions, it is reasonable to use lethal force in the face of lethal force. In these jurisdictions, it probably would be held that the force used by Defendant was a reasonable response to the apparently lethal force threatened by Plaintiff.

Other jurisdictions hold that it is never reasonable to use lethal force when there exists a reasonable means of escape. Since Defendant could have run away without increasing the danger to himself, those jurisdictions would conclude that the force used by Defendant was unreasonable, and, therefore, that Defendant was not privileged by self-defense.

C. **Application to intentional tort:** Since self defense is a privilege to use force against a person, it may be raised as an affirmative defense against any tort involving the intentional use of force against a person. This may include ***battery, assault, false imprisonment, and, under some circumstances, intentional infliction of mental suffering***.

IV. DEFENSE OF OTHERS

A. **General concept:** Defense of others is a privilege to protect other persons against threatened attack.

B. **Essential elements:** The essential elements of ***"defense of others"*** are: (1) ***an attempt to protect another person against a threatened contact or confinement***; and (2) ***use of reasonable force***.

1. **Attempt to prevent tort:** A person is privileged to use force when she is attempting to protect another person against a threatened contact or confinement.

2. **Reasonable force:** The definition of reasonable force in the defense of others is ***identical to that used in connection with self defense*** (*i.e.*, the force which would appear necessary to the reasonable person). A controversy has developed, however, regarding the point of view of the "reasonable" person.

   a. **Reasonable defender:** In some jurisdictions, a person acting in defense of another is ***privileged to use whatever force would appear necessary to the reasonable person in the position of the defender***.

   b. **Privilege same as that of person defended**. In other jurisdictions, a person acting in defense of another is not privileged to use any more force than the person being defended would be privileged to use, *supra*, p. 39.

   Example: Defendant sees Plaintiff and another man beating a smaller man with clubs. In attempting to protect the smaller man against what appears to be an attack, Defendant pushes Plaintiff. Actually Plaintiff is a police officer and, with his partner, is in the act of arresting the smaller man who has attempted to stab them with a knife. Plaintiff subsequently asserts a battery claim against Defendant. Defendant argues that he was privileged to act in the defense of another.

In some jurisdictions, Defendant is permitted to use whatever force would have seemed necessary to the reasonable person in Defendant's position. If the reasonable person in Defendant's position would have believed that the small man was a victim being attacked by ruffians, he would have believed it necessary to use the force that Defendant used. If so, the force was reasonable and Defendant was privileged. In other jurisdictions, Defendant is privileged only to use as much force as the person he was defending would have been privileged to use in defense of himself. Since the small man was resisting a lawful arrest, he would not have been permitted to use any force at all. For this reason, the force used by Defendant was not reasonable and Defendant was not privileged.

C. **Application to intentional tort:** Since defense of another is a privilege to use force against a person, it may be raised as an affirmative defense against any tort involving the intentional use of force against another. This includes ***battery, assault, false imprisonment***, and, under some circumstances, ***intentional infliction of mental harm***.

V. DEFENSE OF PROPERTY

A. **General concept:** Defense of property is a privilege to use reasonable force to protect one's own real or personal property against a threatened trespass.

B. **Essential elements:** The essential elements of ***"defense of property"*** are: (1) ***an attempt to protect ones own property against a trespass***; and (2) ***use of reasonable force***.

1. **Prevention of a trespass:** A defendant is privileged to use force to protect realty against intentional unauthorized entry or to protect personalty against intentional interference. Once a trespass has begun, reasonable force may be used to prevent it from continuing.

2. **Reasonable force:** The definition used for reasonable force as that term is used in self defense and defense of others applies to defense of property as well.

a. Lethal force: Since no property is worth as much as the life of any human, ***lethal or deadly force*** (*i.e.*, force likely to result in death or great bodily harm) is ***never reasonable in defense of property***.

Example: Defendant is the owner of an unused and unoccupied farmhouse. Thieves have often broken into the farmhouse and stolen objects from it. In an attempt to prevent further thefts, Defendant constructs a spring gun consisting of a shotgun loaded, cocked, and aimed at the middle of the doorway. Plaintiff, a thief, breaks into the farmhouse for the purpose of stealing objects. When he opens the door, he is shot and injured by the spring gun. Plaintiff subsequently asserts a battery claim against Defendant. Defendant argues that he was acting in defense of his property.

Because a shotgun is likely to inflict death or great bodily harm, using one to defend property has the potential disadvantage of causing death or serious injury to a human being. The advantage of using a shotgun is the prevention of theft of objects from the farmhouse. Since human life is more valuable than property, the disadvantage resulting from use of a shotgun outweighs the advantage resulting from its use. For this reason, the force used by Defendant was unreasonable, and Defendant was not privileged. *Katko v. Briney*, 183 N.W.2d 657 (Iowa 1971).

b. Escalation: Since the value of property does not exceed the value of human life, it is generally held that only slight force is permitted to defend it. Since that use of force is privileged, however, any resistance which is offered to it may constitute a tort against which the property owner has a privilege to defend himself by using greater force.

Example: Defendant observes Plaintiff attempting to steal Defendant's stove. Defendant demands that Plaintiff let it alone, but Plaintiff continues his attempt to steal it. Defendant places his hands against Plaintiff's shoulders and pushes him gently away from the stove. Plaintiff draws a knife and threatens to stab Defendant. Defendant hits Plaintiff with a club. Plaintiff asserts a battery claim, in response to which Defendant argues that he was privileged to use reasonable force. Plaintiff alleges that the force used by Defendant was excessive and, therefore, unreasonable.

Because a club is capable of inflicting serious physical injury to a person, it probably would not have been reasonable for Defendant to use a club in defense of his stove. In his defense of his stove, however, Defendant used gentle hands against

Plaintiff. Since this initial contact was not likely to inflict any serious injury and since it was likely to prevent the trespass to Defendant's chattel, its advantage probably outweighed its disadvantage, and, therefore, it was reasonable and privileged. Since Defendant was privileged to touch Plaintiff in an attempt to repel him from the stove, Plaintiff had no right to use force in response. For this reason, Plaintiff's attempt to stab Defendant with a knife was a threatened battery. In striking Plaintiff with a club, Defendant was attempting to protect himself against the threatened battery. If the force which he used was reasonable in the face of that threat, it was privileged as self defense. *Hodgeden v. Hubbard*, 18 Vt. 504 (1846).

C. Application to intentional tort: Since defense of property is a privilege to use force against a person, it may be raised as an affirmative defense against any allegation of tort involving the intentional use of force. This may include ***battery, assault, false imprisonment, and, under some circumstances, intentional infliction of mental harm***.

VI. RECAPTURE OF CHATTEL

A. General concept: Although the law is willing to permit the use of force to prevent torts from being committed, it is less willing to permit force to be used against a tortfeasor after the tort is complete. In some cases, the privilege called ***recapture of chattel*** makes an exception for force used in attempting to recapture a chattel which has been wrongfully taken.

B. Essential elements: The essential elements of recapture of chattel are: (1) ***wrongful dispossession of a chattel from the defendant***; (2) ***prompt action to recover it***; and (3) ***use of reasonable force***.

1. Wrongful dispossession: Wrongful dispossession occurs when the ***chattel is removed from the defendant's actual or constructive possession by one who has no right to do so.***

Example: Thief steals Defendant's television and sells it to a second hand store. Plaintiff purchases the television from the store and is carrying it down the street when Defendant sees her. Defendant recognizes his television and uses force against Plaintiff to recapture it. Plaintiff asserts a battery claim. Defendant argues that Plaintiff had converted the television and that Defendant was privileged to use force to recapture it.

Since Plaintiff intentionally acquired possession of the television, and since Defendant had a right to possess it, Plaintiff probably did commit a conversion. Because the television was not in Defendant's possession at the time Plaintiff converted it, however, Plaintiff did not dispossess Defendant of it. For this reason, Defendant was not privileged to use any force at all to recapture it from Plaintiff, and probably will be liable for battery.

2. **Prompt action:** Although the defense of recapture permits the use of force after the tort is complete, it is not a license to fight oneself back into possession of the converted chattel. The privilege to use force only exists when the ***dispossession is discovered immediately, action begins immediately, and there is no interruption and no opportunity to cool down***.

   Example: After seeing Plaintiff stealing his car, Defendant chases him but does not catch him. The next day, Defendant sees Plaintiff driving his car and uses force against Plaintiff to recapture the car. Plaintiff subsequently asserts a claim for battery. Defendant argues that he was privileged to use force to recapture his chattel.

   Although Defendant was wrongfully dispossessed of his car by Plaintiff, and although Defendant acted immediately in attempting to get it back, a day passed between the time the chattel was taken from Defendant and the time the Defendant used force against the Plaintiff. Since this passage of time probably would have given the reasonable person in Defendant's position an opportunity to cool down and use other means to retrieve his car, Defendant's use of force probably was not sufficiently prompt to be privileged as a recapture of chattel.

3. **Reasonable force:** As used in connection with defense of self, others, and property, the term reasonable force in the case of recapture means the force which would appear necessary to the reasonable person. However, since one recapturing a chattel is an aggressor rather than a defender, ***force is reasonable only if it would have been used by a reasonable person who was familiar with all the facts***.

   Example 1: Defendant sees Plaintiff about to strike the windshield of Defendant's car with a baseball bat. Actually, the bat which Plaintiff is swinging is made of plastic foam and cannot possibly damage the windshield, but Defendant reasonably believes it to be made of wood. In an attempt to prevent Plaintiff from damaging his car, Defendant strikes Plaintiff's wrist, knocking the bat out of his hand. Plaintiff asserts a battery claim. Defendant argues that he was acting in defense of his property.

If it was reasonable for Defendant to believe that Plaintiff was about to smash the windshield, Defendant was privileged to use reasonable force in an attempt to prevent it, even though Plaintiff was not actually going to smash the windshield.

Example 2: Defendant's car is stolen by a person who looks exactly like Plaintiff. Defendant chases the thief and sees Plaintiff driving a car identical to that which was stolen from Defendant. Reasonably believing that Plaintiff stole his car and is driving it, Defendant uses force against Plaintiff in an attempt to recapture it.

Defendant was wrongfully dispossessed of his car and acted promptly in an attempt to get it back. Since Plaintiff was not the thief, however, and since the car which Plaintiff was driving was not Defendant's car, the reasonable person who knew all the facts would not have believed it necessary to use any force against Plaintiff to recapture the car from him. For this reason, the force used by Defendant against Plaintiff was not reasonable, and was not privileged. Defendant probably is liable for battery.

C. **Application to intentional tort:** Since recapture of chattel is a privilege to use force against a person, it may be raised as an affirmative defense against any tort involving the intentional use of force. This may include ***battery, assault, false imprisonment***, and, under some circumstances, ***intentional infliction of mental suffering***.

VII. AUTHORITY OF LAW

A. **General concept:** Because responsible members of society are expected to carry out mandates of established law or of the courts, they must be free to do so without fear of tort liability. For this reason, ***conduct which might otherwise be tortious may be privileged if performed under authority of law.*** (See Immunities, *infra*, p. 310.)

B. **Essential elements:** The essential elements of the ***"privilege to act"*** under authority of law are: (1) ***a mandate of the court or of the law***; and (2) ***reasonable conduct in carrying it out***.

1. **Legal mandate:** The source of legal authority may be a statute or an order of the court.

   a. **Invalid order:** Even if an order of the court is invalid, it may provide the basis for this affirmative defense so long as it is "fair on its face." ***A court order is fair on its face if the court which issued it had jurisdiction to issue orders like it and***

if its form and condition would lead a reasonable person acting under it to believe that it is valid.

Example 1: Defendant, a police officer, is directed to execute a warrant for the arrest of Plaintiff. The court which issued the warrant had the jurisdiction to issue arrest warrants, but this particular warrant is invalid because the information on which it was based was not sufficient to give probable cause to believe that Plaintiff was guilty of a crime as required by the United States Constitution. Defendant executes the warrant by placing Plaintiff under arrest. Plaintiff subsequently asserts a false imprisonment claim against Defendant, on the ground that the warrant was invalid.

Since the court which issued the warrant generally had the power to issue arrest warrants, Defendant was privileged to execute it so long as the warrant was fair on its face. The warrant was fair on its face if the reasonable police officer looking at it would have believed that it was valid. Since the face of a warrant does not disclose the basis on which it was issued, there would have been no way for the reasonable police officer to know that the information on which it was based was legally insufficient. For this reason, the warrant was fair on its face and Defendant was privileged by authority of law.

b. **Lack of jurisdiction:** ***If the court*** which issued the order ***did not have jurisdiction to issue orders of that kind, the person executing the order is not privileged.***

Example 2: In Example 1. above, assume that the court which issued the warrant did not have jurisdiction to issue arrest warrants of any kind.

Because the warrant was issued by a court which did not have jurisdiction to issue arrest warrants, the warrant could not be fair on its face. For this reason, Defendant was not privileged to execute it, and may be liable for false imprisonment.

2. **Reasonable conduct:** A defendant is privileged to act reasonably in executing a legal mandate.

a. **Reasonable force or entry:** Authority of law includes the privilege to use ***reasonable force against persons, to make reasonable entry onto real property, or to interfere reasonably with the chattel of another*** for the purpose of carrying out the mandate.

b. **Reasonableness:** As usual, the reasonableness of conduct is ***determined by balancing the advantages against the disadvantages of that conduct.***

Example 1: Pursuant to a valid arrest warrant, Defendant, a police officer, places Plaintiff under arrest. Although Plaintiff does not offer resistance, Defendant handcuffs Plaintiff. Plaintiff subsequently asserts a battery claim against Defendant. Defendant argues that he was privileged by authority of law.

Ordinarily, handcuffs cause only mild discomfort and no real injury to a person who does not struggle against them. For this reason, the disadvantage of using them is relatively slight. On the other hand, persons placed under arrest frequently attack the officers who have arrested them, inflicting great bodily harm or even death. Since the use of handcuffs effectively prevents this from happening, the advantage of using them is comparatively great. Therefore, it probably was reasonable for Defendant to use handcuffs, and their use probably was privileged.

Example 2: Pursuant to a valid arrest warrant, Defendant, a police officer, places Plaintiff under arrest. Although Plaintiff does not offer resistance, Defendant uses a choke hold (*i.e.*, the exertion of pressure on a certain point in the neck which results in unconsciousness and, occasionally, in death) on Plaintiff. Plaintiff subsequently asserts a battery claim against Defendant. Defendant argues that he was privileged by authority of law.

Since a choke hold can result in unconsciousness and occasionally death, the disadvantage of using it was relatively great. Since handcuffs could have effectively protected the arresting officer without inflicting serious harm on Plaintiff, the advantage of using a choke hold to accomplish the same purpose was relatively slight. For this reason, it probably was unreasonable for Defendant to use a choke hold, and its use probably was not privileged.

c. **Must be carrying out mandate:** No matter how reasonably a defendant acts and no matter how good his intentions, if she is ***not actually carrying out a legal mandate, she is not privileged by authority of law.***

Example: In attempting to execute a warrant for the arrest of Mary, Plaintiff's identical twin sister, Defendant, a police officer, arrests Plaintiff instead. Plaintiff subsequently asserts a claim for false imprisonment against Defendant. Defendant argues that since it was reasonable for him to mistake Plaintiff for her sister, he was privileged by authority of law.

Since the warrant was for the arrest of Mary, Defendant was not carrying it out when he arrested Plaintiff. For this reason, Defendant cannot effectively assert the privilege of authority of law.

C. **Application to intentional torts:** Since authority of law is a privilege to use force against a person, it may be raised as a defense to any intentional tort involving the application of force against a person. These include ***battery, assault, false imprisonment, and, in some cases, intentional infliction of mental harm***. Because it also is a privilege to enter realty or interfere with chattels, it may be raised as a defense to any intentional tort involving entry onto realty or interference with a chattel. These include ***trespass to land, trespass to chattel, and conversion***.

VIII. NECESSITY

A. **General concept:** The privileges of necessity permit the violation of property rights for the purpose of protecting persons or property threatened by an emergency.

B. **Public and private necessity:** There are actually two privileges based on necessity: public necessity and private necessity.

1. **Public necessity a complete privilege:** ***Public necessity is a complete or absolute privilege***. This means that a defendant who successfully asserts it, is free from all liability for damage resulting from her act.

2. **Private necessity a qualified privilege:** ***Private necessity is a qualified privilege***. This means that a defendant who successfully asserts it has not committed a trespass, but may be liable for damage resulting from the act.

Example: Defendant breaks into Plaintiff's house in order to put out a fire in his own house next door. In doing so, Defendant damages Plaintiff's door which requires repairs costing $100. Plaintiff subsequently asserts a claim against Defendant for $100, alleging that Defendant committed a trespass to land. Defendant argues that he was privileged by public necessity, or in the alternative, that he was privileged by private necessity.

If it is found that Defendant was not privileged by either public or private necessity, Defendant has committed a trespass to land and will be liable for $100 in damages.

If it is found that Defendant was privileged by public necessity, Defendant has not committed a trespass to land and is free of any liability to Plaintiff.

If it is found that Defendant was privileged by private

necessity, Defendant has not committed a trespass to land, but is liable to Plaintiff for $100 in damages.

C. **Essential elements:** The essential elements of the ***"privilege of necessity"*** are: (1) ***an emergency***; and (2) ***a reasonable invasion of property rights in response to it***.

1. **Emergency:** An emergency is a situation which ***threatens life or property and which requires immediate action***.

a. **Public emergency:** A public emergency is a situation which threatens the lives or property of the general public and which requires immediate action. ***One who reasonably invades property rights to protect the public from a public emergency is privileged by public necessity.***

Example: A fire raging in the city of San Francisco threatens to destroy the property and lives of all persons living in the city. In order to prevent the spread of the fire, Defendant, the mayor, decides to destroy all fuel in its path. Since Plaintiff's house is in the path of the fire, the mayor orders that it be blown up. Plaintiff subsequently asserts a claim against Defendant for trespass. Defendant argues that he was privileged by public necessity.

Since the spread of the fire threatened the lives and property of all people who lived in San Francisco (*i.e.*, of the general public), it constituted a public emergency. For this reason, if Defendant's conduct was reasonable, he was privileged by public necessity. If so, Defendant did not commit a trespass and is not liable for damage. *Surocco v. Geary*, 3 Cal. 69 (1853).

b. **Private emergency:** A private emergency is a situation which threatens the life or property of Defendant, or the lives or property of a limited group of people. ***One who reasonably invades property rights to protect himself or his property, or the lives and property of a limited group of people, is privileged by private necessity.***

Example: Boater is sailing his boat on the lake when a storm begins to blow. Fearful that his boat will be damaged by the storm, Boater ties it to Docker's dock. The storm causes the boat to be thrown repeatedly against the dock, causing $500 damage to the dock. Docker, seeing the boat tied to his dock, cuts its line, casting it adrift. As a result, Boater is injured. Boater asserts a battery claim against Docker for his injuries, in response to which Docker argues that he was acting in defense of property. Docker asserts a trespass to land claim against Boater for damage to the dock, in response to which Boater argues that he was privileged by necessity.

Since Docker cut the line, casting Boater adrift with knowledge that Boater would probably be injured in the storm as a result, Docker has committed a battery unless his act was privileged as a defense of property. This privilege permits the use of reasonable force to defend realty against a trespass. Since Boater was confronted by an emergency to himself and his property, however, he was privileged by private necessity. For this reason, he was not a trespasser, and Docker was not privileged to use force against him. Docker, therefore, may be liable to Boater for battery. *Ploof v. Putnam*, 71 A. 188 (Vt. 1908).

Since Boater was privileged by necessity, tying his boat to the dock was not a trespass. However, since the emergency was a private emergency threatening only him and his property, the privilege was private necessity. While this prevents his conduct from being a trespass, it is only a qualified privilege, which means that he must pay for the damage which resulted from his act. Since his act caused $500 in damage to Docker's dock, Boater is liable to Docker for that amount. *Vincent v. Lake Erie Transportation Co.*, 124 N.W. 221 (Minn. 1910) (see also *infra*).

c. **Emergency created by defendant:** Most jurisdictions agree that a ***person who created an emergency is not privileged by necessity*** when acting in response to that emergency.

Example: Defendant negligently starts a fire which threatens to burn all the houses in town. In an attempt to prevent its spread, Defendant blows up Plaintiff's house. Plaintiff subsequently asserts a trespass claim against Defendant. Defendant argues that he was privileged by necessity. Since Defendant created the emergency, he was not privileged by necessity, and will be held liable for damage to Plaintiff's property.

2. **Reasonable invasion:** In determining whether the invasion of a property right was reasonable, courts usually ***balance the value of the property which was being protected against the value of the right which was invaded***. If the value of the property which was being protected outweighed the value of the right which was invaded, the invasion was reasonable. If the value of the right invaded outweighed the value of the property which was being protected, the invasion was unreasonable.

Example: Boater is sailing his boat on the lake when a storm begins to blow. Fearful that his boat will be damaged by the storm, Boater ties it to Docker's dock. The storm causes the boat to be thrown repeatedly against the dock, causing $500 damage to the dock. Docker asserts a trespass to land claim against

Boater. Boater argues that he was privileged by private necessity.

Since Boater was confronted by an immediate threat to himself and his property, he was faced with a private emergency. This means his entry onto Docker's realty was privileged provided it was reasonable. Since it was possible to save a valuable boat at a relatively small cost by tying it to the dock, it was reasonable for Boater to do so. Since his invasion of Docker's right was reasonable, it was privileged by private necessity, and Boater did not therefore commit a trespass. Since private necessity is a qualified privilege, however, Boater is required to pay for the damage which his conduct caused. *Vincent v. Lake Erie Transport, supra*.

IX. PRIVILEGE TO ENTER REALTY TO RECOVER CHATTEL

A. General concept: Under some circumstances, a person may be privileged to enter the realty of another for the purpose of retrieving a chattel. This privilege is similar to and is often described as a variation on the privilege of private necessity.

B. Essential elements: The essential elements of this privilege are: (1) ***the presence of the defendant's chattel on the plaintiff's realty through no fault of the defendant's***; and (2) ***reasonable entry to retrieve it***.

1. **Lack of fault:** Just as a defendant who creates an emergency ordinarily is not privileged by necessity to protect himself against it by invading the property rights of another, similarly, a ***defendant whose chattel is on the realty of another through his own fault*** is not privileged to enter the realty to get it back.

   a. **Fault by plaintiff:** If the defendant's chattel is on the plaintiff's realty as the result of some fault by the plaintiff, the defendant's privilege to enter and retrieve it is an ***absolute privilege***. This means that a defendant acting under that privilege is not liable for any of the damage that results from his act.

   b. **No fault:** If the defendant's chattel is on the plaintiff's realty without any fault by the plaintiff, the defendant's privilege to enter and retrieve it is a ***qualified privilege***, similar to the privilege of private necessity. This means that although the defendant is not thereby committing a trespass, the defendant will be liable for any damage which results.

Example 1: Defendant negligently fails to close the gate to his corral, allowing his cow to escape and wander into a fenced field on Plaintiff's realty. Defendant cuts the fence to retrieve his cow. Plaintiff asserts a claim for trespass to land, seeking damages to compensate for repairs to the fence. Defendant argues that he was privileged to enter to retake his chattel.

Since the cow was on Plaintiff's realty as a result of Defendant's negligence, Defendant has no privilege to enter and retake the cow. For this reason, Defendant's entry constitutes a trespass and he is liable for the damage to the fence.

Example 2: Same facts as Example 1, except an unforeseeable earthquake has caused the corral gate to open, permitting the corralled cow to escape onto Plaintiff's land.

Since the cow is on Plaintiff's realty with no fault on the part of Defendant, Defendant is privileged to make a reasonable entry to retake the cow. For this reason, Defendant does not commit a trespass if he cuts the fence to retrieve the cow. Since the Plaintiff is not at fault, however, Defendant's privilege is qualified. This means that Defendant must pay for the damage to the fence.

Example 3: Plaintiff steals Defendant's cow and takes it into a fenced field on Plaintiff's realty. Since the only way to get the cow out of the field is to cut the fence, Defendant cuts Plaintiff's fence and retrieves the cow. Plaintiff subsequently asserts a trespass claim for damages to compensate him for repairs to the fence.

Since Defendant's cow was on Plaintiff's realty through no fault of Defendant, Defendant was privileged to make reasonable entry to retake the cow. For this reason, Defendant has not committed a trespass. Since the cow was there as the result of fault by Plaintiff, the privilege was absolute. This means that Defendant is not liable for damage to the fence.

2. **Reasonable entry to retrieve:** In deciding whether the entry was reasonable, courts usually ***balance the value of the chattel being retrieved against the value of the right invaded***. If the value of the chattel exceeds the value of the right invaded, the entry was reasonable. If the value of the right invaded exceeds the value of the chattel, the entry was unreasonable.

Example: Unknown to Plaintiff, thieves steal Defendant's bicycle and put it in Plaintiff's garage. The bicycle is worth $10. The only way for Defendant to retrieve the bicycle is to break down the garage door. Because the garage door was specially made for

Plaintiff, it is worth $2,000. Defendant breaks down the door to retrieve his bicycle, totally destroying the door. Plaintiff subsequently asserts a trespass claim, seeking damages for replacement of the garage door. Defendant argues that he was privileged to enter to retake his chattel.

Since Defendant's chattel was on Plaintiff's realty through no fault of Defendant, Defendant was privileged to enter the realty in a reasonable way to retake it. Since the bicycle was worth only $10, however, and since entry onto the realty involved destruction of a garage door worth $2,000, the entry was not reasonable, and, therefore, not privileged. For this reason, Defendant has committed a trespass and is liable for replacement of the garage door.

CHAPTER 4

NEGLIGENCE

I. GENERAL CONCEPT

A. Distinguished from volitional tortious acts: Volitional tortious acts require knowledge to a substantial degree of certainty that harm will result (*supra*, p. 7). Negligence is based on ***unreasonable conduct in the face of a foreseeable risk that harm may result***.

B. Essential elements: The essential elements of ***"negligence"*** are: (1) ***a duty of reasonable care***; and (2) a ***breach of that duty***.

1. **Duty of reasonable care:** Before unreasonable conduct can qualify as negligence, it must be shown that the defendant owed the plaintiff a duty to act reasonably in whatever the defendant was doing. Ordinarily, a ***defendant owes a plaintiff a duty of reasonable care only if a foreseeable risk to the plaintiff is created by the defendant's conduct***.

   a. **Foreseeable risk:** A foreseeable risk is a ***danger which would be anticipated by the reasonable person in the defendant's position***.

   Example: Defendant leaves a golf club lying on the ground in his back yard. Later that day, Johnny, Defendant's seven year old son, picks up the golf club and attempts to swing it, striking his friend Plaintiff in the head. Plaintiff asserts a negligence claim against Defendant, alleging that it was unreasonable for Defendant to leave the golf club in his yard. Defendant argues that he did not owe Plaintiff a duty of reasonable care.

   Defendant owed Plaintiff a duty of reasonable care if leaving the golf club on the ground created a foreseeable risk. Since there is nothing intrinsically dangerous about a golf club, it may be successfully argued that the reasonable person would not have anticipated that leaving it on the ground would lead to injury, and that, therefore, Defendant did not owe Plaintiff a duty of reasonable care.

   On the other hand, seven year old children frequently try to emulate their parents. For this reason, it was likely that if Johnny found the club, he would attempt to swing it. Since young children usually are not as well coordinated as adults, it was likely that in doing so, he would be unable to control its direction sufficiently to prevent it from striking any child who was with him. For this reason, it may be successfully argued that the reasonable person would have anticipated that leaving it on the ground would lead to injury, and that, therefore, Defendant did owe Plaintiff a duty of reasonable care. *Lubitz v. Wells*, 113. A.2d 147 (Conn. 1955).

b. Risk to plaintiff: Although a defendant's conduct may have created a foreseeable risk to someone, it is usually the rule that a ***defendant does not owe a duty of reasonable care to any specific plaintiff unless it was foreseeable that the defendant's conduct would endanger that particular plaintiff***.

Example: Plaintiff is standing under a tall scale on the platform of a railroad station. As a train pulls out of the station, a man carrying a package wrapped in brown paper rushes to catch it. Defendant, a conductor on the train, grabs the man by the wrist and yanks him aboard the train, causing him to drop the package. The package contains fireworks which explode when they hit the tracks. A shock wave from the explosion causes the scale to fall, striking plaintiff and injuring her. Plaintiff asserts a negligence claim against Defendant, alleging that it was unreasonable for him to yank the man aboard the moving train.

In pulling the man aboard the train, Defendant owed Plaintiff a duty of reasonable care only if his conduct created a foreseeable risk to her. Since there was no way for a reasonable person to know that the package contained fireworks, and since Plaintiff was standing on the platform some distance away, a reasonable person would not have anticipated that yanking the man aboard the train would result in injury to Plaintiff. For this reason, the risk to Plaintiff probably was not foreseeable, and in pulling the man aboard the train, Defendant probably did not owe Plaintiff a duty of reasonable care. *Palsgraf v. Long Island R.R. Co.*, 162 N.E. 99 (N.Y. 1928). (See *supra*, p. 5; *infra*, p. 113.)

i. Duty to rescuer: Generally, it is foreseeable that a rescuer will come along and try to assist a person in peril. "Danger invites rescue" — Judge Cardozo in *Wagner v. International Ry.*, 133 N.E. 437 (N.Y. 1921). For this reason, ***when a defendant acts in a way which foreseeably puts another person in peril, he is also creating a risk to potential rescuers of the imperiled person as well***.

Example: Defendant is operating a railroad train around a curve at an excessive rate of speed. As a result, Passenger, falls out and is injured. Plaintiff, who is Passenger's cousin, attempts to rescue Passenger, who is lying unconscious on the railroad tracks. While doing so, Plaintiff is struck by another train.

Plaintiff asserts a negligence claim against Defendant, alleging that it was unreasonable to operate the train at an excessive rate of speed around a curve. Defendant argues that he did not owe Plaintiff a duty of reasonable care.

Because speeding around a curve frequently causes persons riding on a train to lose their balance and fall, Defendant's conduct created a foreseeable risk to Passenger. Since "danger invites rescue," Defendant's conduct also created a foreseeable risk to Plaintiff as rescuer. For this reason, Defendant owed Plaintiff a duty of reasonable care when operating the train. *Wagner v. International Ry.*, 133 N.E. 437 (N.Y. 1921). (*Supra*; *infra*, p. 90.)

ii. Duty to one who observes injury to another: Because people frequently suffer emotional harm when observing others sustain physical injury, a defendant who negligently injures a person may thereby create risks of emotional injury to anyone observing that physical injury. A controversy exists, however, as to whether the defendant owes those observers a duty of reasonable care.

aa. Zone of physical danger: In the ***majority*** of jurisdictions, a person who injures another owes a duty of reasonable care to observers only if they are in the ***zone of physical danger*** (*i.e.*, in an area in which physical injury to them is foreseeable).

bb. Three part test: In a ***minority*** of jurisdictions, a person who injures another owes a duty of reasonable care to observers who are ***not*** in the zone of physical danger only if (1) they are ***closely related*** to the injured person; (2) they are ***nearby*** when the injury occurs; and (3) they ***perceive the injury with their own senses***.

cc. Foreseeable mental suffering: In a ***small number*** of jurisdictions, a defendant who injures another owes a duty of reasonable care to observers who are ***not*** in the zone of physical danger if it is ***foreseeable that they will experience mental suffering*** as a result of the injury inflicted by the defendant. (See *infra*, p. 138).

Example: Defendant is driving his car at an excessive rate of speed when he strikes and injures Child, a seven year old, who is crossing the street with Sis, her sister. Child's mother, Mom, is watching from a second story window overlooking the street, as is Fred, a close family friend. As a result of seeing Child struck and injured by Defendant's car, Sis, Mom, and Fred experience serious mental suffering. They subsequently assert negligence claims against Defendant, who argues that he did not owe them a duty of reasonable care.

Since Sis was crossing the street with Child, she, too, could have been struck and injured. Because this places her within the zone of physical danger (*i.e.*, physical injury to her was foreseeable), all jurisdictions probably would agree that Defendant owed her a duty of reasonable care in driving his car.

Since Mom and Fred were inside a building and on the second story, it was very unlikely that they would be physically injured by Defendant's car. This means that they were not within the zone of physical danger (*i.e.*, the physical injury to them was not foreseeable). For this reason, the majority of jurisdictions probably would hold that Defendant did not owe them a duty of reasonable care in driving his car.

However, since Mom was related to Child, nearby when the accident occurred, and perceived it with her own senses, a minority of jurisdictions would hold that her mental suffering was sufficiently likely to be foreseeable even though she was not within the zone of physical danger. Courts in these jurisdictions probably would hold that Defendant owed her a duty of reasonable care in driving his car. Although Fred was nearby and perceived the accident with his own senses, he was not related to Child. For this reason, most jurisdictions would hold that his mental suffering was not so likely that harm to him could be regarded as foreseeable, and that, therefore, Defendant did not owe him a duty of reasonable care.

In a very small number of states, it would be held that Defendant owed Fred a duty of reasonable care in driving his car if it was foreseeable that striking Child would cause Fred to experience mental suffering. In making this determination, Fred's presence at the time of the accident, his closeness to the family, and his having perceived the accident with his own senses, are facts to be considered. *Dillon v. Legg*, 441 P.2d 912 (Cal. 1968) (*infra*, p. 138-139).

c. **Risk created by defendant's conduct:** Ordinarily, a ***defendant does not owe a plaintiff a duty of reasonable care to protect against a risk unless that risk was created by the defendant's conduct.***

Example 1: After receiving a threat of physical attack, Plaintiff calls Defendant police department and requests protection. Defendant notifies Plaintiff that it will not protect her. Plaintiff is injured when a paid ruffian throws acid in her face. Plaintiff asserts a negligence claim against Defendant police department, alleging that its failure to protect her was unreasonable. Defendant argues that it did not owe Plaintiff a duty of reasonable care.

Defendant's failure to protect did not create or increase the risk of attack. For this reason, Defendant did not owe Plaintiff a duty of reasonable care to protect her against attack. *Riss v. City of New York*, 293 N.E.2d 860 (N.Y. 1968).

Example 2: Defendant police department advertises that it is seeking the help of the public to apprehend an escaped felon. Plaintiff sees the escaped felon and notifies Defendant. After arresting the felon, Defendant informs the newspapers of Plaintiff's identity, and the newspapers publish that information. Plaintiff is subsequently shot by gangsters in retaliation for helping the police to catch the felon. Plaintiff asserts a negligence claim against Defendant, alleging that Defendant's failure to protect him was unreasonable. Defendant argues that it did not owe Plaintiff a duty of reasonable care to protect him.

By requesting the help of the public, Defendant exposed Plaintiff to a risk which he probably would not otherwise have assumed. In addition, by publicizing Plaintiff's name and address, Defendant created or increased the risk that Plaintiff would be attacked in retaliation for his assistance. Since Defendant's conduct thus created a risk to Plaintiff, Defendant owed Plaintiff a duty of reasonable care to protect him against that risk. *Schuster v. City of New York*, 154 N.E.2d 535 (N.Y. 1958).

i. **Inducing reliance:** Even though a defendant does not create a plaintiff's initial peril, he may increase the risk by promising aid in a way which ***induces the plaintiff's detrimental reliance***.

Example 1: Defendant finds Plaintiff injured and bleeding. Just as Plaintiff is slipping into unconsciousness, Defendant promises to call an ambulance. Defendant does not call an ambulance, and Plaintiff's injuries worsen as a result. Plaintiff asserts a negligence claim alleging that Defendant's failure to call an ambulance was unreasonable. Defendant argues that he did not owe Plaintiff a duty of reasonable care. Defendant did not owe Plaintiff a duty of reasonable care because he did not create Plaintiff's peril and did not increase her risk by promising to call for ambulance.

Example 2: Defendant finds Plaintiff injured and bleeding. As Plaintiff attempts to crawl to a telephone to call for assistance,

Defendant promises to call an ambulance. Relying on Defendant's promise, Plaintiff stops crawling. Defendant does not call an ambulance, and Plaintiff's injury worsens as a result. Plaintiff subsequently asserts a negligence claim against Defendant, alleging that Defendant's failure to call an ambulance was unreasonable. Defendant argues that he did not owe Plaintiff a duty of reasonable care.

Since Defendant's promise induced Plaintiff to stop crawling, Defendant increased the risk that Plaintiff's injury would worsen as the result of lack of medical treatment. For this reason, Defendant owed Plaintiff a duty of reasonable care.

ii. **Interference with other rescuers:** Even though a defendant did not create the initial peril, she may increase the risk by acting in a way which ***interferes with or discourages other rescuers***.

Example: Plaintiff faints in Defendant's department store. Defendant picks Plaintiff up off the floor and carries her to the store infirmary, but does not render or seek any other assistance. Plaintiff dies several hours later, still lying on a couch in the store infirmary. Plaintiff's personal representative asserts a negligence claim against Defendant, alleging that Defendant's failure to render or seek further assistance was unreasonable. Defendant argues that he did not owe Plaintiff a duty of reasonable care.

Although Defendant did not create the initial peril, if Plaintiff had been left lying unconscious on the floor, it is possible that someone else would have assisted her. By removing Plaintiff to the infirmary, Defendant decreased the likelihood that this would happen, thus increasing the risk. For this reason, Defendant owed Plaintiff a duty of reasonable care. *Zelenko v. Gimbel Bros.*, 287 N.Y.S. 134 (N.Y. Sup. Ct. 1935).

iii. **Conduct which causes plaintiff to ignore risk:** Even though a defendant did not create the initial peril, he may increase the risk by acting in a way which ***causes the plaintiff to ignore the risk***.

Example: Plaintiff applies for a job as a test pilot with Defendant airplane manufacturer and is told that he must be examined by the company physician before being hired. In the course of examining Plaintiff, the physician fails to notice symptoms of a disease of which Plaintiff is unaware. As a result, Plaintiff is hired. Plaintiff does not consult with his personal physician until two years later, at which time he learns that he has the disease and that in the past two years it has become incurable. Plaintiff subsequently asserts a negligence claim against Defendant, alleging that its employee's failure to notice his symptoms was unreasonable. Defendant argues that it did not owe Plaintiff a duty of reasonable care.

Although Defendant did not cause Plaintiff to contract the disease, Defendant increased the risk of Plaintiff's death, since his employment as a test pilot led him to believe that he was in good health and did not need to consult with his personal physician. For this reason, Defendant owed Plaintiff a duty of reasonable care. *Coffee v. McDonnell-Douglas Corp.*, 503 P.2d 1366 (Cal. 1972).

iv. **Undertaking to act:** Even though a defendant did not create the initial peril, ***if she attempts to render aid, she owes a duty to do so reasonably.***

Example: Defendant finds Plaintiff intoxicated and unconscious on a city street. Attempting to protect him against further harm, Defendant places Plaintiff in a car and drives him to a golf course outside the city, leaving him on the green to sleep it off. When Plaintiff wakes up, he does not know where he is. Seeing lights, he wanders onto a highway where he is struck by a car and injured. Plaintiff subsequently asserts a negligence claim against Defendant, alleging that it was unreasonable to leave him unconscious on the golf course. Defendant argues that she did not owe Plaintiff a duty of reasonable care.

Although Defendant initially did not owe Plaintiff a duty to render aid, once she began to do so, she altered the risk (*i.e.*, by moving Plaintiff to another location). For this reason, she owed Plaintiff a duty of reasonable care. *Parvi v. City of Kingston*, *supra*, p. 16.

2. **Duty based on relationship:** Sometimes a ***duty of reasonable care results from the existence of a relationship*** and is imposed even though the defendant's conduct has not created a risk.

   a. **Relationship between plaintiff and defendant:** Some relationships are such that one party owes the other a duty of reasonable care.

   Example: Defendant physician is aware that Plaintiff, her patient, is taking dangerous drugs which Defendant did not prescribe. Defendant does not warn Plaintiff of the danger or suggest that Plaintiff stop taking the drugs. Plaintiff is injured as a result of taking the drugs and subsequently asserts a negligence claim against Defendant, alleging that Defendant's failure to warn Plaintiff of the danger was unreasonable. Defendant argues that because she did not prescribe the drug, she did not create the risk, and, therefore, did not owe Plaintiff a duty of reasonable care.

Although Defendant did not create the risk, the relationship between physician and patient probably is such that the physician owes the patient a duty of reasonable care to advise the patient regarding matters which are likely to endanger the patient's health. For this reason, Defendant probably owed Plaintiff a duty of reasonable care.

b. **Relationship between defendant and another:** Sometimes the relationship between the defendant and another person imposes a duty of reasonable care towards a third person.

Example 1: Defendant is aware that his seventeen year old son has a tendency to attack and injure small children. After Defendant's son attacks Plaintiff, Plaintiff asserts a negligence claim against Defendant, alleging that Defendant's failure to protect him was unreasonable. Defendant argues that he did not owe Plaintiff a duty of reasonable care because the risk did not result from his conduct.

Many jurisdictions hold that the relationship between parent and child is such that the parent owes third persons a duty of reasonable care to protect them against the child's known dangerous propensities. In such a jurisdiction, it probably would be held that, since Defendant knew of his child's tendency to attack small children, he owed those children a duty of reasonable care to attempt to protect them. *Linder v. Bidner*, 270 N.Y.S.2d 427 (N.Y. Sup. Ct. 1966).

Example 2: Defendant, a psychiatrist, knows that his patient is likely to attack and kill Plaintiff, but does nothing about it. After the patient kills Plaintiff, Plaintiff's personal representative asserts a negligence claim against Defendant, alleging that Defendant's failure to protect Plaintiff against the patient was unreasonable. Defendant argues that since he did not induce the patient to be violent or otherwise create the risk, he did not owe Plaintiff a duty of reasonable care.

Some jurisdictions hold that the relationship between psychiatrist and patient is such that if the psychiatrist knows that his patient is likely to commit an act of violence against another person, the psychiatrist owes that other person a duty to act reasonably to protect her. In such a jurisdiction, it probably would be held that, since Defendant knew that his patient was likely to commit an act of violence against Plaintiff, Defendant owed

Plaintiff a duty of reasonable care to protect her. *Tarasoff v. Regents of University of California*, 529 P.2d 553 (Cal. 1974).

3. **Limited duty of landholder:** In many jurisdictions, the general duty which a landholder owes to a person who enters onto her land may be limited.

   a. **No duty unless conduct or condition of land creates a foreseeable** risk to plaintiff: The rules regarding the duty of a landholder do not create duties which otherwise would not exist, but instead limit duties which otherwise might exist. This means that ***unless either the defendant's conduct or a condition on her land creates a foreseeable risk to the plaintiff, the defendant does not owe the plaintiff any duty of reasonable care***.

   b. **Majority view:** In a majority of jurisdictions, however, even if the defendant's conduct, or a condition on her land, does create a foreseeable risk to the plaintiff, the duty which the defendant owes the plaintiff may be limited depending on the plaintiff's ***status*** on the land.

      i. **Persons outside the land:** The duty of care which a landholder owes to persons outside the land ***is the same as the duty which he would owe were he not a landholder***.

      Example: Defendant operates a baseball stadium. During a game, a ball is hit out of the stadium and strikes Plaintiff, who is walking on the adjacent sidewalk. Plaintiff asserts a negligence claim against Defendant, alleging that the stadium wall was not high enough to keep balls from leaving the stadium and that it was unreasonable for Defendant to maintain it in this condition. Defendant argues that he did not owe Plaintiff a duty of reasonable care.

      Since Plaintiff was not on Defendant's land when the accident occurred, Defendant owed her the same duty of care which he would have owed had he not been a landholder. Thus, if his conduct or a condition of his land created a foreseeable risk to persons passing on the adjacent sidewalk, he owed those persons a duty of reasonable care. *Salevan v. Wilmington Park Inc.*, 72 A.2d 239 (Del. 1950).

      ii. **Trespassers:** If the plaintiff is a ***trespasser***, defendant owes plaintiff ***no duty of reasonable care***. For this purpose, a trespasser is one who enters without permission.

      aa. **Known trespassers:** If defendant ***knows of a trespasser's presence*** on her land, the defendant owes him the

same duty of care which she would owe ***to a licensee*** (*infra*).

bb. Trespassing children: If it is ***foreseeable that children will trespass and that a trespassing child who is too young to comprehend the risk will be injured, the defendant owes that child the same duty*** of care which she would owe ***to an invitee*** (*infra*, p. 65).

iii. Licensee: If the plaintiff is a licensee, the defendant owes a ***limited*** duty to give ***reasonable warning of known hidden dangers***. For this purpose, a known danger is ***one which the landholder is substantially certain exists***; a hidden danger is one which is ***not likely to be discovered by another without injury***; and a licensee is one who enters the land ***with the landholder's permission***.

aa. Users of highway: A user of the public highway who enters adjacent land for a ***purpose connected with his use of the highway and*** under circumstances which make such ***entry foreseeable*** is regarded as a ***licensee***, even though he enters without permission.

Example: Defendant owns a building which fronts on the public sidewalk. There is a door in the front of the building which opens onto a coal cellar with a twelve foot drop and which, from outside the building, appears to be part of the wall. Plaintiff is walking on the public sidewalk when, to tie his shoe, he stops and leans against the coal cellar door, believing it to be part of the wall. The door opens, and Plaintiff falls twelve feet into the coal cellar, sustaining injury. Plaintiff subsequently asserts a negligence claim against Defendant, alleging that Defendant's failure to post a warning was unreasonable. Defendant argues that since Plaintiff was a trespasser, Defendant owed him no duty of reasonable care.

When he entered Defendant's realty (*i.e.*, leaned against Defendant's building), Plaintiff was a licensee if it was foreseeable that users of the public sidewalk would do so and if Plaintiff did so in connection with his use of the public sidewalk. Since it is unsafe to walk in a shoe with untied laces, Plaintiff's entry onto the door probably was connected with his use of the public sidewalk. Since the building fronted on the public sidewalk, it probably was foreseeable that persons walking on the sidewalk would occasionally lean against the building. For these reasons, Plaintiff probably was a licensee, and was entitled to a warning of known hidden dangers. *Lacanfora v. Goldapel*, 323 N.Y.S.2d 990 (N.Y. Sup. Ct. 1971).

bb. Social guests: ***Social guests are licensees***, even if present in response to a social invitation. This is true even if the guest renders a valuable service, so long as the service is part of the social visit.

Example: While visiting Defendant, Plaintiff agrees to stay and take care of Defendant's sick sister while Defendant goes to church. Plaintiff is injured while doing so and asserts a negligence claim. Plaintiff claims that she was an invitee (*infra*) and Defendant argues that the Plaintiff was a mere licensee.

Ordinarily, a person whose presence confers economic benefit on the landholder is regarded as the landholder's invitee. Since attending to Defendant's sick sister did confer some benefit on Defendant, Plaintiff might be classified as an invitee.

Because Plaintiff was a social guest, however, she was initially a licensee. If staying with Defendant's sick sister was part of the social functions of the visit, Plaintiff would continue to be classified as a licensee, even though her presence conferred benefit on Defendant. *Hall v. Duke*, 513 S.W.2d 716 (Tenn. 1974).

cc. Public employee: A ***public employee*** who enters premises on ***official business which does not confer an economic benefit*** on the landholder does so as a ***licensee***, even if the entry is without the landholder's permission.

Example: Plaintiff, a fire department inspector, enters Defendant's premises for the purpose of issuing a summons for various violations of the City fire code. While on the premises, Plaintiff sustains injury. Subsequently, Plaintiff asserts a negligence claim against Defendant. Defendant argues that she owed Plaintiff no duty of reasonable care because Plaintiff entered without Defendant's permission and, therefore, was a trespasser.

Because Plaintiff was a public employee and entered on official business, he was a licensee even though he entered without Defendant's permission.

iv. Invitee: If the plaintiff is an invitee, the defendant owes plaintiff a ***duty of reasonable care to keep the premises reasonably safe***. There are two ways a person may be classified as an invitee.

aa. Economic benefit: A plaintiff whose presence confers or is likely to confer an ***economic benefit*** on the landholder is an invitee.

Example 1: Father enters Defendant's store with Plaintiff, his two-year-old daughter, for the purpose of purchasing a part for his automobile. While in the store, Plaintiff sustains an injury. Plaintiff subsequently asserts a negligence claim against Defendant, alleging that she was an invitee. Defendant argues that Plaintiff was too young to make a purchase or otherwise confer an economic benefit on him and, therefore, that she was not an invitee.

Since Father probably would not have entered the store if he had not been able to take his daughter with him, Plaintiff's presence made it possible for him to do business with Defendant. For this reason, Plaintiff's presence probably did confer an economic benefit on Defendant and, therefore, Plaintiff was an invitee.

Example 2: Thief is attempting to rob Defendant's store at gunpoint when Plaintiff, a police officer, enters the store to arrest Thief. While there, Plaintiff sustains injury because of a dangerous condition on the premises. Plaintiff subsequently asserts a negligence claim against Defendant, alleging that he was an invitee. Defendant argues that Plaintiff was a licensee, because he was a public employee present on official business.

Since Plaintiff's entry was to prevent a robbery of Defendant, it conferred an economic benefit on Defendant. For this reason, Plaintiff was an invitee.

bb. Public invitation: A plaintiff who enters premises ***in response to an invitation issued to the general public*** is an invitee.

Example: Defendant advertises a free lecture on the hazards of smoking and invites the general public to attend. On the night of the lecture, it is raining hard. Raney, who is waiting for a bus, notices a crowd entering Defendant's lecture hall and, although he has no idea what is going on, he decides to mingle with the crowd and enter the lecture hall to get out of the rain. Lissen, who saw the advertisement and wants to attend the lecture, also enters the lecture hall.

Although Lissen's presence did not confer an economic benefit on Defendant, Lissen entered the premises in response to a public invitation and, therefore, is an invitee. Since Raney was not aware of the public invitation, he could not have entered the hall in response to it. For this reason, and because his presence did not confer an economic benefit on Defendant, Raney is not an invitee.

v. **Status may change:** Since a person who enters the land of another may be welcome in one part of the realty at one time, and be unwelcome in another part of the realty at another time, his status on the realty may change as time passes, or as he moves about.

Example 1: After making a purchase in Defendant's grocery store, Plaintiff asks for a cardboard box for a project on which he is working. Defendant says that Plaintiff can go and look for one in the basement. While doing so, Plaintiff sustains an injury and subsequently asserts a negligence claim against Defendant, alleging that he was an invitee while in the basement. Defendant argues that while in the basement, Plaintiff was a mere licensee.

While Plaintiff was in the store itself making a purchase, his presence conferred an economic benefit on Defendant, and he was clearly an invitee. Since the box for which Plaintiff was looking had nothing to do with Plaintiff's purchase, however, it may successfully be argued that his presence in the basement did not confer an economic benefit on Defendant, and, therefore, that Plaintiff's status had changed from invitee to licensee (because Defendant gave him permission to be in the basement). *Whelan v. Van Natta*, 382 S.W.2d 205 (Ky. 1964).

On the other hand, because shopkeepers know that by pleasing their customers they may induce them to return and make more purchases, it can also be argued that permitting Plaintiff to go into the basement to look for a box was an accommodation which was likely to confer an economic benefit on Defendant, and, therefore, that Plaintiff was an invitee.

Example 2: Plaintiff is attending an alumni reunion at Defendant University. The reunion is held in the reunion building. After making a financial contribution to the alumni fund, Plaintiff leaves the reunion building to go outside and urinate in the bushes. While doing so, Plaintiff is injured by a hidden danger of which he had not been warned. Plaintiff asserts a negligence claim against Defendant, alleging that he was an invitee. Defendant argues that Plaintiff's status had changed from invitee in the building to trespasser in the bushes.

While in the reunion building, Plaintiff's presence was likely to confer an economic benefit on Defendant, particularly since Plaintiff made a financial contribution. For this reason, he was an invitee. When he went outside to urinate in the bushes, however, his status may have changed. If Defendant did not expressly or impliedly permit such behavior, Plaintiff's unauthorized use of the bushes outside the building probably constituted a trespass. On the other hand, if the invitation to the reunion impliedly included permission to urinate in the bushes outside the reunion building, Plaintiff probably continued to be an invitee while doing so. A Connecticut court held, on these facts, that the "free and easy hospitality which exists [at Yale] at reunion time" included implied permission to urinate in the bushes during a reunion. *Guilford v. Yale*, 23 A.2d 917 (Conn. 1942).

Example 3: Plaintiff enters Defendant's amusement park, without a ticket, by sneaking in through the fence. Subsequently, he is seen by an employee who reports the unpaid entry to the manager. The manager approaches Plaintiff and says that he may stay even though he entered without paying. Subsequently, Plaintiff rescues a person who is imperiled, saving Defendant a great deal of money. After the rescue, Plaintiff continues his stay in the park. Some time during the day, Plaintiff is injured under circumstances which make his status relevant.

When Plaintiff entered without permission, he was a trespasser. When Defendant's employees became aware of his presence, he became a known trespasser. When the manager said that he could stay, he became a licensee. As participant in a rescue which saved Defendant money, he was an invitee. After the rescue, he went back to being a licensee. *Basso v. Miller*, 386 N.Y.S.2d 564 (N.Y. 1976).

vi. Plaintiff's status relevant only in determining landholder's duty: The ***plaintiff's status*** on land is ***relevant only in determining the duty owed that plaintiff by the landholder and members of his household***. It is not relevant in determining the duty owed by any other person.

Example: While Defendant power company is working on power lines, it allows one of its wires to come into contact with a fence surrounding the land of Thomas, causing the fence to become electrified. Plaintiff, who is trespassing on the land of Thomas, touches the fence and receives a serious electric shock. Plaintiff asserts a negligence claim against Defendant, alleging that allowing the wire to come into contact with Thomas's fence was unreasonable. Defendant argues that it did not owe Plaintiff a duty of reasonable care because Plaintiff was a trespasser.

The rules controlling the duty owed to a plaintiff injured on the land of another are relevant only in determining the duty owed by the landholder. Because Defendant was not the landholder, the fact that Plaintiff was trespassing is irrelevant in determining what duty Defendant owed Plaintiff. *Humphrey v. Twin State Gas & Electric Co.*, 139 A. 440 (Vt. 1927).

c. **Minority view:** An important ***minority*** of jurisdictions has abolished the rule which makes the duty owed by a landholder depend entirely on the plaintiff's status on the land. These jurisdictions have stated that if a landholder's conduct or a condition of his land creates a foreseeable risk to a plaintiff, the ***landholder owes the plaintiff a duty of reasonable care regardless of the plaintiff's status on the land***. The plaintiff's status may be relevant, however, in determining what is reasonable in that particular case.

d. **Natural and artificial conditions:** In general, the duty which a landholder owes to protect others against conditions on the land depends on whether those conditions are artificial or natural.

   i. **Majority view:** The ***majority*** of jurisdictions holds that a landholder ***does not owe anyone a duty to protect against conditions of the realty unless those conditions are artificial***. For this purpose, a condition is artificial if it was ***created by humans.***

   ii. **Minority view:** A ***minority*** holds that a landholder may owe others a duty to protect them against ***natural conditions on the land as well as artificial conditions***. For this purpose, a natural condition is one which was ***not created by humans***.

Example: Defendant and Plaintiff own realty on a hillside. Defendant's realty is higher than Plaintiff's. After an excessive rain, rocks and soil on Defendant's realty slide downhill and damage Plaintiff's realty. Plaintiff asserts a negligence claim against Defendant, alleging that Defendant unreasonably failed to take steps to prevent this from happening. Defendant argues that he owed Plaintiff no duty of reasonable care to protect against natural conditions of the realty.

In the majority of jurisdictions, it would be held that if the conditions which damaged Plaintiff's realty were natural (rather than artificial) Defendant owed Plaintiff no duty to protect against them.

In a minority of jurisdictions, however, it would be held that if the risk to Plaintiff's realty was foreseeable, Defendant owed Plaintiff a duty to act reasonably in attempting to protect Plaintiff against a condition on Defendant's realty, whether that condition was natural or artificial. *Sprecher v. Adamson*, 178 Cal. Rptr. 783 (1981).

4. **Breach:** In general, the duty of reasonable care is breached when the defendant ***does something that the reasonable person would not have done or fails to do something that the reasonable person would have done***.

   a. **Conclusions must be supported by reasoning:** It is not sufficient to say that what the Defendant did was unreasonable "because the reasonable person would not have done it." It is necessary to develop the facts which prove that this is so.

      i. **Balancing test:** Ordinarily, courts determine whether a particular act or omission was reasonable by weighing the ***advantages which the ordinary person in the defendant's position would expect against the disadvantages which he would*** expect. If the advantages outweigh the disadvantages, the conduct is reasonable. If the disadvantages outweigh the advantages, the conduct is unreasonable.

   Note: Sometimes it is said that the dangers are weighed against the benefits, or that the risks are weighed against the burdens of avoiding them.

   Example: A fleeing felon gets into the taxicab operated by Defendant and points a pistol at Defendant, threatening to kill him. Defendant jumps out of the taxicab, leaving the engine running, the transmission in drive, and the brake off. The cab moves forward and strikes Plaintiff, a pedestrian. Plaintiff asserts a negligence claim against Defendant. Defendant argues that he acted reasonably.

   Defendant's conduct was reasonable if the ordinary person in Defendant's position would have expected the advantages resulting from it to outweigh the disadvantages. The advantage of Defendant's jumping out of the cab without stopping to set the brakes or turn off the engine was that it got him away from the armed felon and probably saved his life. The disadvantage was that it risked the lives of pedestrians in the vicinity.

   On behalf of Plaintiff, it may be argued that since there were likely to be several pedestrians in the vicinity, the life that Defendant was saving was not as valuable as the risk which he was creating, and, therefore, that his conduct was unreasonable. On behalf of Defendant, it may be argued that since he would probably regard his own life as more valuable than any other, it would have appeared to the ordinary person in Defendant's position that the advantage of his conduct (*i.e.*, saving his own life) outweighed the disadvantage (*i.e.*, risking the life of another), and, therefore, that his conduct was reasonable. *Cordas v. Peerless Transport Co.*, 27 N.Y.S.2d 198 (N.Y. 1941).

ii. **Specific allegation:** It is not possible to apply the balancing test unless the conduct alleged to be negligent is specifically identified.

Example 1: Defendant is driving her car. She fails to see Plaintiff in the roadway and strikes him. Plaintiff asserts a negligence claim against Defendant, alleging that Defendant's failure to see him was unreasonable.

Obviously, the disadvantage of not seeing a person in the roadway outweighs the advantage of not seeing a person in the roadway. Failure to see is not conduct or the omission of conduct, however; it is the ***result*** of conduct or omission. For this reason, the balancing test cannot be applied to it. This makes it impossible to argue about the reasonableness of Defendant's conduct.

Example 2: While driving her car, Defendant is attempting to read a map instead of looking at the roadway. As a result, she fails to see Plaintiff in the roadway and strikes him. Plaintiff asserts a negligence claim, alleging that it was unreasonable for Defendant to attempt to read a map instead of look at the roadway.

Because Plaintiff has specifically alleged that certain conduct by Defendant was unreasonable, it is possible to balance the advantage and disadvantage of that conduct. It may be argued, for example, that since looking at a map instead of the roadway makes it impossible to see persons in the roadway, it creates the risk of striking such persons and injuring them, which is a serious disadvantage. The slight advantage in time saved by not pulling over to the side of the road to read the map, is greatly outweighed by the disadvantage, since human life is more valuable than time. Therefore, Defendant's conduct was unreasonable.

iii. **Custom:** Because custom usually indicates how the ordinary person acts, ***evidence of custom may be relevant in deciding whether a defendant's conduct was unreasonable***. Since conduct is unreasonable if its disadvantages outweigh its advantages, however, ***custom alone does not determine whether conduct is reasonable***.

Example: Defendant ophthalmologist examines Plaintiff, a 32 year old patient, without checking for glaucoma. Plaintiff has glaucoma and, because it is undiscovered, eventually loses her eyesight. Plaintiff asserts a negligence claim against Defendant, alleging that his failure to check her for glaucoma was unreasonable. Defendant argues that because glaucoma is rare in people of Plaintiff's age, ophthalmologists customarily do not check them for it. Evidence indicates that the test for glaucoma is simple, painless, inexpensive, and risk-free; also that untreated glaucoma always leads to blindness.

It can be argued that since the glaucoma test is simple, painless, inexpensive, and risk-free, the advantage of not administering it is slight. On the other hand, since untreated glaucoma always leads to blindness, the disadvantage of not testing for it is great, even though its occurrence is not common. For this reason, it can be concluded that Defendant's failure to check for glaucoma was unreasonable in spite of medical custom. *Helling v. Carey*, 519 P.2d 981 (Wash. 1974).

b. Characteristics of the reasonable person: The reasonableness of an act or omission depends on the advantages and disadvantages which would have been expected by the reasonable or ordinary person in the defendant's position. For this purpose, "the reasonable person" is a fiction; a hypothetical character which the law has created for judging conduct. To some extent, the fictitious reasonable person is imagined to have ***characteristics like those of the person whose conduct is being judged***.

i. Knowledge and intelligence: Ordinarily, the reasonable person is imagined to have ***ordinary knowledge and intelligence***, whether or not the defendant actually does.

Example: The tires of Defendant's car are worn to the point where the nylon cords are showing. While Defendant is driving the car, one of the tires blows out, causing the car to go out of control and strike Plaintiff. Plaintiff subsequently asserts a negligence claim, alleging that it was unreasonable for Defendant to drive while her tires were in that condition. Defendant argues that she was unaware that tires in that condition were dangerous.

The ordinary driver probably knows that when tires are so worn that the nylon cords are showing, they are dangerous and are likely to blow out, and, therefore, would expect a blowout and accident to result from driving with tires in that condition — a serious disadvantage to such conduct. The only advantage to driving on such tires is the saving of a relatively small sum of money. Since the disadvantage which the ordinary person would have expected far outweighs the advantage which she would have expected, Defendant's conduct probably was unreasonable even though she herself did not actually expect that disadvantage. *Delair v. McAdoo,* 188 A. 191 (Pa. 1936).

aa. Mental retardation: In judging the conduct of a person who is mentally retarded, most jurisdictions do not use a standard based on the intelligence and knowledge of the ordinary person. ***Allowance is made for the defendant's retardation***; however, no fixed standard has yet been developed.

bb. Insanity: In judging the conduct of a person who can be described as insane, courts generally make no allowance for insanity, applying the ***same standard which would be applied if the person were not insane*** (*i.e.*, balancing the advantages and disadvantages which would have been expected by the ordinary person).

cc. Sudden loss of sanity: In judging the conduct of a person who acts unreasonably because of a sudden loss of sanity, courts usually hold that ***if the loss of sanity was unforeseeable, the conduct which resulted from it was not unreasonable***. On the other hand, ***if the loss of sanity was foreseeable, the conduct which resulted from it may be unreasonable***.

Example: Defendant has long believed that she has been chosen by God to survive the end of the world, that God sometimes takes over the operation of her car, and that under those circumstances she and her car can fly like Batman. One day, while driving, she believes that God has taken over the operation of her car and lets go of the wheel, losing control of the car and striking Plaintiff. Plaintiff subsequently asserts a negligence claim, alleging that it was unreasonable for Defendant to let go of the wheel while driving her car.

Because Defendant's conduct resulted from her sudden loss of sanity, her conduct will be regarded as unreasonable only if it was foreseeable that she would experience such a loss of sanity. Based on her past delusional beliefs, it probably would be found that her loss of sanity was foreseeable. If so, her conduct was unreasonable. *Breunig v. American Family Insurance Co.*, 173 N.W.2d 619 (Wis. 1970).

ii. Physical attributes: In judging the conduct of a person with physical disabilities, most courts visualize the reasonable person as having the ***same physical disabilities***.

Example: Defendant, who is blind, operates a candy stand in a public building. While walking from the stand to the restroom without a cane, Defendant bumps into Plaintiff, injuring him. Plaintiff subsequently asserts a negligence claim against Defendant, alleging that it was unreasonable for Defendant to walk down the corridor without a cane. Defendant argues that, like many blind people, he relied on his "facial sense" instead of a cane.

If the reasonable blind person would not have walked down the corridor without a cane, Defendant's conduct was unreasonable. On the other hand, if the reasonable blind person would have relied on his facial sense instead of a cane, Defendant's conduct was not unreasonable. *Roberts v. Louisiana*, 396 So.2d 566 (La. 1981).

iii. Children: In judging the conduct of a child, most courts compare it to that of the ***reasonable person of the same age, experience, and intelligence as the actor***.

aa. Child: For most purposes, a person is a child until she reaches the age of majority. For purpose of judging the reasonableness of her conduct, however, a person is a child only until she has reached a level of maturity approximating that of an adult. Thus, persons over the age of twelve or thirteen years are not usually regarded as children for this purpose.

bb. Adult activity: No matter what the age of the actor, a ***person engaging in an adult activity is held to the same standard as an adult***. For this purpose, an activity is an ***adult activity if traditionally it is only performed by adults or if it is an activity which is unsafe unless performed by someone with the maturity of an adult***.

Example 1: While deerhunting in a rural area, Defendant child accidentally shoots Plaintiff. Plaintiff asserts a negligence claim, alleging that Defendant was engaged in an adult activity and failed to act like the reasonable adult. Defendant argues that he was not negligent because he acted like the reasonable child of his age, experience and intelligence.

In rural areas of the United States, children are taught to use firearms and to hunt at an early age. For this reason, the use of firearms by children probably is traditional in these areas. If so, it is not an adult activity, and Defendant's conduct would be compared with that of the reasonable child of Defendant's age, experience, and intelligence. *Purtle v. Shelton*, 474 S.W.2d 123 (Ark. 1972).

Example 2: Defendant, who is 11 years of age, is operating a snowmobile when she strikes and injures Plaintiff. Plaintiff asserts a negligence claim, alleging that Defendant failed to act like the reasonable person in the way she operated the snowmobile. Defendant argues that she was not negligent because she acted like the reasonable 11-year-old with her experience and intelligence.

Since snowmobiles are capable of reaching great speeds, and since collisions in which they are involved frequently lead to death and serious injury, snowmobiling probably is an activity which is unsafe unless performed by a person with the maturity of an adult. If so, it is an adult activity, and Defendant's conduct was unreasonable if unlike that of the reasonable adult. *Robinson v. Lindsay*, 598 P.2d 392 (Wash. 1978).

iv. Professional malpractice: If the defendant is a member of a profession, and it is alleged that she was negligent in the way she practiced that profession, the defendant's conduct is compared to that of the ***reasonable member of that profession***. Thus, the defendant acted unreasonably if the reasonable member of her profession would have expected the disadvantage of his conduct to outweigh the advantage. This form of negligence is called ***professional malpractice***.

aa. Need for expert witness: In the usual case, when a plaintiff alleges that a defendant was negligent, the ***plaintiff has the burden*** of proving that the defendant's conduct was unreasonable. Ordinarily, the term "unreasonable" describes conduct unlike that of the reasonable person. Since a jury is competent to decide what the reasonable person would do, the plaintiff ordinarily meets the burden of proof by showing what the defendant did and asking a jury to decide that it was unreasonable.

In a claim for professional malpractice, however, the ***plaintiff has the burden of proving that the defendant failed to act like the reasonable member of her profession***. Since members of a jury usually have not received training in the defendant's profession, they are not competent to decide whether the reasonable member of that profession would have acted in the same way as the defendant. For this reason, it is not enough for the plaintiff to prove what the defendant did. In addition, he must offer evidence as to what the reasonable member of the profession would have done. Since this is a matter of opinion, and since only an expert qualifies to testify to an opinion, it ***usually is necessary for the plaintiff to produce an expert opinion as to what a rea-***

sonable member of the defendant's profession would have done.

Example: Defendant, a physician, is prescribing medicine for Plaintiff, her patient. Although one unit of the medicine would have cured Plaintiff, Defendant prescribes two units. This causes Plaintiff's illness to worsen. Plaintiff asserts a negligence (*i.e.*, professional malpractice) claim against Defendant, alleging that it was unreasonable for Defendant to prescribe two units.

A jury will not be allowed to consider a case unless evidence has been introduced which would make it possible for the jury to find in the plaintiff's favor. Since this is a claim for professional malpractice, Plaintiff must prove that the reasonable physician would not have prescribed two units. Since the dose to prescribe for a particular patient is a matter of professional judgment, it is necessary for Plaintiff to offer the testimony of an expert in medical practice who is of the opinion that the reasonable physician would not have prescribed two units for this Plaintiff. Once that testimony has been presented, the jury may determine whether Defendant acted unreasonably in the light of that expert's opinion. If Plaintiff does not offer the testimony of an expert, the case probably will be dismissed.

bb. Conduct within understanding of lay person: ***Expert testimony is not required if the ordinary lay person is competent to decide*** that the reasonable member of the defendant's profession would not have engaged in conduct like the defendant's.

Example: Trying to obtain leverage while extracting a tooth from Plaintiff, a patient, Defendant dentist presses his finger against Plaintiff's eye, causing damage. Plaintiff asserts a negligence claim, but does not offer the testimony of an expert. Defendant moves to dismiss the case before sending it to the jury.

If Plaintiff does not offer evidence tending to support his allegation that the Defendant acted unreasonably, his case should be dismissed. Ordinarily, in a case of professional malpractice, this requires the opinion of an expert. In this case, however, the issue is whether a reasonable dentist would stick his finger in a patient's eye while trying to extract a tooth. If the court decides that the lay person is competent to answer that question, it may submit the case to the jury.

cc. Informed consent: Many jurisdictions presume that a reasonable member of the medical profession would not treat a patient without obtaining the patient's "*informed consent.*"

This means that *a physician who does not inform her patient of the risks connected with the treatment and the alternatives to that treatment is presumed to be acting unreasonably.* This presumption makes expert testimony in such a case unnecessary.

Example: Defendant physician advises Plaintiff, his patient, to submit to an operation called a biopsy to determine whether Plaintiff's kidney is cancerous. Defendant does not inform Plaintiff that such operations sometimes cause the loss of the kidney. If Plaintiff had known this, he would not have consented to the biopsy. Plaintiff consents and the biopsy is performed. Although the kidney was not cancerous, the biopsy causes it to be lost. Plaintiff asserts a negligence claim against Defendant, alleging that Defendant's failure to inform Plaintiff of the risk was unreasonable. Defendant moves to dismiss the case before it goes to the jury on the ground that Plaintiff has not offered the testimony of an expert who is of the opinion that the reasonable doctor would have informed Plaintiff of the risk.

In many jurisdictions, there is a presumption that the reasonable physician would not have operated without informed consent. Since Defendant did not inform Plaintiff, this presumption makes expert testimony unnecessary. Defendant may attempt to rebut the presumption by proving that the reasonable doctor in that jurisdiction would not have informed the patient.

In other jurisdictions, there is no such presumption, and Plaintiff must offer the testimony of an expert that in his opinion the reasonable doctor would not have performed such an operation without informing the patient of the risk. *Miller v. Kennedy*, 552 P.2d 852 (Wash. Ct. App. 1974).

5. **Proof of negligence:** The plaintiff in any tort case has the burden of proof. This means that the plaintiff must offer evidence which would justify a jury's finding that the facts satisfy all the essential elements of the plaintiff's claim. (Sometimes this is called "making out a prima facie case.") If there is no evidence to justify that conclusion, there is no reason to ask the jury any question at all, and the case will be dismissed before it is sent to the jury. On the other hand, if the plaintiff meets this burden of proof (*i.e.*, offers evidence which would justify a jury's finding in his favor), he does not necessarily win. It is then necessary to submit the case to the jury and ask it to decide whether it does find that the elements of the plaintiff's claim are satisfied. In order to meet the burden of proof in a negligence claim, the plaintiff must offer evidence which would justify the jury's finding that the defendant's conduct created

a foreseeable risk (*i.e.*, that the defendant owed the plaintiff a duty of reasonable care) and that the defendant failed to act reasonably in the face of that risk (*i.e.*, that the duty of reasonable care was breached).

a. **Proof that defendant's conduct was unreasonable:** To meet the burden of proving a breach, the plaintiff usually offers evidence of the defendant's conduct and asks the jury to decide that the conduct was unreasonable (*i.e.*, that the reasonable person in the defendant's position would have expected the resulting disadvantages to outweigh the resulting advantages). Without proving what the defendant did, it usually is impossible to prove that what she did was unreasonable.

b. **Circumstantial evidence:** Circumstantial evidence is proof of one fact from which another fact can be inferred. Sometimes the inferences derived from circumstantial evidence can assist a plaintiff in meeting his burden of proof.

   Example: Every morning Defendant, a dairy farmer, milks his cow and carries the milk in a bucket along the river to Plaintiff's home, where he sells it to Plaintiff at a fixed price per quart. One day, Plaintiff accuses Defendant of adding river water to the milk to increase the quantity sold to Plaintiff. Although Plaintiff has no witness who saw Defendant do this, Plaintiff bases his accusation on the presence of a trout in the milk bucket.

   Since trout do not come from cows' teats, it could not have gotten into the bucket when Defendant was milking the cow. Since trout are often found in rivers, dipping the bucket into the river could have resulted in the subsequent presence of a trout in the bucket. Since there is very little likelihood that the trout got into the bucket in any other way, the presence of the trout is circumstantial evidence that the bucket was dipped in the river. Thus, by proving that there was a trout in the bucket, Plaintiff has raised an inference that the milk was watered.

c. ***Res ipsa loquitur:*** Under some circumstances, the mere fact that a particular accident occurred in a certain way is circumstantial evidence that the defendant did something unreasonable, even though there is no evidence as to what he did. A British judge commenting on the circumstantial evidence in a particular case once said, in Latin, ***"res ipsa loquitur,"*** which translates as, ***"the thing speaks for itself."*** Since then, it has been understood that although a defendant's conduct may be unknown, a certain kind of circumstantial evidence may ***create an inference*** that the defendant did something unreasonable. This has come to be known as the doctrine of *res ipsa loquitur*.

d. Essential elements: ***The occurrence of an accident may be circumstantial evidence that the defendant acted unreasonably (i.e.,*** *res ipsa loquitur* applies) if: (1) the accident is of a kind which does not usually occur without negligence; and (2) the defendant is the only person who could have caused the accident.

Example: Plaintiff is walking on the sidewalk in front of Defendant's flour warehouse when a barrel of flour falls from a second story window, striking and injuring Plaintiff. At the time of the accident, Defendant was the only person inside the building. Plaintiff asserts a negligence claim, but is unable to offer any evidence as to what the Defendant did or failed to do which was unreasonable. Defendant moves to dismiss the case, arguing that Plaintiff has failed to meet his burden of proof.

Since barrels of flour do not usually fall from second story windows unless they are being handled in an unreasonable manner, the fact that the barrel fell may create the inference that it was being handled unreasonably. The fact that Defendant was the only person present at the time creates the inference that he was the one handling the barrel. Thus, the occurrence of the accident may itself create the inference that Defendant was acting unreasonably, even though there is no evidence as to what he actually did. This inference may be sufficient to send the case to the jury to decide whether Defendant did act unreasonably. Thus, Plaintiff may have made out a *prima facie* case, simply by proving that the accident occurred. *Byrne v. Boadle*, 159 Eng. Rep. 299 (Eng. 1863).

i. Accident of a kind which does not usually occur without negligence: It is not necessary to show that the accident could not possibly have occurred without negligence, but only that it is unlikely that anything but negligence caused it.

Example: Plaintiff was a passenger on Defendant airline's plane when it suddenly crashed into the sea. Plaintiff's personal representative asserts a negligence claim against Defendant, relying on *res ipsa loquitur* to create an inference that Defendant acted unreasonably. Defendant argues that there are many possibilities other than its negligence which might have caused the crash.

Although there are other possibilities, airplanes do not usually crash into the sea unless they are being operated or have been maintained unreasonably. The crash itself is sufficient to create the inference that Defendant acted unreasonably. For this reason, the case should be given to the jury to decide whether Defendant did act unreasonably. *Cox v. Northwest Airlines*, 379 F.2d 893 (7th Cir. 1967).

ii. **Defendant was the only person who could have caused the accident:** This is usually established by showing that the defendant was in ***exclusive control*** of the circumstances or instrumentalities which produced the harm. A showing of ***exclusive control is not necessary, however, if other evidence makes it improbable that anyone other than the defendant could have committed the act*** which led to the harm.

Example: Defendant manufactures and bottles grenadine syrup. Defendant delivers several cases of the product to Plaintiff's tavern, carries them to Plaintiff's storeroom, and stacks them there. The product remains there for three months, during which period no one else touches it and during which period there are no changes in temperature or other conditions. After that time, one of the bottles explodes, injuring Plaintiff. Plaintiff asserts a negligence claim against Defendant. At the trial, Plaintiff is unable to show what Defendant did that was unreasonable, but proves that bottles of grenadine syrup do not usually explode unless they are handled negligently. Defendant moves to dismiss on the ground that Plaintiff has failed to make out a *prima facie* case.

Although Defendant was not in control of the product at the time of the explosion, the evidence eliminates the possibility that the product was handled negligently by anyone other than Defendant. Therefore, the happening of the accident probably is sufficient circumstantial evidence to create the inference that Defendant handled the bottle negligently (*i.e.*, *res ipsa loquitur* may be applied), and the case should be given to the jury. *Parrillo v. Giroux Co., Inc.*, 426 A.2d 1313 (R.I. 1981).

iii. **Not available when defendant's conduct known:** When defendant's conduct is known, *res ipsa loquitur* is not a substitute for argument about whether that conduct was unreasonable. In most jurisdictions, *res ipsa loquitur* may not be applied at all when defendant's conduct is known or even when specific allegations are made about what defendant did.

6. **Violation of statute:** In some cases, the fact that a defendant violated a statute ***may help to establish negligence***, without regard to whether that defendant's conduct was unreasonable. This is so only ***when the statute violated was designed*** (1) ***to protect a***

class of persons to which plaintiff belongs; and (2) ***to protect against a class of risks which includes the one which resulted in harm to the plaintiff.***

a. **Legislative history:** Legislative history is ***not usually decisive*** in determining the purpose of a statute. Instead, it is better to argue that a statute is designed to protect all persons who are likely to be protected by it against all risks which the statute is likely to prevent.

b. **Class to which plaintiff belongs:** Unless the plaintiff is a person whom the statute was designed to protect, its violation is not relevant to a negligence claim brought by the Plaintiff against a defendant who violates the statute.

Example: Defendant sells Robber an assault rifle in violation of a statute which prohibits the sale of such weapons. While attempting to hold up a bank, Robber accidentally shoots herself and Teller, a bank employee, with the rifle. Robber and Teller assert negligence claims against Defendant, alleging that Defendant's sale in violation of the statute was negligent.

Since the law does not usually seek to protect criminals against·accidental, self-inflicted injuries, the statute was probably not designed to protect persons like Robber. Its violation by Defendant, therefore, probably does not help to establish that Defendant was negligent as to Robber.

Since an obvious purpose of the statute was to prevent criminals from shooting victims with assault rifles, its violation probably does help to establish that Defendant was negligent as to Teller.

i. **Multiple classes:** A statute may be designed to protect more than one class of persons. For this reason, it may be an ***error in logic to argue that the statute was not designed to protect one class of persons because it was designed to protect another.***

Example: Defendant sells a firearm to a fifteen-year-old in violation of a statute which prohibits selling firearms to children under the age of sixteen. Plaintiff, an adult, is injured when shot by the child, and asserts a negligence claim against Defendant, alleging that the sale in violation of the statute was negligent. Defendant argues that the statutory violation does not help Plaintiff to establish negligence because the statute was designed to prevent children under the age of sixteen from hurting themselves with firearms.

Because children are less likely to be careful with firearms, and since the law usually provides extra protection for children, the statute probably was designed to protect children. Defendant's argument is erroneous, however, since the statute may also have been designed to protect other persons against the risk of being shot by children.

ii. **Protection of general public**: A statute designed to protect the general public protects a class of persons to which all plaintiffs belong.

c. **Class of risks:** A defendant's violation of a statute is relevant in proving that the defendant was negligent only if the statute was designed to protect against a risk like the one which led to the plaintiff's harm.

Example: While Plaintiff is in Defendant's tavern, several persons who have become intoxicated and rowdy start a fight with Plaintiff and injure him. Plaintiff asserts a negligence claim against Defendant, alleging that Defendant's negligence is established by his violation of two statutes: (1) a prohibition against serving alcohol to persons who are already intoxicated; and (2) a prohibition against allowing persons who have become rowdy to remain in a tavern. Defendant argues that the statutes were not designed to prevent barroom fights, and, therefore, that the violations are not relevant in determining whether Defendant was negligent.

People who are intoxicated and rowdy are more likely to get into fights than people who are not. For this reason, a statute which is designed to prevent people from becoming drunk and rowdy, or which is designed to prevent people who are drunk and rowdy from remaining in a tavern, probably is designed to prevent barroom fights. Statute (1) did not prohibit serving alcohol to a person until that person was already drunk, and did not require that he be ejected from the tavern. For this reason, it probably was not designed to protect against the risk of barroom fights, and its violation probably does not help to establish that Defendant was negligent.

Statute (2) specifically prohibited permitting rowdy persons to remain in a tavern. Since rowdy persons are more likely to get into fights, it probably was designed to prevent barroom fights. For this reason, its violation probably does help to establish that Defendant was negligent. *Stachniewicz v. Mar-Cam Corp.*, 488 P.2d 436 (Or. 1971).

i. **Multiple risks:** Some statutes are designed to protect against more than one risk. For this reason, it may be an ***error in logic to argue that the statute was not***

designed to protect against one risk because it was designed to protect against another.

ii. **Foreseeable risks:** Some jurisdictions hold that a statute is designed to protect against all risks which foreseeably result from its violation.

d. **Excuse:** A statutory violation ***does not establish negligence*** if the violation was ***excused.***

i. **Inexcusable violations:** Every jurisdiction recognizes that ***some statutes may not justifiably be violated*** under any circumstances. These statutes vary so much from one state to another that it is always necessary to research the law in a particular jurisdiction before arguing that a statutory violation may be excused.

ii. **Excused violations:** ***Violation of a statute may be excused*** if the violation resulted from: (1) circumstances beyond the violator's control; (2) ignorance of the facts which made the statute applicable; or (3) the existence of an emergency which made obeying the statute more dangerous than violating it. (But *ignorance of the law* is never an excuse.)

Example 1: A statute requires that motorists stop at stop signs. While driving her car, Defendant sees a stop sign and attempts to stop, but is unable to do so because her car skids in a puddle of oil in the roadway. Defendant's car collides with Plaintiff who is walking on the cross street. Plaintiff asserts a negligence claim, alleging that Defendant's violation of the stop sign statute establishes Defendant's negligence. Since the statutory violation resulted from circumstances beyond Defendant's control, her violation may be excused.

Example 2: Defendant is aware of a statute which requires motorists to stop at stop signs, but does not see a stop sign because it is overgrown with vines and covered by leaves. Defendant's car collides with Plaintiff who is walking on the cross street. Plaintiff asserts a negligence claim, alleging that Defendant's violation of the stop sign statute establishes Defendant's negligence. Since the statutory violation resulted from ignorance of the facts which made the statute apply (*i.e.*, that there was a stop sign at that corner), it may be excused.

Example 3: Defendant approaches a stop sign. She is aware that a statute requires motorists to stop, but in her rear view mirror she notices a large truck bearing down rapidly on her. She realizes that if she stops, the truck will strike her. Defendant enters the intersection without stopping and collides with Plaintiff, who is walking on the cross street. Plaintiff asserts a negligence claim, alleging that Defendant's violation of the stop sign statute establishes Defendant's negligence. Since Defendant was confronted with an emergency, it may have been more reasonable to violate the statute than to obey it. If so, her statutory violation may be excused.

e. **Effect of statutory violation:** Depending on the statute and jurisdiction, violation of a statute may result in an irrebuttable presumption of negligence (sometimes called "negligence *per se*"); a rebuttable presumption of negligence (sometimes also called "negligence *per se*"); or an inference (evidence) of negligence.

   i. **Irrebuttable presumption (negligence *per se*):** ***If a statute is such that it may not be justifiably violated*** under any circumstances, its violation results in an ***irrebuttable presumption of negligence***. The court should instruct the jury, "If you find that the defendant violated the statute, you must find that he was negligent."

   ii. **Rebuttable presumption (sometimes also called negligence *per se*):** The ***majority holds*** that violation of most other statutes results in a ***presumption of negligence which may be rebutted*** by proof that the violation was excused. The court should instruct the jury, "If you find that the defendant violated the statute, you must find that he was negligent unless you find that the violation resulted from circumstances beyond the defendant's control, from ignorance of the facts which made the statute apply, or in response to an emergency which made violating the statute less dangerous than obeying it."

   iii. **Inference (evidence) of negligence:** Except for those statutes the violation of which can not be excused under any circumstances, a ***minority*** of jurisdictions holds that the violation of a statute results in an ***inference of negligence*** sufficient to raise a jury question and is evidence which a jury may consider in deciding whether the defendant was negligent. The court should instruct the jury, "If you find that the defendant violated the statute, you may find that he was negligent, but you are not required to do so;" or, "If you find that the defendant violated the statute, you may consider that fact in deciding whether he was negligent."

f. Causation: Even when the violation of a statute helps to establish that the defendant was negligent, ***liability will not be imposed unless the violation is shown to be a cause of the harm*** sustained by the plaintiff.

Example: Defendant practices medicine without being licensed to do so. In the course of treating Plaintiff, Defendant causes her to become paralyzed. Plaintiff asserts a negligence claim against Defendant, alleging that his violation of the licensing statute establishes that he was negligent.

A license to practice medicine does not confer upon the licensee a skill which she otherwise does not have. Similarly, lack of a license does not remove a skill which a person does have. Even a licensed physician may act unreasonably, just as an unlicensed practitioner may act reasonably. For these reasons, there is no direct causal relationship between Defendant's failure to have a license and Plaintiff's injury. *Brown v. Shyne*, 151 N.E. 197 (N.Y. 1926).

g. Effect of compliance: Since negligence is defined as the failure to act reasonably, and since the reasonable person frequently exercises more caution than is required by a statute, ***compliance with a statute does not of itself establish reasonable care or freedom from negligence***.

Example: A federal statute provides that although passenger cars must be equipped with head restraints, pickup trucks need not be so equipped. The absence of head restraints in a pickup truck manufactured by Defendant causes Plaintiff to sustain injury to his cervical spine. Plaintiff asserts a negligence claim, alleging that it was unreasonable to manufacture a vehicle without head restraints. Defendant argues that it complied with the statute and, therefore, was not negligent.

A court may find that the reasonable manufacturer would have equipped the vehicle with head restraints and, therefore, that Defendant was negligent, even though Defendant complied with the federal statute. *Buccery v. General Motors*, 132 Cal. Rptr. 605 (1976).

II. AGGRAVATED NEGLIGENCE

A. General concept: Although qualitatively different from intentional torts and negligence, aggravated negligence (also known as recklessness) generally is not viewed as a separate basis of liability, but rather as a variation on negligence.

B. Definition: Aggravated negligence consists of the ***willful disregard of an obvious risk with a high probability of serious harm***.

C. Legal effect: ***Many jurisdictions permit punitive damages*** (*infra*, p. 128-129) to be awarded against a defendant who is guilty of aggravated negligence.

> **Example:** Defendant, a manufacturer of automobiles, is aware that the location of the gas tank on one of its models will cause the car to burst into flames when struck in the rear at an impact speed in excess of 35 miles per hour, and that this is likely to happen to three or four cars each year. After determining that the cost of redesigning the automobile probably would exceed the damages which Defendant would be required to pay to persons injured in such accidents, Defendant decides to continue selling the automobiles without redesigning them. Plaintiff is driving one of the automobiles when it is struck in the rear at an impact speed in excess of 35 miles per hour and bursts into flames, causing Plaintiff to sustain serious burns. Plaintiff asserts a negligence claim and seeks punitive damages, arguing that Defendant's conduct amounted to aggravated negligence.
>
> Since Defendant's conduct was unreasonable, Plaintiff probably will be successful in making out a case of negligence against Defendant. In addition, since Defendant knew that there was an obvious risk of serious harm and willfully disregarded it by continuing to sell the cars without redesigning them, Defendant's conduct may have amounted to aggravated negligence. If so, Plaintiff may be entitled to recover punitive damages in addition to compensatory damages for his injuries. *Grimshaw v. Ford Motor Co.*, 174 Cal. Rptr. 348 (1981) (*infra*, p. 129-130).

CHAPTER 5

AFFIRMATIVE DEFENSES

I. PLAINTIFF'S NEGLIGENCE

A. Concept: If it ***contributed*** to the plaintiff's injury, the plaintiff's failure to act reasonably may provide the defendant with either a complete or a partial affirmative defense.

B. "All or nothing": Until recently, the majority of American jurisdictions applied the ***"all or nothing"*** rule of contributory negligence. Under the "all or nothing" rule, ***if the plaintiff's negligence contributed to the accident, the plaintiff receives nothing***. The rule has received a great deal of criticism for being unduly harsh. This criticism has led many jurisdictions to replace the rule with a system of ***comparative fault***. In those jurisdictions which continue to apply the "all or nothing" rule, attempts have been made to ameliorate its harshness.

1. **Courts reluctant to find Plaintiff negligent:** Although courts frequently decide as a matter of law that a defendant was negligent, some of the courts which are required to apply the "all or nothing" rule have indicated that they would prefer not to decide as a matter of law that a plaintiff was negligent. They reason that finding a defendant negligent as a matter of law does not necessarily lead to victory for the plaintiff, since the doctrine of proximate cause and other affirmative defenses issues may prevent the defendant from being liable. However, in an "all or nothing" jurisdiction, finding a plaintiff to be negligent must lead to judgment for the defendant.

2. **Last clear chance:** In most "all or nothing" jurisdictions, the doctrine of ***last clear chance*** may make the plaintiff's contributory negligence immaterial. If the ***plaintiff's negligence*** places the plaintiff in a position of peril from which she is unable to extricate herself, that negligence ***does not provide the defendant with an affirmative defense if*** the defendant has had the last clear chance of avoiding the harm. In effect, the doctrine applies only when (1) the ***plaintiff, because of her own negligence or inadvertence, is powerless to avoid injury***; and (2) ***the defendant discovers or should discover the plaintiff's peril and can still avoid the injury by acting reasonably, but fails to do so***.

   Example 1: Plaintiff leaves his horse tethered near a highway, but negligently uses too long a rope. Defendant is driving on the highway when he encounters Plaintiff's horse, which has wandered onto the highway. Although Defendant can swerve to avoid striking the horse, he negligently fails to do so, striking and killing the horse. Plaintiff asserts a negligence claim against Defendant. Defendant argues that he is not liable because Plaintiff was contributorily negligent.

Although Plaintiff was negligent in using a rope so long that the horse had access to the highway, Plaintiff was powerless to extricate the horse from the position of peril which his negligence had created. Since Defendant became aware of the peril in time to avoid causing damage, and since Defendant failed to act reasonably after discovering the peril, Defendant may be said to have had the last clear chance of avoiding the harm. In jurisdictions which apply this doctrine, Plaintiff's contributory negligence will not be available as a defense. *Davies v. Mann*, 152 Eng. Rep. 588 (1842).

Example 2: In the above Example, assume that Defendant does not see Plaintiff's horse because Defendant is negligently attempting to read a map while driving and is not looking at the road.

In most of the jurisdictions which apply the last clear chance doctrine, Plaintiff's contributory negligence will not be available to Defendant as a defense because Defendant would have had the last clear chance to avoid the injury if he had been acting reasonably while driving his car.

Example 3: In the above Example, assume that Defendant's brakes are not working properly and that Defendant knows this when he gets into his car. Although Defendant sees Plaintiff's horse, Defendant cannot stop in time to avoid striking it because his brakes are not working properly.

Many of the jurisdictions which apply the last clear chance doctrine would not apply it to this case because Defendant could not have avoided the injury by acting reasonably after he discovered Plaintiff's peril.

C. Pure comparative negligence (or fault): In many jurisdictions, the "all or nothing" rule has been replaced by a system of ***pure comparative negligence*** in which the plaintiff's negligence does not necessarily prevent the plaintiff from collecting damages. However, those ***damages are measured in proportion to the fault of plaintiff and defendant***.

D. Modified comparative negligence: In some jurisdictions, the plaintiff's recovery is diminished in proportion to plaintiff's fault (as in "pure" comparative negligence systems), but if the plaintiff's fault is ***equal to*** (in some jurisdictions) or ***greater than*** (in some jurisdictions) the defendant's, ***the plaintiff is completely barred from recovering*** (as in the "all or nothing" system).

> **Example:** Defendant's car and Plaintiff's car collide in an intersection. Plaintiff, who is injured in the collision, asserts a negligence claim against Defendant. At the trial, the jury finds that Plaintiff and Defendant were both driving their cars in a negligent manner at the time of the accident. The jury also finds that Plaintiff's damages amounted to $100,000, and that the injury was 40% Defendant's fault and 60% Plaintiff's fault.
>
> In an "all or nothing" jurisdiction, Plaintiff would collect nothing, since Plaintiff's negligence contributed to his own injury.
>
> In a pure comparative negligence jurisdiction, Plaintiff could collect damages in proportion to his own fault. Since the injury was 60% the fault of Plaintiff, Plaintiff can collect $40,000 (*i.e.*, $100,000 reduced by 60%).
>
> In a modified comparative negligence jurisdiction, Plaintiff would recover nothing, since his fault exceeded Defendant's.

II. ASSUMPTION OF THE RISK

A. General concept: A plaintiff who agrees in advance to relieve the defendant of liability for damage resulting from what would otherwise be negligent conduct is ***prevented from recovering damages*** for harm resulting from that conduct.

B. Express assumption: A plaintiff may expressly assume the risk by ***agreeing that the defendant will not be liable for harm resulting from the defendant's specified conduct***. So long as the express agreement does not violate public policy, courts will enforce it by holding that the defendant is not liable.

> **Example:** Defendant is the owner of an automobile race track. Plaintiff, desiring to test his race car on Defendant's track, pays Defendant a fee to do so, and enters into an agreement which provides: "I have inspected the premises and agree to assume all risks of injury which I may sustain while testing my car in and about the premises." While driving his car on the track, Plaintiff strikes a cylinder head which is lying in the track and sustains injury. Plaintiff asserts a negligence claim against Defendant. Defendant argues that Plaintiff expressly assumed the risk.
>
> So long as the parties bargain freely and openly, and so long as the transaction is not one in the public interest (*e.g.*, a transaction involving a hospital or a common carrier), parties may

expressly agree in advance to relieve one another of liability for negligence. Since Plaintiff was given the opportunity to inspect the track and since the transaction was not one ordinarily classified as being in the public interest, Plaintiff's express assumption of the risk probably is enforceable, and Plaintiff's claim probably will fail. *Winterstein v. Wilcom*, 293 A.2d 821 (Md. Ct. Sp. App. 1972).

C. Implied assumption: A plaintiff may ***impliedly assume the risk of damage by voluntarily encountering a known risk.***

1. Voluntary encounter: A plaintiff voluntarily encounters a risk when he freely chooses to do so without any constraint or compulsion.

a. Circumstances interfering with free choice: Even though a plaintiff has exercised free will, courts may find that her encounter with a risk was ***not voluntary if there were circumstances which made it difficult for her to avoid it.***

Example: Knowing that its floor is rotten, Plaintiff uses a wooden privy which is the only toilet which her landlord, Defendant, has provided. When Plaintiff enters the privy, the floor collapses, causing Plaintiff to fall into the accumulation below and sustain injury. Plaintiff asserts a claim against Defendant, alleging that he was negligent in allowing the floor to become rotten. Defendant argues that Plaintiff assumed the risk.

Since Plaintiff had need of a toilet, and since the privy provided by Defendant was the only one available, a court may find that Plaintiff did not act voluntarily when she used it, and that, therefore, she did not assume the risk. *Rush v. Commercial Realty Co.*, 145 A. 476 (N.J. 1929).

b. Rescue: Courts usually hold that a plaintiff who knowingly encounters a risk ***while attempting to rescue an imperiled person is not acting voluntarily*** and, therefore, is not assuming the risk. The reason frequently given for this ruling is that emergencies involving others in distress rob persons of their free will, giving them no choice but to offer aid. Judge Cardozo distilled this argument into three words when he wrote, "Danger invites rescue." *Wagner v. International Ry.*, *supra*, pp. 56-57.

Example: As the result of Defendant's negligence, his car collides with a pole and catches fire, trapping John, a passenger, inside it. Plaintiff, a passer-by, rushes to John's aid and is severely burned while rescuing him. Plaintiff asserts a negligence claim against Defendant. As an affirmative defense, Defendant argues that Plaintiff assumed the risk by voluntarily exposing herself to the flames in her attempt to rescue John.

Since John was in peril, many courts would hold that Plaintiff's attempt to rescue him was involuntary, and that, therefore, Plaintiff did not assume the risk of being burned.

i. **"Fireman's rule":** Since ***persons who are engaged in occupations which involve rescuing others*** (*e.g.*, firefighters, police officers, etc.) voluntarily chose to pursue those occupations, most courts hold that such persons ***voluntarily encounter, and therefore assume, the risks associated with rescues***.

Example: In the above Example, assume that Plaintiff is a police officer who has been called to the scene of John's accident. Since Plaintiff's choice of occupation was not made while Plaintiff was confronted with an emergency, it was made rationally and of Plaintiff's free will. For this reason, Plaintiff's encounter with the risks connected with rescuing John was voluntary, and Plaintiff assumed those risks.

ii. **Reckless conduct:** Courts usually hold that a ***person who acts recklessly*** by undertaking a rescue which is obviously futile, ***is voluntarily exposing himself to risks and therefore assuming them***, even though confronted by an emergency which imperils another.

2. **Known risk:** A plaintiff knows of the risk when he is ***substantially certain that injury probably will occur***.

Example: Plaintiff parks his vehicle in an alleyway while repairing it, believing that he has left enough room for other vehicles to go around it. Defendant is attempting to drive around Plaintiff's vehicle when he strikes the vehicle, injuring Plaintiff. Plaintiff asserts a negligence claim against Defendant. Defendant argues that Plaintiff assumed the risk.

Since Plaintiff did not believe that his vehicle would be struck while he worked on it, he was not substantially certain that injury would occur. For this reason, he did not "know" of the risk, and could not have assumed it. *Hildebrand v. Minyard*, 494 P.2d 1328 (Ariz. 1972).

3. **Same risk:** The only risk which a plaintiff assumes is the risk of which she knows and which she voluntarily encounters. A plaintiff who voluntarily encounters a risk of which she knows, but is injured as the result of a different risk, did not assume the risk which led to her injury.

Example: Plaintiff rents a car from Defendant. As a result of Defendant's negligence, the brakes and steering do not function properly. After driving the car for one mile, Plaintiff discovers that the brakes do not function properly, but continues to drive the car. Plaintiff is subsequently injured when the steering does not function properly. Plaintiff asserts a negligence claim against Defendant. Defendant argues that since Plaintiff knew that the brakes did not function and knew that a car without functioning brakes is dangerous, Plaintiff assumed the risk.

Because Plaintiff voluntarily drove the car with knowledge that the brakes were not functioning properly, and since Plaintiff probably knew that a car without functioning brakes is likely to be involved in an accident, Plaintiff probably assumed the risk of an accident resulting from non-functioning brakes. Since Plaintiff did not know that the steering was not functioning properly, however, Plaintiff did not assume the risk of an accident resulting from non-functioning steering. Since this accident resulted from non-functioning steering, assumption of the risk is not available as a defense.

D. Availability as a defense: The availability of assumption of the risk as a separate and complete affirmative defense is presently a subject of some controversy.

1. **Majority view:** The majority of jurisdictions treat assumption of risk as a ***complete affirmative defense which is separate from contributory/comparative negligence***. In these jurisdictions, a plaintiff who has assumed the risk is completely barred from recovery.

2. **Minority view:** An important minority of jurisdictions has decided that assumption of the risk ***should not be available as a separate and complete defense***. These jurisdictions, all of which have adopted systems of pure comparative negligence, hold that conduct which would have supported an assumption of risk defense ***may be regarded as comparative negligence and considered by the jury in determining the plaintiff's proportion of fault in bringing about the injury***.

Example: Plaintiff rents a car from Defendant. As a result of Defendant's negligence, the brakes do not function properly. After driving the car for one mile, Plaintiff discovers that the brakes do not function properly, but continues to drive the car. Plaintiff is subsequently injured because the brakes do not function properly. Plaintiff asserts a negligence claim against Defendant. Defendant raises the defenses of contributory/ comparative negligence and assumption of the risk.

a. **Jury finding of contributory/comparative negligence**: In this Example, a jury will be asked to decide whether Plaintiff acted unreasonably by driving with knowledge that the brakes were not functioning properly. If they find that he did:

   i. In jurisdictions which apply the all or nothing rule, the jury will be instructed to find for the defendant.

   ii. In jurisdictions which apply the pure comparative negligence rule, the jury will be asked to determine how much of the fault was Plaintiff's and to diminish Plaintiff's recovery in proportion to his fault.

   iii. In jurisdictions which apply a rule of modified comparative negligence, the jury will be asked to determine how much of the fault was Plaintiff's. If Plaintiff's fault was less than Defendant's, the jury will be instructed to reduce Plaintiff's recovery in proportion to his fault. If Plaintiff's fault equaled (in some jurisdictions) or exceeded (in some jurisdictions) that of Defendant, the jury will be instructed to find for Defendant.

b. **Jury finding of assumption of risk**: In the majority of jurisdictions, assumption of the risk is a separate and complete defense. In these jurisdictions, in this Example, the jury will be asked whether Plaintiff's injury resulted from a voluntary encounter with a risk of which he knew. If the jurors decide that it did, they will be instructed to find for Defendant.

   In a minority of jurisdictions, assumption of risk is no longer a separate defense, but is a factor for a jury to consider in applying the comparative negligence rule. In these jurisdictions, the jurors will be asked to reduce Plaintiff's recovery in proportion to his fault. They will also be asked to decide whether Plaintiff voluntarily encountered a known risk. If he did, they will be instructed to consider that fact in determining the extent of his fault.

CHAPTER 6

STRICT LIABILITY

I. GENERAL CONCEPT

A. Liability without fault: While intent and negligence are bases of liability which involve fault, there are certain activities and situations in which the law of torts imposes liability without fault. This is called ***strict liability***. Ordinarily, it is our philosophy that a person who has done nothing "wrong" should not be held responsible for another's damage. This makes it tempting to explain strict liability in terms which analogize it to fault.

Some writers, for example, have said that strict liability is imposed for the breach of an absolute duty to avoid injuring another. This, however, is simply playing with words. ***Strict liability is not imposed for breaching any duty*** at all. It is imposed because our society (through the courts and legislatures) has determined that certain activities should pay their own way; that certain victims should be compensated for their injuries even though the person who caused those injuries may be as innocent as the victim.

> **Example:** In a jurisdiction which imposes strict liability for damage resulting from the use of dynamite, Defendant, a dynamite contractor, charges customers $100 per hour. Most laborers in the area charge $25 per hour. While acting reasonably during the use of some of his dynamite, Defendant causes damage to Plaintiff's realty.
>
> Because the jurisdiction imposes strict liability on those who work with dynamite, Defendant will be liable — without regard to fault — for the damage to Plaintiff's realty. Defendant, knowing that this can happen, has charged his customers $75 more per hour than other laborers in the area. The extra money is used by Defendant to pay for the damages which his work occasionally causes or to purchase insurance which will pay for those damages. In this way, the damage which results from the use of Defendant's dynamite is paid for by all the persons who benefit from its use. The concept of strict liability thus spreads the losses resulting from certain activities among all those who benefit from those activities.

B. Not absolute liability: Courts are careful to distinguish between strict liability and what they sometimes call "absolute liability." Although strict liability is imposed regardless of fault, its imposition is still limited by various factors. Among these factors are proximate cause and the understanding that strict liability is imposed only for damages which result from activity which requires strict liability (*e.g.*, activity which is ultra hazardous). (These limiting factors will be discussed in detail, *infra.*) Courts have stated repeatedly that without such limitations, they would be imposing "absolute liability" and that this would violate public policy.

C. **Basis of many torts:** There are many torts which may be based on the imposition of strict liability. Among these are: the sale of defective products; certain classes of defamation; certain types of misrepresentation; false marketing; invasion of privacy by appropriation of identity; and several others. The traditional development of strict liability has involved three particular fact situations, however. We will discuss these situations in this chapter.

II. ANIMALS

A. **Wild animals:** Although humans have always kept animals, the law has traditionally drawn a distinction between those animals which are customarily kept by humans (*i.e.*, domestic animals) and those animals which are not customarily kept by humans (*i.e.*, wild animals). Ordinarily, ***liability for damage done by domestic animals is not imposed on their keepers without a showing of fault***. On the other hand, ***one who keeps a wild animal is usually held strictly liable for damage done by that animal***.

> **Example:** Defendant keeps a lion in a cage and a cow in a pen. As the result of an unforeseeable earthquake, the lion and the cow are freed from their enclosures. The lion eats Plaintiff's dog, and the cow eats Plaintiff's prize petunias. Plaintiff asserts claims against Defendant, but is unable to show that Defendant acted unreasonably or intended the harm.
>
> Since Plaintiff was unable to show that Defendant acted unreasonably or with intent, Defendant is without fault. Because a cow is a domestic animal and the keeper of a domestic animal is not liable for damage caused by it unless the keeper was at fault, Defendant is not liable for the loss of Plaintiff's petunias. On the other hand, because a lion is a wild animal and the keeper of a wild animal is strictly liable for the damage it causes, Defendant is liable for the loss of Plaintiff's dog.

1. **Domestic animal defined:** A ***"domestic animal"*** is of a species which, because of its nature or its long association with humanity, can safely be kept by humans without special training or restraint.

2. **Wild animal defined:** A ***"wild animal"*** is of a species which cannot safely be kept by humans without special training or restraint.

Example: Defendant keeps a tame lion which is used to perform in television dramas. The lion was born in captivity and has never bitten or injured any person. Defendant also keeps a house cat which has a vicious nature and which has bitten and clawed everyone who has ever come into contact with it.

Although the lion is tame, it belongs to a species which ordinarily cannot safely be kept by man without special training or restraint. For this reason, it is a wild animal. Although the house cat is vicious, it belongs to a species which by its nature and by its long association with humanity, ordinarily can safely be kept without special training or restraint. For this reason it is a domestic animal.

B. **Domestic animals known to have dangerous propensities:** The oldest statutes known to humanity were inscribed on a marble stela in ancient Mesopotamia nearly 4,000 years ago and are known as the Code of Hammurabi. Among these statutes is one which imposes strict liability on the keeper of an animal which is known to have a dangerous propensity. ***Most American jurisdictions apply a similar rule, imposing strict liability for damages on the keeper of a domestic animal who knows of its dangerous propensities***. For this purpose, it is not actually necessary that the animal be vicious. Even a friendly animal may have a dangerous propensity. If it is known to its keeper, it can result in the imposition of strict liability.

Example 1: Defendant keeps a dog which, as defendant knows, has bitten several people. The dog bites Plaintiff. Plaintiff asserts a claim against Defendant, but is unable to show that Defendant acted unreasonably in the way she kept the dog.

Since Defendant knew that her dog had a tendency to bite, and since this is a dangerous propensity, Defendant should be strictly liable for damages resulting from the dog's bite.

Example 2: Defendant is the keeper of a large dog which, as Defendant knows, has the overfriendly tendency to rise onto his hind legs and place his front paws on the shoulders of a person to lick his face. The dog greets Plaintiff, an elderly person, in this manner, causing her to fall and sustain injury. Plaintiff asserts a claim for her damage against Defendant, but is unable to show that Defendant acted unreasonably.

Since the dog's customary greeting is likely to lead to the kind of harm which occurred, it is a dangerous propensity. Since

Defendant knew of it, he may be held strictly liable for the damage which the dog inflicted on Plaintiff.

C. **Variation on negligence:** Some jurisdictions hesitate to impose strict liability for keeping an animal. Instead, they ***hold that it is negligent for a person to keep a wild animal or a domestic animal which, as the owner knows, has a dangerous propensity.***

Example 1: Defendant, who operates a shopping center, arranges to have an elephant displayed in the parking lot as part of a "Grand Opening" ceremony. Although Defendant takes all reasonable precautions for restraining the animal, it escapes and enters Plaintiff's realty, causing Plaintiff to experience fright and other mental suffering with physical manifestations. Plaintiff asserts a claim against Defendant, but is unable to show that Defendant acted unreasonably.

The majority of jurisdictions would hold that, because an elephant is a wild animal, Defendant is strictly liable for damage sustained by Plaintiff as a result of its escape.

In some jurisdictions, however, strict liability would not be applied. Instead, it might be held that Defendant's knowledge of the characteristics of elephants imposed a special duty of reasonable care and that the animal's escape creates an inference that the duty was breached. A court might state that allegations of the animal's nature and of its escape, establish a prima facie case of negligence. *Butt v. Perez*, 408 S.W.2d 576 (Tex. 1966).

Example 2: Defendant is the keeper of a large dog which, as Defendant knows, has the overfriendly tendency to rise onto his hind legs and place his front paws on the shoulders of a person to lick his face. The dog greets Plaintiff, an elderly person, in this manner, causing her to fall and sustain injury. Plaintiff asserts a claim for her damage against Defendant, but is unable to show that Defendant acted unreasonably.

The majority of jurisdictions would hold that, because Defendant knew of his dog's propensity to do harm, Defendant is strictly liable for damage sustained by Plaintiff as a result of that tendency.

In some jurisdictions, however, strict liability would not be applied. Instead, it might be held that Defendant's knowledge of his dog's dangerous propensity imposed upon him a special duty of reasonable care and that his continuing to keep the animal, creates an inference that the duty was breached. A court might hold that allegations that Defendant knew of the animal's nature and that despite such knowledge he continued to keep it, establish a prima facie case of negligence.

D. Harm must relate to dangerous nature of the animal: In the case of wild animals, strict liability is imposed on the keeper because of the inherently dangerous nature of the species to which the animal belongs. In the case of domestic animals with known dangerous propensities, strict liability is imposed on the keeper because of the dangerous nature of the individual member of the species. In either event, however, ***strict liability is imposed only for injuries resulting from the dangerous trait which called for the imposition of strict liability in the first place***.

> **Example:** Defendant takes his pet elephant for a walk on Main Street. Several hours later, Plaintiff, who is strolling on Main Street, slips in a pile of droppings left by Defendant's elephant and falls, sustaining injuries. Plaintiff asserts a claim for her injuries, arguing that, since an elephant is a wild animal, Defendant should be held strictly liable for the damage.
>
> An elephant is a dangerous animal because of its great size, strength, and ferocity. Risks associated with its droppings are no greater than risks associated with the droppings of a horse or other domestic animal. For this reason, the danger associated with elephant droppings probably is not a reason for imposing strict liability on keepers of elephants. Therefore, absent a showing of unreasonable conduct, Defendant probably should not be liable for Plaintiff's injury.

E. Statutory modification: Many jurisdictions have enacted statutes modifying the common law regarding the liability of persons who keep wild or domestic animals. Such statutes should be consulted whenever it is necessary to know the law of a particular jurisdiction.

III. STORAGE OF SUBSTANCES

A. General concept: There are some substances the storage of which can be likened to the keeping of domestic animals. Ordinarily they are harmless, and the keeper should not be liable for damage which they cause. Occasionally, however, these substances have a known tendency to do harm. One who keeps such a substance may be strictly liable for the damage which it causes as in the case of animals with known dangerous propensities. This analogy has given rise to the rule that ***a person who stores a substance which is likely to do great harm if it escapes, should be strictly liable for the harm which it does upon its escape***. Because this principle was first enunciated in a well known English case, it is sometimes called the rule of ***Rylands v. Fletcher***.

B. Essential elements: The ***essential elements*** of this principle are: (1) ***the use of realty in a non-natural manner***; and (2) ***the storage***

of a substance which is ordinarily harmless while stored, but which is likely to do great harm upon its escape.

Example: Defendant maintains a mill pond as part of his milling operation. Through no fault of Defendant, water escapes from the pond and passes through a series of underground mine shafts until it floods and damages Plaintiff's realty. Plaintiff asserts a claim for damage against Defendant, but is unable to show that Defendant failed to act reasonably in maintaining the pond.

Since the storage of water was in a man-made contrivance, it was a non-natural use of the land. Because water is a substance which, although harmless while contained, is likely to do great harm upon its escape from containment, Defendant should be held strictly liable to Plaintiff for the harm resulting from its escape. *Rylands v. Fletcher,* L.R. 3 H.L. 330 (Eng. 1868).

1. **Non-natural use of realty:** In ***Rylands v. Fletcher***, the English court said that the mill pond in which the Defendant stored water was a non-natural use of the realty because it had been constructed by humans. The court suggested that if the water had been kept in a pond which occurred without the help of man, its storage would have been a natural use. Other cases, however, have suggested that what is natural or non-natural may depend on the needs of humans living in the area, and may actually depend on what use is common, rather than "natural."

Example 1: As part of its oil drilling operation in the state of Texas, Defendant maintains a storage reservoir filled with salt water. Through no fault of Defendant, the water escapes from the reservoir and poisons Plaintiff's cattle. Plaintiff asserts a claim for damages under the *Rylands v. Fletcher* theory of strict liability.

Since water is scarce in Texas, it may be argued that storing it, even in man-made reservoirs, is a natural, rather than non-natural, use of the land. In addition, because drilling for oil is a common activity in Texas, and drilling for oil necessitates the storage of salt water, it may be argued that storing salt water is a natural activity in Texas. *Turner v. Big Lake Oil,* 96 S.W.2d 221 (Tex. 1936).

Example 2: Defendant in California runs water through an irrigation ditch to water his fields. Through no fault of Defendant. the walls of the ditch collapse, permitting the water to escape and damage Plaintiff's orchard. Plaintiff asserts a claim for damage under the *Rylands v. Fletcher* theory of strict liability.

Since people in what is now California have been irrigating fields for hundreds of years, it may be argued that the irrigation of fields and the storage of water for that purpose are natural activities in the state of California. *Clark v. DiPrima*, 241 Cal.App.2d 823 (1966).

2. **Storage of substance likely to do harm upon its escape:** Almost all the decisions applying the *Rylands v. Fletcher* theory have involved the storage of water. It probably is true, however, that almost any substance will fall into the same category when stored in sufficiently large quantities.

C. **Nature of risk:** Since strict liability occurs because of the danger that stored substances pose in the event of their escape, ***strict liability is imposed only for injuries which result from the escape of the stored substance***.

Example: Defendant operates a mill pond and stores water for the operation in a reservoir constructed for that purpose. Plaintiff falls into the reservoir and drowns. Plaintiff's personal representative asserts a claim for damage under the *Rylands v. Fletcher* theory of strict liability.

Since Plaintiff's death did not result from the escape of the stored water, strict liability should not be applied.

IV. EXCESSIVELY DANGEROUS ACTIVITIES

A. **General concept:** Some activities are so excessively dangerous that our society has concluded that they should pay their own way. This is accomplished by imposing on persons engaging in those activities strict liability for damages resulting from them.

B. **Ultra-hazardous activities:** The first Restatement of Torts defined ultra-hazardous activities and indicated that persons engaging in them should be held strictly liable for damage which results from those activities. According to the Restatement, an activity is ***ultra-hazardous if***: (1) ***it necessarily involves a serious risk to persons or property which cannot be eliminated by the exercise of reasonable care***; and (2) ***the activity is not a common one***.

1. **Risk which cannot be eliminated by reasonable care:** The factor which makes an activity excessively dangerous is the ***inability to perform it safely by acting reasonably***. Although any activity poses risks, most of the time these risks can be eliminated or substantially decreased by using care in performing the activity. There are some activities, however, which cannot be made safe. Among these are the use of explosives, which may be ignited by

static electricity in the air, or of compressed gases, which may expand and explode upon changes in the weather.

Example: Defendant stores dynamite in a warehouse located on land set aside by the federal government for the storage of explosives. Thieves break into the warehouse and cause an explosion which damages Plaintiff, a nearby property owner. Plaintiff asserts a claim against Defendant, alleging that strict liability should be imposed because the storage of dynamite is an ultra-hazardous activity.

Because dynamite is unstable, the storage of dynamite necessarily involves a serious risk of injury to persons or property. The risk cannot be eliminated by reasonable care. Because of this and because the storage of dynamite is not a common activity, it may be regarded as ultra-hazardous, and Defendant may be held strictly liable for Plaintiff's damage. *Yukon Equipment v. Fireman's Fund Ins. Co.*, 585 P.2d 1206 (Alaska 1978), *infra*.

2. **Not a common activity:** This requirement is roughly analogous to the non-natural use requirement in the *Rylands v. Fletcher* theory (*supra*, p. 99). ***Whether an activity is common is a relative question***, and one upon which courts will differ. ***The most reliable definition of "common" is: "practiced by the great bulk of humanity,"*** but this definition is not always applied.

Example 1: Defendant, an exterminator, uses a cyanide compound to kill insects on premises adjacent to those occupied by Plaintiff. Plaintiff is injured by inhaling some of the compound, which drifts onto his property through no fault of Defendant. Plaintiff asserts a strict liability claim against Defendant on the ground that the use of cyanide compounds is an ultra- hazardous activity.

Since all exterminators use such compounds, it may be argued that their use is common and that, for this reason, the activity is not ultra-hazardous. On the other hand, since very few persons are exterminators, it may be argued that the activity is not a common one and is ultra-hazardous. *Luthringer v. Moore*, 190 P.2d 1 (Cal. 1948).

Example 2: Defendant moves earth in Southern California to create a hillside landfill on which houses are built. During a rain, the landfill collapses, causing damage to Plaintiff's realty. Plaintiff is unable to show any fault on the part of Defendant, and so asserts a strict liability claim on the ground that creating landfills is an ultra-hazardous activity.

Since many houses in southern California are built on hillside landfills, it may be argued that the creation of hillside landfills is a common activity, and, therefore, is not ultra- hazardous. On the other hand, since very few people actually move earth to create such landfills, it may be argued that the activity is not a common one, and, therefore, may be ultra-hazardous. *Beck v. Bel-Air Properties*, 286 P.2d 503 (Cal. 1955).

C. **Abnormally dangerous activities:** The Restatement (2d) of Torts replaces the phrase "ultra-hazardous activity" with "abnormally dangerous activity." It states that in deciding whether to impose strict liability, in addition to the factors listed by the First Restatement, (*supra*, p. 100), ***courts should consider the activity's appropriateness to the location and the extent to which its dangerous attributes are outweighed by its value to the community.***

Example: Defendant stores dynamite in a warehouse located on land set aside by the federal government for the storage of explosives. Thieves break into the warehouse and cause an explosion which damages Plaintiff, a nearby property owner. Plaintiff asserts a claim against Defendant alleging that strict liability should be imposed because the storage of dynamite is an ultra-hazardous activity.

Because dynamite is unstable, the storage of dynamite necessarily involves a serious risk of injury to persons or property. The risk cannot be eliminated by reasonable care. Because of this and because the storage of dynamite is not a common activity, it may be regarded as an ultra-hazardous activity as defined by the First Restatement. Since the activity was conducted in an area specifically set aside for such purpose by federal order, and since the storage of dynamite in relatively safe places is of high social utility, it may be argued that the activity was not an abnormally dangerous one as defined by the Restatement (2d), and that strict liability should not be imposed. *Bridges v. Kentucky Stone*, 425 N.E.2d 125 (Ind. 1981), commenting on *Yukon Equipment v. Fireman's Fund*, (*supra*, p. 101).

D. **False controversy:** Although the difference between ultra- hazardous activity as defined by the first Restatement of Torts and abnormally dangerous activity as defined by the Restatement (2d) appears to be substantial, courts may interpret either definition in a way which makes the difference more dramatic in form than in substance. In reality, the court's conclusion depends more on the way it feels about the activity involved than upon which definition is applied in that jurisdiction.

Example: Plaintiff is an organic farmer (*i.e.*, one who grows crops without the use of chemicals or artificial fertilizers). Neighbor owns the farm adjacent to Plaintiff and grows crops by conventional (*i.e.*, non-organic) methods. Defendant, a crop-duster, is hired by neighbor to spray Neighbor's fields with chemicals from an airplane. Through no fault of Defendant, some of the chemicals drift onto Plaintiff's farm. As a result, Plaintiff's farm can no longer be classified as organic, and this causes Plaintiff to sustain economic loss. Plaintiff asserts a strict liability claim against Defendant on the ground that cropdusting is an abnormally dangerous activity.

Most jurisdictions agree that because of the tendency of air-borne chemicals to drift, cropdusting is an activity which necessarily involves a serious risk of damage to property which cannot be eliminated by reasonable care.

In jurisdictions which apply the First Restatement ultra-hazardous activity concept, it may successfully be argued that since the great bulk of humanity does not spray chemicals from airplanes, the activity is not a common one and, therefore, is ultra-hazardous, necessitating the imposition of strict liability.

On the other hand, it may also be argued that since farming is a common activity, and since farmers frequently do have their fields sprayed with chemicals from airplanes, the activity is a common one, and, therefore, is not ultra-hazardous, and does not require the imposition of strict liability.

In jurisdictions which apply the Restatement (2d) concept, it may successfully be argued that even though the activity is not a common one, its utility is great because it facilitates the efficient production of foods and other important agricultural products. In addition, since it is an activity peculiar to farming, it is appropriate to the location. For these reasons, it is not an abnormally dangerous activity, and strict liability should not be applied.

On the other hand, it may also be argued that although society is benefitted by the aerial spraying of crops, society would be benefitted even further by having those who engage in such activities compensate persons who are damaged thereby. In addition, because chemicals sprayed from an airplane are always likely to drift, the activity is inappropriate to a location where there is an organic farm. For these reasons, it is an abnormally dangerous activity, and strict liability should be applied. *Langan v. Valicopters*, 567 P.2d 218 (Wash. 1977).

E. Nature of risk: Since strict liability is imposed on those who engage in excessively dangerous activities because we believe they should pay their own way, ***strict liability will only be imposed for damage which results directly from the excessively dangerous nature of the activity***.

> **Example:** Defendant is blasting with dynamite one half mile from Plaintiff's mink ranch. Vibrations from the blast frighten mother minks, causing them to destroy their young. Plaintiff asserts a strict liability claim against Defendant on the ground that blasting with dynamite is an excessively dangerous activity.
>
> The hazards which make the use of dynamite excessively dangerous are the risks that shock waves will damage structures or that explosions will hurl debris. Since there are many things which might frighten minks, the possibility that vibrations from a blast will do so is not one of the hazards which makes the use of dynamite excessively dangerous. For this reason, strict liability should not be imposed on Defendant for the loss of Plaintiff's minks. *Foster v. Preston Mill Co.*, 268 P.2d 645 (Wash. 1954).

V. AFFIRMATIVE DEFENSES

A. Contributory and comparative fault:

1. **Majority view**: The majority of jurisdictions holds that, since strict liability is not based on fault by the defendant, ***plaintiff's fault should not be available as an affirmative defense***.
2. **Minority view**: A growing minority of jurisdictions holds that, although the use of a plaintiff's fault as a defense in a case not based on defendant's fault, lacks "semantical symmetry", ***justice demands that it be permitted***. All of these jurisdictions have adopted the pure comparative negligence theory (*supra*, p. 88).

> **Example:** Defendant keeps a horse which, as he knows, has a propensity to attack humans. Plaintiff keeps a horse in the same corral as Defendant's horse. Plaintiff enters the corral to feed grain to his own horse. While he is doing so, Defendant's horse approaches and attempts to eat the grain which Plaintiff is handling. Plaintiff chases Defendant's horse away by waving his arms and shouting, and then turns his back to continue feeding his own horse. Defendant's horse attacks Plaintiff, injuring him. Plaintiff asserts a strict liability claim against Defendant on the ground that Defendant kept a domestic animal with a dangerous propensity of which Defendant knew. Defendant argues that Plaintiff was contributorily negligent.
>
> Since Plaintiff's claim is based on strict liability, and since

strict liability is imposed without regard to fault, the essence of Plaintiff's claim is not fault by Defendant. For this reason, a majority of jurisdictions would not permit fault by Plaintiff to be raised as an affirmative defense. In a minority of jurisdictions, however, Plaintiff's fault may be raised as a defense. *Sandy v. Bushey*, 128 A. 513 (Me. 1925).

B. Assumption of the risk:

1. **Majority view:** Since the essence of assumption of the risk is that the plaintiff has expressly or impliedly consented to relieve the defendant of liability for his acts, (see *supra*, p. 89), the ***majority of jurisdictions permits assumption of the risk to be raised as a defense in a strict liability case.***

2. **Minority view:** The essence of the pure comparative negligence system is the belief that a plaintiff's negligence should not furnish a defendant with a complete affirmative defense, but that the plaintiff's recovery should be reduced in proportion to her own fault. Some jurisdictions have determined that this should be true even where the plaintiff's conduct constitutes an assumption of the risk. For this reason, a ***minority of jurisdictions holds that assumption of the risk is no longer a separate defense to anything, but that facts which would have supported such a defense may now be considered by a jury in determining the plaintiff's comparative fault***. In effect, these jurisdictions have merged assumption of the risk into the concept of pure comparative negligence. In this minority, assumption of the risk ***is no longer a defense in strict liability cases***, but comparative fault (*i.e.*, comparative negligence) is.

   Example: Defendant keeps a horse which, as he knows, has a propensity to attack humans. Plaintiff keeps a horse in the same corral as Defendant's horse. Although Plaintiff knows that Defendant's horse is vicious, Plaintiff enters the corral to feed grain to his own horse, turning his back to Defendant's horse. Defendant's horse attacks Plaintiff, injuring him. Plaintiff asserts a strict liability claim against Defendant on the ground that Defendant kept a domestic animal with a dangerous propensity of which Defendant knew. Defendant argues that Plaintiff was comparatively negligent and that Plaintiff assumed the risk.

   The majority of jurisdictions would not permit Defendant to assert the defense of comparative negligence, since Plaintiff's claim is not based on fault. These jurisdictions would permit the defense of assumption of the risk.

   A minority of jurisdictions has abolished assumption of the

risk as a separate defense, and would not permit Defendant to assert it. These jurisdictions would permit him to assert the defense of comparative negligence, however, and in support of that defense, would permit him to prove that Plaintiff voluntarily encountered a known risk (*i.e.*, assumed the risk).

CHAPTER 7

PROXIMATE CAUSE

I. GENERAL CONCEPT

A. Requirement of proximate cause: Any time a plaintiff seeks compensation for damages resulting from a tort, it is necessary for her to show that the defendant did something which should result in liability (*i.e.*, fault or a basis for imposing liability without fault). In addition, it is necessary to connect the defendant's conduct to the harm sustained by plaintiff by showing that the defendant's conduct was a ***proximate cause*** of that harm.

B. One of the proximate causes: Because of the rule that joint tortfeasors are jointly and severally liable (discussed *infra*, p. 110), in most jurisdictions it is not necessary to show that the defendant's conduct was the sole proximate cause of the plaintiff's harm. Instead, if the plaintiff shows that the ***defendant's conduct was one of the proximate causes of that harm, the defendant may be held liable for the full extent of the harm***.

C. Concept: The relationship of cause-and-effect is a physical one, and whether it exists is entirely a question of fact. It has been said, however, that "cause and effect have their beginning and end in the limitless and unknowable". For this reason, the law requires not only that the defendant's conduct be a cause of the plaintiff's injury, ***but that the relationship of cause (i.e.***, defendant's conduct) ***to effect*** (*i.e.*, plaintiff's injury) be so close that liability is necessary. This is the concept known as proximate cause.

> **Example:** Defendant negligently causes an explosion which frightens John, a bystander, causing him to drop a hammer which strikes and injures Mary's toe. The following day, while Mary is driving her car, the pain in her toe prevents her from stepping on the brake pedal with sufficient pressure to stop her car, causing it to strike and injure Arthur, a pedestrian. John, Mary, and Arthur assert negligence claims against Defendant.
>
> Since Defendant's negligence is a given, and since negligence is liability-forming (*i.e.*, may result in the imposition of liability), the only questions remaining to be answered are whether Defendant's conduct was a proximate cause of the damages sustained by John, Mary, and Arthur.
>
> Since John would not have been frightened, Mary's toe would not have been injured, and Arthur would not have been struck by Mary's car, if not for Defendant's negligence, it may be

said that Defendant's negligence was a cause of all the injuries. It is possible, however, that one or more of the plaintiffs will be unsuccessful, because a court may find that Defendant's conduct was not a proximate cause of the injury sustained.

John's injury: Many jurisdictions hold that negligence is not a proximate cause of mental suffering unless that suffering results from a physical injury or has a physical manifestation (*infra*, p. 135). Since John's only injury was fright (*i.e.*, mental suffering), these jurisdictions would hold that Defendant's conduct was not a proximate cause of damage to him.

Mary's injury: Although John's action (*i.e.*, dropping the hammer) was an intervening cause of Mary's injury, most courts probably would hold that the chain of events which led to Mary's harm was not unusual, and that, therefore, Defendant's conduct was a proximate cause of Mary's injury.

Arthur's injury: Many courts would hold that the chain of events leading from Defendant's negligence to Arthur's injury was sufficiently unusual to prevent Defendant's negligence from being a proximate cause of Arthur's harm. Other courts would hold that Defendant's conduct was a proximate cause of Arthur's harm.

D. Two-step process: As suggested by the foregoing Example, proximate cause determinations require a two-step process. First, it is necessary to decide whether the defendant's conduct was a ***factual cause*** of the plaintiff's harm. If not, the process is ended. If the defendant's conduct was a factual cause of the plaintiff's harm, however, it must be determined whether it was a ***legal cause*** of that harm. ***If the defendant's conduct was both a factual and a legal cause of the plaintiff's injury, then it was a proximate cause of that injury.***

E. Mixed question: The two-step process described above has led commentators to call proximate cause a "mixed question of fact and law." This flows from the obvious truth that factual cause involves a question of fact and legal cause involves a question of law. It may be more helpful, however, to think of proximate cause as a mixed question of reality and philosophy. Factual cause involves the relationship of cause to effect, and is, therefore, rooted in universal realities. If all the necessary evidence is available, there is usually very little controversy whether a particular act caused a particular injury, and a jury is certainly competent to answer the question. This will be called a question of fact. On the other hand, even if it is clear that a defendant's particular conduct was a factual cause of a particular harm, the court may decide that the defendant should not be held financially responsible for the harm done to the plaintiff.

In coming to this conclusion, the court will say that, although the defendant's conduct was a factual cause of the harm, it was not a legal cause. In effect, however, the court is concluding that, for philosophical reasons, the relationship of this cause to this effect is not one for which the law should impose liability. Since this decision is based on legal philosophy, a jury is not competent to decide it. For this reason, it is said to be a question of law.

> **Example:** When involved in a collision, Plaintiff is wearing a motorcycle helmet manufactured by Defendant. As a result of the collision, Plaintiff is thrown eighty feet through the air and lands on her helmeted head. The helmet shatters on impact, causing Plaintiff to sustain brain damage. Plaintiff asserts a negligence claim against Defendant, alleging that her injury resulted from unreasonable conduct in the design and manufacture of the helmet. At the trial, expert bio-mechanical engineers testify and demonstrate that Plaintiff would not have sustained brain damage if she had not been wearing the helmet.
>
> The jury should be asked to decide whether the condition of the helmet was a factual cause of Plaintiff's brain damage. (If the jurors believe the testimony of the experts, they probably will find that it was.) This decision is like any other which a jury is required to make, depending primarily on how credible and convincing they find the evidence which is presented to them. Even if the jury finds that the condition of the helmet was a factual cause of the brain damage, however, the court may determine that it was not a legal cause. The court may state, for example, that it is so unusual for a person wearing such a helmet to fly eighty feet through the air and land on her head, that it would not be fair to require Defendant to pay for the extraordinary injury which resulted. This determination as to what is "fair" is one which depends on legal philosophy and public policy. For this reason, it is not one which a jury is competent to make and must be left for resolution by the court as a matter of law.

1. **Factual cause:** Before deciding whether public policy or legal philosophy requires the imposition of liability on the defendant for injuries sustained by the plaintiff, it is necessary to determine that a cause-and-effect relationship exists between the defendant's conduct and the plaintiff's injury. This relationship has been called a "factual cause", an "actual cause", a "physical cause", a "cause-in-fact", or simply a "cause" of the injury. Courts have developed sev-

eral tests for determining whether a cause-and-effect relationship exists between conduct and injury.

a. **"But for" or *"sine qua non"*:** In most situations, the ***"but for"*** rule can be applied to determine whether a particular conduct was a factual cause of a particular injury. Simply stated, the "but for" rule provides that ***conduct is a factual cause of injury if the injury would not have occurred without (i.e.,*** but for) the conduct.

Example 1: Defendant is operating a railroad train at a speed of 37 miles per hour at a location where operating at any speed in excess of 25 miles per hour is negligent. Plaintiff is driving his car across the railroad tracks when he is struck by Defendant's train. If Defendant had been traveling at a speed of 25 miles per hour, he would not have struck Plaintiff's car. Since the collision would not have occurred without Defendant's negligence, Defendant's negligence was a factual cause of it. *Perkins v. Texas & New Orleans Ry. Co.*, 147 So.2d 646 (La. 1962).

Example 2: Assume the same facts as in Example 1, except that Plaintiff's car stalls on the tracks before it is hit. Even if Defendant had been traveling at a speed of 25 miles per hour, he would have struck Plaintiff's car.

Since the accident would have occurred even without Defendant's negligence, Defendant's negligence was not a factual cause of the accident. *Perkins v. Texas, supra.*

i. **Not necessarily the sole cause:** It is ***not necessary that the conduct in question be the sole factual cause*** of the plaintiff's injury. It is sufficient that it be an act without which the plaintiff's injury would not have occurred.

Example: Defendant is driving his car in a negligent manner when he strikes a wooden power pole. Because the pole is rotted, the collision causes it to fall, injuring Plaintiff. Plaintiff asserts a negligence claim against Defendant, alleging that Defendant's negligent driving was a factual cause of Plaintiff's injury. Defendant argues that the injury was caused by the rotten condition of the pole.

Since the pole would not have fallen if Defendant had not struck it, Defendant's conduct was a factual cause of the injury. This is true even though the rotten condition of the pole may also have been a factual cause of the injury. *Gibson v. Garcia*, 216 P.2d 119 (Cal. Dist. Ct. App. 1950).

ii. **Multiple defendants:** The "but for" approach may successfully be applied in most factual cause problems, including those involving multiple defendants.

Example: Acting independently of each other, John and Mary negligently shoot guns in Plaintiff's direction, both striking Plaintiff. John's bullet causes Plaintiff to lose one pint of blood. Mary's bullet causes Plaintiff to lose one pint of blood. If Plaintiff had lost less than two pints of blood, he would have survived. The loss of two pints of blood brings about Plaintiff's death. Plaintiff's personal representative asserts claims against both John and Mary, alleging that their negligence was a factual cause of Plaintiff's death. John argues that his conduct was not a factual cause of Plaintiff's death because Plaintiff would not have died without Mary's negligence.

Since a loss of less than two pints of blood would not have brought about Plaintiff's death, and since Mary's bullet caused Plaintiff to lose only one pint of blood, Plaintiff would not have died without John's bullet. Therefore, John's negligence was a cause of Plaintiff's death, even though Mary's bullet was also a cause of Plaintiff's death.

b. **Substantial factor:** Where two acts combine to bring about harm which each of them might have brought about by itself, the "but for" approach will not work, since it may be said of each act that the injury might have occurred without it. In this situation, courts apply the "substantial factor" rule. Simply stated, this rule provides that ***conduct is a factual cause of injury if the conduct was a substantial factor in bringing about that injury***. Conduct was a substantial factor in bringing about an injury if it ***contributed to the injury and was, alone, sufficient to bring about that injury***.

Example: Assume the same set of facts as in the previous Example, except that John's bullet and Mary's bullet each causes the loss of two pints of Plaintiff's blood. Applying the "but for" approach to John's conduct might result in a finding that John's conduct was not a factual cause of Plaintiff's death, since Mary's bullet would have brought about Plaintiff's death even if John's bullet had not struck Plaintiff. Applying the "but for" approach to Mary's conduct would result in a finding that Mary's conduct was not a factual cause of Plaintiff's death, since John's bullet would have brought about Plaintiff's death even if Mary's bullet had not struck Plaintiff.

Because this would be an absurd result, it is necessary to apply the substantial factor approach. Since John's bullet contributed to Plaintiff's death and would have brought about Plaintiff's death all by itself, it was a substantial factor in bringing about Plaintiff's death and was, therefore, a factual cause of Plaintiff's death. (The same argument can be made about Mary's bullet in a claim against Mary.)

c. **Alternate liability:** Where two or more defendants commit ***identical acts, either of which could have caused injury to the plaintiff***, but it is ***impossible to determine which*** caused the injury, it may be ***presumed that both caused*** the injury. Each defendant may attempt to rebut the presumption of fault by proving that it was not he who caused the injury.

Example: Acting independently of each other, John and Mary negligently shoot guns in Plaintiff's direction. A bullet from one of the guns strikes Plaintiff, injuring him. Plaintiff asserts negligence claims against John and Mary, but is unable to prove which gun fired the bullet which struck him. John moves to dismiss on the ground that Plaintiff has failed to establish that his conduct was a cause of the injury. Mary makes the same motion.

Since it cannot be proven that John's bullet struck Plaintiff, it cannot be shown that Plaintiff's injury would not have occurred without John's negligence. For this reason, the "but for" approach will not establish that John's conduct was a factual cause of the harm. For the same reason, it cannot be proven that Mary's conduct was a factual cause of the harm.

Also, since it cannot be proven that John's bullet struck Plaintiff, it cannot be shown that John's bullet was a substantial factor in bringing about Plaintiff's harm. For this reason, the "substantial factor" approach cannot be used. For the same reason, it cannot be used to prove that Mary's conduct was a factual cause of the harm.

Since John and Mary committed identical acts of negligence, one of which injured Plaintiff, and since it is impossible to determine which caused the injury, the "alternate liability" approach may be applied. Under this approach, it will be presumed that John and Mary both caused the harm, and each of them will be given the opportunity to rebut this presumption. *Summers v. Tice*, 199 P.2d 1 (Cal. 1948).

i. **Small number of defendants:** It has been held that the principle of alternate liability should not be applied unless the number of wrongdoers is small. In supporting this conclusion, a California court stated that it is not grossly unfair to presume that each of two defendants caused harm which only one of them actually caused, since there is a 50% chance that either actually did cause it. On the other hand, where there are a hundred defendants, it would be grossly unfair to presume that each of them caused the harm which only one of them actually caused. As to each defendant, there is only a 1% chance that he actually did cause it.

ii. **Necessary parties:** The principle of alternate liability can be applied only where it is certain that one of the defendants caused the harm. For this reason, it cannot be applied unless all wrongdoers are named as defendants.

iii. **Not a universal view:** Although the alternate liability approach has been the subject of a great deal of comment, most of it favorable, so far only a few jurisdictions have actually applied it.

2. **Legal cause:** Since there can be no liability unless the defendant's conduct is liability-forming, our discussion of legal cause will be based on the assumption that the defendant's conduct has been found to be actionable (*i.e.*, intentional, negligent, or the kind of activity for which strict liability may be imposed).

After it has been determined that the defendant's conduct was a factual cause of the plaintiff's harm (*i.e.*, that a cause-and-effect relationship existed between conduct and harm), we must necessarily determine whether liability should be imposed on the defendant.

Several rules of law have been developed to help in making this determination. As Judge Andrews pointed out in his famous *Palsgraf* dissent, (*supra*, pp. 5 and 56) this decision is not really based on logic but on practical politics. Like most policy decisions, it is influenced by the court's personal philosophy; or by what Judge Andrews described as a rough sense of justice combined with a rough sense of expediency.

After reaching its conclusion of liability, the court must justify it by reference to accepted legal arguments like those discussed below. Because the arguments are formed after the conclusion has been reached, it frequently seems that decisions, even of the same court, are inconsistent with each other. Indeed, for the same reason, judicial decisions sometimes appear to be inconsistent with the very rule of law on which they claim to be based. To a large extent, this explains the confusion which law students experience when first encountering the study of proximate cause.

Example 1: In a case decided in the mid-nineteenth century, Defendant, a railroad company, negligently operated its locomotive in a way which threw sparks on and set fire to a building which it owned. The fire spread to and destroyed a neighboring building which was owned by Plaintiff. In defense against Plaintiff's negligence claim, Defendant asserted that its conduct was not a legal cause of the damage to Plaintiff's building.

The court began by declaring that conduct is a legal cause of harm if the harm could have been expected to result from the conduct. The court then found that Defendant's conduct was not a legal cause of the destruction of Plaintiff's building because the sparks fell on defendant's building, and ordinarily it cannot be expected that a fire will spread from one building to another. Humans have known for thousands of years that fires often spread from one structure to another. Yet in attempting to justify its conclusion that Defendant did not have to pay for the result of its negligence, the court found itself compelled to argue that the harm to Plaintiff could not have been expected, and thus to state that fires cannot be expected to spread.

At one point in its opinion, the court gave a clue to the real reason for its decision, showing that it had combined a rough sense of justice with a rough sense of expediency before constructing an argument to justify the result. Fire, it said, is our most important source of energy — the force which makes the wheels of industry turn. Fires, it added, can spread, often without any hope of control. Everyone who makes a fire is likely to be negligent at some point. If it were understood that negligence in handling fire could lead to legal responsibility for all the damages resulting from its uncontrolled spread, those who tend the fires of industry might let their hearths grow cold in fear of unlimited liability. In order to avoid this potentially disastrous result, a line must be drawn which confines the liability resulting from the spread of a fire to reasonable limits, *Ryan v. New York Central R.R. Co.*, 35 N.Y. 210 (1866).

Example 2: Defendant negligently causes an explosion which burns John, causing him to drop a hammer which strikes and injures Mary's toe. The following day, while Mary is driving her car, the pain in her toe prevents her from stepping on the brake pedal with sufficient pressure to stop her car, causing it to strike and injure Arthur, a pedestrian, breaking his leg. Because of his injuries, Arthur is unable to work. As a result, Arthur's employer, Boss, loses $5,000 worth of business. The monetary loss makes it impossible for Boss to purchase medicine for her sick child, Sonny, and Sonny dies as a result. While driving to Sonny's funeral, Boss's husband Harold strikes Edna's vehicle, causing Edna to sustain minor injuries. While Edna is being treated for her injuries, a doctor carelessly gives her the wrong medicine, and this makes her permanently paralyzed.

Defendant's negligence was a factual cause of John's burn, Mary's injured toe, Arthur's broken leg, Boss's loss of income, Sonny's death, Edna's minor injury, and Edna's paralysis, since those injuries would not have occurred if Defendant had not negligently caused an explosion.

A court utilizing its rough sense of justice combined with its rough sense of expediency probably would impose liability on Defendant for John's burns, but probably not for Edna's paralysis. Whether liability would be imposed on Defendant for the injuries sustained by the other parties would be more difficult to predict. In deciding the claim of each of them, the court would probably be guided by its instincts and its sense of fair play, but would use an accepted legal argument to support its conclusion.

a. **Restatement (2d) of Torts view:** The plaintiff has the burden of proving all the elements of her claim, including causation; but once it has been established that the defendant's conduct was a factual cause of the plaintiff's injury, issues involving legal cause do not usually arise unless raised by the defendant. The Restatement (2d) explains this by stating that a ***factual cause of harm is a legal cause of that harm unless there is some rule of law to the contrary***.

b. **Direct consequence:** Some cases have held that conduct which is a ***factual cause of harm is a legal cause of that harm if the harm was a "direct consequence"*** of the conduct and was not brought about by the operation of new, independent, intervening causes. Harm is a "direct consequence" of conduct if, ***given the existing context of circumstances and conditions, the harm was a natural and inevitable result*** of that conduct.

Example: The hold of a ship containing cargo is filled with gasoline fumes. While the ship is being loaded, Defendant, a longshoreman, negligently drops a plank into the hold. The plank strikes a piece of cargo, making it fall over and strike another piece of cargo, producing a spark. The spark ignites the gasoline fumes, bringing about an explosion which injures Plaintiff. Plaintiff asserts a negligence claim, alleging that Defendant's negligence was a legal cause of Plaintiff's injury.

Defendant's conduct was a factual cause of the explosion, since the explosion would not have occurred if Defendant had not allowed the plank to fall. Since the hold was filled with gasoline fumes and cargo which was stacked in a particular way, this conduct was a legal cause of the explosion if it was natural and inevitable that a plank dropped into the hold under the circumstances would cause an explosion.

On facts similar to these, an English judge came to the conclusion that the explosion was a direct consequence of the dropped plank (*i.e.*, given the existing circumstances, the explosion was a natural and inevitable result of dropping the plank) and that, therefore, the dropped plank was a legal cause of the explosion. A different judge, however, in whom the rough sense of justice and the rough sense of expediency were combined differently, might have come to a different conclusion. *In Re Polemis*, 3 K.B. 560 (Eng. 1921).

c. **Foreseeability:** Some cases have held that a ***factual cause of harm is a legal cause*** of that harm ***if, with knowledge of the circumstances which existed at the time the defendant acted, the harm could have been foreseen by the reasonable person*** in the defendant's position.

Example: Assume the same facts as in the previous example. Defendant's negligence was a factual cause of the explosion, since the explosion would not have occurred if the plank had not fallen. Defendant's negligence was a legal cause of the explosion if the reasonable person in the defendant's position with knowledge that the hold was filled with gasoline fumes and cargo would have foreseen that an explosion would result from dropping a plank.

i. **Retrospective analysis:** Although this analysis is based on "foreseeability", the concept is somewhat artificial, since the question asked is: What would have been ***anticipated by the reasonable person with knowledge of the existing circumstances***. This question is very different from the question asked to determine negligence: what would have been anticipated by the reasonable person with the knowledge that the defendant had or should have had.

Example: In the above Example, to decide whether Defendant was negligent in the way he handled the plank, (*i.e.*, whether Defendant had and breached a duty to act reasonably), it is necessary to ask whether the reasonable person in Defendant's situation, knowing what Defendant knew or should have known, would have anticipated that dropping the plank would cause some harm.

On the other hand, to decide whether dropping the plank was a legal cause of the explosion, it is necessary to ask whether, knowing all the circumstances and conditions which existed in the hold of the ship, the reasonable person in the defendant's position would have anticipated that dropping the plank would lead to an explosion.

ii. **Unforeseeable extent of harm:** ***If harm was foreseeable, the fact that its extent was not foreseeable does not prevent the defendant's conduct from being a legal cause of the harm.***

Example: Defendant is driving his car in a negligent manner when he strikes the rear of Plaintiff's car, destroying a rare Ming vase worth ten million dollars which Plaintiff is carrying in the trunk. Plaintiff asserts a negligence claim against Defendant. Defendant argues that it was not foreseeable that a vase worth ten million dollars would be in the trunk of Plaintiff's car.

Since it was foreseeable that striking a car in the rear would damage items in its trunk, the conduct which caused the accident was a legal cause of the destruction of the Ming vase even though the reasonable person might not have anticipated that the trunk of Plaintiff's car would contain an object worth ten million dollars.

d. **Not extraordinary in retrospect:** The Restatement (2d) of Torts suggests that conduct is ***not a legal cause*** of harm ***if, looking back from the harm to the negligent conduct, the harm appears to have been a highly extraordinary consequence*** of the conduct.

Example: The hold of a ship contains cargo. It becomes filled with gasoline fumes. While the ship is being loaded, Defendant negligently drops a plank into the hold. The plank strikes a piece of cargo, making it fall over and strike another piece of cargo, producing a spark. The spark ignites the gasoline fumes, bringing about an explosion which injures Plaintiff.

Defendant's conduct was a factual cause of the explosion, since the explosion would not have occurred without it. Given that the hold was filled with gasoline fumes and cargo which was stacked in a particular way, the dropped plank was a legal cause of the explosion only if it does not appear in retrospect that an explosion was a highly extraordinary consequence of dropping a plank into the hold.

e. **Retrospective analysis:** All legal cause theories require a ***retrospective analysis which accepts the circumstances and conditions which existed at the time of the defendant's conduct***. Thus, in determining legal cause issues, it never is relevant to ask whether it was inevitable, or foreseeable, or extraordinary, that the existing conditions were as they were. Instead, courts see these conditions as a "set stage" on which a defendant acts, and ask whether the result was inevitable, or foreseeable, or extraordinary, given the stage setting.

Example: Defendant negligently inflicts a minor cut on Plaintiff's arm. Plaintiff suffers from a rare disease which prevents his blood from clotting, so that when Defendant cuts him, he bleeds to death. Plaintiff's personal representative asserts a negligence claim against Defendant, alleging that Defendant's negligence was a proximate cause of Plaintiff's death. Defendant argues that it was not, because Plaintiff's disease was rare. Defendant's negligence was a factual cause of Plaintiff's death because he would not have bled to death if Defendant had not inflicted the cut.

Direct Consequences: Given the existing circumstances, which included the fact that Plaintiff suffered from a disease which prevented his blood from clotting, Plaintiff's death probably was a natural and inevitable result of Defendant's conduct. For this reason, Defendant's conduct probably was a legal cause of Plaintiff's death.

Foreseeability: Knowing that Plaintiff suffered from a disease which prevented his blood from clotting, the reasonable person probably would have anticipated that Plaintiff would bleed to death if a minor cut was inflicted on him. Therefore, Defendant's conduct probably was a legal cause of Plaintiff's death.

Not Extraordinary: Given that Plaintiff suffered from a disease which prevented his blood from clotting, in retrospect it probably does not appear highly extraordinary that the cut inflicted by Defendant would cause Plaintiff to bleed to death. Therefore, Defendant's conduct probably was a legal cause of Plaintiff's death.

3. **Intervening causes:** Many proximate cause problems are complicated by the fact that there were other causes of harm in addition to the defendant's conduct. Since all legal cause theories require retrospective analysis which accepts as given all circumstances and conditions existing at the time of the defendant's conduct, causes which pre-existed the defendant's conduct (*i.e.*, parts of the stage setting) do not complicate or affect the defendant's liability in any way. Forces which contributed to the plaintiff's injury and which came into being after the defendant's conduct, however, are known as

intervening causes and must be considered in resolving legal cause issues.

Example: Shopper is shopping in Mart grocery store, using a shopping cart provided by Mart. Because of Mart's negligence, there is an uncovered opening in the back of the shopping cart. Shopper places a large glass bottle in the shopping cart. As Shopper wheels the cart past Plaintiff, the bottle falls through the uncovered opening and strikes Plaintiff's foot, fracturing her toe. Plaintiff goes to a hospital where she is treated by Dr. Med who negligently prescribes the wrong medicine, causing Plaintiff to lose her eyesight. Plaintiff asserts negligence claims against Mart, Shopper, and Dr. Med for damage resulting from the injury to her toe and the loss of her eyesight.

Plaintiff v. Mart: If Mart had not negligently provided a shopping cart with an uncovered opening, the bottle would not have fallen on Plaintiff's foot and Plaintiff would not have received treatment by Dr. Med. For this reason, Mart's negligence was a factual cause of the injury to Plaintiff's toe and the loss of her eyesight. Since the injury to Plaintiff's toe would not have occurred if Shopper had not placed the bottle in the cart, and since Shopper did so after Mart furnished the cart, in Plaintiff's claim against Mart, Shopper's conduct was an intervening cause of Plaintiff's fractured toe. Since the loss of Plaintiff's eyesight would not have occurred if Shopper had not placed the bottle in the cart and if Dr. Med had not prescribed the wrong medicine, and since these acts occurred after Mart furnished the cart, in Plaintiff's claim against Mart, the conduct of Shopper and Dr. Med are intervening causes of the loss of Plaintiff's eyesight.

Plaintiff v. Shopper: If Shopper had not placed the bottle in the cart, it would not have fallen on Plaintiff's toe and Plaintiff would not have been treated by Dr. Med. For this reason, Shopper's conduct was a factual cause of both injuries. Mart's conduct was also a cause of both injuries, but since Mart's conduct occurred before Shopper's, in Plaintiff's claim against Shopper, Mart's conduct was not an intervening cause, but was part of the set stage. Since the injury to Plaintiff's toe would have occurred without Dr. Med's conduct, the doctor's conduct is not a cause of that injury. Since the loss of Plaintiff's eyesight would not have occurred without Dr. Med's conduct, and since the doctor's conduct occurred after Shopper's, in Plaintiff's claim against Shopper, Dr. Med's conduct is an intervening cause of the loss of Plaintiff's eyesight.

Plaintiff v. Dr. Med: Since Plaintiff would not have lost her eyesight if Dr. Med had not prescribed the wrong medicine, Dr. Med's conduct was a factual cause of the lost eyesight. The conduct of Mart and Shopper were also factual causes of the loss of Plaintiff's eyesight. Since that conduct occurred before Dr. Med's conduct, however, in Plaintiff's claim against Dr. Med, the acts of Mart and of Shopper are not intervening causes of the loss of Plaintiff's eyesight, but are parts of the set stage. *Gross v. Waldbaum*, 423 N.Y.S.2d 123 (1979).

a. **Definition:** An intervening cause of harm is a force without which the harm would not have occurred or which was a substantial factor in producing the harm (*i.e.*, ***a factual cause of the harm***) and ***which occurred after the defendant's conduct***. It may be attributable to another defendant, to a person who is not a defendant, or even to a natural force.

Example: Defendant negligently allows the roof of its building to become rotten. During a storm, the wind blows part of the roof off the building, and causes it to strike and injure Plaintiff's head. If the roof had not been rotten, the wind would not have blown it off. If there had been no wind, the roof would not have fallen off.

While Plaintiff is being taken to the hospital, the ambulance in which she is riding is struck by Driver, causing injury to Plaintiff's arm. Plaintiff asserts a negligence claim against Defendant for damage resulting from the injuries to her head and arm. Since the roof would not have blown off if Defendant had not allowed it to become rotten, Defendant's conduct was a factual cause of the injury to Plaintiff. Since Plaintiff would not have been riding in the ambulance if not for the injury to her head, Defendant's conduct was also a factual cause of the injury to her arm.

Since the roof would not have fallen off without the wind, and since the wind occurred after Defendant's negligence, in Plaintiff's claim against Defendant, the wind was an intervening cause of both injuries.

Since the injury to Plaintiff's head occurred before the conduct of Driver, Driver's conduct was not a cause of the head injury. Since the injury to Plaintiff's arm would not have occurred without the conduct of Driver, and since that conduct occurred after the negligence of Defendant, in Plaintiff's claim against Defendant, Driver's conduct was an intervening cause of the injury to Plaintiff's arm. *Kimble v. Mackintosh*, 59 A.2d 68 (Pa. 1948).

b. Concurring and superseding causes: The fact that an intervening cause contributed to a plaintiff's harm does not, alone, prevent the defendant's conduct from being a legal cause of that harm. If the court concludes that the intervention was a ***"concurring cause"*** of the harm, the defendant's conduct will still be regarded as a legal cause of the harm and liability may be imposed on the defendant (and may also be imposed on the intervenor).

If the court concludes that the intervention was a ***"superseding cause"*** of the harm, however, the defendant's conduct is no longer regarded as a legal cause of the harm and liability is not imposed on the defendant (although it may be imposed on the intervenor). Courts have developed many theories and arguments in deciding whether an intervention was a concurring or a superseding cause of harm.

Example: In the above Example, in Plaintiff's claim against Defendant, if the court concludes that the wind and Driver's negligence were concurring causes of harm, Defendant's conduct will be regarded as a legal cause of the harm and liability may be imposed on him. On the other hand, if the court concludes that Driver's negligence was a superseding cause of harm, or that the wind was a superseding cause of harm, Defendant's conduct will not be regarded as a legal cause of that harm and liability will not be imposed on him. Note that liability may still be imposed on Driver for the proximate results of his negligence.

i. Dependent and independent intervention: An intervention is a ***concurring cause*** of harm if its occurrence is ***dependent*** on the risk created by the defendant's conduct, and is a ***superseding cause*** of harm if its occurrence is ***not dependent*** on the risk created by the defendant's conduct. The occurrence of an intervention is ***dependent*** on the risk created by the defendant's conduct ***if the likelihood of that intervening occurrence is a foreseeable consequence of the conduct.***

Example: Defendant manufactures and markets a device known as a "heat block", for use in warming the bodies of accident victims as a first aid treatment for shock. Defendant packages the heat block in a box which contains a warning against applying the device directly to the skin without clothing or some other insulating material to protect against burns. Although the device was designed to be refilled and reused many times, the only warning furnished is the one printed on the box; no warning of any kind is printed directly on the device itself.

While giving first aid at an accident scene, a nurse who is unfamiliar with the device applies it directly to the accident victim's skin, causing a severe burn. The particular device has been reused many times, and the box in which it was originally packaged has been lost. Plaintiff asserts a claim against Defendant, alleging that it was unreasonable for Defendant to market the device without a warning printed directly on the heat block itself. Defendant argues that the conduct of the nurse was a superseding cause of harm.

If Defendant's failure to print a warning on the heat block was unreasonable, it was because of the risk that a person unfamiliar with it would use the device improperly. For this reason, the nurse's intervention probably was dependent on the risk created by Defendant and, therefore, was a concurring cause of harm. If so, Defendant's conduct was a legal cause of the harm. *McLaughlin v. Mine Safety Appliances*, 226 N.Y.S.2d 407 (1962).

ii. **Foreseeable intervention:** An intervention is a ***concurring*** cause of harm if its occurrence would have been ***foreseeable to the reasonable person who knew of the circumstances and conditions which existed*** at the time of his actions, and is a ***superseding*** cause of harm if its occurrence would ***not*** have been ***foreseeable to the reasonable person who knew of those circumstances and conditions***.

Example: Defendant manufactures and sells a device known as a "mace pencil", which is designed to discharge an irritating chemical. Because he has been robbed at gunpoint several times while on the job, Plaintiff, a night clerk in a motel, purchases the device after seeing an advertisement which says, "Defend yourself. Amazing self-defense weapon stops attackers instantly in their tracks." During a robbery, Plaintiff attempts to use the mace pencil on an attacker. When it fails to function, the attacker shoots Plaintiff, injuring him. Plaintiff asserts a claim against Defendant for damages resulting from his bullet wound, alleging that Defendant was negligent in the way it manufactured the device. Defendant argues that the robbery was a superseding cause of harm.

Because Plaintiff had been robbed at gunpoint several times while on the job, it probably would have been foreseeable to the reasonable person with knowledge of the circumstances that Plaintiff would be attacked again. For this reason, the robber's act probably was a concurring cause of harm. If so, Defendant's conduct was a legal cause of the harm. *Klages v. General Ordnance*, 367 A.2d 304 (Pa. 1976).

iii. Extraordinary intervention: An intervention is a ***superseding*** cause of harm ***if in retrospect its occurrence appears to have been highly extraordinary***, and is a ***concurring*** cause of harm ***if in retrospect its occurrence does not appear to have been highly extraordinary***.

Example: Defendant, a lumber dealer, sells a unit of lumber to Bildco, a building contractor, knowing that the lumber will be used to build a scaffold and knowing also that one of the boards in the unit is defective. Bildco, who is aware of the defective board, uses it to construct the scaffold. Bildco knows that workers including Plaintiff will be standing or walking on the scaffold, and that, if it collapses, they are likely to sustain serious injury. Plaintiff, a painter, is standing on the scaffold when the defective board breaks, causing the scaffold to collapse and injure Plaintiff. Plaintiff asserts a negligence claim against Defendant.

Since Bildco was a building contractor, it must have known that a defective board would weaken a structure in which it was used and that its use in the scaffold was likely to cause it to collapse. Since it is in a building contractor's best interest to avoid jobsite accidents, Bildco's use of the defective board in a scaffold appears highly extraordinary in the face of its knowledge. Therefore, Bildco's intervention probably was a superseding cause of Plaintiff's injury. If so, Defendant's conduct was not a legal cause of the harm. *Stultz v. Benson Lumber*, 59 P.2d 100 (Cal. 1936).

iv. Same type of harm: Where the defendant's conduct creates a risk of a particular type of harm, an ***intervention which brings about that very type of harm is a concurring cause of that harm, unless the intervenor intentionally brought the harm about***, in which case the intervention is a superseding cause of harm.

Example 1: Defendant manufactures a cleaning compound which is highly explosive when exposed to flame. Mary accidentally drops a match into the compound causing it to explode and injure Plaintiff. Plaintiff asserts a claim, alleging that Defendant's negligence made the cleaning compound explosive, and that this negligence was a proximate cause of Plaintiff's injury. Defendant argues that Mary's intervention was a superseding cause of harm.

Since the alleged negligence created the likelihood of explosion, and since Mary's intervention precipitated the explosion, Mary's intervention probably was a concurring cause of Plaintiff's harm.

Example 2: In the above Example, assume that Mary knows that the compound is explosive and deliberately drops a match into the compound, intentionally causing it to explode and injure Plaintiff.

Since Mary deliberately dropped a match into the compound with the intent to cause an explosion, her intervention probably was a superseding cause of harm. For this reason, the defect in the product probably was not a legal cause, even though the harm which occurred is the type of harm of which the defect created a risk.

v. **Normal intervention:** Even if it is not foreseeable or common, an intervention is a ***concurring cause*** of harm if it is ***within the range of normal responses to a situation created by Defendant's conduct***. An intervention is a superseding cause of harm if it is so far outside the scope of what may be expected as to be regarded as an abnormal event.

Example 1: As a result of Defendant's negligent driving, she is unable to stop her car in time to avoid striking a cow. The cow is rendered unconscious but regains consciousness a few moments later and, crazed by pain, charges a crowd of onlookers, injuring Plaintiff. Plaintiff asserts a negligence claim against Defendant. Defendant argues that the cow's charge was a superseding cause of Plaintiff's injury.

Although the events which occurred may be highly unusual and, therefore, unforeseeable, the cow's conduct was within the scope of normal bovine responses to pain, and, therefore, probably was a concurring cause of harm.

Example 2: Plaintiff, an infant, is a passenger in an automobile manufactured by Defendant. As a result of Defendant's negligence, the horn in the car begins to sound and will not stop. Frightened to the point of hysteria, Plaintiff's mother throws Plaintiff from the car, intending to save her from being hurt. Plaintiff is injured and asserts a negligence claim against Defendant for her injuries. Defendant argues that the conduct of Plaintiff's mother was a superseding cause of the injury.

Although it probably is foreseeable that a passenger in an automobile will be frightened by the sound of a horn which will not stop sounding, and although it probably is foreseeable that she would therefore take some step to protect her infant child, the mother's response was probably so far outside the scope of normal behavior that it was a superseding cause of the injuries sustained by Plaintiff.

vi. **Negligent and criminal acts:** An intervention consisting of the ***negligent act of a third person is generally viewed as a concurring cause*** of harm because it is generally regarded as foreseeable that persons will be negligent. An intervention consisting of the ***criminal act of a third person is generally viewed as a superseding cause*** of harm because criminal acts are generally regarded as unforeseeable.

Note: These rules should be used as ***guidelines only***. In many cases, courts have found specific intervening acts of negligence to be so unforeseeable (or extraordinary, or independent, etc.) that they have held them to be superseding causes of harm. Similarly, many courts have found specific intervening criminal acts to be so foreseeable (or non-extraordinary, or dependent, etc.) that they have held them to be concurring causes of harm.

Example 1: Defendant railroad negligently allows gasoline to leak into the street. Mary is walking by when she carelessly drops her lit cigarette into the gasoline spill, causing an explosion which injures Plaintiff. Plaintiff asserts a negligence claim against Defendant, who argues that Mary's conduct was a superseding cause of the injury.

Since Mary's intervening act of dropping a lit cigarette into the gasoline was negligent, it probably was foreseeable and, therefore, a concurring cause of the explosion. For this reason, Defendant's negligence probably was a legal cause of Plaintiff's injury. *Watson v. Kentucky & Indiana Bridge & R.R.*, 126 S.W. 146 (Ky. 1910).

Example 2: In the above Example, assume that Mary deliberately throws a lit cigarette into the gasoline, intending to cause the explosion which injures Plaintiff.

Since Mary's act of dropping the lit cigarette into the gasoline was criminal, it probably was unforeseeable and, therefore, a superseding cause of the explosion. For this reason, Defendant's negligence probably was not a legal cause of Plaintiff's injury.

Example 3: Defendant physician negligently misdiagnoses Plaintiff's illness as syphilis. When Plaintiff tells her husband, he beats her, fracturing her jaw. Plaintiff asserts a negligence claim against Defendant, alleging that Defendant's negligence was a proximate cause of her fractured jaw. Defendant argues that the husband's attack was a superseding cause.

Generally, an intervening cause of harm is a superseding cause if it would not have been foreseen by the reasonable person. Ordinarily, it is held that criminal conduct is to be unforeseeable, and that, for this reason, if criminal conduct is an intervening cause of harm, it is a superseding cause.

However, many married persons become violent when they learn that their spouses have been unfaithful to them. For this reason, and since syphilis is a sexually transmitted disease, it may be argued that the husband's attack on Plaintiff was foreseeable even though it was criminal. If this argument succeeds, the husband's conduct will be held to be a concurring cause of Plaintiff's fractured jaw, and Defendant's negligence will be held to be a proximate cause of it. *Hensley v. Heavrin*, 282 S.E.2d 854 (S.C. 1981).

4. **Particular types of damage:** In the next section we will deal with the requirement of damage in torts cases. We will explain why certain types of damage are not ordinarily recoverable. Some cases argue that the injury of which the plaintiff complains is not recognized as damage. In other cases, the same result is reached by arguing that the conduct of which the plaintiff complains is not a proximate cause of the plaintiff's damage. For the sake of simplicity, we will discuss whether the injuries complained of are "damage". Students should recognize, however, that a discussion of whether the conduct complained of was a proximate cause of the injury sustained, would be equally correct.

Example: Plaintiff is pregnant when she develops rubella, a disease which causes deformities in babies born to pregnant women who contract it. Plaintiff consults with Defendant physician, explaining that if her baby is going to be born defective, she wants to abort the pregnancy. Defendant negligently performs diagnostic tests and erroneously concludes and advises Plaintiff that her baby will not be affected by the disease. Plaintiff does not abort the pregnancy and gives birth to a baby with physical defects which resulted from the rubella. Plaintiff asserts a malpractice claim against Defendant, alleging that his negligence was a proximate cause of the birth of a defective child.

The majority of jurisdictions would not permit Plaintiff to recover for damages resulting from the birth of her child. Some of the courts would explain their conclusion by saying that the birth of a child is not "damage" in a negligence case. Others would say that damage resulting from the birth of an unwanted child is not proximately caused by negligence. *Procanik v. Cillo*, 478 A.2d 755 (N.J. 1984).

CHAPTER 8

DAMAGE

I. IN GENERAL

A. Essential element of liability: With only a few exceptions (including battery, assault, false imprisonment, and trespass to land), damage is an essential element of all tort claims. This means that in most cases, there can be no recovery without proof of some actual damage. As noted, *supra*, p. 85, courts sometimes rule that in spite of conduct by the defendant which resulted in harm to the plaintiff, the plaintiff is precluded from recovery. Some courts justify this conclusion by holding that the defendant's conduct was not a proximate cause of the harm which the plaintiff sustained. Other courts hold that the plaintiff's harm was not "damage" as required by law.

B. "Damage" and "damages" distinguished: Semantic precision distinguishes between the terms "damage" and "damages". "Damage" refers to the harm or injury which the plaintiff sustained. "Damages" refers to a sum of money awarded to the plaintiff as a remedy for the damage which he sustained.

II. TYPES OF DAMAGES

A. Nominal damages: Nominal damages consist of a ***token sum of money — usually six cents or one dollar — which is awarded to a plaintiff who has made out a case but has failed to prove any actual damage***. Although there has been no actual loss, nominal damages are awarded to vindicate the plaintiff whose rights have been invaded. Since damage is an essential element of most tort cases, a plaintiff cannot usually make out a case without also establishing that he sustained actual damage. For this reason, nominal damages are not available in most tort cases.

B. Punitive or exemplary damages: Punitive or exemplary damages may be awarded to the plaintiff ***to punish or to make an example of the defendant, because the defendant's conduct was reprehensible or base***. Although the award is motivated by the defendant's conduct, the plaintiff is the beneficiary of the award. For this reason, the award is sometimes referred to as "smart money" and is said to be awarded for the purpose of easing the plaintiff's smart or sting.

1. **Intentional tort**: Since a defendant may be liable for an intentional tort without having any evil motive, punitive damages are ***not available in all intentional tort cases. If it can be shown***

that the defendant acted with malice, however, punitive damages may be available. For this purpose, "malice" is defined as ***ill will*** or ***a desire to cause harm***.

Example 1: As a joke, Defendant sets off a firecracker to frighten his friend Plaintiff by making her believe that shots are being fired at her. Plaintiff is so frightened that she has a heart attack. Plaintiff subsequently asserts a claim for assault, seeking compensatory and punitive damages.

Since Defendant desired that his act make Plaintiff apprehensive, Defendant had the intent necessary to make him liable for assault, and for compensatory damages. Since he meant to play a joke, his motive probably was not sufficiently malicious to make him liable for punitive damages.

Example 2: Knowing that Plaintiff suffers from heart disease and hoping to frighten her into having a heart attack, Defendant sets off a firecracker to make her believe that shots are being fired at her. Plaintiff becomes frightened, but does not have a heart attack. Plaintiff subsequently asserts a claim for assault, seeking compensatory and punitive damages.

Since Defendant desired to frighten Plaintiff, he had the intent necessary to be liable for assault. Since he desired to inflict injury, his motive probably was sufficiently malicious to make him liable for punitive damages as well.

Note: Liability for punitive damages does not depend on the seriousness of Plaintiff's injury, but rather on Defendant's state of mind.

2. **Aggravated negligence**: Since it is recognized that even a person with the best of motives may occasionally act unreasonably, punitive damages are ***not ordinarily available in negligence cases***. If it can be shown that defendant's conduct amounted to ***aggravated negligence or recklessness***, however, punitive damages may be available. As previously seen, aggravated negligence or recklessness consists of the willful disregard of an obvious risk with a high probability of serious harm (see *supra*, p. 86).

Example: Defendant, a manufacturer of cars, learns that, because of the placement of the gas tank, one of its models is very likely to burst into flames when struck in the rear at an impact speed in excess of thirty-five miles per hour. After determining that the cost of compensating victims will be less than the cost of redesigning the car, Defendant decides to continue manufacturing the cars with the gas tank so placed. Plaintiff is driving a car manufactured by Defendant when it is struck in the rear at an impact speed in excess of thirty-five miles per hour and bursts into flames, causing Plaintiff to be severely burned. Plaintiff asserts a claim for compensatory and punitive damages against Defendant.

Since Defendant wilfully disregarded an obvious risk with a high probability of serious harm, Defendant's conduct probably amounted to aggravated negligence. For this reason, Defendant probably is liable for punitive damages. *Grimshaw v. Ford*, 174 Cal. Rptr. 348 (1981) (*supra*, p. 86).

3. **Strict liability:** A plaintiff who sues on a strict liability theory may recover compensatory damages without showing fault on the part of the defendant (*supra*, p. 94). ***If the plaintiff seeks punitive damages***, however, the plaintiff must also ***show*** that the defendant's conduct was ***reckless***.

4. **Plaintiff must make out a case**: ***Punitive damages*** may ***not be*** awarded unless it is found that the plaintiff is entitled at least to ***nominal or compensatory damages***.

5. **Relationship to compensatory damages**: Some jurisdictions hold that the amount of punitive damages must bear some rational relationship to the amount of compensatory damages awarded to the plaintiff. Other jurisdictions hold that since punitive damages are based on the defendant's evil state of mind rather than on the harm suffered by the plaintiff, the amount awarded in punitive damages need not bear any relationship to the amount of compensatory damages awarded to the plaintiff.

6. **Relationship to defendant's wealth**: Since the primary purpose of punitive damages is to punish the defendant for improper conduct, and since the punitive effect of such an award is likely to vary with the defendant's personal wealth, many jurisdictions admit ***evidence of the defendant's personal wealth*** in order to help the jury determine what award would be appropriate.

7. **Functions of court and jury**: If a plaintiff asserts a claim for punitive damages the court must decide, after all the proof is in, whether an award of punitive damages will be permitted. Punitive damages are ***never available as of right***, however. This means that even if the court determines that punitive damages may be awarded, it will still be up to the jury to determine whether or not to award punitive damages.

8. **Minority view**: Since punitive damages are quasi-penal in nature, some courts hold that punitive damages may never be awarded in civil suits.

C. Compensatory damages: Compensatory damages consist of a sum of money awarded to the plaintiff ***to compensate her for the damage (i.e.***, harm) which she has sustained.

1. **General and special damages**: Compensatory damages are usually characterized as either general damages or special damages. ***General damages*** are awarded to compensate for damage which flowed ***as a natural and necessary consequence of the harm suffered, without regard to the particular circumstances or character of the plaintiff. Special damages*** are awarded to compensate for damage which flowed ***as a natural, but not a necessary consequence of the harm suffered by this plaintiff, requiring reference to the particular circumstances of the plaintiff***. (Different kinds of evidence are required for measuring and fixing general and special damages. This is best left for courses in Evidence and Remedies.)

 Example: As the result of Defendant's negligence, Plaintiff suffers a broken arm. Plaintiff is admitted to a hospital and treated by physicians. He experiences great physical pain and mental suffering. This makes it impossible for Plaintiff to attend to his ordinary activities, causing him to lose earnings and requiring him to hire a housekeeper. Plaintiff will be disabled for a long period of time and will continue to lose earnings as a result. He asserts a claim for damages against Defendant.

 Since a person with a broken arm will necessarily experience physical pain and mental suffering, and also the inability to attend to ordinary activities, these are all items of general damage and may be compensated as such.

 However, since a person with a broken arm will not necessarily be admitted to a hospital, lose past and future earnings, and hire a housekeeper, these are items of special damage caused by the plaintiff's special circumstances, and may be compensated as such.

2. **Functions of court and jury**: The amount of damages necessary to compensate a plaintiff for his damage is a question of fact and should be determined by the jury. Any question of fact may become a question of law, however, when reasonable minds would not differ as to its answer, or, as Judge Cardozo put it, when one conclusion and one only is permissible for rational and candid minds.

 Since the amount of damages necessary to compensate a plaintiff for personal injury will always be the subject of some disagreement among rational and candid minds, it is always the jury's function to fix this amount initially. It is possible, however, that rational and candid minds would all agree that the jury has awarded too much or too little to compensate the plaintiff properly. For this reason, a court may conclude as a matter of law that the jury's verdict is excessive or inadequate. In deciding that a verdict is excessive or inadequate, the court does not determine what amount should have been awarded. Instead, the court must decide what are the highest or the lowest limits upon which rational and candid minds would agree. Anything higher than the highest limit is excessive as a matter of law, and anything lower than the lowest limit is inadequate as a matter of law.

a. ***Remittitur***: A court which finds that a jury's verdict is excessive may enter judgment for a lower amount which the court decides is the maximum sum which rational and candid minds would find reasonable. Such a judgment is called a *remittitur.*

b. ***Additur***: A court which finds that a jury's verdict is inadequate may enter judgment for a higher amount which the court decides is the minimal sum which rational and candid minds would find reasonable. Such a judgment is called an *additur.*

c. **Alternatives**: As alternatives to *additur* or *remittitur,* a court may order a new trial on the issue of damages, or enter a conditional order granting a new trial unless the parties agree to settle for a sum named by the court.

Example 1: As the result of Defendant's negligence, and without any fault on the part of Plaintiff, Plaintiff sustains a simple fracture of his little finger. Plaintiff asserts a claim against Defendant, and the jury awards him one million dollars as compensatory damages. Defendant moves to set aside the verdict on the ground that it is excessive. The court determines that rational and candid minds would find that any sum above fourteen thousand dollars is excessive compensation for Plaintiff's fractured finger.

The court may enter a *remittitur,* reducing the award to fourteen thousand dollars. As an alternative, the court may order a new trial on the issue of damages or order a new trial unless the parties agree to settle for fourteen thousand dollars.

Example 2: As the result of Defendant's negligence and without any fault on the part of Plaintiff, Plaintiff is rendered permanently blind. Plaintiff asserts a claim against Defendant, and the jury awards him one hundred dollars as compensatory damages. Plaintiff moves to set aside the verdict on the ground that it is inadequate. The court determines that rational and candid minds would find that any sum below five hundred thousand dollars is inadequate compensation for Plaintiff's blindness.

The court may enter an *additur*, increasing the award to five hundred thousand dollars. As an alternative, the court may order a new trial on the issue of damages or order a new trial unless the parties agree to settle for five hundred thousand dollars.

3. **Avoidable consequences**: A defendant who is liable for the plaintiff's damage is ***not liable for complications or consequences which the plaintiff could have avoided by acting reasonably after the injury occurred***. Sometimes it is said that the plaintiff has a duty to ***mitigate*** (*i.e.*, minimize) her damage, and that the defendant is relieved of liability for damage resulting from the plaintiff's failure to do so.

   Example: As the result of Defendant's negligence, Plaintiff sustains an injury to the cartilage in her knee. If the injured cartilage remains in Plaintiff's knee, Plaintiff will walk with a limp for the rest of her life. The damaged cartilage can be surgically removed and full use of Plaintiff's knee restored, but Plaintiff refuses to submit to the surgery. Plaintiff asserts a negligence claim against Defendant in which she seeks damages to compensate her for a permanent limp.

   Since the permanent limp can be avoided if Plaintiff submits to surgery, a jury will have to decide whether the reasonable person would submit to surgery. If so, Plaintiff's refusal to do so is unreasonable and Defendant is not liable for damage resulting from the permanent limp (although Defendant would continue to be liable for the injury and for the pain and expenses associated with surgery). If, on the other hand, Plaintiff's refusal to submit to surgery is reasonable, Defendant will be liable for damage resulting from the permanent limp. *Zimmerman v. Ausland*, 513 P.2d 1167 (Or. 1973).

4. **Collateral sources**: The majority of jurisdictions hold that ***compensation which a plaintiff receives from a collateral source (i.e.***, not on behalf of a tortfeasor) is not relevant in measuring damages which the plaintiff is entitled to collect from the defendant.

   Example: As the result of Defendant's negligence, Plaintiff sustains a broken leg. Plaintiff's cousin, a physician, gives Plaintiff one thousand dollars worth of treatment without charge. Although Plaintiff is absent from work for a period of one month, his employer pays him a sum equal to his regular salary of one thousand dollars as a gesture of good will. Plaintiff also collects under an insurance policy which he owns and which calls for payment of one thousand dollars in the event the policy holder sustains a fracture of any limb.

Plaintiff asserts a claim against Defendant in which he seeks damages for pain and suffering and other damages including one thousand dollars for the reasonable value of medical treatment received and one thousand dollars in lost earnings. At the trial, Defendant attempts to offer evidence that the medical treatment which Plaintiff received was rendered without charge, and that Plaintiff's employer paid him a sum equivalent to his regular salary. Defendant also argues that since Plaintiff received one thousand dollars under his insurance policy, his award for pain and suffering should be reduced by this amount.

Since Plaintiff's employer, Plaintiff's insurer, and the physician who rendered medical treatment without charge were not tortfeasors and were not acting on behalf of tortfeasors, they were collateral sources. Under the collateral sources rule, the benefits which they gave to Plaintiff are not relevant in measuring the damages which Plaintiff is entitled to recover from Defendant. For this reason, the evidence which Defendant attempted to offer at the trial is not admissible, and Plaintiff's award for pain and suffering should not be reduced by the amounts which he has received.

5. **Taking plaintiff as found**: It has been said that a ***defendant takes the plaintiff as he finds her***. This means that a defendant is liable for the full extent of the injuries proximately caused by his conduct even though their severity may have resulted, in part, from an unusual pre-existing condition of the plaintiff.

Example: Plaintiff has a predisposition to schizophrenia which requires a precipitating factor to produce an occurrence of the disease. As the result of Defendant's negligence, Plaintiff sustains a minor physical injury in an automobile accident. The accident serves as the precipitating factor which brings on her schizophrenia. Plaintiff asserts a claim against Defendant seeking damages for her schizophrenia. Defendant argues that he is not liable for these damages because Plaintiff was already predisposed to schizophrenia.

Because of the rule that a defendant takes the plaintiff as he finds her, the fact that Plaintiff was already predisposed to schizophrenia does not relieve Defendant of the damage resulting from the outbreak of the disease.

If we examine the proximate cause aspects of this Example, it is possible to argue that since Defendant's conduct was a proximate cause of whatever harm was foreseeable in view of the existing circumstances, and since Plaintiff's predisposition to schizophrenia was an existing circumstance which made it foreseeable that an automobile accident would produce an occurrence of the disease, Defendant's negligence was a proximate cause of the occurrence. *Steinhauser v. Hertz Corp.*, 421 F.2d 1169 (2d Cir. 1970).

6. **Bodily injury**: Where appropriate, damages for injury to the plaintiff's body may be recovered under all theories of tort liability.

7. **Mental suffering**: Damages for mental suffering may be available, depending on the circumstances and the basis of tort liability.

   a. **Intentional tort**: Damages for mental suffering are available in tort actions for intentional interference with the person. These include battery, assault, and false imprisonment. In cases of intentional infliction of mental harm, however, some jurisdictions hold that the plaintiff's mental suffering can not be sufficiently severe to result in any liability unless that suffering has a physical manifestation. (*supra*, p. 19).

   b. **Negligence and strict liability**: In claims based on negligence or strict liability, damages for mental suffering are available according to the following rules:

      i. **Resulting from bodily injury**: All jurisdictions agree that damages may be recovered for mental suffering which ***results from injury to the plaintiff's body***.

   Example: As the result of Defendant's negligence, Plaintiff sustains a laceration of the face which results in a disfiguring scar. Plaintiff asserts a claim against Defendant in which he seeks damages for his injury, including compensation for the mental suffering which he experiences every time he sees his face in the mirror.

   Since Plaintiff's mental suffering is the result of a physical injury to his body which was proximately caused by Defendant's negligence, Plaintiff may recover damages to compensate him for his mental suffering.

      ii. **Physical manifestations**: If mental suffering is not the result of a physical injury to the plaintiff's body, a ***majority*** of jurisdictions holds that the plaintiff may recover damages for it if the mental suffering has a ***physical manifestation***.

   Example: Defendant operates his car in a negligent manner, almost striking John and Mary. Mary is so frightened that she has to be treated by a psychiatrist every day for four years. John becomes so frightened that he vomits many times. Both assert claims against Defendant.

Since John and Mary both experienced mental suffering which did not result from a physical injury, the majority of jurisdictions would permit them to recover damages only if their mental suffering had a physical manifestation. Since John's suffering caused him to vomit, and since vomiting is a physical manifestation, John may recover damages from Defendant. Since Mary's suffering, although severe, did not result in physical manifestations, Mary may not recover damages from Defendant.

iii. **Physical impact**: If mental suffering is not the result of a physical injury to the plaintiff's body, a small ***minority*** of jurisdictions holds that the plaintiff may recover damages for it only if the suffering resulted from some ***physical impact*** with plaintiff's body.

Example: As the result of Defendant's negligence, his car collides with a pole near where John and Mary are standing. Mary is so frightened by the noise of the collision that she requires psychiatric treatment. John is struck by a piece of Defendant's car. Although the contact does not injure him physically, he becomes so frightened by it that he requires psychiatric treatment.

Since John and Mary both experienced mental suffering which did not result from a physical injury, a small minority of jurisdictions would permit them to recover damages only if their mental suffering resulted from a physical impact with their bodies. Since Mary's body was not touched, she will be unable to recover damages from Defendant in these jurisdictions. Since John's mental suffering was accompanied by an impact with his body, he will be able to recover damages from Defendant in these jurisdictions.

iv. **Foreseeable mental suffering**: If mental suffering is not the result of a physical injury to the plaintiff's body, a ***small minority*** of jurisdictions holds that the plaintiff may recover damages for it ***if the mental suffering was a foreseeable result of the defendant's conduct***.

Example: As the result of the negligence of Defendant physician, Plaintiff's wife is incorrectly diagnosed as having a sexually transmitted disease. Since she has not engaged in sexual intercourse with any man other than Plaintiff, she concludes that she contracted the disease from him and that he has been unfaithful to her. As a result, she divorces Plaintiff. Plaintiff experiences severe mental suffering because of the divorce and because he believes that his wife contracted the disease by being unfaithful to him.

Since Plaintiff's mental suffering did not result from a physical injury and did not have a physical manifestation, the majority of jurisdictions would not permit him to recover damages from Defendant.

But since married persons who contract sexually transmitted diseases frequently suspect their spouses of infidelity, and since such a belief usually leads to anguish and marital difficulties, it probably was foreseeable that the spouse of a person negligently misdiagnosed as having such a disease would experience mental suffering. For this reason, a minority of jurisdictions would permit Plaintiff to recover damages from Defendant. *Molien v. Kaiser Foundation Hosp.*, 616 P.2d 813 (Cal. 1980).

v. **Phobias:** In some jurisdictions, a phobia (*i.e.*, a chronic, abnormal fear of something) which a plaintiff develops as the result of a defendant's conduct, but not necessarily as the result of a physical injury, is a form of mental suffering for which the plaintiff may recover damages, subject to the above principles.

Example: After working for twenty years as an installer of insulation manufactured by Defendant, Plaintiff learns that frequent and prolonged exposure to ingredients in the insulation is likely to cause cancer. Although Plaintiff does not develop cancer, he experiences "cancerphobia", a chronic, abnormal fear that he will develop cancer. His cancerphobia makes it impossible for him to work and causes him to require treatment by a psychiatrist, but it does not cause any physical manifestations. Plaintiff asserts a strict products liability claim (*infra*, P. 233) against Defendant on the ground that the presence of cancer-causing ingredients in the product is a defect which makes the product unreasonably dangerous. The court agrees.

Some jurisdictions would not regard Plaintiff's cancerphobia as sufficient mental suffering to entitle him to damages under any circumstances. Other jurisdictions would regard Plaintiff's cancerphobia as mental suffering and would permit or deny recovery according to the rules stated *supra*, p. 135.

In the majority of jurisdictions, Plaintiff would not be permitted to recover damages from Defendant because his mental suffering did not have a physical manifestation.

In the minority which requires physical impact, Plaintiff would be permitted to recover damages from Defendant on the theory that his handling of the insulation satisfied the requirement of a physical impact with his body.

In the minority which permits recovery for foreseeable mental suffering, Plaintiff may be permitted to recover damages from Defendant if the court finds that cancerphobia is a foreseeable result of the presence of cancer-causing substances in the insulation which Plaintiff installed for twenty years. *Jackson v. Johns-Manville*, 781 F.2d 394 (5th Cir. 1986).

vi. Observing harm to another: If a plaintiff experiences mental suffering as the result of observing physical injury to another person, many jurisdictions continue to apply one or another of the general rules outlined *supra*. Other jurisdictions have developed special rules, however, which they apply either instead of these rules or in combination with them.

Note: Some cases have treated this as a question of whether the defendant owed the plaintiff a duty of reasonable care (*supra*, p. 57). Other cases have treated this as a proximate cause problem.

aa. Zone of physical danger: In the ***majority*** of jurisdictions, a person who injures another is liable for damage suffered by observers only if they are in the ***zone of physical danger*** (*i.e.*, in an area in which physical injury to them is foreseeable) (*supra*, p. 57).

bb. Three-part test: In a ***minority*** of jurisdictions, a person who injures another is liable for damage suffered by observers who are not in the zone of physical danger so long as they are ***closely related*** to the injured person, are ***nearby*** when the injury occurs, and ***perceive the injury with their own senses*** (*supra*, p. 57).

cc. Foreseeable mental suffering: In a ***small minority*** of jurisdictions, a person who injures another is liable for damage suffered by observers who are not in the zone of physical danger if it is ***foreseeable that they will experience mental suffering*** as a result of the injury inflicted by the defendant (*supra*, p. 57).

Example: Defendant is driving his car at an excessive rate of speed when he strikes and injures Child, a seven year old, who is crossing the street with Sis, her sister. Child's mother, Mom, is watching from a second story window overlooking the street, as is Fred, a close family friend. As a result of seeing Child struck and injured by Defendant's car, Sis, Mom and Fred experience serious mental suffering. They subsequently assert negligence claims against Defendant.

Since Sis was crossing the street with Child, she, too, could have been struck and injured, and so was within the zone of physical danger. In some jurisdictions, this would be sufficient to permit her to recover damages for her mental suffering. In other jurisdictions, she would be eligible to recover damages from Defendant only if her mental suffering had a physical manifestation. In jurisdictions which apply the impact rule, she could recover for her mental suffering only if there was some physical impact with her body.

Since Mom and Fred were inside a building, on the second story, it was very unlikely that they would be physically injured by Defendant's car. This means that they probably were not within the zone of physical danger. For this reason, the majority of jurisdictions probably would hold that Defendant is not liable to them for their mental suffering.

Since Mom was closely related to Child, was nearby when the accident occurred, and perceived it with her own senses, a minority of jurisdictions would allow her to recover damages for her mental suffering even though she was not within the zone of physical danger. Some of these would make her recovery subject to the rules regarding physical manifestation and physical impact.

Although Fred was nearby and perceived the accident with his own senses, he was not closely related to Child. For this reason, most jurisdictions would hold that Defendant is not liable for Fred's mental suffering. In a very small minority, it would be held that Defendant might be liable if it was foreseeable that striking Child would cause Fred to experience mental suffering. In making this determination, Fred's presence at the time of the accident, his closeness to the family, and his having perceived the accident with his own senses are facts to be considered. All of the jurisdictions in this minority have dispensed with the requirements of physical manifestation and physical impact. *Dillon v. Legg*, 441 P.2d 912 (Cal. 1968) (*supra*, p. 57-58).

8. **Death**: The death of an injured plaintiff may require consideration of two distinct concepts in tort law: the survival of personal injury actions, and the recovery of damages resulting from wrongful death. To avoid confusion, we should have a separate understanding of each.

   a. **Survival of personal injury actions**: At one time, it was generally understood that the right to sue for injuries to the body was so personal that the plaintiff's death, from any cause, terminated that right and resulted in the dismissal of any cause of action already instituted by the decedent. Today, however, most jurisdictions regard the right to sue for personal injuries as inheritable property. This means that when an injured person dies, her right to sue for the injuries which she sustained prior to her death does not terminate, but survives (*i.e.*, outlives) her and is inherited by her heirs and distributees.

i. **Survival statutes:** In most jurisdictions, the survival of a personal injury claim results from the provisions of statutes. Since these statutes vary from one jurisdiction to another, it is always necessary to check the existing "survival statute" in the jurisdiction in question. In general, survival statutes treat a right to sue as an item of property which is inherited in the same way as any other item of property. This means that if the decedent died testate (*i.e.*, with a will), the provisions of his will may determine who inherits the lawsuit. If the decedent died intestate (*i.e.*, without a will), the laws of intestate distribution will determine who inherits the lawsuit. In some jurisdictions, the survival statutes themselves determine who inherits the lawsuit, or specify that the lawsuit is to be brought by the decedent's personal representative (*i.e.*, administrator, administratrix, executrix, executor) for the benefit of persons specifically identified by the statute.

ii. **Case law:** In some jurisdictions, the survival of a personal injury action is not the result of statute but of judicial decision. These jurisdictions also vary in the details controlling survival of actions, making specific research necessary. In general, however, the rules which have developed judicially are similar to those which have developed by statute.

iii. **Cause of death**: The survival of personal injury actions is based on the recognition that a right to sue for personal injury damages is an item of property which should be inheritable as is any other item of property. For this reason, the survival of a personal injury action does not depend on the cause of the decedent's death. Thus, an action may survive whether the decedent died from the injuries which furnish the basis of the action or from unrelated causes.

Example: As the result of Defendant's negligence, decedent sustains a fracture of his toe. Two months later, after the toe has completely healed, decedent is struck by lightning and dies.

Since decedent died while owning the right to assert a claim against Defendant for damages resulting from the injury to his toe, the right to sue will survive him, and the lawsuit may be brought for the benefit of the appropriate heir, even though the death was unrelated to the injury which gave rise to the right of action.

iv. **Institution of action**: Some survival statutes provide that an action survives death only if it had already been instituted at the time of the decedent's death. In most jurisdictions, however, the right to sue survives even if no action had been instituted prior to the decedent's death.

v. **Recoverable damages**: In general, the surviving personal injury action protects the same rights which the decedent would have had if she had not died, and permits recovery of whatever damages the decedent would have been able to recover at the moment before her death.

Example: As the result of an explosion at Defendant's dynamite factory, decedent sustains serious personal injuries which cause physical pain and mental suffering, cause decedent to lose earnings, and require treatment by a physician. Under the statutes of the jurisdiction, Plaintiff asserts an appropriate surviving personal injury claim against Defendant on a strict liability theory.

If Plaintiff is successful, she may recover damages for the pain and suffering experienced by decedent, as well as for decedent's lost earnings and medical expenses.

vi. **Defenses**: Since the surviving personal injury action is identical to the action which the decedent would have brought had he lived, it is generally understood that any defenses which could have been raised against the decedent can be raised against the plaintiff.

Example: Defendant is a manufacturer of automobiles. As a result of Defendant's negligence, the door latch on an automobile which it manufactured does not function properly. Wilma's husband Harold is driving the automobile without wearing a seat belt when the automobile is struck by another car. Because the door latch does not function properly, Harold is ejected from the car, striking the pavement and sustaining an injury to his head. If Harold had been wearing a seat belt, he would have sustained no injury at all. Harold subsequently dies due to causes unrelated to the injury. Under an appropriate statute in the jurisdiction, Wilma institutes a surviving personal injury action against Defendant. Defendant claims that it was unreasonable for Harold to drive without a seat belt and attempts to assert the defense of comparative negligence against Wilma in the action.

Since the surviving personal injury action brought by Wilma is identical to the action which Harold would have brought had he survived, Defendant can assert a defense based on Harold's negligence, even though Harold is not the plaintiff in the action.

b. **Wrongful death**: In causing the death of another person, a defendant may be inflicting serious economic injury on the decedent's dependents. With this in mind, a nineteenth century English statute known as ***Lord Campbell's Act*** declared that defendent's tort might be a tort against the decedent's spouse, children, and parents if the decedent's death denied them financial support on which they had previously relied. After the English Parliament's enactment of this law, every one of the United States adopted a similar rule. As a result, the tort known as ***"wrongful death"*** is now recognized in every state.

   i. **Variations**: Although the tort of wrongful death was originally the creature of statute in every U.S. jurisdiction, there are now several courts which hold that it has become part of the common law. Either way, its details vary from state to state, requiring specific research to determine the form which it takes in any particular jurisdiction.

   ii. **Concept**: In concept, wrongful death is based on the understanding that by tortiously causing the death of a human being, a defendant has committed a tort against the interests of certain surviving relatives of the decedent.

   iii. **Interests protected**: The majority of jurisdictions hold that wrongful death is an invasion of economic interests only. This means that a wrongful death plaintiff can only recover damages resulting from economic losses. In general, these include the costs of disposing of the decedent's remains, as well as the loss of financial benefit which the plaintiff would have derived from the decedent's continued life. In a minority of jurisdictions, however, the wrongful death plaintiff may also be able to recover damages resulting from the grief occasioned by the decedent's death.

Example: As the result of a battery committed by Defendant against Plaintiff's mother, Plaintiff's mother dies. Had Plaintiff's mother lived, she would have contributed a total of seventy thousand dollars to Plaintiff's support in the course of Plaintiff's lifetime. As a result of his mother's death, Plaintiff experiences severe mental suffering and requires treatment by a psychiatrist. Plaintiff asserts a wrongful death claim against Defendant on a battery theory.

In the majority of jurisdictions, Plaintiff's recovery is limited to his pecuniary loss — the seventy thousand dollars which his mother would have contributed to his support in the course of his lifetime and whatever it cost him to bury her. A minority of jurisdictions, however, would also allow him to recover damages to compensate him for his mental anguish and his expenses in treating it.

iv. **Parties**: All jurisdictions agree that the wrongful death action is available for the benefit of the decedent's surviving spouse, children, and parents. Some jurisdictions add other relatives to this list. In some jurisdictions, the action must be brought on behalf of these beneficiaries by the decedent's personal representative, while in other jurisdictions the beneficiaries may bring the action on their own behalf.

v. **Stillbirth**: In many jurisdictions, the parents of a stillborn child (*i.e.*, a child born dead) may recover for wrongful death. Other jurisdictions hold that since the child never lived independently of its mother, it was not a human being, and that, therefore, there is no action for wrongfully causing its death.

vi. **Cause of death**: Since the essence of this tort is that the defendant has injured the plaintiff by causing the decedent's death, the plaintiff must show that the decedent's death proximately resulted from the defendant's conduct.

vii. **Defenses**: Since the action for wrongful death is based on a claim that the defendant wrongfully caused the death of the decedent, the defendant may raise any argument which would prove that the decedent's death was not the result of defendent's tort. For this reason, any defense which could have been asserted against decedent in an action brought on his own behalf can be raised in the wrongful death action.

Example: Defendant mechanic negligently repairs the brakes on the automobile of Plaintiff's wife, who drives the car although she knows that the brakes are not working properly. As a result, she is involved in a collision which causes her death. Plaintiff asserts a negligence claim against Defendant for wrongfully causing the death of his wife.

Since the decedent knew of the risk and voluntarily encountered it, it may be argued that she assumed the risk, and that Defendant is, therefore, not legally responsible for her injury. If this argument is successful, it will defeat the rights of Plaintiff, even though Plaintiff did not, himself, assume any risk at all.

viii.Damages: Since the tort of wrongful death is committed by causing the decedent's death, recovery is permitted only for damages resulting from the death. For this reason, *they begin to accrue at the moment of death.*

aa. Compared to surviving personal injury actions: Since the surviving personal injury action is identical to the action which the decedent had at the moment of her death, and since the decedent can not have sustained damage after death, in a surviving personal injury action damages stop accruing at the moment of the decedent's death. On the other hand, since the wrongful death action is for damage resulting from the decedent's death, damages for wrongful death begin to accrue at the moment of death.

bb. Limitation: Some wrongful death statutes impose limits on the amount of damages which may be recovered for wrongful death.

c. Election and merger: In most jurisdictions, surviving personal injury actions and wrongful death actions are distinct causes of action and may coexist without limitation. According to statutes in some jurisdictions, however, an ***election*** must be made between actions. A potential plaintiff is required to choose one or the other. In other jurisdictions, the two actions merge into one.

d. Rights of creditors: Since the surviving personal injury action is, in effect, a lawsuit which belonged to the decedent but has been inherited by someone else, creditors of the decedent are entitled to collect against the proceeds of the surviving personal injury action. On the other hand, since the wrongful death action never was the property of the decedent, creditors of the decedent have no rights against its proceeds.

Example: As the result of an explosion in Defendant's dynamite factory, Mary is injured. The following day, Mary dies of her injuries. At the time of Mary's death, she owed five thousand dollars to Creditor. Mary's will leaves all her property to her husband, Plaintiff. Under statutes existing in the jurisdiction, Plaintiff asserts Mary's surviving strict liability claim against Defendant, and asserts a wrongful death claim on his own behalf against Defendant on a strict liability theory. Plaintiff wins both claims, receiving an award of four thousand dollars in the surviving personal injury claim and an award of ten thousand dollars in the wrongful death claim. Creditor now seeks to collect from the proceeds of these claims.

Since the surviving personal injury claim was Mary's property at the time of her death, Creditor is entitled to collect against it and may receive the entire four thousand dollars (assuming that there are no creditors with superior rights). Although one thousand dollars of Mary's debt to Creditor remains unpaid, Creditor is not entitled to collect it from the proceeds of the wrongful death claim, since these funds never belonged to Mary.

9. **Loss of consortium**: It is generally recognized that a married person is entitled to the ***society, services, and sexual attentions*** of his spouse. This bundle of rights is known as "consortium." In many jurisdictions, if a defendant wrongfully injures a plaintiff's spouse in a way which interferes with the plaintiffs right of consortium, the plaintiff is entitled to recover damages resulting from that loss. Some jurisdictions do not recognize this right at all. Among those which do, most recognize that such damages may be recovered by a wife who has been deprived of her husband's consortium, as well as by a husband who has been deprived of his wife's consortium. For questionable historical reasons, some jurisdictions hold that such damages are only available to a husband.

Example: As the result of negligence by Defendant, Plaintiff's husband sustains an injury to his back. Prior to the injury, Plaintiff and her husband enjoyed spending time together watching television. In addition, Plaintiff's husband used to prepare dinner for her three nights a week, and they used to engage in sexual relations. Since the injury, the time they spend together is no longer enjoyable; he is unable to prepare dinner; and he is in too much pain to engage in sexual relations. Plaintiff asserts a negligence claim against Defendant for loss of consortium.

Since Defendant's conduct resulted in an interference with Plaintiff's rights to her husband's society, services, and sexual attention, Defendant has wrongfully interfered with her right of consortium. In some jurisdictions, damages are never recoverable for interference with this right. In other jurisdictions, damages may be recovered only by a husband who has lost the right to his wife's consortium. In these two groups of jurisdictions, Plaintiff may not recover for the loss of her husband's consortium. In some jurisdictions, however, Plaintiff will be entitled to recover damages from Defendant to compensate her for interference with her right of consortium. .

10. Fetal injuries: All jurisdictions agree that a ***child born with injuries which were inflicted prior to birth and which resulted from the defendant's conduct may recover*** damages for those injuries. Some jurisdictions hold that such a cause of action is available only if the child had reached a particular stage of fetal development before sustaining the pre-natal (*i.e.*, before birth) injury.

a. **Requirement of viability**: In some jurisdictions, no recovery is permitted unless the fetus was ***viable*** at the time the injury was inflicted. For this purpose, a fetus is viable if it was ***capable of independent life*** if separated from its mother.

b. **Requirement of quickening**: In some jurisdictions, no recovery is permitted unless the fetus had begun ***quickening*** prior to the time the injury was inflicted. For this purpose, quickening begins when the fetus begins to ***move independently within the womb*** (*i.e.*, the sensation which many pregnant mothers describe when they say, "the baby is kicking").

c. **Stillborn children**: All jurisdictions agree that ***no cause of action exists on behalf of a fetus which is not born alive***.

Example: As the result of negligence by Defendant, a woman is injured while pregnant with twins, whom she has decided to name Jacob and Esau. At the time of the injury, the twins have begun to "kick" within the womb, but would not be capable of independent life if separated from their mother. As a result of the injury, Jacob is stillborn (*i.e.*, born dead). Esau is born alive, but with a permanent disability of the arm. Claims are brought on behalf of Jacob and Esau.

Since Jacob was not born alive, all jurisdictions would agree that no cause of action is available on his behalf. Some jurisdictions would permit the mother to maintain a wrongful death action for damages which she sustained as the result of Jacob's stillbirth; others would not. See discussion of *wrongful death* (*supra*, p. 142).

Since Esau was born alive with a pre-natal injury which resulted from Defendant's conduct, he may be permitted to recover damages from Defendant. In jurisdictions which allow recovery for pre-natal injuries sustained after quickening, he will be permitted to recover, since he had begun to kick (*i.e.*, quicken) prior to the injury. In jurisdictions which allow recovery only for pre-natal injuries sustained after the fetus becomes viable, he will not be permitted to recover since at the time the injury was inflicted he was not yet capable of independent life.

d. **Pre-conception injuries**: A small minority of jurisdictions permits a child to recover for injuries with which the child was born as the result of a tort committed against the child's parent(s) prior to the child's conception.

Example: Defendant is the manufacturer of a defoliant used to kill plants. Because of Defendant's negligence, persons who are exposed to the product suffer damage to their chromosomes (*i.e.*, the parts of reproductive cells which control an offspring's characteristics). Plaintiff's father sustains chromosome damage as a result of exposure to Defendant's product. Unaware of the chromosome damage, Plaintiff's father subsequently engages in sexual intercourse which results in the conception of Plaintiff. As a result of the damage to his father's chromosomes, Plaintiff is born with permanent disability and asserts a claim for resulting damages.

In a few jurisdictions, Plaintiff may be permitted to recover damages from Defendant for his injuries even though they were inflicted prior to Plaintiff's conception. Based on *In Re Agent Orange Product Liability Litigation*, 597 F.Supp. 740 (E.D.N.Y. 1984).

11. **Wrongful life:** If a defendant's conduct causes a child to be born who otherwise would not have been born, most jurisdictions hold that the child is not entitled to recover damages for her "wrongful life." It is said that to measure damages, it would be necessary to compare the value of being born with the value of not being born, and that since it is impossible to imagine what it means not to be born, it is impossible to make this comparison. In effect, then, these courts are saying either that being born is not an injury or that if it is, it is not an injury for which damages can be fixed.

    A small minority of jurisdictions has granted recovery to a child who was born as a result of a defendant's conduct. So far, all such cases have involved children ***born with birth defects***. Damages consist of the sum necessary to compensate the child for the pain, suffering, and discomfort resulting from the birth defect.

12. **Wrongful birth:** If a defendant's conduct causes a plaintiff to give birth to (or become the father of) a child which otherwise would not have been born, most jurisdictions hold that the parent is not entitled to recover damages for the "wrongful birth." A rationale given for this holding is that to measure damages it would be necessary to compare the value of becoming the parent of such a child with the value of not becoming the parent of such a child, and that since it is

impossible to appreciate all the blessings of parenthood it is impossible to make this comparison.

In effect, then, such courts are saying either that becoming the parent of an unwanted child is not an injury or that, if it is, it is not an injury for which damages can be fixed. ***A small minority of jurisdictions has permitted recovery by a plaintiff who became the parent of an unwanted child as the result of a defendant's conduct***. So far, all such cases have involved a child ***born with birth defects***. Damages consist of the difference between the cost of raising a normal child and the cost of raising the child with birth defects.

Example 1: As the result of Defendant's negligence, a birth control device manufactured by Defendant fails, causing Martha and Fred to conceive a child which they do not want to have. Charity, the child, is born healthy and normal.

Since Charity is healthy and normal, no jurisdiction will permit Charity to recover damages for wrongful life, or permit Martha and Fred to recover damages for wrongful birth.

Example 2: Tay-Sachs disease is a hereditary and congenital illness which disables an infant and substantially shortens its life. Mary, who has a history of Tay-Sachs disease in her family, conceives a child with her husband Ferdinand. While pregnant, Mary asks Defendant, her doctor, to perform a test to determine whether the fetus in her womb will be born with Tay-Sachs disease. It is her intention, and Ferdinand's, to abort the pregnancy if the test results are positive. As the result of negligence by Defendant, the test results are negative. Based on the result, Mary and Ferdinand decide not to abort. In fact, the child, Channing, is born with Tay-Sachs disease. (Defendant's negligence did not cause the disease, but induced the parents' decision not to abort.) Channing is a helpless invalid and she dies of the disease at the age of five years. Mary and Ferdinand assert a wrongful birth claim, and Channing asserts a wrongful life claim against Defendant on a negligence theory.

The majority of jurisdictions would not permit any of the plaintiffs to recover damages from Defendant, on the ground that no injury had been sustained. A small minority of jurisdictions would permit Mary and Ferdinand to recover damages consisting of the difference between the expenses of raising a normal child and the expenses of raising Channing. A smaller minority would permit Channing to recover damages to compensate her for the pain, suffering, and discomfort occasioned by the disease. *Curlender v. Bio-Science*, 165 Cal. Rptr. 477 (1980).

13. **Property damage:** Damages to compensate a plaintiff for damage to his property consist of: the ***reasonable cost of repair***ing the damaged property, the ***reduction in the property's value*** resulting from the damage, or the ***total value*** of the property immediately prior to the damage, ***whichever is the least***.

Example: Defendant is driving negligently when he strikes Plaintiff's parked car, causing it to be seriously damaged. Plaintiff's vehicle was worth two thousand dollars before the accident and is worth one hundred dollars after the accident. For three thousand dollars, it can be restored to the condition in which it was before the accident. Plaintiff asserts a negligence claim against Defendant for the damage to his automobile.

Since the value of the vehicle before the accident was two thousand dollars and after the accident was one hundred dollars, the property has been reduced in value by one thousand nine hundred dollars. Since this is less than either the total value of the car immediately prior to the accident (*i.e.*, two thousand dollars) or the cost of repair (*i.e.*, three thousand dollars), Plaintiff may recover one thousand nine hundred dollars.

14. **Commercial losses:** ***Lost profits or other financial losses*** which do not result from injury to the plaintiff's person or property are generally ***not items*** for which a plaintiff can recover damages in actions founded on ***negligence or strict liability*** theories.

Example: In the previous Example, assume that as the result of the damage to Plaintiff's car, Plaintiff is unable to get to a business meeting where he would have earned ten thousand dollars in profits, and that Plaintiff asserts a negligence claim against Defendant for his lost profits.

Since Plaintiff's theory is negligence, and since damages for lost profits ordinarily are not available in a negligence claim, Plaintiff probably will be unable to recover from Defendant.

CHAPTER 9

VICARIOUS LIABILITY

I. IN GENERAL

A. Concept: Ordinarily, a defendant is legally responsible only for damage which results proximately from his own conduct. In special situations, however, the relationship between a defendant and another person may make the defendant legally responsible for damage which results proximately from that other person's conduct. When this happens, the defendant is said to be ***"vicariously liable"***. ("Vicarious" means through or by identification with another.) Sometimes it is said that the defendant is responsible for the tortfeasor's act by "imputed negligence", or that the tortfeasor's negligence is imputed to the defendant. ("Imputed" means attributed.) Since the relationship between a defendant and a tortfeasor may result in the imposition of liability on defendant no matter what conduct is involved, we will use the general phrase "vicarious liability" instead of the more limited "imputed negligence".

B. No vicarious liability without tort: Since the concept of vicarious liability does nothing more than make one person responsible for the tort of another, there can be ***no vicarious liability unless a tort has been committed***. For this reason, the defendant ordinarily will not be vicariously liable unless the tortfeasor is herself liable.

> **Example:** While acting within the scope of his employment, John, a clerk in Defendant's department store, sells Plaintiff an ax. John is not negligent and his conduct is not tortious in any other way. The ax is fit for ordinary use and is not defective. Plaintiff is using the ax when she cuts herself on its blade. Plaintiff asserts a claim against Defendant, alleging that the relationship between Defendant and John makes Defendant vicariously liable for Plaintiff's injury.
>
> Since John did not engage in any tortious conduct, he would not be liable for Plaintiff's injury. Since John would not be liable, Defendant cannot be held vicariously liable.

C. Encompasses all theories of liability: So long as the relationship between defendant and tortfeasor is sufficient to impose vicarious liability on the defendant, it will be imposed ***regardless of the plaintiff's theory of recovery***.

> **Example:** While attempting to collect a bill, John, an employee of Defendant, deliberately punches Plaintiff, intending to injure

her. Plaintiff is injured and asserts a battery claim against Defendant, alleging that the relationship between Defendant and John makes Defendant vicariously liable for John's tort.

Since John intended to make harmful contact with Plaintiff and did so, he will probably be liable to her for battery. If John was acting within the scope of employment for Defendant (see *respondeat superior*, *infra*, p. 152), Defendant is vicariously liable to Plaintiff for John's battery. *Murrell v. Goertz*, 597 P.2d 1223 (Okla. Ct. App. 1979).

D. Defenses: Because vicarious liability will not be imposed unless a tort was committed, a defendant against whom a plaintiff seeks to impose vicarious liability, may raise any defense which could be raised by the tortfeasor.

> **Example:** Plaintiff is injured when her car collides in an uncontrolled intersection with the vehicle operated by Defendant's employee, John. Both Plaintiff and John were driving negligently at the time of the accident. Plaintiff asserts a claim against Defendant, arguing that he is vicariously liable for John's negligence under the doctrine of *respondeat superior.* Defendant raises the defense of contributory negligence, in a jurisdiction which applies the "all or nothing" rule (*supra*, p. 87).
>
> If Plaintiff had sued John, John would have been entitled to assert contributory negligence as a defense. Since Plaintiff seeks to hold Defendant vicariously liable for John's conduct, Defendant can raise any defense which John could have raised. Since the jurisdiction applies the "all or nothing" rule, and since Plaintiff's negligence contributed to the accident, judgment will probably be entered for Defendant.

E. Not a defense: The fact that someone else is vicariously liable for a tort does not prevent the tortfeasor from being liable for his own act as well. For this reason, the ***vicarious liability of another is never a defense***.

F. Indemnity: All jurisdictions recognize that when one person has been held vicariously liable for a tort committed by another, he ***is entitled to indemnity (i.e.***, repayment) from the one who actually committed the tort.

> **Example:** Mary, a chef employed in Defendant's restaurant, negligently permits a toxic ingredient to get into food which she is preparing for Plaintiff, a customer of the restaurant. As a result, Plaintiff is injured. Plaintiff asserts a claim against Defendant, alleging that Defendant is vicariously liable for Mary's negligence. Finding that the relationship between Defen-

dant and Mary is sufficient to make Defendant vicariously liable for Mary's negligence, the court enters judgment for Plaintiff against Defendant. After satisfying the judgment, Defendant asserts a claim against Mary for indemnity.

Since Mary caused the loss for which Defendant was required to compensate Plaintiff, Defendant is entitled to indemnity from Mary. The court should award judgment for Defendant against Mary in the sum which Defendant was required to pay Plaintiff (and, in some jurisdictions, for certain expenses incident thereto).

II. RESPONDEAT SUPERIOR

A. General concept: Under the doctrine of ***respondeat superior***, an employer is vicariously liable for certain acts and omissions of her employees.

B. Essential elements: The essential elements of respondeat superior are: (1) the tortfeasor was an ***employee of the defendant***, and (2) when the tort was committed, the employee was acting within the ***scope of employment***.

1. **Employer**: In applying the doctrine of respondeat superior, an "employer" is anyone who hires or employs another to perform services.

2. **Employee**: An employer is vicariously liable for torts committed by a person working for him ***only if that person is an employee***. For this reason, it is often necessary to distinguish between one who works as an employee and one who works as an independent contractor. Courts take many factors into consideration in making this determination.

   a. **Control of details**: The most important factor in determining whether the tortfeasor was employed as an employee or as an independent contractor is the extent of the ***right of the employer to control details of the work*** being performed. If the worker has the right to control details of the work being performed, the worker is more likely to be considered an independent contractor. If the employer has the right to control details of the work being performed, the worker is more likely to be considered an employee.

   Example 1: Defendant is a manufacturer of widgets. Mary is employed by Defendant to sell the widgets door-to-door. Each morning, Defendant phones Mary to tell her where to sell that day and during what hours. Frequently, Defendant tells Mary how to dress when carrying out that day's assignment. From time to time, Defendant furnishes Mary with a printed sales "pitch" which Mary is required to use when discussing the product with customers. As a result of Mary's negligence, Plaintiff is injured by a widget which Mary sold her. Plaintiff asserts a negligence claim against Defendant, alleging that under the doctrine of respondeat superior Defendant should be held vicariously liable for Mary's negligence. Defendant argues that the doctrine of respondeat superior should not be applied because Mary is an independent contractor.

Since Defendant selected the location and hours where Mary was to sell each day, and told Mary what to wear when selling, and what words to use when discussing the product, a court probably would find that Defendant had the right to control the details of Mary's work. For this reason, Mary probably was an employee and the doctrine of respondeat superior probably would be applied.

Example 2: Defendant is a manufacturer of widgets. Mary is employed by Defendant to sell the widgets door-to-door. Each morning, Mary decides where to sell that day and during what hours. Mary decides how to dress most effectively to carry out each day's work. Although Defendant makes suggestions by furnishing Mary with a printed sales "pitch", Mary is expected to use her own judgment in deciding what to say when discussing the product with customers. As the result of Mary's negligence, Plaintiff is injured by a widget which Mary sold her. Plaintiff asserts a negligence claim against Defendant, alleging that under the doctrine of respondeat superior Defendant should be held vicariously liable for Mary's negligence. Defendant argues that the doctrine of respondeat superior should not be applied because Mary was an independent contractor.

Since Mary selected the location where she would sell each day and the hours of work, and decided what to wear when selling and what words to use when discussing the product, a court probably would find that Mary had the right to control the details of her own work. For this reason, Mary probably was an independent contractor and the doctrine of respondeat superior would not be applied.

b. **Negotiating with contractor**: Even in employing an independent contractor, an employer may determine some details of the work by negotiating for conditions in the contract between them. This does not make the worker an employee, since the conditions of work were the result of negotiation and agreement by the parties prior to the commencement of the work. If, however, the contract is such that the employer has the ***right to add or change conditions*** after the work has begun, the contractor is more likely to be classified as an employee.

Example: Defendant is a manufacturer of widgets. John and Fred are employed by Defendant to sell the widgets door-to-door. It is agreed that John and Fred will wear ties every day, have their shoes shined at least twice per week, and drive cars no more than five years old. It is further agreed that they will not begin selling before 9 AM or continue selling past 9 PM. Each morning, Defendant phones John to tell him where to sell that day and during what hours. Frequently, Defendant tells John what colors to wear when carrying out that day's assignment. From time to time, Defendant furnishes John with a printed sales "pitch" which John is required to use when discussing the product with customers.

Each morning, Fred himself decides where to sell that day and during what hours. Fred decides what colors to wear to most effectively carry out each day's work. Although Defendant makes suggestions by furnishing Fred with a printed sales "pitch", Fred is free to use his own judgment in deciding what to say when discussing the product with customers. As the result of negligence by John and Fred, Plaintiffs are injured by widgets which John and Fred sold them. Plaintiffs assert negligence claims against Defendant, alleging that under the doctrine of respondeat superior, Defendant should be held vicariously liable for the negligence of John and Fred. Defendant argues that the doctrine of respondeat superior should not be applied because John and Fred were independent contractors.

Since Defendant selected the location and hours of John's workday, and told John what colors to wear when selling, and what words to use when discussing the product, a court probably will find that Defendant had the right to control the details of John's work. For this reason, John probably was an employee, and the doctrine of respondeat superior will be applied.

Although Defendant had bargained for certain conditions (*e.g.*, requiring tie and late model car), Fred selected the location and hours of his work day, and decided what colors to wear when selling and what words to use when discussing the product. For this reason, a court probably will find that Fred had the right to control the details of his own work. Therefore, Fred probably was an independent contractor, and the doctrine of respondeat superior will not be applied.

c. **Furnishing tools**: The furnishing of tools or implements of work is another, less important, factor which courts consider in deciding whether a worker is an employee or independent contractor. A worker who furnishes her own tools is more likely to be regarded as an independent contractor than one to whom tools are furnished by the employer.

d. **Method of payment**: A worker who is paid by time unit (*e.g.*, hour, week, month, year) is more likely to be regarded as an employee than a worker who is paid for a result.

Example: Defendant employs John and Fred as used car salesmen. John is paid $100 per day regardless of his sales. Fred is paid a commission of 5% of the price of every car he sells.

Since John is paid by the day and Fred is paid for sales (*i.e.*, results), John is more likely to be regarded as an employee and Fred is more likely to be regarded as an independent contractor.

3. **Scope of employment**: The doctrine of respondeat superior makes an employer vicariously liable for an employee's tort, but only if the employee was acting ***within the scope of employment*** at the time the tort was committed. In deciding whether an employee was acting within the scope of employment, courts consider the factors of ***benefit and control***.

a. **Benefit**: An employee was not acting within the scope of employment unless at the time the tort was committed, his conduct was ***intended or likely to benefit the employer***.

i. **Actual benefit not required**: In deciding whether conduct was intended to or likely to benefit the employer, the courts do not consider whether the employer actually received benefit, but whether the conduct was ***consistent with an intent to benefit the employer***.

Example: Tender is employed as manager of Defendant's tavern. One night, after taking out the trash, Tender negligently burns it in an alley behind the tavern. The fire spreads, damaging the tavern and Plaintiff's building which is next door. Plaintiff asserts a claim against Defendant, alleging that Defendant should be held vicariously liable for the negligence of Tender. Defendant argues that Tender was not acting within the scope of employment, because his act damaged rather than benefitted Defendant.

Since Tender's purpose was to dispose of trash from Defendant's tavern, his act was intended to benefit Defendant. The fact that it actually damaged Defendant does not take the act out of the scope of employment. For this reason, Defendant probably will be held vicariously liable for the damage sustained by Plaintiff. *Poydras v. Parker*, 392 So.2d 94 (La. App. 1980).

ii. Incidental needs of employee: For the purpose of applying the doctrine of respondeat superior, an employer may be said to receive a benefit even when an employee leaves the job temporarily to satisfy a ***personal need***, so long as the need is ***incidental to the employment*** and the employee cannot reasonably be expected to work without satisfying it.

Example: John, who is employed as quality control inspector in Defendant's widget factory, is required to examine every widget as it comes off the production line. One day, because he is hungry, John leaves the production line to get a sandwich, allowing several widgets to be packaged without inspection and failing to discover a flaw in one of them. Plaintiff is injured when the flaw causes the widget to explode while she is holding it. Plaintiff brings a claim against Defendant, asserting that Defendant should be held vicariously liable for John's negligence. Defendant argues that John was not acting within the scope of employment when he failed to inspect the widgets, because Defendant derived no benefit from John's conduct.

A court may hold that since an employee cannot be expected to work without eating, John was conferring a benefit on Defendant even when he went for a sandwich, and, therefore, was still acting within the scope of employment. If it comes to this conclusion, the court will apply the doctrine of respondeat superior.

iii. Independent frolic: An employee who acts for ***reasons which are purely personal and not in any way related to the employer's business is sometimes said to be on an "independent frolic," and not acting within the scope of employment***.

Example: Manny, who is employed as manager of Defendant's supermarket, sends Plaintiff a package containing a dead rat instead of the loaf of bread which she had ordered. Plaintiff experiences mental suffering and asserts a claim against Defendant, alleging that it should be held vicariously liable for Manny's tort. At the trial, there is conflicting testimony, one witness stating that Manny sent the dead rat as a joke, and another witness stating that Manny sent the package containing the rat by mistake, thinking it contained a loaf of bread.

If Manny knew that the package contained a rat and sent it as a joke, he probably was acting for his own amusement rather than to benefit his employer. If so, Manny may be said to have been on an independent frolic, and Defendant will not be held vicariously liable for his tort.

If Manny sent the package by mistake, thinking that it contained the loaf of bread which Plaintiff had ordered, his act was intended to benefit Defendant, and Defendant probably will be held vicariously liable for Manny's tort (*i.e.*, negligence). *Great A & P v. Roch*, 153 A. 22 (Md. 1931).

b. Control: An employee is not acting within the scope of employment unless, at the time the tort was committed, the employer had the ***right to control the employee's behavior***.

Example 1: John is employed by Defendant as an engineer on a project located 80 miles from John's home. During the week, John stays at a hotel near the jobsite, but on weekends he drives home. Defendant compensates John for the use of his car to drive to and from his home on weekends. One weekend, while driving home from the jobsite, John negligently collides with Plaintiff's car, causing Plaintiff to sustain injury. Plaintiff asserts a claim against Defendant, alleging that Defendant should be held vicariously liable for John's negligence. Defendant argues that John was not acting within the scope of employment at the time of the accident.

Although Defendant compensated John for the use of his car while driving to and from his home while John was commuting, Defendant probably had no right to tell John how fast to drive or what route to take, or otherwise to control his conduct. For this reason, John probably was not acting within the scope of his employment, and Defendant is not vicariously liable for his negligence. *Lundberg v. State*, 306 N.Y.S.2d 947 (1969).

Example 2: Mary, who is employed by Defendant as a salesperson, travels to a sales convention in a distant town. Before she leaves, Defendant tells Mary that during her free time while at the convention, she should socialize as much as possible with more experienced salespersons. One evening, Mary drives from the hotel where the convention is being held to a bar, for the purpose of socializing with other salespersons. While driving back to the hotel, she negligently strikes and injures Plaintiff. Plaintiff asserts a claim against Defendant, alleging that Defendant should be held vicariously liable for Mary's negligence. Defendant argues that Mary was not acting within the scope of employment while traveling from a bar to her hotel.

Since Defendant instructed Mary to socialize during her free time, it may be argued that Defendant probably had the right to exercise control over Mary's conduct during the entire time that she was away for the convention. For this reason, we may conclude that Mary was acting within the scope of employment, and Defendant probably is vicariously liable for her negligence. *Fruit v. Schreiner*, 502 P.2d 133 (Alaska 1972).

i. **Power to control not required**: So long as an employer has the *right* to control the employee's behavior, it is ***immaterial that the employer lacked the ability to exercise such control***.

Example: John is employed as a clerk in Defendant's grocery store. While Defendant is away from the store, John is operating the cash register when Plaintiff, a customer, enters the store and, as a joke, says "Stick 'em up." Believing that the store is being robbed, John shoots Plaintiff. Plaintiff asserts a claim against Defendant, alleging that Defendant should be held vicariously liable for John's tort. Defendant argues that he should not be vicariously liable because he was not present to control John's conduct.

Since John was working in Defendant's store, Defendant had the right to tell John how to behave. Thus, although Defendant lacked the ability to exercise control over John in his absence, he had the right to exercise such control. For this reason, John probably was acting within the scope of employment, and Defendant is vicariously liable for John's tort. *Frederick v. Collins*, 378 S.W.2d 617 (Ky. 1964).

ii. **Violation of employer's instructions**: So long as the employer has a right to exercise control over the employee's behavior, the ***employee may be acting within the scope of employment even when violating the employer's instructions or orders***.

Example: Mike is employed as manager of Defendant's supermarket. Defendant has repeatedly instructed Mike not to take any action at all against suspected shoplifters. After observing Plaintiff, a twelve year old girl, steal a piece of penny candy, Mike takes five dollars from her, beats her, hangs her by her wrists from a roof rafter, threatens her with a pistol, displays her to other customers, and refuses to let her go until her mother pays a ransom. Plaintiff asserts a claim against Defendant, alleging that Defendant should be held vicariously liable for Mike's torts. Defendant argues that Mike was not acting within the scope of employment because he violated specific instructions from Defendant.

Although Mike violated his employer's instructions, Defendant had the right to give such instructions. Mike was thus subject to Defendant's control. Since his conduct was designed to discourage shoplifting, it was intended to benefit Defendant. For these combined reasons, Mike probably was acting within the scope of employment, and Defendant is vicariously liable for his torts. *Great A & P v. Dowling*, 159 S.E. 609 (Ga. 1931).

III. INDEPENDENT CONTRACTORS

A. In general: Although the employer of an independent contractor is not generally liable for the torts of the contractor, ***there are some situations in which a person who employs an independent contractor may be held vicariously liable for the contractor's torts***.

B. Particular risk: If an independent contractor is employed to perform a job with which ***a particular risk*** is associated, the employer may be held vicariously liable for damage resulting from the ***contractor's unreasonable conduct in the face of that particular risk***.

Example: Defendant ice cream company employs Mary as an independent contractor to sell ice cream to children from an ice cream truck. As the result of Mary's negligence in operating her truck, Plaintiff, a child seeking to purchase ice cream from Mary, is injured. Plaintiff asserts a claim against Defendant, alleging that Defendant should be held vicariously liable for Mary's negligence. Defendant argues that it should not be vicariously liable because Mary was an independent contractor.

Since selling ice cream to children from a truck involves certain risks which are peculiar to that kind of enterprise, it may be successfully argued that Defendant should be held vicariously liable for Mary's negligence in the face of those risks, even though she is an independent contractor. *Wilson v. Good Humor Corp.*, 757 F.2d 1293 (D.C. Cir. 1985).

C. Non-delegable duty: If a ***statute or administrative regulation creates*** a duty to provide specified safeguards for the protection of others, an employer who hires an independent contractor to provide those safeguards may be held vicariously liable for the contractor's negligence in doing so. In justifying this conclusion, courts sometimes say that the defendant had a ***"non-delegable duty."***

Example: Defendant hires Mary, an independent contractor, to repair the brakes on Defendant's automobile. Mary does so in a negligent manner. As a result, Defendant is unable to stop her car and collides with Plaintiff's car, injuring Plaintiff. A statute in the jurisdiction requires all vehicles driven on public highways to have brakes which function properly. Plaintiff asserts a claim, alleging that Defendant is vicariously liable for Mary's negligence in repairing the brakes. Defendant argues that she should not be held vicariously liable for Mary's negligence because Mary is an independent contractor.

Since the statute imposed the obligation to have effective brakes as a safeguard to other users of the highway, it may be argued that it created a non-delegable duty. If this argument is successful, Defendant will be held vicariously liable for Mary's negligence, even though she was an independent contractor. *Maloney v. Rath*, 71 Cal. Rptr. 897 (1968).

D. Extremely dangerous activities: A landholder who employs an independent contractor to work on the land at an ***activity for which strict liability is imposed*** (*supra*, p. 100), is vicariously liable for damages resulting from the independent contractor's activity.

Example: Defendant, who is having a swimming pool built in his yard, hires Blastco to dynamite rock. Although Blastco acts reasonably, shockwaves from the explosions cause damage to the home of Plaintiff, Defendant's neighbor. Plaintiff asserts a strict liability claim against Defendant, alleging that blasting is an abnormally dangerous activity and that Defendant is vicariously liable for the damage caused by it. Defendant argues that he is not vicariously liable for damage resulting from Blastco's activity because Blastco was an independent contractor.

Since blasting with explosives is usually regarded as an ultra- hazardous or abnormally dangerous activity for which strict liability is imposed, and since Defendant hired Blastco to engage in that activity on Defendant's realty, Defendant may be held vicariously liable for resulting damage, even though Blastco was an independent contractor.

E. Employer's negligence: Sometimes, when the negligence of an independent contractor results in harm to a plaintiff, it is possible to show that the employer of that contractor was also negligent. In such a case, the essence of the plaintiff's claim is not that vicarious liability should be imposed on the employer, but rather that some element of the ***employer's negligent conduct*** was, itself, a proximate cause of the plaintiff's harm.

1. **Negligent selection**: If an employer of an independent contractor fails to use reasonable care in selecting the contractor, she may be liable for the proximate results of her ***selection***.

2. **Negligent management**: If an employer of an independent contractor fails to use reasonable care in instructing, supervising, or

inspecting the work of the contractor, she may be liable for the proximate results of her negligent ***management***.

> **Example:** Defendant is a retailer of bicycles. The bicycles are delivered to Defendant in a dismantled condition and Defendant employs Bilder, an independent contractor, to put them together before Defendant sells them to customers. Although Defendant is aware that Bilder has no experience in assembling bicycles, Defendant gives Bilder no instructions and does not supervise Bilder's work in any way. Without inspecting it, Defendant sells Plaintiff a bicycle which was assembled by Bilder. Because the bicycle was improperly assembled, it collapses soon after Plaintiff begins using it, causing Plaintiff to sustain injury. Plaintiff asserts a negligence claim against Defendant.
>
> Since Bilder was an independent contractor, vicarious liability under the doctrine of respondeat superior will not be imposed on Defendant for Bilder's negligence. If a jury finds, however, that Defendant acted unreasonably in the way it selected Bilder for the job, or that Defendant's failure to instruct or supervise Bilder's work was unreasonable, or that it was unreasonable for Defendant to sell Plaintiff the bicycle without inspecting it, Defendant may be held liable to Plaintiff for its own negligence.

IV. ENTERPRISE LIABILITY

A. General concept: The relationship between persons participating together in a business activity may make one vicariously liable for the tort of another.

B. Enterprise liability: ***Members of a joint enterprise are vicariously liable for torts committed by other members of the joint enterprise acting within the scope of the enterprise.***

1. **Joint enterprise defined**: For the purpose of determining whether vicarious liability should be imposed, a joint enterprise is defined as an ***undertaking for profit*** by two or more persons who ***agree to share control*** over the undertaking.

> **Example:** Defendant and John are co-owners of an airplane which they fly for pleasure. Each has an equal say in how the plane is to be used. One day Defendant, Plaintiff, and John go up in the plane as part of a volunteer search and rescue operation. While John flies, Defendant and Plaintiff observe the ground below with binoculars. As a result of John's negligence, the plane crashes, causing Plaintiff to sustain injury. Plaintiff asserts a

claim against Defendant, alleging that he and John were joint enterprisers, and that, therefore, Defendant was vicariously liable for John's negligence.

Although Defendant and John were involved in a joint undertaking, and although they shared the power to decide how the plane was to be used, their undertaking had no profit motive. For this reason, joint enterprise liability probably will not be applied. *Shoemaker v. Estate of Whistler*, 513 S.W.2d 10 (Tex. 1974).

C. Members of commercial chain usually not joint enterprisers: Unless some special agreement exists between them, members of a chain of commercial distribution (*i.e.*, manufacturer, wholesaler, retailer) ordinarily are not involved in a joint enterprise.

Example: Defendant is a retailer of electrical appliances. He purchases them at wholesale prices from manufacturers and resells them at a profit to the general public. As the result of negligence by the manufacturer, a toaster sold by Defendant has a sharp and jagged edge. Plaintiff, who purchases the toaster from Defendant, cuts her hand on the sharp edge while using it. Plaintiff brings a claim against Defendant, asserting that Defendant should be held vicariously liable for the manufacturer's negligence.

Since Defendant simply purchased toasters for resale from the manufacturer, Defendant probably had no control over the manufacturing process. Similarly, the manufacturer who simply sold the toasters to Defendant probably had no control over the retailing process. For this reason, Defendant was not involved in a joint enterprise with the manufacturer and, therefore, will not be held vicariously liable for the manufacturer's negligence. Defendant may be liable under other products liability theories (*infra*, p. 209 *et seq.*).

D. Concert of action: Even where persons have not agreed to a joint undertaking and have not agreed to share control, a court may find that they are engaged in a ***concert of action*** sufficient to make each vicariously liable for the other's torts as if they were joint enterprisers. For this purpose, a concert of action may be found to exist when one person ***aids, assists, or tacitly encourages*** another in accomplishing a commercial purpose.

Example: Defendant, a drug manufacturer, applies for and receives government permission to sell DES, a synthetic hormone used in attempting to prevent miscarriage. Other drug manufacturers receive government permission to sell DES by imitating Defendant's application. Plaintiff is injured as the result of a defect common to all DES, but is unable to identify the manufacturer of the particular DES tablets which injured her. Plaintiff asserts a strict products liability claim against Defendant, arguing that Defendant was involved in a concert of action with all other manufacturers of DES and that vicarious liability should, therefore, be imposed on Defendant, no matter which manufacturer made the particular tablets which injured Plaintiff.

Since all drug manufacturers who manufactured and sold DES had received government permission to do so by imitating Defendant's application, it may be found that Defendant tacitly encouraged them in their enterprise. If so, a court may decide that Defendant was involved in a concert of action with all the other manufacturers of DES. The result of such a finding would be the imposition of vicarious liability on Defendant for the actions of the manufacturer which actually did produce the tablets that injured Plaintiff, even though Plaintiff may be unable to establish which manufacturer that was. *Bichler v. Eli Lilly*, 450 N.Y.S.2d 776 (1982).

CHAPTER 10

NUISANCE

I. GENERAL CONCEPT

A. Subject of confusion: Although the names given to torts usually suggest the nature of the defendant's conduct, the term ***"nuisance"*** does not. This has led to so much confusion about the law of nuisance that Dean William Prosser once wrote that in the entire law of torts there is no jungle more impenetrable than that which surrounds the term "nuisance."

B. Characterization of right invaded: One of the reasons the law of nuisance is surrounded by confusion is that instead of describing the defendant's conduct, the term "nuisance" characterizes the right which was invaded.

C. Two separate torts: Further confusion results from the fact that there are actually two separate areas of tort liability which are covered by the term "nuisance." These are ***"public nuisance"*** and ***"private nuisance"***. In truth, the only thing that they have in common is that they both employ the word "nuisance" and are both torts.

D. Public and private nuisance distinguished: A ***"public nuisance"*** is a liability-forming invasion of ***some right of the general public***. A ***"private nuisance"*** is a liability-forming invasion of the ***plaintiff's right to use and enjoy real property***.

E. Liability forming conduct: As we have already discussed, there are three kinds of conduct which the law of torts recognizes as liability forming: ***intentional conduct, negligent conduct, and conduct for which strict liability may be applied*** (*supra*, p. 3, *et seq.*). Any of these may be the basis of an action for nuisance if the conduct results in the necessary invasion of right.

1. **Intent**: A nuisance is based on ***intentional*** conduct ***if the defendant acted with a desire (or knowledge to a substantial certainty) that his conduct result in an invasion of a public right (public nuisance) or of the plaintiff's right to use and enjoy his realty (private nuisance)***.

   Example: In the city of Towne, Defendant operates a refinery which emits obnoxious odors and gases. Defendant is unaware that gases from the plant are making residents of Towne sick and are killing shrubs which grow on Plaintiff's realty. Plaintiff, a resident of Towne, tells defendant about the damage to his shrubs. After being so informed, Defendant continues to operate the refinery without making any change in the method of operation, causing residents of Towne to become sicker and causing more of Plaintiff's shrubs to die.

Since the gases from Defendant's refinery made the residents of Towne sick, they probably invaded a public right. Since they killed shrubs growing on Plaintiff's realty, they probably invaded Plaintiff's right to use and enjoy the realty.

So long as Defendant was unaware of these effects, however, her invasion of those rights was not intentional. After being informed by Plaintiff, Defendant knew that her conduct was invading the public right to clean air and Plaintiff's right to use and enjoy his realty. For this reason, the invasions which occurred after Defendant was informed were intentional. *Morgan v. High Penn Oil Co.*, 77 S.E.2d 682 (N.C. 1953).

2. **Negligence**: A nuisance is based on ***negligence if the invasion of a public right (public nuisance) or of the plaintiff's right to use and enjoy realty (private nuisance) resulted from the defendant's failure to act reasonably in the face of a foreseeable risk.***

Example: In the city of Towne, Defendant operates a refinery which emits obnoxious odors and gases. Defendant is unaware that gases from the refinery are making residents of Towne sick and are killing shrubs which grow on Plaintiff's realty, but the reasonable person in Defendant's situation would have expected this to happen. Defendant could avoid emitting odors and gases by equipping the smokestacks of her refinery with a low-cost device which will remove them from the emissions, but Defendant fails to do so.

Since the reasonable person would have expected that the operation of Defendant's refinery would invade the public's right to clean air and Plaintiff's right to use and enjoy his realty, the risk of such invasion was foreseeable. Since Defendant could have avoided the harm by installing a low-cost device and failed to do so, Defendant's conduct probably was unreasonable. For these reasons, Defendant's conduct probably was negligent.

3. **Strict liability**: A nuisance may be based on ***strict liability if the invasion of a public right (public nuisance) or of the plaintiff's right to use and enjoy realty (private nuisance) results from the defendant's participation in an activity for which strict liability is imposed.***

Example: In the city of Towne, Defendant operates an explosives factory. Each day, Defendant tests his product in a reasonable manner by setting off explosions. The resulting shock waves frighten residents of Towne and reduce the property value of realty owned by Plaintiff in Towne. Defendant is unaware that his conduct is causing these results.

Since the public is entitled to feelings of security, Defendant's conduct probably invaded a public right by inducing fright. In addition, it probably invaded Plaintiff's right to use and enjoy realty by reducing the value of his realty. Because Defendant was unaware that his conduct was producing those results, the invasions of right were not intentional. Because Defendant behaved in a reasonable manner, his conduct was not negligent. Since the use of explosives is usually regarded as an ultra-hazardous or abnormally-dangerous activity, however, it is one for which strict liability may be imposed. For this reason, it may be the basis of claims for public and private nuisance.

F. Invasion of right: Like all torts, both kinds of nuisance involve an invasion of right. Unlike most other torts, however, ***no invasion of right can be termed a nuisance unless it is substantial***. For this purpose, an invasion of right is substantial if it will ***seriously inconvenience the ordinary person*** (*e.g.*, a person making ordinary use of land).

Example 1: Defendant, a church, rings its bell every half hour during daylight. Plaintiff, who is recuperating from an illness and needs to sleep all day, complains that the ringing of the bell interferes with the public's right to peace and quiet, and, therefore, is a public nuisance.

Unless the invasion of a public right is substantial, it does not constitute a public nuisance. An invasion of public right is not substantial unless the ordinary member of the public would be inconvenienced by it. Since most people do not sleep during the daytime, and since the ringing of a church bell is generally enjoyable, the ordinary member of the general public probably would not be substantially inconvenienced by Defendant's conduct. For this reason, it probably is not sufficiently substantial to be a public nuisance. *Rogers v. Elliot*, 15 N.E. 768 (Mass. 1888).

Example 2: Defendant is the operator of a racetrack which features horse racing at night. To illuminate the races, Defendant turns on lights nine times per night for approximately two minutes each time. Plaintiff operates a drive-in motion picture theater next to Defendant's racetrack. Because Defendant's lights cast as much light as a full moon, Plaintiff's customers are unable to see the movie screen when they are on. This causes a decrease in Plaintiff's business. Plaintiff asserts a claim for private nuisance.

The invasion of Plaintiff's right is not sufficiently substantial to constitute a private nuisance unless Defendant's conduct would seriously inconvenience an ordinary person in the use of his land (*i.e.*, a person making ordinary use of land). Since the light of the full moon nine times per night for two minutes each time probably would not seriously inconvenience an ordinary person in the ordinary use of land, Defendant's lights probably do not constitute a private nuisance. *Amphitheaters v. Portland Meadows*, 198 P.2d 847 (Or. 1948).

II. PUBLIC NUISANCE

A. Definition: A ***public nuisance*** is an invasion of a right of ***the general public*** which results from conduct of the defendant.

1. **Public right**: A right of the general public is a right which all members of the public are entitled to exercise.

   Example: Defendant intentionally obstructs a public highway. Since all members of the general public are entitled to make use of public highways, Defendant's conduct is an invasion of a right of the general public.

2. **Not necessary that entire public be affected**: If the right invaded is one which the entire public is entitled to exercise, it is a public right even though not all members of the general public actually exercise it.

   Example: As part of a religious ceremony, Defendant handles poisonous snakes and passes them around among members of his congregation.

   Since poisonous snakes endanger the public safety, the entire public is entitled to protection against them. Thus, by exposing even a few members of the public to poisonous snakes, Defendant invaded a public right. *Swann v. Pack*, 527 S.W.2d 99 (Tenn. 1975).

B. Criminal consequences: Although modern law defines a crime as a violation of a penal statute, a crime can be conceptually defined as "any act done in violation of those duties which an individual owes to the community." *Black's Law Dictionary*, Fifth Ed. Since a public nuisance is an invasion of a public right, it necessarily involves a violation of a duty owed to the community and is more properly regarded as a crime than a tort. In most jurisdictions, statutes in general terms prohibit intentional or negligent invasions of public rights, characterizing such invasions as "nuisances" or "public nuisances."

C. **Public nuisance as a tort**: Since damage to the public is likely to result from any invasion of a public right, conduct which constitutes a public nuisance may be classified as a tort as well as a crime.

1. **Kinds of invasion**: Invasions of public right which have been called public nuisances include interferences with the public health, safety, morals, comfort, and convenience.

2. **Public is plaintiff**: In a public nuisance tort action, the injured party is the general public. For this reason, the ***public is usually the plaintiff***.

3. **Representation by public attorney**: Since the public is the plaintiff, the action for public nuisance is usually brought on its behalf by a public officer who is designated as the public attorney.

4. **Remedies**: Remedies available to the public for a public nuisance include ***damages and injunction***.

a. **Damages**: Damages for public nuisance are calculated to compensate the general public for the harm which it has sustained. The damages thus recovered are paid into the public treasury for the benefit of the entire public.

b. **Injunctions**: When damages are not a sufficient remedy, the public may also be entitled to equitable relief in the form of an injunction directing the defendant to refrain from the conduct which resulted in the nuisance or to modify the conduct to avoid further interference with the public right.

Example: Defendant's power plant emits noxious gases which drift over Chicago, causing pollution of the air. This affects residents by interfering with their health, safety, and comfort.

A public nuisance claim may be asserted on behalf of the people of Chicago. If so, it should be brought by the city attorney or such other public official as is designated to represent the people of the city. If successful, the plaintiff should receive a judgment for damages to compensate the people of Chicago for harm which has resulted from the pollution of its air. In addition, since damages are probably not a sufficient remedy in the face of continuing emissions of gases by Defendant, the plaintiff probably is entitled to an injunction directing Defendant to avoid further emission of the gases. *City of Chicago v. Commonwealth Edison*, 321 N.E.2d 412 (Ill. 1974).

5. **Action by private individual**: A private individual may maintain an action for public nuisance ***if a public nuisance existed***

which caused him to sustain damage different from that sustained by the general public.

a. **Damage different in kind**: In order to maintain a private action for public nuisance, the plaintiff must show that the harm which he sustained was ***different in kind and not merely in degree*** from that sustained by the general public. In effect, this means that the plaintiff's harm must be so far outside the limits of the harm sustained by the public that damages to compensate for his harm would not be included in damages recovered by the public in its action.

Example 1: Defendant maintains a settling pond which emits noxious gases which make residents of the nearby town sick and uncomfortable. Inhalation of the gases results in the death of Plaintiff's decedent. Plaintiff asserts a private claim for public nuisance, seeking compensation for the death of decedent.

Since Defendant's conduct resulted in sickness and discomfort among the general public, the public attorney may assert a claim for public nuisance in which she seeks to recover damages to compensate the public for its sickness and discomfort. Since Plaintiff's decedent was the only member of the public who died, however, his death was different from the harm sustained by the general public. For this reason, the public attorney may not seek compensation for the death of Plaintiff's decedent in the public nuisance action. This establishes that the harm sustained by Plaintiff's decedent was sufficiently different from the harm sustained by the general public as to permit recovery for it in Plaintiff's private action for public nuisance. *Hosmer v. Republic Iron*, 60 So. 801 (Ala. 1913).

Example 2: Defendant negligently pollutes the bay, poisoning fish and making it impractical to engage in commercial or pleasure fishing. Plaintiff, a commercial fisherman, asserts a private claim for public nuisance, seeking damages to compensate him for the loss of his livelihood.

Since all members of the general public had the right to fish in the bay, Defendant may argue that Plaintiff, who fishes more than most other members of the public, has sustained harm which is different only in degree, but not in kind, from that sustained by the general public. If this argument is successful, Plaintiff should not be permitted to maintain a private action for public nuisance. *Burgess v. M/V Tamano*, 370 F. Supp. 247 (D. Me. 1973).

On the other hand, since the general public ordinarily fishes only for pleasure, and since Plaintiff fishes for a livelihood, Plaintiff may argue that his harm (*i.e.*, interference with his livelihood) is different in kind and not merely degree from that sustained by the general public (*i.e.*, interference with pleasure). If this argument is successful, Plaintiff should be permitted to maintain a private action for public nuisance.

b. **Damages only**: Since the basis of the plaintiff's claim is that she has sustained "particular" or "special" damage (*i.e.*, damage different from that of the general public) as the result of a violation of the public's right, most jurisdictions hold that the plaintiff is entitled to recovery only for that damage. Since the right violated was a public right, only the public is entitled to seek injunctive relief.

Example: In the Example (*supra*, p. 169), citing the case of *Hosmer v. Republic Iron*, Plaintiff may recover damages for the death of his decedent. Only the public attorney suing on behalf of the residents of the town may seek an injunction against further maintenance of the pond.

III. PRIVATE NUISANCE

A. **Definition**: A private nuisance is an interference with the plaintiff's right ***to use and enjoy realty*** which results from the defendant's liability-forming conduct.

B. **Distinguished from trespass**: Although some authorities define private nuisance as a non-trespassory invasion of the right to use and enjoy real property, an intrusion onto realty may be a private nuisance. The requirements of substantial interference (*supra*, p. 166) and unreasonable interference (*infra*, p. 173) make it more difficult to establish a claim for private nuisance than a claim for trespass. For this reason, if the defendant's conduct constitutes a trespass to land (*supra* p. 20, *et seq.*), there may be no need to treat it as a private nuisance. There are, however, invasions which cannot be classified as trespass.

1. **Intent requirement**: In modern law, trespass to land is an intentional tort in that it requires the desire (or knowledge) by the defendant that her conduct result in a physical contact with the realty involved. Nuisance liability, however, may be founded on intent, negligence ***or*** strict liability.

2. **Physical entry**: Trespass to land requires a physical entry onto the plaintiff's realty. If such an entry occurs, the defendant who intentionally causes it may be held liable for almost any kind of resulting damage. If no such entry occurs, however, the defendant cannot be held liable on a trespass theory. On the other hand, pri-

vate nuisance involves an invasion of the plaintiff's right to use and enjoy the realty, without regard to whether the invasion results from a physical entry.

Example: Defendant operates a smelter with knowledge that the operation results in the emission of gases and particulate matter (*i.e.*, particles too small to be detected by the human senses) which settle on Plaintiff's realty, reducing its value. Plaintiff asserts claims for trespass to land and for private nuisance.

Although there are a few decisions to the contrary, most jurisdictions hold that gases and substances which cannot be detected by the human senses are not sufficiently tangible to constitute an entry onto realty. Thus, even though Defendant intended that its conduct cause these substances to go onto Plaintiff's land, most jurisdictions would not impose trespass liability.

On the other hand, since the settling of these substances caused the value of Plaintiff's realty to be reduced, it interfered with Plaintiff's use and enjoyment of the realty, and, therefore, may have been a private nuisance. *Bradley v. American Smelting & Refining Co.*, 709 P.2d 782 (Wash. 1985) (*supra*, p. 23).

C. Distinguished from negligence and strict liability claims: Negligence and strict liability may be the bases of a private nuisance claim. If so, the plaintiff must prove the elements of negligence or strict liability in establishing that the defendant's conduct was wrongful. The requirements of substantial interference and unreasonable interference make it more difficult to establish a claim for private nuisance than a claim for negligence or strict liability, however. For this reason, if the plaintiff can make out a claim for negligence or strict liability, there is no reason to call it a private nuisance. Since there are certain kinds of damage which ordinarily are not recoverable in negligence or strict liability claims, however, it may be necessary for the plaintiff to argue that the defendant's negligence or participation in an ultra-hazardous or abnormally dangerous activity resulted in a private nuisance.

1. **Economic losses**: Ordinarily, economic losses which are not connected with damage to persons or property are not recoverable in actions based on negligence or strict liability. If the defendant's negligent conduct or his participation in excessively dangerous activities resulted in an interference with the plaintiff's right to use and enjoy realty, Plaintiff's damage may be recoverable in an action for private nuisance.

2. **Peace of mind**: Ordinarily, damages for mental suffering are not recoverable in an action based on negligence or strict liability unless

the mental suffering is associated with a physical injury or the manifestation of a physical injury. If the mental suffering results from an interference with the plaintiff's right to use and enjoy realty, however, it may be recoverable in an action for private nuisance.

Example: Defendant operates an explosives factory in the vicinity of Plaintiff's property. As the result of Defendant's negligence, an explosion occurs at the factory which does no physical damage to Plaintiff's realty. Following the explosion, Plaintiff is frightened that there may be another explosion which will injure him and his family. This feeling becomes common in the area, and the value of Plaintiff's realty is diminished. Plaintiff asserts claims against the defendant on theories of negligence, strict liability, and private nuisance.

Since the explosion resulted from Defendant's negligence, and since working with explosives is generally recognized to be an ultra-hazardous or abnormally dangerous activity, Plaintiff can establish some of the elements of his negligence and strict liability claims. Because his damages consist solely of economic losses and mental suffering, however, neither of which involved physical injury to Plaintiff's person or property, Plaintiff will not be able to recover damages under either of these theories.

Because the right to maintain the value of realty is part of the right to use and enjoy realty, the reduction in the value of Plaintiff's land may constitute a private nuisance. Because the right to feel safe and secure is also part of the right to use and enjoy realty, the fright which Plaintiff experienced while on his land may also constitute a private nuisance. If so, Plaintiff may recover damages in an action for private nuisance to compensate for his economic losses and mental suffering.

D. Possessory right: The action for private nuisance is available only to plaintiffs who have ***a possessory right*** in the realty the use and enjoyment of which has been invaded.

Example: Defendant negligently operates a fat-rendering plant in a way which causes obnoxious odors to pass over Blackacre, a nearby parcel of realty owned by Owner. The odors reduce the value of the realty and disturb the comfort of Tenant, the lessee of the realty, and of Visitor, Tenant's guest. Claims for private nuisance are asserted by Owner, Tenant, and Visitor.

The invasion resulting from Defendant's conduct may constitute a private nuisance since it was caused by negligence and led to interference with the use and enjoyment of Blackacre. Since he has a future possessory interest in the realty (*i.e.*, a reversion), owner owns Blackacre, and therefore, is entitled to maintain the action. Because Tenant is a lessee of Blackacre, she has a present possessory interest ln the realty (*i.e.*, a leasehold) and, therefore, is entitled to maintain the action. Because Visitor is a mere guest, he has no present or future possessory interest in Blackacre and, therefore, is not entitled to maintain the action.

E. **Unreasonable invasion**: Because the basis of a private nuisance claim usually is the allegation that the defendant's use of his realty is interfering with the plaintiff's use of her realty, it is necessary to balance the respective rights of the parties. In performing this balancing process, courts frequently say that ***an invasion of the right to use and enjoy realty is a private nuisance only if that invasion is unreasonable***. Care should be taken, however, not to confuse this requirement with the requirement that the defendant's conduct be liability-forming. Frequently, defendant's conduct is liability-forming because it is negligent. Negligence is based on the unreasonableness of the defendant's conduct, which may be entirely unrelated to the unreasonableness of the invasion which the plaintiff has suffered.

1. **Restatement view**: The Restatement (2d) of Torts holds that an invasion of the right to use and enjoy realty may be unreasonable in two different ways:

   a. **Gravity of harm v. Utility of conduct**: The ***invasion of the plaintiff's right is unreasonable if the gravity of the harm to the plaintiff outweighs the utility of the defendant's conduct***. In making this determination, consideration should be given to the following factors:

      i. **Gravity of harm**: The gravity of the plaintiff's harm depends on the extent and type of the harm, the social importance of the plaintiff's use of his realty, and its appropriateness to the location.

      ii. **Utility of conduct**: The utility of the defendant's conduct depends on how burdensome it would be to avoid harming the plaintiff, the social importance of defendant's use of his realty, and its appropriateness to the location.

      iii. **Chronology**: Although ***the order in which the parties began their respective uses*** of the realty may be significant in determining which activity is more appropriate to the location, it is ***not the only factor in determining the reasonableness of the invasion***.

   Example: Defendant has been operating his feedlot for thirty years in the same location. When he began operating, the nearest habitation was five miles away. In the last few years, the area in which Defendant operates has become residential. Plaintiff, a real estate developer who is building homes in the area, asserts a private nuisance claim against Defendant on the ground that odors and flies generated by the feedlot are interfering with the use and enjoyment of realty by residents of Plaintiff's development. Defendant argues that its use began long before Plaintiff came to the area.

In deciding whether Defendant's conduct has caused an unreasonable invasion of Plaintiff's right, it is necessary to consider the appropriateness to the area of each activity involved. Although Defendant's activity preceded Plaintiff's, the fact that the area has become residential probably makes Defendant's operation of a feedlot less appropriate than Plaintiff's development of residential realty. For this reason, Defendant's conduct probably is the cause of a private nuisance. *Spur Industries v. Del E. Webb Development Co.*, 494 P.2d 700 (Ariz. 1972).

b. Serious harm: The invasion of the plaintiff's right may also be termed unreasonable if harm to the plaintiff ***is serious***, and compensating the plaintiff for it ***would not prevent*** the defendant from continuing her activity.

Example: Defendant operates a power plant with knowledge that emissions from it are affecting the crops of Plaintiff, a nearby farmer. As a result of the emissions, Plaintiff sustains crop damage totaling $995. Plaintiff asserts a private nuisance claim against Defendant. Defendant argues that its activity is as socially important as Plaintiff's and is as appropriate to the location, and that, therefore, the invasion of Plaintiff's right is not unreasonable.

Although Defendant's activity may be as worthy of protection as Plaintiff's, the damage which the Plaintiff sustained is serious but can still be measured in dollars, and compensating Plaintiff for it would not prevent the Defendant from continuing operations. For this reason, the invasion of Plaintiff's right may be characterized as unreasonable, and Defendant may be required to compensate Plaintiff for it. *Jost v. Dairyland Power*, 172 N.W.2d 647 (Wis. 1970).

F. Remedies: A successful plaintiff in a private nuisance action may recover damages to compensate for harm which results from the interference with his use and enjoyment of realty. If damages are not a sufficient remedy, he may also be entitled to injunctive relief.

G. Affirmative defenses: The affirmative defenses available in private nuisance actions depend on the basis of liability alleged by the plaintiff.

If the plaintiff proceeds on a theory involving intent, the defendant may assert the defenses available in intentional tort cases. If the plaintiff proceeds on negligence or strict liability theories, the defendant may assert defenses available in those cases.

> **Example:** Defendant dumps warm water into a ditch by the side of the road on a cold day. As a result, a dense fog forms which interferes with visibility on the road. Plaintiff drives into the fog without slowing and strikes a stalled truck which was left in the road. Plaintiff asserts a private claim for public nuisance against Defendant. As an affirmative defense, Defendant argues that Plaintiff was contributorily negligent.
>
> If Defendant knew that its conduct would result in an accident on the highway, the public nuisance resulted from defendant's intent. Since contributory negligence is not a defense to intentional tort, Defendant's argument would be ineffective.
>
> On the other hand, if Defendant did not know that its conduct would result in an accident, but should have known it, then the public nuisance resulted from negligence. Since contributory negligence is a defense to negligence, Defendant's argument would be effective. *Timmons v. Reed*, 569 P.2d 112 (Wyo. 1977).

IV. PRIVILEGE TO ABATE A NUISANCE BY SELF-HELP

A. General concept: A person who is confronted by a nuisance may be privileged to enter realty and to use force to abate it. This privilege may provide a defense to criminal charges stemming from such entry and to tort actions for battery, assault, trespass to land, and trespass to chattel.

B. Essential elements: A defendant is privileged to abate a nuisance by self-help if: (1) ***there is a public or private nuisance***; (2) ***waiting for a judicial determination would result in irreparable harm***; and (3) ***the defendant acts reasonably under all the circumstances***.

> **Example:** Plaintiff is shooting at paper targets in his back yard with an assault rifle. Frequently, stray bullets strike Defendant's house, nearly striking his children. Defendant asks Plaintiff to stop shooting, but Plaintiff refuses. Defendant enters Plaintiff's yard and physically takes the assault rifle from Plaintiff. Plaintiff asserts claims against Defendant for trespass to land, trespass to chattel, and battery. Defendant argues that he was abating a nuisance by self-help.

Since Plaintiff's conduct was intentional, and substantially and unreasonably invaded Defendant's right to use and enjoy his realty, it probably was a private nuisance. Since a bullet might have seriously injured a member of Defendant's family or damaged his home, irreparable harm could have resulted from waiting for a judicial determination.

Under the circumstances, it probably was reasonable for Defendant to enter the yard and take the assault rifle, because in doing so he protected more than he risked. For this reason, Defendant was probably privileged.

CHAPTER 11
MISREPRESENTATION

I. GENERAL CONCEPT

A. Two torts: At common law, there are two different, but closely related, torts, both of which involve misrepresentation. These are ***intentional misrepresentation*** (also known as ***"fraud" or "deceit"***) and ***negligent misrepresentation***.

B. Elements in common: Intentional misrepresentation and negligent misrepresentation have the following elements in common: (1) ***a misrepresentation***; (2) ***the plaintiff's justified reliance***; and (3) ***damage.***

1. **Misrepresentation:** The defendant must have made a ***misrepresentation***. A misrepresentation is a ***false assertion of material fact made with the intent to induce the plaintiff's reliance.***

   a. **False:** An assertion is false if it is ***not substantially true.***

   b. **Assertion:** An assertion is a statement made either expressly or impliedly.

      i. **Express assertion:** An express assertion is a statement made in ***words or in a substitute for words.***

      Example: A box containing a product has the word "helmet" printed on it along with a photograph of a person riding a motorcycle while wearing a product like the one in the box. Plaintiff uses the product as head protection while riding a motorcycle and is injured because it is not suitable for that purpose. Plaintiff asserts a misrepresentation claim against Defendant. Defendant argues that it never represented the product to be suitable as head protection while riding a motorcycle.

      Since a "helmet" is a protective head covering, the box expressly asserted (*i.e.*, stated in words) that it contained a protective head covering. Since the box displayed a photograph of a person wearing a helmet like the one in the box while riding a motorcycle, and since a photograph is a substitute for words, the box expressly asserted that the helmet which it contained was suitable for use while riding a motorcycle. *Winkler v. American Safety Equipment*, 604 P.2d 693 (Colo. 1979), *infra*, p. 216.

      ii. **Implied assertion:** An implied assertion is a statement which is not made in words or a substitute for words but which would be ***inferred or gathered*** by the reasonable person after observing the defendant's conduct or the circumstances.

Example: Defendant magazine affixes its "seal of approval" to a product advertised in its pages. Plaintiff is injured because the product is unfit for ordinary use. Plaintiff brings a misrepresentation claim against Defendant, alleging that Defendant asserted that the product was fit. Defendant denies having made such an assertion.

If the reasonable person would infer such an assertion from Defendant's "seal of approval", it may be held that Defendant's "seal of approval" impliedly asserted that Defendant knew about products like the one in question, that Defendant had tested the product in question, and that Defendant had found it to be suitable for ordinary use. *Hanberry v. Hearst,* 81 Cal. Rptr. 519 (Cal. Ct. App. 1969) (*infra*, p. 184).

iii. Assertion implied by non-disclosure: If a defendant was under a legal ***duty to disclose*** the existence of a particular fact, the ***failure to disclose that fact may be an assertion*** that the fact did not exist.

Example: Defendant sells Plaintiff a house without telling Plaintiff that the house is infested with termites. Plaintiff subsequently brings a claim for misrepresentation, alleging that Defendant asserted that the house was free of termites. Defendant argues that it did not make such an assertion.

If the law recognizes an obligation to disclose the presence of termites in a house being sold, then Defendant's silence was an implied assertion that the house was free of termites. On the other hand, if the law does not require such a disclosure, then Defendant's silence did not assert anything. *Swinton v. Whitinsville Savings Bank*, 42 N.E.2d 808 (Mass. 1942).

aa. Partial disclosure: If the seller made a ***partial disclosure which was likely to mislead*** the reasonable person or which the seller knew would mislead the buyer, the seller is under an obligation to make full disclosure to avoid misunderstanding.

Example: While negotiating for the purchase of a franchise from Defendant, Plaintiff asks why there is not already a franchise in operation in that location. Defendant answers, "We are selling franchises in the area now." In fact, there was a franchise in operation in the area, but the operator went out of business because of lack of profit. Plaintiff purchases the franchise, and subsequently asserts a misrepresentation claim against Defendant. Defendant argues that its statement was not false.

Although Defendant's statement was true, it was only a partial disclosure of the truth. If it was likely to mislead the reasonable person in Plaintiff's position, Defendant had a duty to make full disclosure, and his failure to do so was an implied assertion that there had never been a franchise in the area before.

bb. Discovery of additional information: If the seller makes an assertion which is true when he makes it, but learns, prior to the sale, that circumstances have changed, he may be under an obligation to advise the buyer of the ***change in circumstances.***

Example: While negotiating for the sale of his business to Plaintiff, Defendant truthfully tells Plaintiff that the business makes gross sales of $10,000 per month. Before the sale is completed, sales drop to $1,000 per month. If Plaintiff was aware of this, she would not purchase the business, but Defendant does not tell her and she does purchase the business. Plaintiff subsequently asserts a misrepresentation claim against Defendant. Defendant argues that he made no false statement.

Although Defendant's statement was true when he made it, Defendant had a duty to advise Plaintiff of the change in circumstances since it was obvious that Plaintiff would rely on the statement. His failure to do so may be regarded as an implied assertion that there was no change in circumstances, and thus as a misrepresentation as well. *Guastella v. Wardell*, 198 So.2d 227 (Miss. 1967).

cc. Active concealment: A seller who has taken steps to ***actively conceal*** a fact from the purchaser is under an obligation to disclose that fact.

Example: Before selling an automobile to Plaintiff, Defendant fills and paints a crack in the automobile's engine block. Plaintiff purchases the automobile and subsequently brings a misrepresentation claim against Defendant, alleging that Defendant's failure to disclose the existence of the crack was a misrepresentation. Defendant denies having made any assertion regarding the engine block.

Although originally Defendant may not have been under a duty to disclose the presence of the crack in the engine block, his active steps to conceal it probably imposed upon him a duty to disclose it, and his failure to do so was an implied representation that there was no crack. *Lindberg Cadillac v. Aron*, 371 S.W.2d 651 (Mo. Ct. App. 1963).

dd. Facts material to the transaction: Some jurisdictions hold that a seller is under an affirmative obligation to disclose any facts which go to the *essence of the transaction* and of which the *reasonable buyer would expect disclosure.*

Example: Defendant sells Plaintiff a parcel of realty without disclosing that the soil is sterile. Plaintiff subsequently brings a misrepresentation claim, alleging that Defendant's non-disclosure was a misrepresentation.

Since the fertility of soil usually goes to the essence of a transaction in real estate, Defendant was under an obligation to disclose that the soil was sterile if the reasonable buyer would have expected such a disclosure to be made. *Griffith v. Byers Constr. Co. of Kansas, Inc.*, 510 P.2d 198 (Kan. 1973).

c. Material: An assertion is material if it is about something which would be ***important to the reasonable person*** in the position of the party to whom it was made.

Example: In selling Plaintiff a new car, Defendant states that the car was originally ordered by a doctor who then changed her mind and refused to go through with the transaction. In fact, the person who originally ordered the car was an accountant. After purchasing the car, Plaintiff brings a misrepresentation claim against Defendant.

Since the occupation of the person who had originally ordered a car which is now for sale probably would not be important to the reasonable buyer, Defendant's assertion, although false, probably is not material. Thus, although Defendant made a false assertion it was not a misrepresentation.

d. Fact: An assertion is of fact if it is ***capable of objective truth or falsity and does not contain an expression of doubt or equivocation***. A statement which concerns a ***subjective*** matter or which equivocates or expresses doubt is an assertion of ***opinion*** rather than of fact.

Example 1: In negotiating for the sale of his vacuum cleaner manufacturing business, Defendant tells Plaintiff that the vacuum cleaners which he produces (1) are the best on the market, and (2) have never before been sold. Plaintiff purchases the business and subsequently brings a misrepresentation claim, alleging that both statements were misrepresentations.

Since what makes one vacuum cleaner better than another

is a subjective matter, statement (1) probably was an expression of opinion. Since the statement that the vacuum cleaner had never been on the market before is capable of objective truth, statement (2) probably was an assertion of fact. *Vulcan Metals v. Simmons*, 248 F. 853 (2d Cir. 1918) (*infra*, p. 188).

Example 2: In selling timberland to Plaintiff, Defendant states that "about 20 acres have been burned". In fact, 60 acres had been burned. After purchasing the land, Plaintiff brings a misrepresentation claim against Defendant, alleging that he had misstated a fact. Defendant argues that his statement was an assertion of opinion.

The word "about" indicates that the speaker is not certain. This expression of uncertainty or equivocation probably makes defendant's statement an expression of opinion rather than an assertion of fact. *Saxby v. Southern Land Co.*, 63 S.E. 423 (Va. 1909) (*infra*, p. 188).

Example 3: In selling Plaintiff a resort, Defendant states that (1) he intends to build a railroad to the area; and (2) when the railroad is completed, the resort will earn $150,000 per year. The railroad is never completed, and Plaintiff alleges that statements (1) and (2) were misrepresentations. Defendant argues that they were not assertions of fact.

Whether a person actually intends to do a thing is capable of objective truth (i.e., he either does or does not actually intend to do it). Thus, statement (1) was an assertion of fact. If, when he made the statement, Defendant actually did intend to build the railroad, his statement was true (whether or not he ever actually got around to building it.) If, when he made the statement, Defendant did not actually intend to build the railroad, his statement was false, and may have been a misrepresentation.

At the time a prediction about the future is made, it is not capable of objective truth (*e.g.*, when Defendant said that the resort would earn $150,000 per year, there was no way to determine then whether the statement was true). For this reason, statement (2) probably was an expression of opinion rather than an assertion of fact. *McElrath v. Electric Investment Co.*, 131 N.W. 380 (Minn. 1911).

i. **Assertion that Defendant holds a particular opinion:** It is sometimes held that in expressing an opinion, a defendant is asserting ***as a fact that he actually holds that opinion.***

Example: In selling Plaintiff a car, Defendant says, "I think the windshield is shatterproof." After sustaining an injury because the windshield is not shatterproof, Plaintiff brings a misrepresentation claim against Defendant. Defendant denies having asserted a fact.

Since the phrase "I think..." is an expression of qualified knowledge, Defendant's statement is an opinion rather than an assertion of fact. It may be held, however, that in stating his opinion, Defendant also asserted that he did, in fact, believe that the windshield was shatterproof.

ii. **Falsity of assertion that defendant holds a particular opinion:** ***If the defendant actually did hold the opinion*** which she said she held, the ***assertion of fact was true***, even if the opinion was incorrect. ***If she actually did not hold that opinion, her assertion was false.***

Example 1: In selling Plaintiff a car, Defendant says, "I think the windshield is shatterproof." In fact, the windshield is not shatterproof, but Defendant believes that it is. After sustaining an injury because the windshield is not shatterproof, Plaintiff brings a misrepresentation claim against Defendant. Defendant denies having falsely asserted a fact.

Although the windshield was not shatterproof, Defendant's assertion that "I think the windshield is shatterproof" was true, since Defendant actually did think that the windshield was shatterproof.

Example 2: In selling Plaintiff a car, Defendant says, "I think the windshield is shatterproof." In fact, the windshield is not shatterproof, and Defendant knows this. After sustaining an injury because the windshield is not shatterproof, Plaintiff brings a misrepresentation claim against Defendant. Defendant denies having falsely asserted a fact.

Although the statement "I think the windshield is shatterproof" was an expression of opinion, it also asserted as a fact that Defendant actually did hold that opinion (*i.e.*, that Defendant actually believed that the windshield was shatterproof). Since Defendant did not actually hold this opinion the statement of fact was false.

iii. **Assertion that defendant holds a particular opinion not usually material:** Even if a defendant's expression of opinion asserts as a fact that she holds that particular opinion, ***frequently that fact*** (*i.e.*, ***that the defendant actually holds a particular opinion) is not material***. The reason for this is that a seller is likely to be influenced by different factors than a buyer, and, knowing this, a reasonable buyer does not usually consider a seller's opinion to be important.

Example: In selling Plaintiff an automobile, Defendant states, "I really believe that this is a safe car." In fact, Defendant does not believe that the car is safe. After sustaining injury in the car, Plaintiff brings a misrepresentation claim against Defendant. Defendant denies having falsely asserted a material fact.

Since Defendant said that he believed the car to be safe when in fact he did not believe the car to be safe, he made a false assertion of fact (*i.e.*, about what he believed). Although that assertion was false, however, it probably was not material, since the reasonable buyer is not likely to regard as persuasive the seller's opinion about whether a car is safe.

iv. **Assertion that defendant holds a particular opinion may be material:** A seller's assertion that he holds a particular opinion ***may be material if the reasonable buyer would consider that seller's opinion important***. This is particularly so where the seller is an ***expert*** in connection with the product being sold.

Example: In selling Plaintiff paint for use in a nursery, Defendant, a paint dealer, says, "I don't think that there are any toxic ingredients in this paint." In fact, Defendant knows that the paint contains toxic ingredients. Plaintiff uses the paint in the nursery, and Plaintiff's child is injured because the paint contains a toxic ingredient. Plaintiff brings a misrepresentation claim against Defendant. Defendant argues that he made no false assertion of fact about the ingredients in the paint.

Defendant's use of the phrase "I don't think...," probably expressed sufficient lack of certainty to be an opinion rather than an assertion of fact. But Defendant's statement asserted as a fact that Defendant ***believed*** that the paint was non-toxic. Since Defendant did not really hold that opinion, his statement was false. Ordinarily, a seller's opinion is not material. Here, however, since the seller was a paint dealer, and presumably an expert, the reasonable buyer would probably regard the seller's opinion as to the toxicity of the paint to be important. For this reason, Defendant's assertion that he was of the opinion that the paint was non-toxic was material.

v. **Expression of opinion may impliedly assert fact:** A seller who expresses an opinion about the thing sold may be impliedly asserting that he knows of facts which justify his opinion. If he does not know of such facts, the expression of opinion may imply a false statement of fact.

Example: Defendant affixes its "seal of approval" to a product, stating that it considers the product to be a good one. Plaintiff purchases the product and subsequently asserts a misrepresentation claim against Defendant. Defendant argues that it made no false assertion of fact.

If the reasonable person would infer such an assertion from Defendant's "seal of approval", it may be held that Defendant's "seal of approval" impliedly asserted that Defendant knew about products like the one in question, that Defendant had tested the product in question, and that Defendant had found it to be suitable for ordinary use. *Hanberry v. Hearst, supra*, p. 178.

e. **Intent to induce plaintiff's reliance:** Not every assertion of fact is a representation. Unless an assertion was made with the ***desire (or knowledge) that it induce the plaintiff's reliance***, it was not a representation, and, therefore, even if false, could not be a misrepresentation.

Example: Seeking to impress his neighbor, Defendant tells her that his new car is equipped with bulletproof glass, although Defendant knows that this is not true. Unknown to Defendant, Plaintiff overhears the statement. The following day, believing that the glass is bulletproof, Plaintiff purchases the car from Defendant. Upon learning that the glass is not bulletproof, Plaintiff asserts a misrepresentation claim against Defendant. Defendant argues that he did not make a misrepresentation.

Since Defendant did not intend (or know) that Plaintiff hear and believe this statement, he did not make it for the purpose of inducing Plaintiff's reliance. Thus, the assertion was not a representation and could not have been a misrepresentation, even though it was false.

i. **Statement to someone other than plaintiff:** A statement made to someone other than the plaintiff may have been made with the intent to induce the plaintiff's reliance if the defendant ***desired (or knew) that the plaintiff*** learn of the statement, believe it, and ***rely*** on it.

Example: Before selling a load of beans to Plaintiff, Seller hires Defendant, a public weigher, to certify their weight. Defendant weighs the beans and issues an inaccurate certificate to Seller. Because of the inaccuracy, Plaintiff overpays Seller for the beans. Plaintiff subsequently asserts a misrepresentation claim against Defendant. Defendant argues that, since he was not in privity with Plaintiff, he lacked the intent to induce Plaintiff's reliance.

Since Defendant knew that the weight certificate was to be used by Seller in determining the price at which to sell the beans, Defendant knew that someone in Plaintiff's position (*i.e.*, a buyer) would be relying on the weight certificate. For this reason, Defendant had the necessary intent to induce Plaintiff's reliance, and may be held liable for misrepresentation. *Glanzer v. Shepard*, 135 N.E. 275 (N.Y. 1922).

ii. **Class including plaintiff:** Even if a defendant is not aware of the identity of a particular plaintiff, his ***knowledge that the statement will be relied upon by members of a class of persons to which the plaintiff belongs***, is sufficient to result in a finding that he acted with the intent to induce the plaintiff's reliance.

Example: Defendant sells an automobile to Saleco, a car dealer, falsely representing that she holds title to it. Plaintiff purchases the car from the dealer, but does not receive good title because the dealer has none to convey. Plaintiff subsequently asserts a misrepresentation claim against Defendant. Defendant argues that she did not have the intent to induce Plaintiff's reliance.

Because a car dealer would not buy a car without receiving what he believed to be good title, when Defendant falsely represented that she held title to the car, she intended to induce Saleco's reliance. Since Saleco was a dealer, Defendant must have known that the car would be resold to a purchaser who would rely on Saleco's representation regarding title. Thus, although Defendant did not know Plaintiff's identity, she knew that somewhere along the line, a purchaser like Plaintiff would rely on her representation. For this reason, Defendant had the intent to induce Plaintiff's reliance and may be liable to Plaintiff for misrepresentation. *Varwig v. Anderson-Behel Porsche Audi, Inc.*, 141 Cal. Rptr. 539 (Cal. Ct. App. 1975).

2. **Inducing plaintiff's justified reliance:** Unless the plaintiff ***actually relies*** on the defendant's statement and is ***justified*** in doing so, no liability for misrepresentation will be imposed.

a. **Reliance:** A plaintiff relied on the representation if it was a ***significant factor in the plaintiff's decision***.

i. **Knowledge of representation:** If ***plaintiff does not know of the representation***, she does not rely on it.

Example: Defendant, a car manufacturer, distributes a brochure representing that its cars are equipped with shatterproof glass. Without seeing the brochure and without knowing that Defendant has represented the glass to be shatterproof, Plaintiff purchases a car from Defendant. Plaintiff is subsequently injured when the glass shatters, and asserts a misrepresentation claim against Defendant. Defendant argues that Plaintiff did not rely on the representation.

Since Plaintiff did not know of the representation, she could not have relied on it, and Defendant cannot be liable to her for misrepresentation.

ii. **Belief in representation:** Unless the plaintiff ***believes*** that Defendant's statement is true, she does not rely on it.

Example: In selling Plaintiff a car, Defendant represents that it is equipped with shatterproof glass. Plaintiff does not believe that the glass is shatterproof, but buys the car. Plaintiff is subsequently injured when the glass shatters. She asserts a misrepresentation claim against Defendant. Defendant argues that Plaintiff did not rely on the representation.

Since Plaintiff did not believe that the glass was shatterproof, Defendant's representation could not have been a significant factor in Plaintiff's decision to purchase the car. For this reason, Plaintiff did not rely on the representation, and Defendant cannot be liable for misrepresentation.

iii. **Independent investigation:** It is frequently held that a plaintiff who investigates the truth of the defendant's representation is ***relying on his own investigation*** rather than on the representation.

Example 1: In negotiating the sale of a horse to Plaintiff, Defendant represents that the horse is in good health. Before purchasing the animal, Plaintiff has it examined by a veterinarian who certifies that the horse is in good health. After purchasing the horse, Plaintiff finds that it is not in good health and asserts a misrepresentation claim against Defendant. Defendant argues that Plaintiff did not rely on his representation.

Since Plaintiff had the horse examined by a veterinarian for the purpose of determining whether it was in good health, he probably was not relying on Defendant's representation. For this reason, Defendant probably is not liable for misrepresentation. *Sessa v. Riegle*, 427 F.Supp. 760 (E.D. Pa., 1977) (*infra*, p. 224-225).

iv. **Significant factor:** Unless the representation was a ***significant factor*** in the plaintiff's decision, he did not rely on it. A representation may be a significant factor in a plaintiff's decision, even though it is ***not the only factor.***

Example: In selling a car to Plaintiff, Defendant represents that it is equipped with bulletproof glass and that it gets 26 miles to a gallon of gasoline. Plaintiff has no need for bulletproof glass and does not care whether or not the car is equipped with it. Plaintiff purchases the car because of its make, its condition, its color, and the fact that it gets 26 miles to the gallon of gas. The car is not equipped with bulletproof glass and actually gets only 15 miles to the gallon of gas. Plaintiff subsequently asserts a misrepresentation claim against Defendant. Defendant argues that Plaintiff did not rely on the representations.

Since Plaintiff did not care whether or not the glass was bulletproof, Defendant's statement that it was bulletproof was not a significant factor in Plaintiff's decision to buy the car. For this reason, Plaintiff did not rely on the bulletproof glass representation, and Defendant probably is not liable for making it.

Since Plaintiff did care about the gas mileage, however, and since Defendant's representation concerning it was one of the reasons for Plaintiff's decision to purchase, Plaintiff did rely on that representation, and Defendant may be liable for making it.

b. **Justified reliance:** Liability is not imposed unless the plaintiff's reliance was justified. A plaintiff's reliance is justified if the ***reasonable person in the plaintiff's position would have relied.***

i. **Obvious falsity:** Since the reasonable person would not believe a statement which is ***obviously false***, a plaintiff is not justified in relying on such a statement.

Example: Defendant sells Plaintiff a load of beans, showing them to Plaintiff and saying that they are oats. Plaintiff subsequently asserts a misrepresentation claim against Defendant, who argues that Plaintiff's reliance was not justified.

Since the reasonable person knows the difference between beans and oats, Defendant's statement was so obviously false that the reasonable person would not have relied on it. For this reason, Plaintiff's reliance was not justified, and Defendant is not liable.

ii. **Puffing:** A plaintiff is not justified in relying on ***general statements which a seller makes in praise of his own***

wares (sometimes called ***"puffing"***), if the reasonable person would not have taken those statements seriously.

Example: In selling a vacuum cleaner to Plaintiff, Defendant says that it is absolutely perfect in every detail; it is so simple a child of six can operate it; it will last a lifetime; and perfect satisfaction will result from its use. After purchasing the vacuum cleaner, Plaintiff is dissatisfied with it and asserts a misrepresentation claim against Defendant. Defendant argues that Plaintiff was not justified in relying on his statements.

Since Defendant's statements were the kind of general praises of his product that every seller is likely to make, the reasonable person probably would not have taken them seriously. For this reason, Plaintiff probably was not justified in relying on them. *Vulcan Metals v. Simmons*, (*supra*, p. 180-181.)

iii. Opinions and predictions: Because the reasonable person is not usually influenced by a seller's ***predictions or opinions*** regarding the subject of the sale, ordinarily a plaintiff is not justified in relying on them. (See discussion of materiality, *supra*, p. 181.)

Example: Defendant sells Plaintiff land, stating that the timber on the land will probably bring $200 per cord when sold as firewood, and that, once the land is cleared, Plaintiff can probably grow 100 bushels of potatoes per acre. After purchasing the land, Plaintiff is unable to get $200 per cord for the firewood, and the land does not yield 100 bushels of potatoes per acre. Plaintiff asserts a misrepresentation claim. Defendant argues that Plaintiff's reliance was not justified.

Since there was no particular reason why Defendant's opinions and predictions about the price of firewood or the potential agricultural yield of the land were likely to be accurate, the reasonable person in Plaintiff's position probably would not have relied upon them. For this reason, Plaintiff's reliance is not justified. *Saxby v. Southern Land*, *supra*, p. 180-181.

iv. Failure to investigate: Although there are some statements which the reasonable person would believe without investigation, a plaintiff is ***not justified*** in relying on a defendant's representation ***if the reasonable person would have investigated*** its truth before relying on it.

Example: In negotiating the purchase of a house, Plaintiff notices water stains on the ceiling and asks whether the roof leaks. Defendant tells Plaintiff that the roof used to leak but that it has been fixed. To determine whether the roof actually has been fixed, it would be necessary to perform costly and destructive tests. Instead, Plaintiff chooses to believe Defendant. After purchasing the house, Plaintiff discovers that the roof still leaks and asserts a misrepresentation claim against Defendant. Defendant argues that the water stains would have led the reasonable person to investigate the truth of his representation, and, therefore, that Plaintiff was not justified in relying on it.

Since an investigation would have been costly and destructive, the reasonable person probably would not have made one unless there was some reason to disbelieve Defendant. Since water stains do not go away after a roof has been fixed, their presence was not inconsistent with Defendant's representation. For this reason, the reasonable person probably would not have investigated, and Plaintiff probably was justified in relying. *Sippy v. Cristich*, 609 P.2d 204 (Kan. Ct. App. 1980).

v. **Known gullibility or mental deficiency:** If the defendant is ***aware that the plaintiff is so gullible or mentally deficient*** that he will believe and rely on the defendant's statement, the plaintiff may recover damages resulting from his reliance even though that reliance may not have been justified (*i.e.*, the reasonable person would not have relied).

Example: Knowing that the Plaintiff was extremely gullible, Defendant offered to sell him a roadhouse for $35,000, telling him that it was worth more than that but that if Plaintiff asked anyone's advice about its value, word would get out that it was a bargain and somebody else would buy it before Plaintiff could. Plaintiff purchased in reliance on Defendant's statements. After learning that the property was worth far less than Defendant had represented, Plaintiff asserted a misrepresentation claim. Defendant argued that Plaintiff's reliance was not justified because the reasonable person would have made an investigation before buying.

Since Defendant knew that Plaintiff was extremely gullible and took advantage of that fact in making misrepresentations on which he knew Plaintiff would rely, Plaintiff's reliance was foreseeable and justified even if the reasonable person would have made an independent investigation. *Adan v. Steinbrecher*, 133 N.W. 477 (Minn. 1911).

3. **Damage:** There are two accepted methods of calculating damage in a misrepresentation case: the "benefit of the bargain" approach and the "out of pocket" approach.

a. **Benefit of the bargain:** The majority of jurisdictions favor the ***benefit of the bargain*** approach, which is designed to give to the plaintiff the value which the defendant represented she would receive. Using this approach, plaintiff's damage consists of the ***difference between the value actually received and the value which the plaintiff would have received if things had been as the defendant represented them to be***.

b. **Out of pocket:** A minority of jurisdictions favors the ***out of pocket*** approach, which is designed to restore the plaintiff to her position before she relied on the defendant's misrepresentation. Using this approach, plaintiff's damage consists of the ***difference between the price which the plaintiff paid and the value which she received.***

Example: Defendant sells Plaintiff an ounce of metal for $300, telling Plaintiff that it is gold. If it were gold, it would be worth $400. In fact, the metal is frammisite, worth only $10. Plaintiff asserts a misrepresentation claim against Defendant.

In a ***benefit of the bargain*** jurisdiction, Plaintiff's damage consists of the difference between the value he should have received (*i.e.*, gold) and the value he actually did receive. Since an ounce of gold would have been worth $400, and an ounce of frammisite was worth only $10, Plaintiff's damage is $390.

In an ***out of pocket*** jurisdiction, Plaintiff's damage consists of the difference between what he paid and the value which he received. Since Plaintiff paid $300 and received frammisite worth $10, his damage is $290.

c. **Rule of flexibility:** Some of the jurisdictions which generally apply the ***benefit of the bargain*** approach, have adopted a ***rule of flexibility*** which permits a plaintiff to ***elect*** the ***out of pocket*** approach when it is impossible to prove the extent of his ***benefit of the bargain*** loss.

Example: Defendant sells Plaintiff a cubic zirconium for $1,000, telling her that it is a diamond. In fact, the cubic zirconium is worth only $10. Since the value of a diamond varies according to several factors, it is impossible to determine what the stone would have been worth if it had actually been a diamond.

In jurisdictions which inflexibly apply the *benefit of the bargain* approach, Plaintiff's damage is measured by the difference between the value which she received, and the value which the stone would have had if it had been a diamond. Since Plaintiff is unable to prove what that value would have been, she cannot prove damage and her case may be dismissed.

In jurisdictions which apply the rule of flexibility, however, Plaintiff may elect to apply the *out of pocket* approach instead. Under this approach, Plaintiff's damage consists of the difference between what she paid (*i.e.*, $1,000) and what she received (*i.e.*, $10). Since this sum can be determined (*i.e.*, $990), Plaintiff can prove damage, and her case will not be dismissed.

C. Liability without fault: In exceptional cases, ***misrepresentation liability has been imposed without fault***. Usually, however, these cases have involved ***statements which qualified as express warranties***. Since liability for breaching a warranty has traditionally been imposed without regard to fault, the only feature which distinguishes these "misrepresentation" cases from actions for breach of warranty is the characterization given to the plaintiff's allegations.

Example: During negotiation for the sale of realty to Plaintiff, Defendant, a real estate developer, gives Plaintiff a plot plan indicating that the house on the subject realty is located twenty feet from the boundary line. Plaintiff purchases in reliance on this description, but subsequently discovers that the front of the house is only one foot from the boundary line, requiring Plaintiff to trespass on his neighbor's land whenever he enters or leaves the house. Plaintiff asserts a claim for misrepresentation, but is unable to show that inaccuracies in the plot plan resulted from fault by Defendant. Defendant moves to dismiss on the ground that, since he has not established fault, Plaintiff has failed to make out a prima facie case of misrepresentation.

An express warranty is an assertion of fact which becomes part of the basis of the bargain. The plot plan asserted facts about the location of the house. Since Plaintiff relied on them in purchasing the realty, they became part of the basis of the bargain. For this reason, it may be argued that assertions contained in the plot plan were warranties. If this argument is successful, warranty or misrepresentation liability may be imposed on Defendant without regard to fault. *Richard v. A. Waldman & Sons, Inc.*, 232 A.2d 307 (Conn. 1967).

D. Fault: In most cases, fault is an essential element of torts based on misrepresentation. The specific fault required is what distinguishes "fraud" or "deceit" (*i.e.*, intentional misrepresentation) from negligent misrepresentation.

II. INTENTIONAL MISREPRESENTATION

A. **Intent sufficient fault:** ***All jurisdictions agree that intent to deceive is sufficient fault*** to result in liability for misrepresentation if all the other elements are satisfied.

B. **Definition:** A defendant has the necessary "intent" to misrepresent if, when he makes the statement, he ***knows that the statement is false*** or acts with a ***reckless disregard*** for the truth.

1. **Knowledge of falsity:** Knowledge of falsity consists of a ***substantial certainty that*** the statement which the defendant is making is ***not true***. Sometimes this is called the requirement of ***"scienter"*** (*i.e.*, knowledge). So long as the belief is not reckless, a defendant who believes that his statement is true does not have the requisite intent even if the reasonable person in his position would have known that the statement was false.

   Example: Plaintiff purchases stock in Defendant's trolley line in reliance on Defendant's statement that necessary permits have been obtained so that the line can run on steam power. Although Defendant actually believes this statement to be true, it is not. In fact, the permits are never obtained, and the line operates at a loss. Plaintiff asserts a deceit claim against Defendant. Defendant moves to dismiss on the ground that Plaintiff has failed to establish the necessary fault.

   Since Defendant believed his statement to be true, he did not intend to make a false statement. Because intent is an essential element of deceit, Plaintiff's case should be dismissed. *Derry v. Peek*, 14 App. Cas. 337 (Eng. 1889).

2. **Reckless disregard:** A defendant acts with a reckless disregard for the truth if she makes a statement under circumstances indicating that she ***does not care whether it is true or false.***

   a. **No belief in truth:** Circumstances indicate that a defendant does not care whether her statement is true if, when she makes the statement, she ***does not believe*** that it is true.

   b. **Knowledge that defendant does not know:** Circumstances indicate that a defendant does not care whether her statement is true if, when she makes the statement, she ***is aware that*** she ***has no knowledge*** whether or not it is true.

   Example: The corporation of which Defendant is president owes money to Plaintiff. Relying on Defendant's statement that the corporation is solvent, Plaintiff does not sue. When Defendant makes the statement, he realizes that he does not know whether or not it is true, and there is no reason for him to believe that it is. The statement is in fact false, and, as a result, Plaintiff loses money when the corporation goes into bankruptcy. Plaintiff asserts a claim against Defendant for deceit, but is unable to prove that Defendant knew that the corporation was insolvent when he said that it was solvent. Defendant moves to dismiss on the ground that Plaintiff has failed to establish the requisite intent.

Since Defendant had no reason to believe that the statement was true, he probably did not believe it to be true. If this was so, he acted with a reckless disregard for the truth, and had the necessary intent to deceive. Since Defendant was aware that he had no knowledge whether or not the statement was true, he could not have believed that it was true. Therefore, he acted with a reckless disregard for the truth and probably had the necessary intent. *Sovereign Pocohontas v. Bond*, 120 F.2d 39 (D.C. Cir. 1941).

III. NEGLIGENT MISREPRESENTATION

A. Commercial losses resulting from negligence: Liability is not usually imposed for commercial losses (*i.e.*, loss of profits) which result from negligence. Some courts say that this is because such losses are not "damage." Other courts say that negligence is not a proximate cause of these losses.

B. Negligent misrepresentation: Because of this rule (concerning commercial losses resulting from negligence), ***approximately half the jurisdictions in the United States do not impose liability for negligent misrepresentation***, except to award damages for resulting injury to the person or property of plaintiff. In some jurisdictions, however, liability may be imposed for loss of profits resulting from negligent misrepresentation.

Example: In purchasing steel beams from Defendant, Plaintiff, a bridgebuilder, justifiably relies on Defendant's statement about how much weight the beams can support. Because of Defendant's negligence, the statement is false. As a result, a bridge which Plaintiff builds with the beams collapses, causing Plaintiff to fall and break a leg. In addition, Plaintiff loses profits which he was to receive for building the bridge. Plaintiff asserts negligent misrepresentation claims against Defendant for his loss of profits and for damage resulting from his broken leg. Defendant moves to dismiss.

Since all jurisdictions agree that negligence may be a proximate cause of a broken leg (or that a broken leg is damage in a negligence case), Plaintiff's claim for damage resulting from his broken leg probably will not be dismissed.

As to Plaintiff's claim for lost profit, in a jurisdiction which holds that commercial losses are not recoverable in an action for negligent misrepresentation because such losses are not proximately caused by negligence (or are not damage in a negligence case), Plaintiff's claim for lost profits probably will be dismissed.

In a jurisdiction which holds that loss of profits resulting from negligent misrepresentation is recoverable as an exception to the general rule regarding negligently caused commercial losses, Plaintiff's case probably will not be dismissed.

C. **Definition of negligent misrepresentation:** A defendant makes a negligent misrepresentation if he owes the plaintiff a ***duty to act reasonably in ascertaining the truth*** of the representations he is making, and ***breaches that duty.***

Example: Plaintiff calls Defendant about merchandise which Plaintiff has stored in Defendant's warehouse. Explaining that he wishes to insure the merchandise, Plaintiff asks Defendant for its exact location. Because he carelessly reads the wrong line in his record book, Defendant incorrectly tells Plaintiff that the goods are stored in building A, when they are actually stored in building B.

In reliance on the statement, Plaintiff purchases fire insurance on goods stored in building A. When building B burns down, Plaintiff is unable to collect on his fire insurance policy, because the policy only covered goods stored in building A. Plaintiff asserts a claim against Defendant in a jurisdiction which imposes liability for commercial losses resulting from negligent misrepresentation.

Since Plaintiff rented warehouse space from Defendant, and since Defendant knew that Plaintiff would be relying on Defendant's statement in insuring his goods, Defendant owed Plaintiff a duty to act reasonably in ascertaining the truth of the statement which Defendant was making. Since he failed to do so, he breached that duty, and probably will be liable for negligent misrepresentation. *International Products v. Erie RR*, 155 N.E. 662 (N.Y. 1927).

1. **Duty of reasonable care:** Even though a defendant has acted unreasonably in ascertaining the truth of her representations, she is not negligent as to the plaintiff unless she owes the plaintiff a duty of reasonable care.

    a. **Privity:** Most cases which permit recovery for negligent misrepresentation hold that a defendant does not owe the plaintiff a duty of reasonable care in ascertaining the truth of the defendant's representations unless plaintiff and defendant are in privity.

b. **Close relationship:** Some cases have held that a defendant may owe the plaintiff a duty of reasonable care in ascertaining the truth of defendant's representations even if they are not in privity, so long as plaintiff and defendant are in a ***close relationship which is similar to privity.***

c. **Foreseeable reliance:** In ordinary negligence cases, a defendant owes a plaintiff a duty of reasonable care if the defendant's conduct creates a foreseeable risk to the plaintiff. Some jurisdictions extend this to mean that in a case of negligent misrepresentation the defendant owes the plaintiff a duty of acting reasonably in ascertaining the truth of the defendant's representations when it is ***foreseeable that the plaintiff will rely*** on those representations.

Example: Borrower seeks to borrow money from Plaintiff. During the course of their transaction, Plaintiff requires a financial statement from Borrower and meets several times with Defendant, who is Borrower's accountant. Plaintiff lends money to Borrower in reliance on a financial statement prepared by Defendant. Plaintiff loses money because of inaccuracies in the statement which result from unreasonable conduct by Defendant, who failed to check the truth of representations contained in the statement. Plaintiff asserts a claim against Defendant for negligent misrepresentation. Defendant argues that he did not owe Plaintiff a duty of reasonable care in preparing the financial statement.

In some jurisdictions, Plaintiff's claim will be dismissed because liability is not imposed for negligent misrepresentations which result in commercial losses.

In some of the jurisdictions which impose liability for negligent misrepresentation, it will nevertheless be held that Defendant did not owe Plaintiff a duty of reasonable care because Plaintiff and Defendant were not in privity. *Ultramares v. Touche, Niven & Co.*, 174 N.E. 441 (N.Y. 1931).

In some of the jurisdictions which impose liability for negligent misrepresentation, it will be held that because Defendant met several times with Plaintiff and knew that Plaintiff wanted the financial statement and would rely on it, the relationship between Defendant and Plaintiff was sufficiently close to result in a duty of reasonable care even though they were not in privity. *Credit Alliance v. Arthur Andersen*, 493 N.Y.S.2d 435 (1985).

In other jurisdictions, if defendant could foresee that Plaintiff would rely on the financial statement prepared by him, it will be held that Defendant owed Plaintiff a duty to act reasonably in preparing the statement even if there was no relationship at all between Plaintiff and Defendant. *Citizens State Bank v. Timm, Schmidt & Co.*, 335 N.W.2d 361 (Wis. 1983).

2. **Breach:** When a duty of reasonable care exists, defendant breaches it by either ***performing an act which the reasonable person would not have performed or failing to perform an act which the reasonable person would have performed***. In deciding these cases, courts usually ***compare the benefit*** resulting from defendant's conduct ***with the disadvantage*** resulting from that conduct. If the benefit outweighs the disadvantage, the conduct is reasonable. If the disadvantage outweighs the benefit, the conduct is unreasonable.

Example: Defendant, an accountant, prepares a financial statement for her client, Borrower, knowing that Borrower will use it in obtaining a loan from Plaintiff. In the course of preparing the statement, Defendant asks Borrower for the value of inventory contained in Borrower's warehouse, but makes no attempt to verify the information which Borrower furnishes. Because Borrower grossly overstates the value of inventory, the financial statement contains serious inaccuracies which cause Plaintiff to lose money. Plaintiff asserts a claim against Defendant for negligent misrepresentation. Defendant admits that she owed Plaintiff a duty of reasonable care, but denies that she breached it.

If the disadvantage of not verifying the information concerning inventory outweighed the benefit of not verifying it, then it was unreasonable for Defendant to accept the information provided by Borrower without verifying it, and she breached the duty of reasonable care which she owed Plaintiff. On the other hand, if the benefit of not verifying the inventory outweighed the disadvantage, then Defendant acted reasonably and did not breach the duty of reasonable care.

CHAPTER 12

INTERFERENCE WITH BUSINESS ADVANTAGE

I. INTERFERENCE WITH PROSPECTIVE BUSINESS ADVANTAGE

A. Conflicting goals: In our free enterprise system, the profit motive combines with the rules of free competition to assure the best possible deal for both the consumer and the supplier. In order to keep the system working at maximum efficiency, the law of torts must protect the right to make a profit without interfering with the freedom to compete in the marketplace. In recognizing the tort known as interference with prospective business advantage, the law protects the expectation of profit against improper invasions. In making malice one of its essential elements, however, the law protects the freedom to compete.

B. Essential elements: The essential elements of "interference with prospective business advantage" are (1) ***malice***; (2) ***interference with the plaintiff's prospective business advantage***; and (3) ***damage***.

1. **Malice:** Although "malice" generally means ill will or the desire to inflict harm, each tort requiring malice depends on its own unique definition. In connection with this tort, an ***individual is said to act with malice if his primary motive is to injure another rather than to make a profit, or*** if, driven by the profit motive, he acts in a way which is either ***unlawful or highly unethical***.

   Example 1: Defendant hires a barber to open a barber shop across the street from Plaintiff's barber shop. Defendant pays his employee $5 per haircut, but charges the public $1 per haircut. Defendant's purpose is to drive Plaintiff out of business and then to raise his own price to $7 per haircut. When Plaintiff sues for interference with prospective business advantage, Defendant moves to dismiss the claim on the ground that he lacked malice. Since Defendant's purpose was to make a profit, he probably was not acting out of malice, and Plaintiff's claim should be dismissed. *Tuttle v. Buck*, 119 N.W. 946 (Minn. 1909) (*infra*, p. 200).

   Example 2: In the above Example, assume that Defendant's purpose was to drive Plaintiff out of business and then to go out of business himself.

Since Defendant's purpose was not to make a profit, but rather to inflict an injury on Plaintiff, Defendant did act out of malice and Plaintiff's case should not be dismissed. *Tuttle v. Buck*.

Example 3: Defendant opens a barbershop across the street from Plaintiff's barbershop. Defendant charges the same price as Plaintiff, but hires a gunman to stand in front of Plaintiff's shop and threaten to harm Plaintiff's customers unless they go into Defendant's shop. Plaintiff sues for interference with prospective business advantage. Defendant argues that because his purpose was to make a profit, he did not have malice and Plaintiff's case should be dismissed.

Although Defendant's primary purpose was to make a profit, his method of competition was unlawful, and, therefore, satisfies the malice requirement. For this reason, Plaintiff's case should not be dismissed.

Example 4: Defendant, an attorney, is a member of Plaintiff's law firm. Defendant leaves the firm with the intention of starting his own law practice. After leaving Plaintiff's firm, Defendant communicates with Plaintiff's clients, soliciting their business in an unethical manner. Plaintiff sues for interference with prospective business advantage. Defendant moves to dismiss on the ground that since his primary purpose was to make a profit, he lacked the requisite malice.

Although Defendant's primary purpose was to make a profit, his method was unethical. For this reason, the malice requirement is satisfied and Plaintiff's case should not be dismissed. *Adler, Barish, et al v. Epstein*, 393 A.2d 1175 (Pa. 1978).

a. **Intent not sufficient:** Since the essence of the free enterprise system is competition, and since competition includes the right to induce prospective customers to do business with one's firm instead of with a business rival, the mere intent to get customers to transfer their business is not sufficient to create liability.

Example: Defendant is aware that Plaintiff is offering to sell Customer widgets at $10 each. Defendant offers to sell Customer comparable widgets at $9 each. Customer purchases the widgets from Defendant instead of Plaintiff. Plaintiff sues for interference with prospective business advantage.

Since Defendant's primary purpose was to make a profit, and since offering to sell products at a lower price than a business rival is a legitimate means of competing, Defendant did not have malice and will not be liable for interference with prospective business advantage.

b. **Negligence not sufficient:** It is generally held that ***negligence does not lead to liability for lost profits or losses which are merely economic***. For this reason, as well as to protect free competition, negligence is not a basis of liability for interference with prospective business advantage.

Example: Defendant's ship negligently collides with another ship, resulting in a chemical spill which prevents commercial use of the waterways for several days, causing Plaintiff, who is a fishermen, to lose profit. Plaintiff sues Defendant for his lost profit on the theory of interference with prospective business advantage.

Since there is no indication that his purpose was to injure Plaintiff, Defendant lacked the necessary malice to be liable for this tort. Since economic losses are not usually recoverable in a negligence action, Plaintiff's claim should be dismissed. *Louisiana ex rel: Guste v. M/V Testbank*, 752 F.2d 1019 (5th Cir. 1985 *en banc*).

c. **Exceptions:** Exceptions to the malice requirement exist for the variations on this tort known as interference with contract, false marketing, and injurious falsehood.

2. **Interference**: An interference occurs when the defendant's act results in a ***reduction in the value of an economic benefit which the plaintiff legitimately expected to derive***.

Example: Plaintiff works for Butcher as a livestock buyer, attending auctions and purchasing livestock for Butcher's account. Butcher pays Plaintiff a commission based on the prices paid for the livestock. Defendant, the owner of a livestock auction facility, prohibits Plaintiff from attending auctions held at Defendant's facility. As a result, Plaintiff is unable to make purchases for Butcher and loses commissions which he would have earned. Plaintiff sues for interference with prospective business advantage.

Since Defendant's act has diminished Plaintiff's opportunities of earning commissions by purchasing for Butcher's account, Defendant has interfered with Plaintiff's prospective business advantage. *Bacon v. St. Paul Union Stockyards*, 201 N.W. 326 (Minn. 1924).

3. **Prospective business advantage:** ***A prospective business advantage is a legitimate expectation of financial gain***.

Example: Plaintiff's Aunt Martha prepares a will leaving certain valuable property to Plaintiff. Defendant, Plaintiff's cousin, induces Aunt Martha to change her will, cutting Plaintiff out of it and leaving the property to Defendant instead. Plaintiff sues Defendant for interference with prospective business advantage. Defendant argues that the possibility of taking under a will is not a prospective business advantage.

Since a will does not speak until the death of the testatrix and since the testatrix is free to change her will for any reason at all at any time prior to her death, some jurisdictions hold that the possibility of taking under a will is not a legitimate expectation of financial gain and, therefore, not a prospective business advantage.

On the other hand, since the testatrix probably would not have cut plaintiff out of the will without Defendant's instigation, other jurisdictions would hold that the Plaintiff's possibility of taking under the will was a legitimate expectation of financial gain and, therefore, was a prospective business advantage. *Harmon v. Harmon*, 404 A.2d 1020 (Me. 1979).

4. **Damage:** Because the essence of the plaintiff's claim is a missed opportunity, and juries should not be permitted to speculate as to the value of any business opportunity, the ***majority of jurisdictions require proof of special damage***. A small minority permits proof of general damage when circumstances make it impossible to show exactly how much was lost as the result of the defendant's conduct.

Example: Defendant hires a barber to open a barbershop across the street from Plaintiff's barbershop and to give haircuts for $1. His sole purpose is to injure Plaintiff by putting him out of business. Plaintiff is driven out of business and asserts a claim for interference with prospective business advantage, but is unable to show how much profit he would have derived if he had stayed in business. Defendant moves to dismiss on the ground that Plaintiff has failed to establish special damage.

Since Plaintiff was unable to prove how much money he lost as a result of the Defendant's interference with his prospective business advantage, the majority of jurisdictions would dismiss Plaintiff's claim. A small minority would permit the case to go the jury on the question of damages even though Plaintiff did not prove a monetary loss. *Tuttle v. Buck* (*supra*, p. 197).

II. INTERFERENCE WITH CONTRACT

A. Special protection for contracts: The enforceability of contracts is a feature of our legal system which gives continuity to commerce and business. Although our society encourages business rivals to compete with each other, it seeks to discourage any behavior which would disturb relationships which are based on contractual agreement. For this reason, interference with a contract is a special form of interference with prospective advantage, but with elements which differ substantially from those of the tort of interference with prospective business advantage.

B. **Essential elements:** The essential elements of ***"interference with contract"*** are: (1) ***intent***; (2) ***interference***; and (3) ***a valid and existing contract right***.

1. **Intent:** Defendant intends an interference with Plaintiff's contract right when she desires (or knows to a substantial degree of certainty) that her act result in an interference with that right.

a. **Scienter required:** Since intent requires a desire (or knowledge) that the plaintiff's contract right be invaded, the necessary ***intent cannot exist unless the defendant knows of the contract to which the plaintiff is a party.***

Example: Defendant is aware that Plaintiff is negotiating to sell Customer widgets at $10 per widget, but is not aware that Plaintiff and Customer have entered into an agreement to that effect. Defendant offers to sell Customer widgets at $9 per widget. When Customer receives Defendant's offer, Customer notifies Plaintiff that Customer will not purchase from Plaintiff as agreed. Plaintiff sues Defendant for interference with contract.

Since Defendant was not aware that Plaintiff and Customer had entered into a contract, Defendant could not have known to a substantial degree of certainty that his act would interfere with plaintiff's contract right. For this reason, Defendant lacked the requisite intent and Plaintiff's claim should be dismissed.

b. **Interference need not be primary purpose:** So long as the defendant knows that his act will interfere with the plaintiff's contract right, the interference need not be the defendant's primary purpose in acting.

Example: Plaintiff is in the business of selling razor blades. Defendant, a salesman employed by Plaintiff, is aware that there are one million blades in Plaintiff's warehouse waiting for delivery to one of Plaintiff's customers. Defendant steals the blades from Plaintiff's warehouse and sells them on his own account. Plaintiff asserts a claim for interference with contract. Defendant moves to dismiss on the ground that his purpose was not to interfere with Plaintiff's rights, but to make a profit for himself.

Since Defendant knew that Plaintiff had contracted to sell

the blades and that if he stole the blades, Plaintiff would be unable to fulfill his contractual obligational and thus be unable to derive a profit, Defendant had the intent to interfere with Plaintiff's contract rights and Plaintiff's case should not be dismissed.

2. **Interference:** An ***"interference"*** occurs when there is a ***reduction in the value of the plaintiff's contract right***.

   a. **Inducing breach:** Conduct which induces a third person to breach or fail to perform a contract which she has with the plaintiff is an interference with the plaintiff's contract right.

   Example: Plaintiff, the owner of an opera house, contracts with Singer who agrees to perform at Plaintiff's opera house for a fixed fee. Defendant induces Singer to breach her contract with Plaintiff and to sing at Defendant's opera house instead. Plaintiff asserts a claim for interference with contract.

   Since Singer's performance was of value to Plaintiff, and since Plaintiff was deprived of it as the result of Defendant's act, Defendant's act was an interference with Plaintiff's contract right. *Lumley v. Gye*, 118 Eng. Rep. 749 (Q.B. 1853).

   b. **Making plaintiff's performance more difficult:** An act which makes the plaintiff's performance under a contract more difficult reduces the profit which the plaintiff is likely to derive as the result of his performance, and, therefore, is an interference with the plaintiff's contract right.

   Example: Plaintiff, a trash disposal company, contracts with the city to clean the city streets as often as they need cleaning for a fixed price per year. Defendant deliberately dirties the streets so that Plaintiff has to clean them more often than otherwise would be necessary. Plaintiff asserts a claim for interference with contract. Defendant argues that there has been no interference because no breach has been induced.

   Since Defendant's conduct made Plaintiff's performance more costly, it reduced the value of the profit which Plaintiff would derive and, therefore, was an interference with Plaintiff's contract right.

3. **Plaintiff's contract right:** For liability to attach, the interference must be with an expectation of making a profit under a contract to which the plaintiff is a party.

   a. **Contracts terminable at will or unenforceable over objection:** Since the expectation of profit under a contract which is terminable at will or unenforceable over objection is not certain, a controversy exists among the jurisdictions whether such a contract will support an action for interference.

i. **Prospective business advantage:** Some jurisdictions hold that the expectation of profit under a contract which is terminable at will or which is unenforceable over objection is at best a prospective business advantage. These jurisdictions hold that interference with such an expectation does not lead to liability unless it results from malice.

ii. **Contract right:** Other jurisdictions hold that since a contract which is terminable at will is enforceable until it is terminated, and since a contract which is unenforceable over objection (*e.g.*, one which violates the statute of frauds) is enforceable until an effective objection is raised, any interference with an expectation of profit under such a contract is an interference with contract right, which may result in liability without malice.

Example 1: Pursuant to a contract between Plaintiff and the Dairyman's Association, Plaintiff is to transport milk for Association members at a fixed rate. According to the terms of the contract, either party may terminate it upon one day's notice. Defendant persuades the Association to hire him instead of Plaintiff to transport the milk. Plaintiff sues Defendant for interference with contract.

Since Plaintiff's contract with the Association was terminable at will, some jurisdictions would hold that it was nothing more than a prospective business advantage. In these jurisdictions, Defendant would not be liable to the Plaintiff so long as Defendant's primary purpose was to derive a profit (*i.e.*, Defendant did not have malice).

Since the contract was enforceable until terminated, however, other jurisdictions would hold that Defendant's conduct interfered with Plaintiff's contract right. The fact that the contract was terminable at will, however, might affect the value of that right and the damages awarded for the interference. *Terry v. Dairyman's League*, 157 N.Y.S.2d 71 (1956).

Example 2: Under an oral agreement, Plaintiff is to sell Customer 500 widgets at a price of $2 per widget. Under a written agreement, Plaintiff is to sell Child, a minor, another 500 widgets at a price of $2 per widget. Defendant, who is also in the widget business, offers to sell widgets at a price of $1.50 each to Customer and Child, thus inducing them to cancel their contracts with Plaintiff. Plaintiff asserts claims against Defendant for interference with contract.

Because the contract with customer called for the sale of goods at a price in excess of $500, it falls within the provisions of the statute of frauds. Because it was not in writing, it was unenforceable over objection. Since Child was a minor, any contract which he made was voidable at his election. For these reasons, some jurisdictions would hold that Plaintiff's expectations under these contracts were nothing more than prospective business advantage, and that Defendant would not be liable unless he acted with malice.

Other jurisdictions would hold that since both contracts were enforceable until effective objections to them were raised, Plaintiff's expectations were contract rights, and Defendant could be liable even without a showing of malice.

4. **Damage:** The ***majority of jurisdictions*** presumes that a contract right has a value and, therefore, ***do not require proof of special damage***.

III. AFFIRMATIVE DEFENSE

A. **Justification:** As an affirmative defense to allegations of interference with prospective business advantage and interference with contract, a defendant may assert the ***privilege of justification***.

1. **Essential elements:** The essential elements of the ***"privilege of justification"*** are: (1) ***an attempt to protect a legitimate interest***; and (2) ***use of reasonable means***.

a. **Legitimate interest:** The courts usually hold that it is legitimate to protect one's own financial interest, the interests of society, or the interests of another person to whom the defendant owes a moral obligation.

Example: Plaintiff is a theatrical company which underpays and otherwise mistreats its employees. Defendant, a representative of an entertainers' guild, communicates with theaters which have contracted with Plaintiff and with theaters with which Plaintiff is negotiating, requesting that they not permit Plaintiff's troupe to perform until Plaintiff improves the conditions of its employees. As a result, some theaters refuse to honor their contracts with Plaintiff and others refuse to enter into contracts with Plaintiff. Plaintiff asserts claims against Defendant for interference with contract and interference with prospective business advantage. Defendant raises the defense of justification.

Since Defendant was a representative of an entertainers' association, he owed the entertainers employed by Plaintiff an obligation to attempt to improve their lot. Defendant was attempting to protect a legitimate interest. *Brimelow v. Casson*, 1 Ch. 302 (Eng. 1923).

b. Reasonable means: The means which a defendant uses to protect a legitimate interest are reasonable if the advantages likely to result from his use of them outweigh the disadvantages likely to result, considering the rights of the parties involved and the needs of society.

Example: In the above Example, if the improvement of conditions among Plaintiff's employees resulting from Defendant's act outweighs the harm resulting from his act, Defendant's act was reasonable.

IV. FALSE MARKETING

A. General concept: The free enterprise system induces business persons to expend substantial sums in developing marks and symbols by which consumers can readily identify their products. The law of torts protects these marks by imposing liability on anyone who uses the mark of another in a way which is likely to mislead the public.

B. Essential elements: The essential elements of ***"false marketing"*** are: (1) ***use of the plaintiff's mark***; (2) ***in a way which is likely to mislead the public***.

1. Plaintiff's mark: A mark is ***any symbol, logo, phrase, or other communication which identifies a product or service with the plaintiff***.

a. Not necessary that mark be registered: Although statutes provide special protection for a mark which is registered with an appropriate government office, the law of torts does not require such registration.

Example: Plaintiff is a comedian known as Johnny Carson. When he appears on television or in a nightclub, he is always introduced with the phrase, "Here's Johnny." Defendant, who is in the business of renting portable toilets, calls his company "Here's Johnny." Plaintiff asserts a claim for false marketing. Defendant argues that the phrase "Here's Johnny" is not a trademark because Plaintiff has not registered it as such.

Since Plaintiff is identified by the phrase "Here's Johnny," it qualifies as a mark even though it is not registered as such with any government office. *Carson v. Here's Johnny Portable Toilets, Inc.*, 698 F.2d 831 (6th Cir. 1983).

b. **Fanciful and descriptive phrases:** In order to qualify as a mark, a phrase must be fanciful, rather than descriptive.

Example 1: Plaintiff is the manufacturer of a product consisting of bits of absorbent cotton on the ends of short rolled paper sticks known as "Q-tips cotton swabs." Defendant markets a similar product under the name of "J brand cotton swabs." Plaintiff asserts a claim for false marketing on the ground that "cotton swabs" is its mark.

If the phrase "cotton swabs" is descriptive of the product rather than fanciful, it cannot be a mark. If, on the other hand, the phrase is considered to be a fanciful one, it may be a mark.

Example 2: In the above Example, assume that Defendant markets a similar product under the name "Cute-tips." Plaintiff asserts a claim for false marketing, alleging that the phrase "Cute-tips" sounds like its mark, "Q-tips." Defendant argues that the word "tips" is descriptive of the product and, therefore, cannot be a mark.

Since the name "Q" does not describe the product, it is clearly a fanciful name and may be a mark. If the word "tips" is also fanciful rather than descriptive, then "Q-tips" may be Plaintiff's mark. On the other hand, if the word "tips" is descriptive of the product, it probably will not be regarded as a mark, and "Q" will be Plaintiff's only mark.

2. **Likely to mislead the public:** Since the essence of the tort of false marketing is the claim that the defendant has passed off his product as the plaintiff's, there is ***no liability unless the defendant's use of the plaintiff's mark is likely to mislead the public into believing that it is buying plaintiff's product or service.***

Example: Plaintiff is a comedian known by the mark, "Here's Johnny." Defendant, who is in the business of renting portable toilets, calls his company "Here's Johnny." Plaintiff asserts a claim for false marketing.

Even though Defendant is using Plaintiff's mark, no liability will be imposed unless Plaintiff can establish that consumers dealing with Defendant's business are likely to believe that they are dealing with Plaintiff. *Carson v. Here's Johnny Portable Toilets, Inc., supra.*

3. **Negative effect:** A few courts have imposed liability for false marketing where the defendant's use of plaintiff's mark was likely

to cause the public to have negative thoughts about the plaintiff's product, even though the defendant's use of the plaintiff's mark was not likely to mislead the public.

Example: Plaintiff, the manufacturer of a beer known as "Bud", uses the mark, "Where there's life, there's Bud." Defendant, the manufacturer of an insecticide, uses a television commercial in which a camera focuses on live cockroaches while an off-camera voice says, "Where there's life, there's bugs". Plaintiff asserts a claim for false marketing. Defendant argues that its commercial was not likely to lead the public into believing that its products were manufactured by Plaintiff.

The difference between the two products probably would prevent members of the public from believing that Plaintiff was associated with the insecticide manufactured by Defendant. It is likely, however, that Defendant's use of a slogan sounding like Plaintiff's would lead consumers to think about cockroaches when seeing or thinking about Plaintiff's product. Since this association is likely to induce them to purchase a different product instead, some courts would impose liability for false marketing.

4. **Strict liability:** If a defendant uses a plaintiff's mark in a way which is likely to mislead the public, the defendant is realizing a profit which should actually be the plaintiff's. For this reason, ***liability is imposed regardless of fault***.

Example: Using the mark "Mt. Everest," Plaintiff manufactures and sells an expensive pen to a small market. Defendant begins to market his own expensive pen under the name "Mt. Everest." Because Plaintiff's market is small, Defendant does not know, and the reasonable person in her situation would not know, that the Plaintiff is using this mark. Plaintiff asserts a claim for false marketing, and proves that Defendant's use of the mark is likely to mislead the public into believing that Defendant's product is the same as Plaintiff's.

Since "Mt. Everest" is Plaintiff's mark, and since Defendant's use of it is likely to mislead the public into believing that Defendant's product is Plaintiff's, Plaintiff should recover damages from Defendant, even though Defendant did not intend to violate Plaintiff's rights and even though Defendant did not act unreasonably.

5. **Damages:** Damages usually consist of the profit which the defendant realized as a result of the confusion which led consumers to believe that the defendant's product was the plaintiff's.

Example: In the above Example, Plaintiff may recover the profit which Defendant derived from sales of the pen to persons who believed that they were purchasing the Plaintiff's product.

6. **Statutory modification:** Federal statutes prohibiting unfair competition create causes of action similar to the common law action for false marketing. These statutes are not discussed in this outline.

CHAPTER 13

PRODUCTS LIABILITY

I. GENERAL CONCEPT

A. Definition: Although the term "Products Liability" has been used and misused in a number of ways, all it really does is characterize a type of fact pattern in which the ***plaintiff claims to have been damaged as the result of contact or other association with a product which was furnished or handled by the defendant.***

B. Common products liability theories: As in any tort case, a plaintiff suing for damage resulting from contact with defendant's product must show that the defendant engaged in some liability-forming conduct. In products liability cases, liability may be imposed if the result was ***intended***, or if the conduct was ***negligent***. Liability may also be imposed if the defendant ***breached a warranty***, if the defendant made a ***misrepresentation***, or simply if the defendant furnished a ***defective product*** (*i.e.*, strict liability or liability without fault).

II. INTENT

A. General concept: A defendant who furnishes a product with the ***desire (or knowledge to a substantial certainty) that plaintiff***, or one similarly situated, ***be injured*** by it, may be committing an intentional tort.

1. Battery: A defendant who places a product on the market knowing to a substantial degree of certainty that a harmful or offensive contact with a customer will result ***may be liable for battery if such contact results***, *supra*, p. 8.

Example 1: Defendant, who manufactures medicine in capsules, is aware that terrorists have infiltrated its factory and poisoned some of the capsules before they were placed in bottles. Defendant sells the bottles, knowing that some of its customers will be poisoned by ingesting the capsules. Plaintiff purchases a bottle of capsules and is poisoned. Plaintiff subsequently asserts a claim for battery.

Since Defendant knew to a substantial degree of certainty that its volitional act (*i.e.*, selling the capsules) would result in a harmful contact (*i.e.*, ingestion of the poison) with unspecified plaintiffs, and since such contact resulted, Defendant may be held liable for battery.

Example 2: Defendant, who manufactures a prescription medicine, is aware that some persons are allergic to an ingredient in the medicine and will become ill if they ingest it. Defendant notifies all physicians who are likely to prescribe the medicine. A physician prescribes the medicine for Plaintiff, who is allergic to the ingredient and is injured as a result. Plaintiff asserts a battery claim against Defendant.

Since Defendant could reasonably rely on the likelihood that physicians would avoid prescribing the drug for patients with the allergy, Defendant could not be substantially certain that anyone would be injured by the medicine. Defendant probably is not liable for battery.

2. **Assault**: A defendant who places a product on the market with knowledge to a substantial degree of certainty that contact with the product ***will induce a consumer's apprehension of*** imminent harmful or offensive contact, may be held liable for assault if ***such apprehension results***, *supra*, p. 11.

Example: Defendant, a bottler of carbonated beverages, is aware that flaws in some of the bottles contained in a particular shipment will cause them to explode when handled by a consumer, but sells the bottles anyway. Plaintiff purchases one of the bottles and is attempting to open it when it explodes, showering her with broken glass which frightens and injures her. Plaintiff subsequently asserts claims for battery and assault.

Since Defendant knew that a bottle was likely to explode when handled, and since an exploding bottle is substantially certain to injure the person handling it, Defendant had the intent necessary to be liable for battery and assault. Since Plaintiff was injured by pieces of broken glass, Defendant may be held liable for battery. Since Plaintiff was frightened, Defendant may be held liable for assault.

3. **Intentional infliction of mental harm**: If a defendant acts outrageously by marketing a product with a substantial certainty that it ***will produce mental suffering in a consumer***, and if that product produces severe mental suffering, ***the defendant may be liable for intentional infliction of mental harm***, *supra*, p. 18.

Example: Defendant manufactures a white bathing suit, knowing that when it becomes wet, it becomes translucent. Plaintiff purchases the bathing suit and wears it while swimming at a public pool. After the suit becomes wet, Plaintiff realizes that it is translucent and is embarrassed. Plaintiff subsequently asserts a claim for intentional infliction of mental harm.

If Defendant was substantially certain that a person wearing the bathing suit would experience mental suffering as a result of the product's condition, Defendant had the intent necessary for a finding of intentional infliction of mental suffering. If Defendant's conduct exceeded all bounds normally tolerated by decent society and was extremely likely to produce mental suffering, Defendant's conduct was outrageous. Since Plaintiff experienced nothing more than temporary embarrassment, however, Plaintiff probably did not suffer severe mental suffering. For this reason, Defendant may not be liable for intentional infliction of mental harm. *Holden v. Kayser-Roth*, 235 N.E.2d 426 (Ill. 1968), *infra*, pp. 19-20.

B. **Unlikely theory**: It is possible that injuries which result from a plaintiff's contact with a product will be the basis of claims for battery, assault, and intentional infliction of mental harm. In a commercial setting, however, it is unusual for a provider of products to market them with the intent that such products cause harm. For this reason, few products liability cases are brought on intentional tort theories.

III. NEGLIGENCE

A. **General concept**: Negligence is a breach of the duty of reasonable care. (See discussion of Negligence, *supra*, pp. 55-86.) Thus, one who acts unreasonably in furnishing or handling a product may be held liable for negligence to a person to whom she owes a duty of reasonable care and who is injured as a result of the breach of that duty.

1. **Duty of reasonable care**: Before unreasonable conduct can qualify as negligence, it must be shown that the defendant owed the plaintiff a duty to act reasonably in doing whatever the defendant was doing.

   a. **Privity formerly required**: At one time, it was held that a manufacturer of products did not owe a duty of reasonable care to anyone who was not in ***privity of contract*** with the manufacturer. Since, even then, most manufacturers did not sell directly to consumers, but rather to middlepersons who sold to consumers, it was generally held that manufacturers did not owe consumers a duty to act reasonably in designing or fabricating their products.

   b. **Privity no longer required**: The rule now is that, ***in designing, fabricating, or otherwise handling products, a defendant owes a plaintiff a duty of reasonable care whenever***

it is foreseeable that what the defendant is doing will create a risk to that plaintiff.

i. **Foreseeable risk**: As in any negligence case, Defendant's duty of reasonable care ***applies only to those risks which are foreseeable.***

Example: Plaintiff is driving an automobile manufactured by Defendant when another vehicle collides with it through no fault of Plaintiff. As a result of the collision, Plaintiff injures his knee by striking it on an interior door handle. Plaintiff brings a negligence claim against Defendant, alleging that Defendant acted unreasonably by placing the door handle in a location where a driver's knee was likely to strike it in a collision. Defendant argues that it has no obligation to protect Plaintiff against injuries which result from accidents which are not caused by Defendant.

If it is foreseeable that an automobile will be involved in a collision, its manufacturer owes the car's occupants a duty to act reasonably in constructing an automobile which will be reasonably safe when involved in a collision (*i.e.*, which will be reasonably "crashworthy"). Some jurisdictions hold that automobile collisions are not foreseeable, and a manufacturer therefore does not owe anyone a duty to act reasonably to make a crashworthy automobile. Other jurisdictions hold that automobile collisions are foreseeable, and that a manufacturer therefore owes a duty to act reasonably in making make a crashworthy automobile. *Turner v. General Motors*, 514 S.W.2d 497 (Tex. Civ. App. 1974).

ii. **Foreseeable plaintiff**: Since a product which is not made in a reasonable manner is likely to harm a user of it, it is generally understood that a supplier's duty of reasonable care is ***owed to anyone who will foreseeably use it.*** Since non-users are frequently in the vicinity of products while they are being used by others, it is generally held that a supplier owes the same duty of reasonable care to ***non-users who will foreseeably be affected by the product***, as it does to users.

Example: Defendant, a manufacturer of automobiles, sells to a dealer an automobile which Defendant has manufactured in an unreasonable manner. The dealer resells the car to Driver. Because of Defendant's negligence, the automobile goes out of control while Driver is driving it, injuring Driver, a passenger, the occupants of another car on the road, and a pedestrian, all of whom bring negligence claims against Defendant. In response, Defendant asserts that he did not owe any of the plaintiffs a duty of reasonable care.

Since automobiles travel along the highways at great speed, and since many people use the highways, it probably is foreseeable that an automobile which is not built in a reasonable manner will endanger its driver, its passengers, the occupants of other vehicles on the highways, and pedestrians. For this reason, Defendant probably owed to all of these persons a duty to act reasonably in attempting to protect them against the foreseeable dangers of its products.

c. **Duty to act reasonably**: In analyzing the duty to the plaintiff, it may be unnecessarily confusing to be specific about what constitutes reasonable care in a particular case.

Example: Plaintiff claims that Defendant's negligence consisted of failing to tighten a certain bolt when manufacturing a product.

Instead of attempting to decide whether Defendant owed Plaintiff a duty to tighten the bolt, the problem should be analyzed in terms of two separate issues: (1) did the Defendant owe Plaintiff a duty to act reasonably; and (2) if so, was the defendant's failure to tighten the bolt unreasonable.

2. **Breach**: In general, the duty of reasonable care is breached when the defendant does something that the reasonable person would not have done under the circumstances or fails to do something that the reasonable person would have done. Ordinarily, courts determine whether a particular act or omission was reasonable by weighing the advantages foreseeable from the act or omission against the foreseeable disadvantages. If the advantages outweigh the disadvantages, the conduct is reasonable. If the disadvantages outweigh the advantages, the conduct is unreasonable.

Example: Defendant manufactures a van with the engine in the rear. Plaintiff is a passenger in the van when it collides with the vehicle in front of it, crushing Plaintiff's legs. Plaintiff asserts a negligence claim against Defendant, alleging that it was unreasonable to design a van with the engine in the rear because this left nothing in front to protect the legs of a passenger. Defendant proves that placing the engine in the rear increased available cargo space and made construction of the van cheaper.

Since placing the engine in the rear increased the cargo space and made the van cheaper, it may have resulted in advantages which outweighed the resulting disadvantages. If so, it was reasonable to design the van that way. This probably will be a question for a jury. *Volkswagen of America v. Young*, 321 A.2d 737 (Md. 1974).

a. **Specific allegation**: It is not possible to apply the balancing test unless the conduct alleged to be negligent is specifically identified.

Example: In the above Example, assume that Plaintiff simply asserts that Defendant was negligent, without specifying the conduct which constituted the alleged negligence.

Since the conduct constituting the negligence has not been specified, it is not possible to balance advantages against disadvantages, and, therefore, not possible to determine whether the conduct was unreasonable.

b. ***Res Ipsa Loquitur***: The doctrine of *res ipsa loquitur* (*supra*, p. 78) may be applied to products liability cases ***when the plaintiff's theory is negligence***.

i. **Foreign substances in food**: ***If a substance found in a food product is not normally associated with that kind of food***, it is unlikely that it got there without negligence, and *res ipsa loquitur* probably will be applied. On the other hand, if a substance found in food is normally associated with that kind of food, there is a likelihood that it got there without negligence, and, therefore, no inference of negligence will result from its presence (*i.e.*, *res ipsa loquitur* will not apply).

Example 1: Plaintiff breaks a tooth on a cherry pit in a cherry pie manufactured by Defendant. Plaintiff asserts a negligence claim against Defendant. At trial, Plaintiff's only evidence that Defendant acted unreasonably is the presence of the cherry pit. Plaintiff attempts to rely on *res ipsa loquitur.*

Since cherry pits are normally associated with cherries, it is likely that the pit got into the pie without negligence by the manufacturer. For this reason, the presence of the cherry pit is not sufficient circumstantial evidence to create the inference that Defendant was negligent. (*i.e.*, *res ipsa loquitur* does not apply.) Plaintiff may still attempt to make out a case by showing affirmatively that Defendant did something in the baking of the pie which was unreasonable.

Example 2: Plaintiff breaks a tooth on a cherry pit in a chicken pot pie manufactured by Defendant. Plaintiff asserts a negligence claim against Defendant. At trial, Plaintiff's only evidence that Defendant acted unreasonably is the presence of the cherry pit. Plaintiff attempts to rely on *res ipsa loquitur.*

Since cherry pits are not normally associated with chicken

or the other ingredients of chicken pot pie, it is not likely that the pit got into the pie without some negligence by the manufacturer. Since Defendant was the manufacturer, the presence of the cherry pit is probably sufficient circumstantial evidence to establish that Defendant did something unreasonable in the course of the manufacturing process. (*i.e.*, *res ipsa loquitur* may be applied.)

ii. **Applicable only to negligence**: When applicable at all, *res ipsa loquitur* is applicable only in negligence cases, and only for the purpose of creating an inference that the defendant did something unreasonable. It does not establish that a duty of care existed and it does not establish causation. It is ***not relevant to any other theory of liability.***

iii. **Not available when defendant's conduct known**: When defendant's conduct is known, *res ipsa loquitur* is not a substitute for proof whether that conduct was unreasonable.

c. **Violation of statute**: In some cases, the fact ***that a defendant violated a statute may help to establish negligence***, without regard to whether that defendant's conduct was unreasonable (*supra*, p. 80-83).

Example: Defendant sells an unlabeled bottle of poison to Plaintiff's decedent in violation of a statute which requires all poisons to be labeled as such. Plaintiff's decedent ingests the poison and dies. Plaintiff asserts a negligence claim against Defendant, alleging that Defendant's violation of the statute establishes that Defendant was negligent.

If the statute was designed to protect a class of persons which included Plaintiff's decedent, against the danger of ingesting an unlabeled poison, its violation helps to establish that Defendant was negligent. In some jurisdictions, the violation will raise an irrebuttable presumption of negligence. In other jurisdictions it will raise a rebuttable presumption of negligence. In a minority of jurisdictions, it will raise an inference of negligence. *Osborne v. McMasters*, 41 N.W. 543, (Minn. 1889).

IV. BREACH OF WARRANTY

A. **"Bastard child"**: Dean Prosser once called the Breach of Warranty theory of products liability "the bastard child of an illicit union" of the law of torts with the law of contracts. It is helpful to remember that while the law of torts has borrowed the warranty concept for use in products liability claims, the concept is essentially based on contracts principles. Most important is the absence of a fault requirement. Traditionally, tort liability has been based on fault, but contract liability has not. It is generally recognized that one who makes an enforceable promise is ***liable, without regard to fault***, for damage which results proximately from his failure to keep the promise.

B. Warranty defined: In the products liability context, a ***warranty is*** nothing more than a ***promise regarding the quality or condition of a product***. Like any other promise, a warranty may be express or implied.

1. **Express warranty**: A warranty is ***express*** if it is ***stated in words or a substitute for words***.

   Example: Defendant manufactures a helmet which it packages in a box decorated with a photograph showing a person wearing a similar helmet while riding a motorcycle. Plaintiff purchases the helmet to wear as head protection while riding a motorcycle and is injured because the helmet was not suitable for that purpose. Plaintiff asserts a claim against Defendant for breach of express warranty. Defendant argues that it never made a warranty.

   Although no words were used, the photograph probably served as a substitute for words and expressly warranted that the product contained in the box was suitable for use as a motorcycle helmet. *Winkler v. American Safety Equipment* (*supra*, p. 177).

2. **Implied warranty**: A warranty is ***implied*** if it would be ***gathered or inferred*** by the reasonable person from all the circumstances and the defendant's conduct.

   Example: When Plaintiff says, "I need a deodorant which won't irritate my skin," Defendant, a shopkeeper, hands him a particular brand of deodorant. Plaintiff purchases it and subsequently suffers a skin irritation as a result of its use. Plaintiff asserts a claim against Defendant for breach of implied warranty, alleging that Defendant warranted that the product would not irritate Plaintiff's skin. Defendant denies that she made an implied warranty.

   Since Defendant handed Plaintiff the product in response to Plaintiff's request, the reasonable person observing Defendant's conduct probably would gather or infer that Defendant was thereby indicating that the product would not irritate Plaintiff's skin. Defendant, therefore, has probably made an implied warranty to that effect.

C. Liability without fault: ***Liability for breach of express warranty is imposed regardless of fault by the defendant.***

D. Essential elements: The essential elements of any claim for breach of warranty are: (1) ***the existence of a warranty***; (2) ***the requisite relationship between the defendant and the plaintiff***; (3) ***breach of the warranty***; and (4) ***a causal relationship between the breach and the damage.***

E. Breach of Express Warranty theory: A defendant who has made an express warranty regarding a product is liable to any plaintiff to whom the warranty flowed, for any damage which resulted proximately from a breach of the warranty.

1. **Existence of warranty**: An express warranty exists when an ***assertion of fact*** is made which becomes part of the ***basis of the bargain.***

   a. **No particular language required**: Even without the traditional language of promise, a statement which asserts a fact and which becomes part of the basis of the bargain may be regarded as an express warranty. It is not necessary that a word such as "warrant", "promise", or "warranty" be used.

   Example: Defendant, the manufacturer of a pickup truck, uses a television commercial which shows its product being driven off the road over rough terrain while a voice chants the phrase, "Fun pickup. Fun pickup." Plaintiff purchases the truck and is injured when driving it off the road over rough terrain, because the truck is not suitable for such use. Plaintiff asserts a claim against Defendant for breach of express warranty, alleging that the truck did not live up to the promise that it could be driven off the road over rough terrain. Defendant denies having made such a promise.

   Combined with the phrase "Fun pickup", the filmed depiction of the vehicle being used in a particular way probably amounted to an assertion that it was suitable for that type of use. The commercial, therefore, may have constituted a warranty that the pickup truck could safely be driven off the road over rough terrain.

   b. **Assertion must be of fact**: An assertion is of fact if it ***does not equivocate or express doubt*** and if it concerns a matter which is ***capable of objective truth.***

   Example 1: Defendant, a car dealer, says to Plaintiff, "I think this windshield is shatterproof." Plaintiff purchases the car and is injured when the windshield shatters in an accident. Plaintiff asserts a claim against Defendant for breach of express warranty. Defendant argues that he made no assertion of fact.

Since Defendant's words "I think..." indicated that he was not certain, they equivocated or expressed doubt. The statement, therefore, was probably not an assertion of fact and, therefore, not an express warranty.

Example 2: Defendant, a used car dealer, says, "This is a safe car." Plaintiff purchases the car and is subsequently injured in an accident. Plaintiff asserts a claim against Defendant for breach of express warranty. Defendant argues that she made no assertion of fact.

The word "safe" is subjective in meaning, since different people have different ideas about what is "safe". For this reason, Defendant's statement is not about a matter which is capable of objective truth and, therefore, is probably not an assertion of fact or an express warranty.

c. **Basis of the bargain**: An assertion is part of the ***basis of the bargain*** if its subject matter is ***important to the plaintiff, the plaintiff knows it has been made and believes it, and it is a factor*** in the plaintiff's decision to purchase.

Example 1: Defendant sells a refrigerator to Plaintiff, telling her that it works properly. Plaintiff, who is buying it for use as a theatrical prop, does not intend to use it as a refrigerator and does not care whether it works or not. Subsequently, Plaintiff attempts to use the refrigerator as a refrigerator and is injured because it is not working properly. Plaintiff asserts a claim against Defendant for breach of express warranty.

Since the content of Defendant's statement was not important to Plaintiff, it probably was not part of the basis of the bargain and, thus, not an express warranty.

Example 2: Defendant advertises that its car is made with a shatterproof windshield. Plaintiff purchases the car without ever having seen or heard the advertisement and is unaware that the Defendant claims that its windshield is shatterproof. Plaintiff is subsequently injured when the glass shatters, and asserts a claim against Defendant for breach of express warranty.

Since Plaintiff did not know about Defendant's statement and it was not a factor in Plaintiff's decision to purchase, it was not part of the basis of the bargain and, therefore, not an express warranty.

Example 3: Defendant, a car dealer, tells Plaintiff that the windshield of a certain car is bullet proof. Plaintiff does not believe the statement, but purchases the car for other reasons. While driving the car on the highway, Plaintiff is injured when a sniper's bullet shatters the windshield and strikes her. Plaintiff asserts a claim against Defendant for breach of express warranty.

Since Plaintiff did not believe Defendant's statement, and it was not a factor in Plaintiff's decision to purchase, it was not part of the basis of the bargain and, therefore, was not an express warranty.

2. **Warranty must flow from defendant to plaintiff**: Promises are generally enforceable only by those to whom they have been made. This is the traditional requirement of "privity", which is simply a name for the relationship between parties to a contract. Under the breach-of-express-warranty theory of products liability, however, it is generally understood that an express warranty flows ***from any party who makes it to any party who relies on it***.

Example: Defendant car manufacturer advertises that its cars are equipped with shatterproof windshields. In reliance on Defendant's advertisements, Plaintiff purchases a car manufactured by Defendant from an independent dealer and is subsequently injured because the glass is not shatterproof. Plaintiff asserts a claim against Defendant for breach of express warranty. Defendant argues that it is not liable to Plaintiff because they were not in privity.

Since Defendant made the assertion of fact, and since Plaintiff relied on it, the warranty flowed from Defendant to Plaintiff. If the warranty was breached, Plaintiff may recover damages from Defendant. *Baxter v. Ford*, 12 P.2d 409 (Wash. 1932).

3. **Breach**: An express warranty is breached if the product ***fails to conform to the promise*** which was made about it.

Example: Plaintiff, a farmer, needs a product to prevent corn rootworm larvae from destroying his corn crop. Defendant, an agrichemical company, sells Plaintiff a chemical bearing a label which contains the phrase, "For control of corn rootworm larvae." Although Plaintiff uses the chemical on his corn, the crop becomes infested with corn rootworm larvae and is lost as a result. Plaintiff asserts a claim against Defendant for breach of express warranty.

Because Defendant warranted that the product would control corn rootworm larvae and it did not, the warranty was breached. *Swenson v. Chevron Chemical*, 234 N.W.2d 38 (S.D. 1975).

F. **Breach of Implied Warranty of Merchantability**: When a product is sold with an implied warranty that it is merchantable, the seller is liable ***without fault*** for damage which results proximately from the product's failure to be fit for the use intended.

1. **Existence of warranty**: Uniform Commercial Code Section 2-314 provides that in the absence of a valid disclaimer ***every sale by a merchant implies a warranty that the product sold is merchantable***.

   a. **New products only**: Many courts have interpreted this section to apply to ***new products only***, holding that the sale of a second-hand product by a merchant does not necessarily imply a warranty of merchantability, unless it can be specifically inferred or gathered from the seller's conduct or the surrounding circumstances.

   b. **Disclaimer**: The UCC (in Section 2-316) provides that in order to disclaim the implied warranty of merchantability, the disclaimer must appear in conspicuous print and ***must contain the word "merchantability", or a phrase such as "as is", "with all faults"***, or other language which in common understanding indicates that there are no implied warranties.

   c. **Definition of merchant**: Under UCC Section 2-104 a "merchant" is a person in the ***business of buying and selling*** the kind of products involved, or who ***holds himself out to have special knowledge*** about products like the one involved, or who ***employs a person who has or holds herself out to have special knowledge*** about the products.

   d. **Definition of merchantable**: Under UCC Section 2-314, a product is merchantable if it is ***fit for ordinary use*** in the manner intended.

2. **Warranty must flow from defendant to plaintiff**: Promises, even implied promises, are generally enforceable only by those to whom they have been made. This is the traditional requirement of "privity", which is simply a name for the relationship between parties to a contract. Under the breach-of-implied-warranty-of-merchantability theory of products liability, however, the traditional rules have been modified.

   a. **From whom the warranty flows**: The implied warranty of merchantability is made at the time a retail sale takes place and, under traditional contract law, flows directly from the retail merchant to the purchaser. Most courts agree, however, that although it is made by the retail seller, it ***flows to the purchaser from all members of "the vertical chain of distribution."*** This refers to all persons handling the finished product from the time it was manufactured, and includes the manufacturer, all wholesalers and middle persons, and the retailer. Many jurisdictions hold that ***suppliers of component parts*** which were used in making the finished product are ***not members of this vertical chain***, and that the implied warranty of merchantability does not flow from them.

Example: Glasser supplies windshields which are used by Maker in manufacturing automobiles. Maker sells the automobiles to Distributor who resells them to dealers who sell them to the general public. Plaintiff purchases one of these automobiles from Saleco, a dealer, and is injured when a flaw causes the windshield to shatter. Plaintiff asserts claims for breach of the implied warranty of merchantability.

Since Saleco is an automobile merchant, its sale to Plaintiff created an implied warranty of merchantability. This warranty also flowed from Maker and Distributor because they were members of the vertical chain of distribution. Many jurisdictions would hold that the warranty did not flow from Glasser, since it was a supplier of component parts and, therefore, not a member of the vertical chain of distribution of the automobile. This conclusion would not prevent Glasser from being liable to Plaintiff on some other theory.

b. To whom the warranty flows: Since the implied warranty of merchantability is made at the time of sale, it flows to the purchaser. Under the traditional privity concept, this would make the purchaser the only person who can enforce the warranty (*i.e.*, the only person to whom it flows). By the time the UCC was adopted, however, many courts had extended the protection of the implied warranty of merchantability to include persons other than the purchaser. UCC Section 2-318 was an attempt to codify this modification of the traditional view. Since there was disagreement among the jurisdictions as to how far the protection should be extended, the people who drafted the UCC wrote Section 2-318 in three alternative forms, labeled Alternatives A, B, and C.

i. Alternative A: Alternative A extends the protection of the warranty to all ***members of the purchaser's household*** who foreseeably will be affected by the product and who sustain personal injury.

ii. **Alternative B**: Alternative B extends the protection of the warranty to all ***natural persons who foreseeably will be affected by the product and who sustain personal injury***.

iii. **Alternative C**: Alternative C extends the protection of the warranty to all ***natural and artificial persons who (which) foreseeably will be affected by the product and who sustain either personal injury or property damage***.

Example: Seller, a merchant, sells Harry a widget manufactured by Maker. Harry lends the widget to his neighbor Nathan. Nathan takes the widget with him when he takes Harry and Harry's wife, Wilma, for a ride in a truck which belongs to Nathan's employer, X Corporation. The widget is unmerchantable, and it explodes, injuring Harry, Wilma, and Nathan. In addition, the explosion damages Nathan's toolbox and the truck. Harry, Wilma, Nathan, and X Corporation all assert claims against Seller and Maker for breach of the implied warranty of merchantability.

Most jurisdictions would agree that a warranty of merchantability flowed from both Seller and Maker, because both were members of the vertical chain of distribution.

All jurisdictions would agree that the warranty flowed to Harry because he was in privity with the merchant who made the warranty.

Alternative A jurisdictions would hold that the warranty also flowed to Wilma because she was a member of Harry's household who foreseeably was affected by the widget and sustained personal injury, but that it did not flow to Nathan or X Corporation because they were not members of Harry's household.

Alternative B jurisdictions would hold that the warranty flowed to Wilma and to Nathan because they are human beings who foreseeably were affected by the widget and sustained personal injury. Alternative B jurisdictions would not permit Nathan to recover for the damage to his toolbox, however, since this was not a personal injury, and would not permit X Corporation to recover for damage to the truck for the same reason, and because X was not a natural person.

Alternative C jurisdictions would hold that the warranty flowed to Wilma and to Nathan because they were natural persons who foreseeably were affected by the widget and sustained personal injury and, in Nathan's case, property damage. Alternative C jurisdictions would also hold that the warranty flowed to X Corporation because it was an artificial person which foreseeably was affected by the widget and sustained property damage.

3. **Breach**: The implied warranty of merchantability is breached if the product is ***unfit for ordinary use***.

   a. **Ordinary use**: ***Ordinary use*** includes the kind of use which is common, even though such use was not intended by the manufacturer.

   Example: Plaintiff purchases a dinette chair from Defendant, a furniture dealer. Subsequently, Plaintiff stands on the chair in an attempt to reach something on top of her refrigerator and is injured when the chair collapses because it is not strong enough to hold the weight of a standing person. Plaintiff asserts a claim against Defendant for breach of the implied warranty of merchantability. Defendant argues that chairs are intended for sitting, not standing.

   Although chairs are intended for sitting rather than standing, it is a common practice to use dinette chairs as stepladders in the kitchen. For this reason, it could be held that the chair was unfit for ordinary use (*i.e.*, unmerchantable) because it was not strong enough to hold the weight of a standing person. *Phillips v. Ogle Aluminum Furniture, Inc.*, 235 P.2d 857 (Cal. 1951).

   b. **Ordinary user**: Ordinary use is use by the ***kind of person who could reasonably be expected to use or come into contact with such a product***.

   Example 1: Plaintiff takes an over-the-counter headache remedy and becomes blind as the result of an allergic reaction to the product. A similar allergic reaction would occur in one out of every ten persons using the product. Plaintiff asserts a claim against Defendant for breach of the implied warranty of merchantability.

   Since the ordinary use of an over-the-counter headache remedy involves relatively safe ingestion by a wide cross-section of people, and since one in ten persons had the same allergy as the plaintiff, ordinary use probably included use by a person with such an allergy. Since the headache remedy was not fit for use by such people, it probably was unfit for ordinary use (*i.e.*, unmerchantable).

   Example 2: Same facts as previous Example, except that a similar allergic reaction would occur in only one out of every ten billion persons using the product.

   Since only one in ten billion people had the allergy, the

allergic reaction was extraordinary, and ordinary use of the product probably did not include use by people with the allergy. Since the product was safe for use by everyone else, it probably was fit for ordinary use.

c. **Ordinary negligent use**: Ordinary use may include such improper or negligent use of the product as is foreseeable.

Example: A vacuum cleaner manufactured by Defendant is equipped with a filter which has to be removed when the device is being cleaned. Ordinarily, the filter covers the opening in front of the vacuum cleaner's fan, but whenever the filter is removed, the blades of the fan are exposed. Plaintiff's mother removes the filter for cleaning but forgets to replace it. Plaintiff, aged eleven years, starts the vacuum cleaner and inserts his penis into the fan, sustaining injury. Plaintiff asserts a claim against Defendant for breach of the implied warranty of merchantability. Defendant argues that both Plaintiff and his mother made negligent use of the vacuum cleaner.

If it was foreseeable that a user of the product would fail to replace the filter and would permit a child to have access to it, and if it was foreseeable that the a child would insert his penis into the unguarded opening, ordinary use of the vacuum cleaner probably included such conduct, even if it was negligent. Since the product was not safe when used in that way, it probably was unfit for ordinary use. *LaRue v. National Union Elec. Corp.*, 571 F.2d 51 (1st Cir. 1978).

d. **Ordinary imperfection**: If it is common for a type of product to perform imperfectly, such a product may be fit for ordinary use even though it does not perform perfectly.

Example: Plaintiff purchases a racehorse from Defendant, a horse merchant. Soon after he receives the horse, Plaintiff discovers that the horse has tendonitis. As a result, the horse cannot run in races for a period of two years. After that time, it runs in thirteen races, winning four of them, and is subsequently used as a breeding stallion. Plaintiff asserts a claim against Defendant for breach of the implied warranty of merchantability on the ground that a racehorse with tendonitis is not fit for ordinary use.

Since it is common for racehorses to be disabled for years at a time, and to lose more races than they win, and since many racehorses are eventually relegated to careers as breeding stallions, the horse may have been fit for ordinary use in spite of the tendonitis. *Sessa v. Riegle*, 427 F.Supp. 760 (E.D. Pa. 1977), *supra*, 186.

e. **Injury not sufficient to establish breach**: The fact that a product causes an injury is not alone sufficient to show that it is unfit for ordinary use.

Example: Plaintiff purchases a hammer from defendant and, while using it, drops it on his toe, sustaining injury because of the weight of the hammer. Plaintiff asserts a claim against Defendant for breach of the implied warranty of merchantability.

Users of hammers frequently drop them on their toes and should expect to be hurt when they do so, because a hammer would not do its job if it were not heavy and hard. A hammer which causes injury when dropped on the user's toe is not unfit for ordinary use.

G. **Implied Warranty of Fitness for Buyer's Particular Purpose**: If a seller impliedly warrants that the product sold is fit for the particular purpose which the buyer had in mind when purchasing it, that seller is liable ***without fault*** for damage which results proximately from the product's failure to be fit for that purpose.

1. **Existence of warranty**: UCC Section 2-315 provides that when a ***seller knows of a buyer's particular purpose*** in purchasing a product ***and knows that the buyer is relying on the seller's skill and judgment*** in furnishing a product to fit that purpose, the ***sale implies a warranty that the product is fit for the buyer's particular purpose***.

Example 1: Intending to climb Mt. Everest, Plaintiff asks Defendant shoe seller for a pair of hiking boots. Defendant sells Plaintiff a pair of boots. While Plaintiff is climbing Mt. Everest, she is injured because the boots which she purchased from Defendant are not fit for climbing Mt. Everest. Plaintiff asserts a claim against Defendant for breach of the implied warranty of fitness for the buyer's particular purpose.

Since Defendant was a merchant, the sale was accompanied by an implied warranty that the boots were fit for ordinary use. Since Defendant was unaware of Plaintiff's particular purpose in purchasing the boots, however, there was no implied warranty that the boots were fit for climbing Mt. Everest.

Example 2: Intending to climb Mt. Everest, Plaintiff says to Defendant shoe seller, "I'm climbing Mt. Everest next week. Give me a pair of Bootco boots." Defendant sells Plaintiff a pair of Bootco boots. While Plaintiff is climbing Mt. Everest, he is injured because the boots which he purchased from Defendant are not fit for climbing Mt. Everest. Plaintiff asserts a claim against Defendant for breach of the implied warranty of fitness for the buyer's particular purpose.

Since Plaintiff selected the boots himself, he was not relying on Defendant's skill and judgment in furnishing a product to suit Plaintiff's purpose. For this reason, there was no implied warranty that the boots were fit for Plaintiff's particular purpose.

Example 3: Plaintiff says to Defendant shoe seller, "I need a pair of boots for climbing Mt. Everest next week." Defendant selects and sells Plaintiff a pair of boots. While Plaintiff is climbing Mt. Everest, she is injured because the boots which she purchased from Defendant are not fit for climbing Mt. Everest. Plaintiff asserts a claim against Defendant for breach of the implied warranty of fitness for the buyer's particular purpose.

Since Defendant knew Plaintiff's purpose in buying the boots and knew that Plaintiff was relying on Defendant to select boots to suit that purpose, the sale implied a warranty that the boots were fit for climbing Mt. Everest.

2. **Warranty must flow from defendant to plaintiff**: Although privity traditionally was required for the enforcement of an implied promise, modern law has changed this requirement.

   a. **From whom the warranty flows**: Since the warranty arises only when the seller knows the buyer's particular purpose and knows that the buyer is relying on the seller's skill and judgment in selecting a product to suit that purpose, the warranty of fitness for the buyer's particular purpose ***flows only from the seller*** who selected the product.

   b. **To whom the warranty flows**: Since, by its terms, UCC Section 2-318, *supra*, p. 221, applies to all implied warranties, the implied warranty of fitness for the buyer's particular purpose flows to members of the group specified by whichever alternative form of UCC Section 2-318 is adopted by the particular jurisdiction.

3. **Breach**: The implied warranty of fitness for buyer's particular purpose is breached ***if the product is unfit for the buyer's particular purpose***.

Example: Plaintiff says to Defendant shoe seller, "I need a pair of boots for climbing Mt. Everest next week." Defendant selects and sells Plaintiff a pair of boots. While Plaintiff is climbing Mt. Everest, she is injured because the boots which she purchased from Defendant are not fit for climbing Mt. Everest. Plaintiff asserts a claim against Defendant for breach of the implied warranty of fitness for the buyer's particular purpose.

Since Defendant knew Plaintiff's purpose in buying the boots and knew that Plaintiff was relying on Defendant to select boots to suit that purpose, the sale implied a warranty that the boots were fit for climbing Mt. Everest. Since the boots were unfit for climbing Mt. Everest, the warranty was breached, and Defendant is liable, without regard to fault, for damages which resulted proximately from the breach.

H. Exclusion or modification of warranties: Although the law provides for the existence and enforcement of warranties, ***parties are free to contract to exclude or modify these warranties***.

1. **Express warranty**: Under UCC Section 2-316, ***words or conduct which tend to create an express warranty and words or conduct which tend to negate or exclude such a warranty shall be construed as consistent with each other wherever reasonable***. UCC 2-316 further provides, however, that negation and limitation are inoperative to the extent that their application would be unreasonable. This means that ***if there is no reasonable way to interpret the warranty and negation as being consistent with each other, the negation fails***.

Example: Defendant markets a household cleaning product which bears a label stating, "This product is guaranteed safe when used properly and guaranteed to contain no harmful or poisonous ingredients. Warning: Do not expose to temperatures in excess of 120 degrees fahrenheit. May cause death if swallowed." Plaintiff, who is injured by exposing the product to temperatures in excess of 120 degrees and by ingesting some of it, asserts a claim against Defendant for breach of express warranty. Defendant argues that the warnings negated the existence of express warranties.

Under the UCC, language creating a warranty and language negating a warranty should be interpreted as being consistent with each other wherever reasonable.

Since the phrase "when used properly" is somewhat vague, the warning against exposing the product to high temperatures may be consistent with the warranty, if it is interpreted as an explanation of what use is proper. For this reason, the warranty may be interpreted to mean, "Safe if used at temperatures below 120 degrees."

On the other hand, the warning that ingestion can cause death cannot reasonably be interpreted as consistent with the phrase, "guaranteed to contain no harmful or poisonous ingredients." For this reason, it may be held that this warning does not negate or modify the warranty.

2. **Implied warranties**: Under UCC Section 2-316, implied warranties may be excluded or modified by conspicuous writing in language which, in common understanding, makes it clear that there are no implied warranties (*e.g.*, "There are no warranties which extend beyond the description on the face hereof," or ***"as is"*** or ***"with all faults"***).

   a. **Warranty of merchantability**: A written attempt to modify the implied warranty of merchantability must contain the word "merchantability."

   b. **Inspection by buyer**: If, before entering into a contract for sale, the ***buyer has examined*** the goods as fully as he desired ***or*** has ***refused*** to examine them, there is ***no implied warranty*** with respect to defects that an examination would have disclosed to a reasonable person.

      i. **Limitation of remedy**: UCC Section 2-719, provides that parties may agree to ***limit*** remedies ***or*** to ***provide for exclusive remedies*** for breach of warranty.

   Example: Plaintiff purchases a widget from Defendant for $4, pursuant to a sales contract which provides that in the event of product failure, the buyer's only remedy is replacement of the widget. The widget fails, causing Plaintiff to sustain incidental and consequential damages of $10,000. Plaintiff asserts a breach of warranty claim against Defendant for $10,000. Defendant argues that Plaintiff is not entitled to anything other than replacement of the widget.

   Since the agreement provided that replacement was the exclusive remedy, the buyer is probably entitled only to replacement of the widget.

      aa. Not exclusive unless so specified: Unless the agreement provides that specified remedies are the exclusive remedies, common law and UCC remedies continue to be available.

   Example: Plaintiff purchases a widget from Defendant for $4, pursuant to a sales contract which provides that in the event of product failure, the buyer is entitled to replacement of the widget. The widget fails, causing Plaintiff to sustain incidental and consequential damage of $10,000. Plaintiff asserts a breach of warranty claim against Defendant for $10,000. Defendant argues that Plaintiff is not entitled to anything other than replacement of the widget.

Since the agreement did not specify that replacement was the only remedy, Plaintiff is probably entitled to recover damages consisting of $4 to replace the widget and $10,000 as incidental and consequential damages, all of which are available at common law and under the UCC.

bb. Remedy which fails of its purpose: Where circumstances make an exclusive or limited remedy ***fail of its essential purpose, all other remedies continue to be available***.

Example: Plaintiff purchases a new automobile from Defendant pursuant to a contract which provides that in the event of breach of warranty, the buyer's exclusive remedy is replacement of any defective part. After Plaintiff drives only one mile, a defective wire under the dashboard causes the automobile to catch fire and to be totally destroyed. Plaintiff asserts a breach of warranty claim against Defendant for the value of the automobile. Defendant claims that Plaintiff is limited to replacement of the defective wire as her only remedy.

Since replacement of the defective wire would make the remedy for breach fail of its essential purpose (which is to make the buyer whole), Plaintiff probably is entitled to other common law or UCC remedies, including the replacement value of the vehicle. *Russo v. Hilltop Lincoln Mercury*, 479 S.W.2d 211 (Mo. 1972).

cc. Unconscionable limitation: An agreement which limits or excludes consequential damages is enforceable ***unless it is unconscionable***. Limitation of consequential damages ***for personal injury is prima facie unconscionable***.

V. MISREPRESENTATION

A. Common law: Since suppliers of products frequently make representations concerning those products, it may be possible for a plaintiff to proceed on a misrepresentation theory if she is injured because such statements are false. (See discussion of Misrepresentation, *supra*, p. 177.) Ordinarily, a plaintiff proceeding on this theory is required to prove fault. This may consist of proof that the defendant knew the statement to be false or recklessly disregarded the truth (*i.e.*, intentional misrepresentation), or that the defendant owed the plaintiff a duty to act reasonably in ascertaining the truth of the representations which he was making and breached that duty (*i.e.*, negligent misrepresentation).

B. Restatement (2d) of Torts, Section 402B: Some jurisdictions have adopted the view expressed in Section 402B of the Restatement (2d) of Torts, which imposes liability without fault for a certain kind of misrepresentation regarding a product.

1. **General concept**: Under the Restatement view, if the defendant is a professional seller of products and makes a public misrepresentation concerning the quality or condition of a product, liability may be imposed without regard to fault or privity, for damages which result proximately from the plaintiff's justified reliance.

2. **Essential elements**: The essential elements of liability under Restatement (2nd) Section 402B are: (1) Defendant is a ***professional seller*** (2) who made a ***public misrepresentation***; (3) which induced ***plaintiff's justified reliance***; and (4) resulting in ***damage***.

   a. **Professional sellers**: The Restatement applies only where the defendant is a professional seller of chattels. This may include wholesalers and manufacturers as well as retailers. If, however, the defendant is not in the business of selling chattels, this section does not apply.

   Example: Defendant wins an automobile on a television game show and decides to sell it. In advertising it for sale, Defendant refers to its windshield as shatterproof. Although Defendant believes this to be true, in fact it is not. After purchasing the automobile from Defendant in reliance on the representation that the windshield is shatterproof, Plaintiff is injured when the windshield shatters in an accident. Plaintiff brings a claim for misrepresentation under Restatement Section 402B.

   Since Defendant was not in the business of selling automobiles, the provisions of Section 402B are not applicable. For this reason, Defendant probably is not liable for misrepresentation in the absence of fault.

   b. **Public misrepresentation**: The Restatement Section 402B specifies that it applies where the misrepresentation is made in ***labeling, advertising, or otherwise to the public***. In comments which follow the section, the persons who drafted it state that they express no opinion as to whether it should apply to misrepresentations made to a single plaintiff only. So far, none of the states which have adopted the Rule have applied it to misrepresentations which were not made publicly.

Example: In attempting to sell Plaintiff a car, Defendant, a car dealer, states that the car is equipped with a shatterproof windshield. He believes the statement to be true. This statement is not made in any advertisements for the automobile, or in any other way to the general public. Although Defendant reasonably believes that the windshield is shatterproof, in fact, it is not. After purchasing the car in reliance on the assertion that the windshield is shatterproof, Plaintiff is injured when the windshield shatters in an accident. Plaintiff brings a claim for misrepresentation under Restatement Section 402B.

Since Defendant believed his assertion, he did not intend that it be false. Because Defendant's belief was reasonable, the falsity did not result from negligence. Defendant thus lacked fault in making the misrepresentation. Although Section 402B imposes liability without fault, it does so only when a professional seller makes a public misrepresentation. Since Defendant did not make the assertion publicly, he probably is not liable under Section 402B.

c. **Plaintiff's justified reliance**: Under the Restatement view, this requirement of reliance by the plaintiff is identical to its counterpart in the common law view. (See discussion of Misrepresentation, *supra*, p. 184.)

Example: In advertising a pain-relieving drug to physicians, Defendant states that it is absolutely non-addictive and as safe as aspirin. Plaintiff's physician prescribes the drug for Plaintiff in reliance on Defendant's statement. Plaintiff purchases and uses the drug on the advice of his physician. Plaintiff becomes addicted to the drug and eventually dies as a result. Plaintiff's personal representative brings a claim for misrepresentation under Restatement Section 402B. Defendant argues that Plaintiff did not rely on its statement.

Under Restatement Section 402B, liability may be imposed regardless of fault, so long as Plaintiff's damage resulted from his justified reliance on Defendant's representation. It may be argued that since the doctor relied on Defendant's representation in prescribing the drug and since ordinarily it is reasonable for a patient to rely on a doctor's prescription, Plaintiff justifiably relied on the representation. If this argument is successful, liability may be imposed on Defendant. *Crocker v. Winthrop Labs*, 514 S.W.2d 429 (Tex. 1974).

3. **Liability without regard to fault or privity**: Where applicable, the Restatement Section modifies the common law by ***elimi-***

nating the requirements of fault (i.e., intent or negligence) and privity.

Example: In advertising a pain-relieving drug to physicians, Defendant states that it is absolutely non-addictive and as safe as aspirin. Plaintiff purchases and uses the drug in reliance on Defendant's statement, but becomes addicted to it and is injured as a result. Plaintiff asserts a claim against Defendant for misrepresentation under Restatement Section 402B. At trial, a jury finds specifically that Plaintiff's addiction is the result of an unusual congenital response to medication which Defendant could not have foreseen. Defendant moves to dismiss on the ground that the jury has found it to be free of fault.

Since Defendant could not have foreseen Plaintiff's reaction, the falsity of Defendant's statement as applied to Plaintiff did not result from Defendant's fault. Since Defendant is in the business of manufacturing drugs, it is a professional supplier. Since its statement that the drug would not cause addiction was made in advertising, it was a public statement. For these reasons, Defendant may be held liable under Restatement Section 402B without regard to fault. Therefore, Plaintiff's case should not be dismissed. *Crocker v. Winthrop Labs, supra.*

4. **Distinguished from express warranty**: Because of the similarities between the misrepresentation theory and breach of express warranty, good practice requires that both be considered whenever either of them may be applicable. They differ in two important respects, however.

   a. **Professional seller of chattels**: ***Misrepresentation liability is imposed without fault*** under Restatement Section 402B ***only when the defendant is a professional seller*** of chattels. ***On the other hand, liability for breach of express warranty is always imposed regardless of fault and may be imposed on any person*** who makes and breaches an express warranty.

   Example: Defendant wins an automobile on a television game show and decides to sell it. In advertising it for sale, Defendant refers to its windshield as shatterproof. Although Defendant reasonably believes this to be true, in fact, it is not. After purchasing the automobile from Defendant in reliance on the representation that the windshield is shatterproof, Plaintiff is injured when the windshield shatters in an accident. Plaintiff brings claims for misrepresentation under Restatement Section 402B and for breach of express warranty.

Since Defendant was not in the business of selling automobiles, the provisions of Section 402B are not applicable. For this reason, Defendant probably is not liable for misrepresentation in the absence of fault.

Since Defendant's statement that the windshield was shatterproof was an assertion of fact which became part of the basis of the bargain, however, it was an express warranty, and Defendant may be liable for breaching it, without regard to fault.

b. **Public misrepresentation**: Misrepresentation liability is imposed without fault under Restatement Section 402B ***only when the misrepresentation is made in labeling, advertising, or otherwise publicly***. Liability without fault is imposed for breach of express warranty ***whether the warranty is made publicly or privately***.

Example: In attempting to sell Plaintiff a car, Defendant, a car dealer, states that the car is equipped with a shatterproof windshield. This statement is not made in any advertisement for the automobile or in any other way to the general public. Although Defendant reasonably believes that the windshield is shatterproof, in fact it is not. After purchasing the car in reliance on the assertion that the windshield is shatterproof, Plaintiff is injured when the windshield shatters in an accident. Plaintiff brings claims for misrepresentation under Restatement Section 402B and for breach of express warranty.

Since Defendant believed his assertion, he did not intend that it be false, and since Defendant's belief was reasonable, the falsity did not result from negligence. Defendant thus lacked fault in making the misrepresentation. Since Defendant did not make the assertion publicly, he probably is not liable under Section 402B.

Since Defendant expressly asserted that the windshield was shatterproof, and this assertion became part of the basis of the bargain, Defendant made an express warranty which was breached when the windshield shattered. For this reason, Defendant may be held liable for breach of express warranty, without regard to fault.

VI. STRICT PRODUCTS LIABILITY (STRICT LIABILITY IN TORT)

A. **Historical background**: The law of torts has traditionally imposed liability without fault (*i.e.*, strict liability) for damage resulting from certain activities (*e.g.*, blasting, keeping wild animals, etc.). (For full discussion, see *supra*, p. 94 *et seq.*) The law of contracts has traditionally imposed liability without fault for any breach of an enforceable contract. As the notion grew that a merchant impliedly warrants any product which he sells to be fit for ordinary use (*i.e.*, merchantable), tort lawyers found a way to impose liability without fault on the sellers of unfit products by basing their claims on breach of this implied warranty.

As the concept of privity evolved, situations in which strict liability was imposed for personal injury became more common. In 1963, this led a California court to state (in *Greenman v. Yuba Power Products Inc.*, 337 P.2d 897 (Cal. 1963) that although courts had been using the language of contracts to impose liability without fault in products cases, they were really recognizing a new form of "strict liability in tort." The phrase caught on and is frequently interchanged with the phrase "strict products liability" to characterize the imposition of liability without fault on one who places or moves a defective product in the stream of commerce. Although the *Greenman* case was one of the first to apply the concept, most jurisdictions follow the view set forth in Section 402A of the Restatement (2d) of Torts.

B. Restatement Section 402A: Section 402A of the Restatement (2d) of Torts provides that a professional seller of a product which was expected to and did in fact reach the consumer substantially unchanged, should be held strictly liable for personal injury or property damage which resulted proximately from a defect in the product which made it unreasonably dangerous. To these most courts have added a requirement that the plaintiff be a person whose harm was foreseeable.

C. Essential elements: In order for liability to be imposed under the Restatement view as modified by judicial decisions, the following essential elements must be satisfied: (1) it was ***foreseeable*** that the plaintiff would be affected by the product; (2) the defendant was a ***professional seller or supplier***; (3) the product was expected to and did in fact reach the consumer in a ***substantially unchanged*** condition after leaving the defendant's hands; (4) the product was ***defective*** when the defendant placed it in the stream of commerce; and (5) the defect made the product ***unreasonably dangerous***.

1. **Foreseeable plaintiff**: At first a controversy existed whether strict products liability could be applied for the benefit of anyone other than a user or consumer of the product (*e.g.*, for a bystander). Most jurisdictions have resolved the question by applying the section for the benefit of any person whose injury could have been foreseen.

Example 1: Defendant manufactures an automobile with a defective steering gear. As a result of the defect, a driver loses control of the vehicle, and it strikes Plaintiff, a pedestrian crossing the street. Plaintiff brings a strict products liability claim against Defendant. Defendant argues that Plaintiff cannot recover on this theory because she was not a user or consumer of the automobile.

In most jurisdictions, a plaintiff may successfully recover on a strict products liability theory if it was foreseeable that she would be affected by the product. Since pedestrians frequently walk across streets, and since automobiles are driven on the streets, it probably is foreseeable that a defective automobile will affect a pedestrian. Since plaintiff was a pedestrian, it was foreseeable that she would be affected by the product. For this reason, Defendant may be strictly liable to Plaintiff under the rule set forth in Restatement Section 402A.

Example 2: Defendant is the manufacturer of a farm forage wagon which is defective and unreasonably dangerous because it lacks a safety guard to protect the hands of a user from gears and other moving parts. Plaintiff, a four year old child, is playing on the farm forage wagon while it is in operation. She inserts her arm into an opening which is not protected by a safety guard and sustains an injury to her hand. Plaintiff brings a strict products liability claim against Defendant. Defendant argues that Plaintiff may not proceed on this theory because her contact with the product was not foreseeable.

Since a farm forage wagon is a dangerous and complex piece of farm equipment, and since farming is a business which rarely involves small children, it may be argued that it was not foreseeable that a four year old child would be playing on the forage wagon while it was in use. If Plaintiff's contact with the forage wagon was not foreseeable, Defendant probably is not strictly liable to Plaintiff. *Winnett v. Winnett*, 310 N.E.2d 1 (Ill. 1974).

2. **Professional seller**: Strict products liability is imposed only if the defendant ***is in the business*** of selling products like the one involved.

Example: Defendant wins an automobile on a television game show and sells it to Plaintiff while it is still new. After purchasing the automobile, Plaintiff is injured as the result of a defect which makes it unreasonably dangerous and which existed at the time of the sale. Plaintiff brings a strict products liability claim against Defendant. Defendant argues that he is not in the business of selling automobiles.

Strict products liability is imposed on the seller of a defective product only if that person is in the business of selling that product. Since Defendant is not in the business of selling automobiles, Defendant will not be strictly liable under Restatement Section 402A.

a. All members of chain of commercial distribution: Strict products liability may be imposed on ***all sellers and suppliers of the finished product, including manufacturers, wholesalers, middlepersons, and retailers.*** Most jurisdictions have been unwilling to extend this liability to manufacturers of parts which went into the finished product.

Example: Partco manufactures an altimeter and sells it to Planeco which builds it into an airplane. Planeco sells the airplane to Distributor which sells it to Dealer which sells it to Flyco which flies it commercially. Because the altimeter does not work, the airplane crashes, injuring Plaintiff, a passenger who purchased passage from Flyco. Plaintiff brings strict products liability claims against Partco, Planeco, Distributor, Dealer, and Flyco, all of whom deny liability.

Since the non-functioning altimeter made the airplane defective, Planeco (the plane's manufacturer), Distributor (the wholesaler) and Dealer (the retailer) may all be held strictly liable to Plaintiff, because they all placed or moved the finished product (*i.e.*, the airplane) in the stream of commerce.

A few cases have imposed strict products liability on a supplier of component parts. In most jurisdictions, however, Partco would not be held strictly liable because it did not sell the finished product (*i.e.*, the airplane), and because the product which it did sell (*i.e.*, the altimeter) did not reach the consumer in a substantially unchanged condition (*i.e.*, it was built into the airplane).

Flyco would not be strictly liable on this theory in any jurisdiction because it did not sell any part of the product. *Goldberg v. Kollsman Instrument Corp.*, 240 N.Y.S.2d 592 (1963), *infra*, p. 240.

b. Suppliers other than sellers: ***Some jurisdictions*** have imposed strict products liability on ***lessors, professionals who furnish products as part of the professional services rendered, and other suppliers, although they are non-sellers.***

Example 1: Defendant, a car rental company, leases Plaintiff a car with defective brakes. As a result of the defect, Plaintiff is injured. Plaintiff brings a strict products liability claim against Defendant. Defendant argues that it did not sell a defective product.

In some jurisdictions, Defendant will not be held strictly liable because it is not a seller of cars. In other jurisdictions, strict liability may be imposed on Defendant because it supplied the car, even though it did not sell it. *Cintrone v. Hertz*, 212 A.2d 769 (N.J. 1965).

Example 2: Defendant, a beautician, uses a defective product to color Plaintiff's hair. As a result, Plaintiff sustains injury to his scalp. Plaintiff brings a strict products liability claim against Defendant. Defendant argues that she did not sell the product.

In some jurisdictions, Defendant will not be held strictly liable because she did not sell Plaintiff the product, but merely furnished it as part of the professional service which she was rendering (*i.e.*, coloring Plaintiff's hair). In other jurisdictions, strict liability may be imposed on Defendant because she supplied the product, even though she did not sell it as such. *Newmark v. Gimbel's, Inc.*, 258 A.2d 697 (N.J. 1969).

Example 3: Defendant, a seller of propane gas, lends a piece of farm equipment called a potato vine burner to any farmer- customer who purchases propane for use with the equipment. Plaintiff, a customer to whom defendant lends the potato vine burner, is injured as the result of a defect in it. Plaintiff brings a strict products liability claim against Defendant. Defendant argues that it did not sell the burner.

In some jurisdictions, Defendant will not be held strictly liable because it did not sell the potato vine burner, but merely furnished it as an accommodation to customers. In other jurisdictions, strict liability may be imposed on Defendant because it supplied the burner even though it did not sell it. *Fulbright v. Klamath Gas Co.*, 533 P.2d 316 (Or. 1975).

c. **Real estate developers**: Although it is generally the rule that strict products liability is imposed only on sellers of chattels, ***some jurisdictions have imposed strict liability on real estate developers*** whom they characterize as mass producers of dwellings, even though houses are real property rather than chattels.

Example: Defendant, a builder, constructs a housing development and sells Plaintiff one of the houses in it. Because of a defect in the house, Plaintiff is injured. Plaintiff brings a strict products liability claim against Defendant. Defendant argues that strict liability should not be imposed, because a house is realty rather than chattel.

In most jurisdictions, Defendant will not be held strictly liable because a house is not a chattel and Defendant is not a seller of chattels. In some jurisdictions, however, strict liability may be imposed on Defendant because Plaintiff was injured by a defect in a dwelling which was mass produced and supplied. *Schipper v. Levitt & Sons, Inc.*, 207 A.2d 314 (N.J. 1965).

3. **Product must reach consumer substantially unchanged**: In order for strict products liability to be imposed, the product must have been expected to reach the ultimate consumer without undergoing any substantial change in its condition, and must in fact have done so.

Example: Drugco manufactures medicine in capsules which are free of defects when they leave Drugco's factory. While they are in Mart grocery store awaiting sale, criminals poison several of the capsules. Plaintiff purchases the capsules from Mart and is injured as the result of ingesting the poison. Plaintiff brings strict products liability claims against Drugco and Mart.

Although a poisoned medicine capsule is defective and unreasonably dangerous, the defect resulted from a substantial change in the condition of the product which occurred after it left Drugco's hands. Since the product was substantially changed before reaching the Plaintiff, strict products liability probably will not be imposed on Drugco.

Since the product was defective and unreasonably dangerous when it left Mart's hands, however, and since it did not subsequently undergo any substantial change before injuring Plaintiff, strict products liability probably will be imposed on Mart.

a. **Knowledge that changes will be made**: Some cases have held that strict liability may be imposed on a defendant who sells a product with ***knowledge that substantial changes will be made*** in it before it reaches the consumer and that such changes will make the product defective and unreasonably dangerous.

Example: Defendant manufactures and sells plastic in 500 pound blocks. The plastic contains an ingredient which makes it toxic when placed in the mouth. Knowing that the plastic is to be made into picnic spoons, Defendant sells a block of the plastic to a company for that purpose. Plaintiff is injured as a result of placing a picnic spoon in his mouth. Plaintiff brings a strict products liability claim against Defendant.

Although a substantial change was made in the plastic after it left Defendant's hands (*i.e.*, it was changed from a 500 pound block to picnic spoons), Defendant knew that this change would take place before the product reached the consumer. For this reason, some courts will permit the imposition of strict liability.

b. Minor changes: ***Minor changes*** in the product, or changes which do not make the product more dangerous than it was when it left the defendant's hands, ***do not prevent the imposition of strict liability***.

Example: Defendant manufactures automobiles which it sells to dealers for resale to the public. It is understood that before a dealer delivers an automobile to a purchaser, the dealer will perform a process called "new car prep" which consists of putting oil in the engine, cleaning the interior and exterior, and installing a battery.

Plaintiff purchases one of the automobiles from a dealer who performs "new car prep", and Plaintiff is injured as the result of a defect in the braking system which existed when the automobile left Defendant's factory. Plaintiff brings a strict products liability claim against Defendant. Defendant argues that strict liability should not be imposed because changes were made in the product before it reached Plaintiff.

Although changes were made in the automobile before it was delivered to Plaintiff, the changes were minor ones and did not affect the braking system or make it more dangerous. For this reason, the changes were not sufficiently substantial to prevent strict liability from being imposed on Defendant.

c. Expected changes in packaging: Some cases hold that ***changes in packaging*** which were made before the product reached the consumer and ***about which the defendant knew*** or should have known, are not sufficiently substantial to prevent strict liability from being imposed on the defendant.

Example: Defendant manufactures chemicals which it sells in two ounce containers to X. Defendant knows that X makes "do-it-yourself fireworks kits" which consist of three containers of Defendant's chemicals and instructions on how to combine them to make fireworks, and that X then sells the kits to the general public.

Plaintiff purchases one of the kits from X, uses it to make fireworks, and is injured when the fireworks explode with more force than Plaintiff expects. Plaintiff brings a strict products liability claim against Defendant. Defendant argues that strict liability should not be imposed on Defendant because a substantial change in packaging occurred before the product reached Plaintiff.

Since the chemicals would not have exploded without being combined, it may be argued that packaging them as a fireworks kit was a change sufficiently substantial to prevent strict liability from being imposed on Defendant. Some courts would hold, however, that since Defendant knew about the way X would package the product, the change was not sufficiently substantial to prevent strict liability from being imposed on Defendant. *Suchomajcz v. Hummel Chemical Co.*, 524 F.2d 19 (3d Cir. 1975).

d. Component parts: ***Most cases hold*** that component parts are substantially changed when built into a finished product. For this reason, they hold ***that suppliers of component parts are not strictly liable***, even if a defect in the component part causes the finished product to fail, injuring a plaintiff. Some jurisdictions make exceptions to this general rule based on the principles set forth in a., b., and c. above.

Example: Partco manufactures an altimeter and sells it to Planeco which builds it into an airplane. Because of a defect, the altimeter does not work, causing the airplane to crash and injure Plaintiff, a passenger. Plaintiff brings a strict products liability claim against Partco.

Since the non-functioning altimeter could not have injured anyone until it was built into an airplane, its use in the plane was a substantial change which was made before it reached the consumer. In most jurisdictions, this would prevent strict liability from being imposed on Partco. In some jurisdictions, however, strict liability would be imposed on Partco because Partco sold the altimeter to Planeco with knowledge that it would be built into an airplane. (See discussion under 3.a., *supra*, p. 238.) *Goldberg v. Kollsman Instrument Corp.*, *supra*, p. 236.

4. Defective condition: Among other ways, a product may be defective because it contains harmful ingredients; because it contains foreign objects; because it has deteriorated or decayed prior to sale; because of the way it was designed; because of the way it was prepared; because of the instructions and warnings which did or did not accompany it; or because of the way it was packaged. In any case, several tests and definitions have been developed to determine whether a product is in a defective condition. Most jurisdictions favor one or the other, but are prepared to use any or all of them in the appropriate case. Since it would be impossible to list all the definitions which courts have fashioned and are continuing to fashion, we will concentrate on those most commonly used.

a. **Consumer contemplation**: Most commonly, a product defect is defined in terms of consumer contemplation. Under this approach, a product is defective if its condition would ***defeat the reasonable expectations of the reasonable consumer***.

Example 1: Defendant manufactures an ax which is so sharp that when Plaintiff accidentally strikes his leg with it, it cuts him. Plaintiff brings a strict products liability claim against Defendant, asserting that the sharp edge is a defect.

Since an ax is used for cutting wood, the reasonable consumer expects it to be sharp. For this reason, the ax manufactured by Defendant probably was not defective.

Example 2: Defendant manufactures a drinking glass with a jagged edge which is so sharp that when Plaintiff attempts to drink from it, it cuts his lip. Plaintiff brings a strict products liability claim against Defendant, asserting that the sharp edge is a defect.

Since a drinking glass is intended to come into contact with the lips of a user, the reasonable consumer does not expect it to have a sharp, jagged edge. For this reason, the drinking glass manufactured by Defendant probably was defective.

i. **Foreseeable misuse**: If a product is likely to be misused in a particular way, the reasonable consumer would probably expect it to be safe when used that way. Thus, ***a condition of the product which makes it dangerous when subjected to foreseeable misuse may constitute a defect***, unless a proper warning is given.

Example: Defendant manufactures "burning alcohol" for dental technicians to use as fuel in an alcohol torch. Although the alcohol is toxic, the label contains only the following statement: "Alcohol. For use in the burning torch." Plaintiff, a prisoner employed in the prison dental laboratory, drinks the product, believing it to be potable, and is injured as a result of its toxicity. Plaintiff brings a strict products liability claim against Defendant. Defendant argues that the product was fit for its intended use, and that, therefore, it was not defective.

Since most people believe that "alcohol" is drinkable, it probably was foreseeable that someone would attempt to drink the product. Since the label did not warn of the danger of drinking it, the reasonable consumer would expect it to be drinkable.

Since it was toxic, its condition defeated that expectation and was defective, even though drinking it may have been a misuse of it. *Barnes v. Litton*, 555 F.2d 1184 (4th Cir. 1977).

ii. **Inadequate packaging**: Since a product and the container in which it comes are purchased as an integrated whole, they ordinarily cannot be distinguished from each other. Thus, ***a product which is safe but which is packaged in a dangerous or inadequate container may be regarded as defective***.

Example: Defendant manufactures and sells a carbonated beverage in a glass bottle which has a minute crack in it. When Plaintiff picks up the bottle, it explodes as a result of the crack, causing Plaintiff to be injured. Plaintiff brings a strict products liability claim against Defendant. Defendant argues that the beverage itself was not defective, and therefore, that strict liability should not be applied.

Although the carbonated beverage was not defective, the reasonable consumer (or the reasonable seller) would expect such a product to be packaged in a container which would not explode under normal conditions. For this reason, the condition of the bottle would probably be considered a product defect.

iii. **Inadequate warning or instructions**: Since the reasonable consumer's expectations are influenced by warnings and instructions affixed to a product, the ***absence or inadequacy of warnings or instructions can make a product defective***. Conversely, the presence of warnings can prevent a product from being defective.

Example: Defendant, the manufacturer of a cleaning solution which is poisonous if taken internally, prints the following statement on the product label: "Warning. Ingestion of this product could lead to permanent and total cessation of respiratory function." Plaintiff uses the product to clean her false teeth and is poisoned by it when she places the teeth in her mouth. Plaintiff brings a strict products liability claim against Defendant. Defendant argues that the product was not defective because it was accompanied by a warning.

If the language of the warning did not adequately describe the toxicity of the product, the reasonable consumer probably would not expect it to be toxic. For this reason, its toxicity probably was a defect.

iv. **Unavoidably unsafe products**: There are some products which are incapable of being made safe for their intended or ordinary use, ***but which are necessary or desirable***. Such products are ***not defective if accompanied by proper instructions and warnings***.

Example: Defendant manufactures a medicine which cures a certain form of cancer, but which creates a 5% risk of leukemia. This risk cannot be eliminated. Defendant markets the medicine, properly warning of the risk. After receiving Defendant's warning, Plaintiff consents to treatment with the medicine. As a result, Plaintiff develops leukemia. Plaintiff brings a strict products liability claim against Defendant. Defendant argues that even though the product caused leukemia it was not defective.

Since the product cannot be made completely safe, the warning made a 5% risk of leukemia part of the reasonable consumer's expectation. Thus, the existence of that risk probably did not constitute a product defect.

b. **Reasonable seller with knowledge**: Some cases have stated that a product is defective if a reasonable seller with knowledge of its condition would not have sold it. This is often confusing because reference to "the reasonable seller with knowledge" makes people think of negligence. Strict liability is not based on negligence, however. For this test, it is necessary to imagine a hypothetical "reasonable seller" who knows all about the condition of the product. If that ***imaginary "reasonable seller with knowledge" would not be willing to sell the product in its actual condition, then that condition may be called defective***. Some courts have said that since the reasonable seller's expectations are identical with those of the reasonable buyer, this is just another way of describing the "consumer contemplation" test.

Example 1: Defendant manufactures an ax which is so sharp that when Plaintiff accidentally strikes his leg with it, it cuts him. Plaintiff brings a strict products liability claim against Defendant, asserting that the sharp edge is a defect.

Since an ax is used for cutting wood, the reasonable seller probably would have sold it even if she had known how sharp it was. For this reason, the ax manufactured by Defendant probably was not defective.

Example 2: Defendant manufactures a drinking glass with a jagged edge which is so sharp that when Plaintiff attempts to drink from it, it cuts his lip. Plaintiff brings a strict products liability claim against Defendant, asserting that the sharp edge is a defect.

Since a drinking glass is intended to come into contact with the lips of a user, the reasonable seller probably would not have sold this glass if she had known that it had a sharp, jagged edge. For this reason, the drinking glass manufactured by Defendant probably was defective.

c. **Design defects and manufacturing defects**: In a particular case, it may be necessary to distinguish between design defects and manufacturing defects. This is because ***some jurisdictions have held that liability for injuries resulting from a design defect will not be imposed unless the design was negligent***. In effect, this means that in these jurisdictions, strict liability is not imposed for injuries resulting from a design defect.

Example: Defendant manufactures a forklift according to a design which does not include a seat for the operator. Plaintiff attempts to start the forklift while standing beside it and is injured when the forklift surges forward knocking plaintiff to the ground. Plaintiff brings a strict products liability claim against Defendant, alleging that the absence of a seat for the operator was a design defect. At trial, Plaintiff fails to prove that Defendant acted negligently in designing the forklift. Defendant moves to dismiss Plaintiff's case.

In many jurisdictions, strict products liability will be imposed on a defendant who furnishes a product which is defective in any way, including its design. In such jurisdictions, Plaintiff's case probably will not be dismissed.

In some jurisdictions, however, strict liability is not imposed for design defects. In these jurisdictions, Plaintiff's case will be dismissed unless Plaintiff can establish negligence in the design of the product. *Prentis v. Yale Mfg. Co.*, 365 N.W.2d 176 (Mich. 1984).

i. **Design defect**: If the ***product is made the way it was designed to be made, but still is defective*** (*i.e.*, defeats the reasonable expectation of the reasonable consumer) it is said to be defective in design or to have a ***design defect***.

ii. **Manufacturing defect**: If the product is defective because it was ***not made the way it was designed to be made***, it is said to be defective in manufacture or to have a ***manufacturing defect***.

Example: In the previous Example, if we assume that the absence of a seat was a defect, and that the design called for the forklift to be manufactured without a seat, the absence of a seat was a design defect. If the design called for the forklift to be manufactured with a seat, but it was manufactured without a seat, the absence of a seat was a manufacturing defect.

5. **Unreasonably dangerous condition**: In many jurisdictions, the rules used to determine whether a product is "defective" may also be used to determine whether a product is "unreasonably dangerous." The result is a blending of the two concepts, so that frequently they become synonymous. For clearer understanding, however, it is a good idea to think of them separately.

   a. **Restatement view**: Restatement Section 402A, comment (i), states that a product is unreasonably dangerous if it is ***dangerous "to an extent beyond that which would be contemplated by the ordinary consumer*** who purchases it, with the ordinary knowledge common to the community as to its characteristics." In practice, this is so much like the "consumer contemplation" test for product defects that it is difficult to distinguish between the two concepts.

      Example 1: Plaintiff suffers a heart attack because the butter which he ate and which was manufactured by Defendant, deposited cholesterol in his arteries. Plaintiff brings a strict products liability claim against Defendant. Defendant argues that the butter was neither defective nor unreasonably dangerous.

      Since the ordinary consumer knows that butter is high in fat and expects it to deposit cholesterol in the arteries of anyone who consumes it, the butter probably was not unreasonably dangerous. (It may also be argued that since the reasonable consumer expects butter to raise human cholesterol levels, the butter was not defective.)

      Example 2: Plaintiff is injured because he eats butter manufactured by Defendant which contains poisonous fish oil. Plaintiff brings a strict products liability claim against Defendant. Defendant argues that the butter was neither defective nor unreasonably dangerous.

      Since the ordinary consumer does not expect butter to contain poisonous fish oil and does not expect it to poison anyone, the butter was unreasonably dangerous. (It may also be argued that since the reasonable consumer does not expect butter to contain poisonous fish oil, the butter was defective.)

   b. **Balancing disadvantages against advantages**: Traditionally, in deciding whether conduct is reasonable, courts balance the foreseeable benefit (*i.e.*, advantage) against the foreseeable risk (*i.e.*, disadvantage). If the benefit foreseeably resulting from particular conduct outweighs the risk, the conduct is said to be unreasonable. Although strict products liability does not depend on the unreasonableness of a defendant's conduct, many courts use a similar process to determine whether a product's condition is unreasonably dangerous. If the ***condition of a product creates more risk (i.e.***, disadvantage) than benefit (*i.e.*, advantage), it is said to be unreasonably dangerous. On the other hand, if the benefit outweighs the risk, the product's condition is not unreasonably dangerous.

Example: Defendant manufactures and sells a van built with the engine located behind the passenger compartment in order to increase the van's cargo space. As a result, there is nothing in front of the front-seat passenger's legs but the thin sheet metal of the van's body. Plaintiff is riding in the front seat when the van strikes another vehicle, crushing Plaintiff's legs. Plaintiff brings a strict products liability claim against Defendant, alleging that the lack of protection for the legs of a front seat passenger makes the van unreasonably dangerous. Defendant argues that the van is not unreasonably dangerous because the risks created by its condition are outweighed by its advantages.

Since the construction of the van increased the available cargo space, a question of fact arises whether the advantage derived is outweighed by the resulting risk. Similarly, since the addition of safety features would have increased the price of the van, a question of fact arises whether the benefit derived from a lower price is outweighed by the resulting risk. *Volkswagen of America v. Young*, 321 A.2d 737 (Md. 1974).

c. **Distinguished from negligence**: Since strict liability does not depend on fault, determining whether a product is unreasonably dangerous does not depend on whether its manufacturer (or any other seller) was negligent. To decide whether a defendant was negligent, however, the benefits resulting from his conduct must be compared with the disadvantages resulting from that conduct. To do this, we must examine the defendant's conduct and consider what benefits and disadvantages could have been foreseen by the reasonable person in the defendant's shoes at the time the defendant acted. If no disadvantage was reasonably foreseeable, the defendant's conduct could not have been unreasonable.

On the other hand, a product may be unreasonably dangerous even if the conduct of its manufacturer (or other sellers) was reasonable. To determine whether a product is unreasonably dangerous, it is not necessary, or even relevant, to examine the conduct of the person who manufactured and/or marketed it. Nor is it necessary to determine what benefits and disadvantages would have been foreseen by the reasonable person in the defendant's shoes at the time he acted. Instead, the actual benefits must be compared with the actual disadvantages, even though the reasonable person could not have foreseen or known of them.

Example 1: Defendant manufactures Dammitol, a drug which cures mild tension headaches. Although safe and effective for 99% of the users, Dammitol is likely to kill 1% of the users. Since information to this effect has been published in several relevant professional journals, Defendant should know this, but does not. Plaintiff takes Defendant's drug for a mild tension headache and dies from its effects. Plaintiff's personal representative brings claims against Defendant on theories of strict products liability and negligence.

Since mild tension headaches are not especially dangerous or debilitating, and since many less dangerous headache remedies are available, the benefits derived from the use of Dammitol probably are outweighed by the disadvantages. For this reason, the product probably is unreasonably dangerous, and strict products liability may be imposed.

Since Defendant should have known of the disadvantages, it probably was unreasonable for him to market the drug. For this reason, negligence liability may be imposed.

Example 2: Defendant manufactures Dammitol, a drug which cures mild tension headaches. Although safe and effective for 99% of the users, Dammitol is likely to kill 1% of the users. Although all reasonable tests have been performed, neither Defendant nor anyone else has discovered that the drug will kill 1% of its users. At the time Defendant markets the drug, it can not be reasonably foreseen that the drug will kill any of its users. Plaintiff takes the drug for a mild tension headache and dies from its effects. Plaintiff's personal representative brings claims against Defendant on theories of strict products liability and negligence.

Since mild tension headaches are not especially dangerous or debilitating, benefits derived from the use of Dammitol are outweighed by the disadvantages. For this reason, the product probably is unreasonably dangerous, and strict products liability may be imposed.

Since Defendant in our Example could not have foreseen or known of the disadvantages, it was probably reasonable for him to market the drug. For this reason, negligence liability will not be imposed.

D. Minority views: ***Under the Restatement view, strict liability is not imposed unless the product is both defective and unreasonably dangerous***. Since the same definition is often used for both "defect" and "unreasonable danger", however, the evidence which justifies a finding that the product is defective may also justify a finding that the product is unreasonably dangerous. Thus, although both requirements exist, satisfying one frequently satisfies the other. In ***some jurisdictions, the courts reason that only one of these requirements exists***.

1. **Defect only**: Some cases have held that strict liability for harm to a foreseeable plaintiff may be imposed on a professional seller of a product which was expected to and did in fact reach the consumer substantially unchanged, if the product was in a defective condition when it left the seller's hands.

2. **Unreasonable danger only**: Some cases have held that strict liability for harm to a foreseeable plaintiff may be imposed on a professional seller of a product which was expected to and did in fact reach the consumer substantially unchanged, if the product was in an unreasonably dangerous condition when it left the seller's hands.

3. **Defect or unreasonable danger**: Some cases have held that strict liability for harm to a foreseeable plaintiff may be imposed on a professional seller of a product which was expected to and did in fact reach the consumer substantially unchanged, if the product was in either a defective condition or an unreasonably dangerous condition when it left the seller's hands.

CHAPTER 14

DEFAMATION

I. GENERAL CONCEPT

A. Protection of reputation: Defamation is the generic name given to libel and slander, torts which involve damage to the plaintiff's reputation.

B. Libel and slander distinguished: The difference between libel and slander consists primarily of the way in which damage to the plaintiff's reputation is accomplished. Defamatory statements which are made in writing are called libel, while the same statements, when made orally, are called slander. Under English common law, libel and slander were crimes. Libel, a felony, was punishable by death. Slander, a misdemeanor, was punishable by imprisonment. Today, the distinction between libel and slander is less significant.

C. Essential elements: The ***essential elements*** of defamation are: (1) ***a defamatory statement concerning Plaintiff***; (2) ***its falsity***; (3) ***fault***; (4) ***publication***; and (5) ***damage***.

II. ESSENTIAL ELEMENTS

A. Defamatory statement concerning plaintiff: Liability for defamation will not be imposed unless the defendant has made a defamatory statement concerning the plaintiff.

1. **Defamatory**: A statement is defamatory if it tends to injure the plaintiff's reputation by holding the plaintiff up to ***shame, disgrace, or ridicule***. Without the aspect of shame, disgrace, or ridicule, a statement is not defamatory even if it is false and has the effect of injuring the plaintiff's reputation.

   Example: Defendant falsely states that Plaintiff is not a member of the Republican party. As a result, many Republicans vote against Plaintiff, and Plaintiff loses an election. Plaintiff asserts a claim against Defendant for defamation.

   Since there is no shame or disgrace in not being a member of the Republican party, and since non-membership in the Republican party does not usually result in ridicule, Defendant's statement probably was not defamatory, even though it caused Plaintiff to lose the election. *Frinzi v. Hanson*, 140 N.W.2d 259 (Wis. 1966) (*infra*, p. 252).

a. **Substantial group of respectable people**: A person's reputation depends on what others think of her. Since some people find shameful or disgraceful what others find laudatory, it is necessary for the definition of "defamatory" in a particular case to be specific. For this reason, courts usually hold that a statement is not defamatory unless it would cause ***a substantial group of respectable people*** to attach shame, disgrace, or ridicule to the person about whom it has been made.

Example: Plaintiff is a detective who often obtains important information from acquaintances who are professional criminals. Defendant newspaper incorrectly reports that Plaintiff was instrumental in catching a criminal. As a result, most professional criminals think that Plaintiff is a shameful and disgraceful person and stop associating with him. This prevents Plaintiff from obtaining information and reduces his effectiveness as a detective. Plaintiff asserts a defamation claim against Defendant. Defendant argues that its statement was not defamatory.

Although Defendant's statement caused some people to associate shame or disgrace with Plaintiff, those people were not themselves respectable. Since respectable people do not find it shameful or disgraceful to assist the police, Defendant's statement that Plaintiff did so probably is not defamatory.

b. **Not necessary that audience be respectable**: Although courts refer to the responses of "a substantial group of respectable people" when deciding whether a particular statement is defamatory, it is not necessary that the defendant's statement be heard by such a group.

Example: Defendant states that Plaintiff is a thief. The only people who hear the statement are thieves, all of whom gain respect for Plaintiff as a result. Plaintiff asserts a defamation claim against Defendant. Defendant argues that the statement was not defamatory because it did not injure Plaintiff's reputation in the eyes of the persons who heard it.

Since most people find theft to be disgraceful, there probably is a substantial group of respectable people who would associate disgrace with any person who is a thief. For this reason, Defendant's statement probably is defamatory, even though it was not made to respectable people and did not actually damage Plaintiff's reputation before the people to whom it was made.

c. **Ambiguous statements**: Since words and phrases frequently have several meanings, it is sometimes necessary to determine what a statement means before deciding whether it is defamatory. Courts usually hold that ***a statement means whatever the reasonable person hearing (or reading) it would think it means***.

Example: Defendant publishes an article which refers to Plaintiff as a certain person's "mouthpiece". Plaintiff, an attorney, asserts a defamation claim. At the trial, Plaintiff produces a dictionary which defines "mouthpiece" as a dishonest lawyer. Defendant produces a dictionary which defines "mouthpiece" as a spokesperson.

If the reasonable person reading Defendant's article would understand "mouthpiece" to mean dishonest lawyer, then the statement probably is defamatory because respectable people usually regard a dishonest lawyer as an object of shame. On the other hand, if the reasonable person reading the article would understand "mouthpiece" to mean spokesperson, then the statement probably is not defamatory, since respectable people usually do not regard a spokesperson as an object of shame. *Rudin v. Dow Jones*, 510 F.Supp. 210 (S.D. N.Y. 1981).

d. **Defamation by innuendo**: If a statement contains all the facts necessary to damage the plaintiff's reputation, it is said to be ***defamatory on its face***. If the statement alone would not damage the plaintiff's reputation, but there exists a fact ***not mentioned in the statement*** which when taken with the statement would tend to damage the plaintiff's reputation, the statement is said to be ***defamatory by innuendo***. The defamatory meaning which thus results is called ***the innuendo. In such a case, the extrinsic fact (i.e.***, the fact which exists but which was not mentioned in the statement) is called the ***inducement***.

Example 1: The Koh-i-noor diamond is stolen at 3:00 P.M. (yesterday). Defendant says, "The Koh-i-noor diamond was stolen yesterday at 3 PM, and at 3:01 PM, Plaintiff had it in his pocket." Plaintiff asserts a defamation claim.

Since a person who has possession of a thing one minute after it is stolen is probably the thief, the reasonable person hearing Defendant's statement would understand it to mean that Plaintiff stole the diamond. If so, the statement is defamatory, since most respectable people think that theft is shameful or disgraceful. Since the statement itself could produce that inference without reference to any fact not mentioned in the statement, it is defamatory on its face.

Example 2: The Koh-i-noor diamond is stolen at 3:00 P.M. (yesterday). Defendant says, "At 3:01 PM yesterday, Plaintiff had the Koh-i-noor diamond in his pocket." Plaintiff asserts a defamation claim.

Since the Koh-i-noor diamond was stolen at 3 PM, the person who had it in his pocket at 3:01 PM was probably the thief. For this reason, Defendant's statement accused Plaintiff of stealing the diamond, and was thus defamatory for the reasons given in the previous Example. Since Defendant's statement did not mention the fact that the diamond had been stolen, however, and since that extrinsic fact was necessary to establish its defamatory meaning, the statement was defamatory by innuendo. The defamatory innuendo is that Plaintiff is a thief, and the inducement is that the diamond was stolen yesterday at 3 PM.

Example 3: Plaintiff, a candidate for public office, states publicly that she is a member of the Republican party. Defendant falsely states that Plaintiff is not a member of the Republican party. Plaintiff asserts a claim against Defendant for defamation.

Since there is no shame or disgrace in not being a member of the Republican party, Defendant's statement probably is not defamatory on its face. Since Plaintiff has stated that she is a member of the Republican party, however, Defendant's statement asserts that Plaintiff is a liar. Because respectable people usually regard lying as disgraceful, the statement probably is defamatory. Since the defamatory meaning (*i.e.*, that Plaintiff is a liar) depends on an extrinsic fact (*i.e.*, that Plaintiff has stated that she is a member of the Republican party), the statement is defamatory by innuendo. (*Frinzi v. Hanson*, *supra*, p. 249).

2. **Statement**: A statement is ***any communication***, and need not be made in words.

Example: Plaintiff is a well-known actor with a distinctive and recognizable voice. Defendant produces radio commercials using an actor with a voice substantially similar to Plaintiff's. Plaintiff asserts a defamation claim, alleging that Defendant has stated that Plaintiff stooped below his class by making radio commercials. Defendant argues that he made no statement about Plaintiff.

If the reasonable person hearing the commercial believed that he was hearing Plaintiff's voice, the commercial communicated the assertion that Plaintiff had appeared in a radio commercial. The use of a voice matching Plaintiff's would thus be a statement about Plaintiff. *Lahr v. Adell Chemical Co.*, 300 F.2d 256 (1st Cir. 1962) (*infra*, p. 286).

3. **Concerning plaintiff**: A statement is one concerning the plaintiff ***if the reasonable person with knowledge of the plaintiff or of the plaintiff's attributes would believe that the statement was about the plaintiff***.

Example: Defendant writes a novel about a character who conducts nude marathon encounter therapy sessions. Plaintiff, who is unlike the character in many ways, asserts a defamation claim against Defendant, arguing that the book is about him because he is the only person in the United States who conducts nude marathon encounter therapy sessions. Defendant argues that statements made in the book are not about Plaintiff, but are about a fictional character.

The fact that Plaintiff is in the same business as the book's main character, or even that Plaintiff is the only person in that business, probably is not enough by itself to justify the conclusion that statements made in the book are statements concerning Plaintiff. If, however, all the attributes in the book would lead the reasonable person to believe that the character was Plaintiff, then the statements contained in the book are statements concerning Plaintiff. Whether or not this is so is a question of fact. *Bindrim v. Mitchell*, 155 Cal. Rptr. 29 (Cal. Ct. App. 1979).

a. **Not necessary that audience know Plaintiff**: Although courts refer to the responses of "the reasonable person who knows the plaintiff" when deciding whether a particular statement is one concerning the plaintiff, it is not necessary that the defendant's statement be heard by such a person.

b. **Group to which plaintiff belongs**: If a defamatory statement is made about ***a group*** of persons to which the plaintiff belongs, it is a statement concerning the plaintiff ***if the reasonable person who knows that the plaintiff is a member of the group would believe that the statement is about the plaintiff***. Usually, this is so if the group is a small one, but not if the group is a large one. Courts frequently treat a defamatory statement about some members of a group as if it were made about all members of that group.

Example: Writing about the employees of a certain department store, Defendant publishes defamatory statements about "all the models", of whom there are 9; "some of the salesmen", of whom there are 22; and "all of the saleswomen", of whom there are 382. Mod, a model, Sal, a salesman, and Wendy, a saleswoman, assert defamation claims. Defendant argues that the statements did not concern the plaintiffs.

Since there were only 9 models, the reasonable person probably would think that a statement about all the models was about each of them. For this reason, Mod probably will be successful.

Since there were 382 saleswomen, a large number, the reasonable person probably would not believe that a statement about all the saleswomen applied to any one of them in particular. For this reason, Wendy probably will be unsuccessful.

Since a statement about some members of a group casts suspicion on all of them, Defendant's statement about some of the salesmen will be treated as though it may have been made about all of the salesmen. A group of 22 is probably neither small enough nor large enough to permit certainty as to the result. For this reason, a jury probably will be asked to decide whether the reasonable person hearing a statement about a group of 22 would believe that the statement applied to any one particular member of the group. If so, Sal will be successful. If not, Sal will not be successful. *Neiman-Marcus v. Lait*, 13 F.R.D. 311 (S.D.N.Y. 1952).

c. **Living person only**: Most jurisdictions agree that ***only a living person can be defamed***. Statements about a decedent ordinarily will not lead to recovery in a defamation action brought on behalf of that decedent. If defamatory statements are made about a living person who dies subsequent to publication of the statements, but prior to instituting or completing a claim, the claim may survive the decedent, depending on the jurisdiction's survival statute.

Example: One week after John's death, Defendant states that John and Mary robbed a bank. Without having asserted a claim, Mary dies one week after Defendant makes the statement. Personal representatives of John and Mary assert defamation claims against Defendant. Defendant moves to dismiss on the ground that John and Mary are deceased.

Since John was deceased when the statement was made, most jurisdictions will agree that he was never defamed by Defendant and that his estate is not entitled to assert the claim. For this reason, the claim asserted on behalf of John's estate will be dismissed.

Since Mary was alive when the statement was made, she was defamed and was entitled to assert a claim during her life. Since she died before recovering on such a claim, however, her estate will be unable to assert it unless it survived her. Whether or not a defamation claim survives the death of the plaintiff depends on the provisions of the "survival statute" in the applicable jurisdiction.

B. Falsity: In most defamation cases, the plaintiff is required to prove that the defamatory statement made by the defendant was false.

1. **Historical background**: Until recently, the plaintiff in a defamation action was aided by a presumption that all defamatory statements are false. This imposed on the defendant the burden of showing that the statement which he made was true. If he could meet this burden, liability was not imposed. For this reason, it was said that "truth" was an affirmative defense.

2. **Constitutional requirement**: In recent decisions, the United States Supreme Court has ruled that in a defamation claim brought by a private person against a media defendant or brought by a public person against anybody, the First Amendment to the United States Constitution imposes on the plaintiff the burden of proving that the defamatory statement was false. So far, the Supreme Court has not treated the Constitutional issues in a defamation claim brought by a private person against a non- media defendant.

3. **Definition:** A statement is false if it is ***not substantially true***.

   Example: Defendant states that Plaintiff embezzled $50 from X bank. Plaintiff asserts a claim for defamation. During the trial, Plaintiff testifies that he did not steal from X bank. Defendant proves that Plaintiff embezzled $100 from Y bank, and argues that liability should not be imposed because the statement was true.

   Since Defendant's statement was that Plaintiff embezzled from X bank, and since Plaintiff has testified that he did not do so, Plaintiff has sustained the burden of establishing falsity. Although Defendant proves that Plaintiff embezzled money, he has not proven the truth of his statement that Plaintiff stole from X bank. Since Defendant's statement was not substantially true, it was false (based on a hypothetical used by the court in *Kilian v. Doubleday*, 79 A.2d 657 (Pa. 1951).

4. **Meaning of statement**: As discussed above, a statement which is capable of more than one meaning means what the reasonable person hearing or reading it would think it means. In determining whether a statement is true or false, it is this meaning which must be considered. If one of the statement's possible meanings is true, but the meaning which the reasonable person would give it is false, the statement is false.

Example: Defendant says that Plaintiff works in a whorehouse. Plaintiff asserts a claim for defamation. At the trial, Defendant proves that Plaintiff works in a dancehall, and that prostitution is practiced in the dancehall, although not by Plaintiff. Defendant argues that the dancehall was therefore a whorehouse, and that his statement was true.

Although the statement may have been literally true, it must be given the meaning which the reasonable person would give it. If the reasonable person would think that Defendant's statement meant that Plaintiff was a prostitute, the statement was false, since Plaintiff was not a prostitute. *Crelling v. Thomas*, 247 P.2d 264 (Utah 1952).

5. **Opinion**: The United States Supreme Court has stated that there is no such thing as a false opinion. For this reason, a ***statement of opinion cannot be false, and cannot result in liability for defamation***.

   a. **Definition**: An opinion is a statement which is ***not capable of objective truth or falsity***.

   Example: Defendant publicly says, "Mary is a thief, and John is not a nice person." Mary and John assert claims for defamation.

   A thief is a person who steals. If Mary steals, she is a thief. If Mary does not steal, she is not a thief. Defendant's statement about Mary is thus capable of objective truth (*i.e.*, Mary steals) or falsity (*i.e.*, Mary does not steal). For this reason, it is an assertion of fact and may be the basis of defamation liability.

   Whether or not a person is "nice" depends on how "nice" is defined. Since each person has her own definition of "nice", it is a subjective statement, and, therefore, not capable of objective truth or falsity. For this reason, Defendant's statement about John is an expression of opinion and may not be the basis of defamation liability.

   b. **Expression of doubt not sufficient to make statement an opinion**: If the statement made about the plaintiff is capable of objective truth or falsity, it is an assertion of fact, and expressions of doubt annexed to the statement do not change it into an expression of opinion.

   Example 1: Defendant publicly says, "Someone robbed the bank, and, although I'm not certain this is so, I think it was Plaintiff." Plaintiff asserts a claim for defamation. Defendant argues that the claim should be dismissed because her expression of doubt made the statement an expression of opinion.

   The essence of Defendant's statement is that Plaintiff

robbed the bank. Since this is capable of objective truth or falsity, it is an assertion of fact and may result in defamation liability.

Example 2: Defendant states publicly, "I know for a fact that Plaintiff is not a kind person." Plaintiff asserts a claim for defamation. Defendant argues that the claim should be dismissed because her statement was an expression of opinion.

Whether or not a person is kind is a subjective matter since each of us has his own definition of "kind." Since it is not capable of objective truth or falsity, Defendant's statement is, therefore, an expression of opinion, even though it contains no word of doubt.

c. **Ambiguous statements**: Some words or phrases have two meanings, one of which is capable of objective truth or falsity, and the other of which is not. In deciding whether these words or phrases are expressions of fact or opinion it is necessary to determine which of the meanings the reasonable person hearing or reading them would understand them to have.

Example 1: Defendant publicly refers to Plaintiff as "that bastard." Plaintiff asserts a claim for defamation. Defendant argues that the claim should be dismissed because his statement was an expression of opinion.

The word "bastard" literally means a person of illegitimate birth. Since there probably is a substantial group of respectable people in our society which would regard a person born out of wedlock as an object of shame or disgrace, the word probably is defamatory if used in that sense. On the other hand, the word "bastard" is also used colloquially to indicate that the speaker finds the person so described to be distasteful. Since this is a subjective matter and, therefore, not capable of objective truth or falsity, the word expresses an opinion if used in that sense.

In determining the meaning of any statement which is capable of having more than one meaning, it is necessary to determine how the reasonable person hearing or reading the statement would have understood it. Thus, if the reasonable person hearing Defendant call Plaintiff a "bastard" would have thought that Defendant was stating that Plaintiff was of illegitimate birth, the statement would be an expression of fact. On the other hand, if the reasonable person would have believed that Defendant was simply expressing his dislike for Plaintiff, the statement would be an expression of opinion.

Example 2: Plaintiff, a real estate developer doing business with a city, appears at the city council meeting to discuss two transactions between himself and the city. Plaintiff refuses to cooperate on one of the transactions unless the city agrees to give him what he wants on the other transaction. Following the meeting, Defendant publicly states that "Plaintiff blackmailed the city council." Plaintiff asserts a claim for defamation. Defendant argues that the claim should be dismissed because his statement was an expression of opinion.

The word "blackmail" literally describes a crime consisting of obtaining money from another by unlawfully threatening his economic interests. A statement that Plaintiff committed this crime is capable of objective truth or falsity, and, therefore, would be an assertion of fact which might lead to defamation liability.

On the other hand, the word "blackmail" may also be used to describe a negotiating technique in which the negotiator takes a hard-line position and attempts to take advantage of the desperate needs of his adversary (*i.e.*, takes advantage of the fact that his adversary is "over a barrel"). Used in this manner, the word does not have a meaning which is capable of objective truth or falsity, and, therefore, is an expression of opinion which cannot be the basis of defamation liability.

In deciding which meaning to give the word, it is necessary to determine how the reasonable person reading or hearing it would have understood it.

Note: In the case on which this example is based, the United States Supreme Court held as a matter of law that the reasonable person would have understood the word to be nothing more than an expression of the opinion that Plaintiff drove a hard bargain. *Greenbelt Public Ass. v. Bresler*, 398 U.S. 6 (1970).

d. **Four-part test**: Several Circuits of the U.S. Court of Appeals have recognized a four-part test to determine whether an ambiguous statement should be regarded as an expression of fact or of opinion. The four factors to be considered are as follows:

  i. **Precision**: The more precise a statement is, the more likely it is to be an assertion of fact.

  ii. **Verifiability**: The more a statement is subject to verification, the more likely it is to be an assertion of fact.

  iii. **Literary context**: The literary context in which a statement appears is helpful in determining whether it is an expression of fact or opinion. If it appears in a publication which concentrates on stating opinions, it is more likely to be an expression of opinion than if it appears in a news article.

iv. **Public context**: The public context in which a statement is made is helpful in determining whether it is an expression of fact or of opinion. If it is part of a public controversy in which a freeflowing exchange of opinions is taking place, it is more likely to be regarded as an expression of opinion than if it stands alone.

Example: During an election in which Plaintiff is a candidate, Defendant publishes an article in *Newsweek* magazine suggesting that Plaintiff, a public prosecutor, was motivated by a desire for revenge for past insults when he prosecuted a certain person. Plaintiff asserts a defamation claim. Defendant argues that the claim should be dismissed because the statements contained in the article are expressions of opinion.

Since Defendant's statement suggested that Plaintiff was motivated by a desire for revenge, its lack of precision was more likely to make it an expression of opinion than of fact. Since Plaintiff's motivation was not readily verifiable, it was more likely to be an expression of opinion than of fact. Since *Newsweek* magazine is known to be a forum for the expression of opinions, the literary context in which the statement appeared made it more likely to be an expression of opinion than fact. Since the statement was made during a political campaign when opinions are freely expressed, the public context in which it was made was more likely to make it an expression of opinion than of fact. *Janklow v. Newsweek, Inc.*, 788 F.2d 1300 (8th Cir. 1986).

6. **Consider Defamatory part of statement only**: In deciding whether the statement was false, it is necessary to consider ***only the defamatory part of the statement***.

Example 1: Defendant publicly says, "Roses are red; violets are blue; sugar is sweet; and Plaintiff is a thief." Plaintiff asserts a defamation claim. At the trial, Defendant proves that roses are red, that violets are blue, and that sugar is sweet. Defendant moves to dismiss on the ground that her statement was true.

Although parts of the statement were true, these parts were not defamatory. The defamatory part of the statement was, "Plaintiff is a thief." Unless Plaintiff is a thief, this statement is false and may result in defamation liability.

Example 2: Defendant publicly says, "Mary told me that Plaintiff is a thief." Plaintiff asserts a defamation claim. At the trial, Defendant proves that Mary told him that Plaintiff was a thief and moves to dismiss on the ground that his statement was true.

Part of the statement was true (*i.e.*, that Mary told Defendant something); this part was not defamatory. The defamatory part of the statement was, "Plaintiff is a thief." Unless Plaintiff is a thief, this statement is false and may result in defamation liability.

C. Fault: Until the mid nineteen-sixties, defamation liability was imposed without regard to fault. Then, the United States Supreme Court issued a series of decisions based on the conclusion that the First Amendment protection of free expression required that fault be established in most defamation cases. Although there is one group of cases to which the Supreme Court has not yet applied this conclusion, we will treat fault as an essential element of defamation liability, discussing, where appropriate, the group of cases of which this may not be so.

1. **Plaintiff's status**: In deciding what, if any, fault must be proven, it is necessary to determine plaintiff's status. For this purpose, defamation plaintiffs are classified as ***public officials, public figures, or private persons***.

   a. **Public official**: The United States Supreme Court has defined a public official as ***an employee in the hierarchy of government who has or reasonably appears to have substantial control over the conduct of public affairs***. By way of further clarification, the Court added that a public official is one who holds a position of such apparent importance that the public has an ***independent interest*** in her qualifications and performance beyond the interest which it has in the qualifications and performance of government employees generally.

   Example: As director of a state recreation area, Plaintiff is responsible for controlling expenditures.

   Since one who controls the use of public funds is in a position to exercise control over the conduct of public affairs, Plaintiff probably is a public official. *Rosenblatt v. Baer*, 383 U.S. 75 (1966).

   b. **Public figure**: The United States Supreme Court has described two kinds of public figures.

      i. **Involuntary public figure**: An involuntary public figure is a person who, ***without necessarily seeking to do so***, has achieved such pervasive fame and notoriety that he is known to the great mass of society. This type of public figure has also been called a ***public figure for all purposes***. So far, there has been no case in which the United States Supreme

Court has identified the plaintiff as an involuntary public figure.

ii. **Voluntary public figure**: A voluntary public figure is a person who has ***injected himself into a public controversy for the purpose of influencing public opinion***. Using a graphic metaphor, the United States Supreme Court has said that in order to become a voluntary public figure, it is necessary for a person to "mount the rostrum." This type of public figure has also been called a ***limited issue public figure***.

Example 1: Plaintiff is a well-respected trial attorney who serves as honorary president of a city Civic Association. Other than representing the interests of his clients in court, he has made no attempt to influence public opinion.

Since Plaintiff has not "mounted the rostrum" he probably is not a voluntary public figure. *Gertz v. Robert Welch, Inc.*, 418 U.S. 323 (1974).

Example 2: Plaintiff, a retired U.S. Army general, makes several public speeches in opposition to the racial integration of a state university. After Plaintiff makes such a speech in front of the state university, Defendant publishes an article falsely stating that Plaintiff led a band of armed persons against U.S. military forces. Plaintiff asserts a claim for defamation. Defendant argues that Plaintiff is a public official because of his status as a retired military officer and that he is a public figure because of his speechmaking activity.

Since Plaintiff is no longer active as a military officer, he no longer has or appears to have any control at all over the conduct of public affairs, and, therefore, is not a public official. Since Plaintiff has "mounted the rostrum," however, by voluntarily injecting himself into a public controversy for the purpose of influencing public opinion, he probably is a voluntary (*i.e.*, limited issue) public figure. *Associated Press v. Walker*, 388 U.S. 130 (1967).

c. **Private person**: A private person is a plaintiff who is neither a public official nor a public figure.

2. **Defendant's status**: In determining whether fault must be proven, it may also be necessary to determine whether a defendant is a media publisher or a non-media publisher.

a. **Media publisher**: A media publisher is a defendant which (who) customarily publishes information.

b. Non-media publisher: A non-media publisher is a defendant who (which) does not customarily publish information.

Example: Daily, a newspaper, publishes an article containing false defamatory statements about Plaintiff. Reader sees the article, clips it out of the newspaper, and sends a copy of it to Plaintiff's spouse. Plaintiff asserts defamation claims against Daily and Reader.

Since Daily is a newspaper, it is in the business of publishing information, and can be classified as a media publisher. Since Reader does not ordinarily publish information, she should not be classified as a media publisher.

3. Kinds of fault: The law of torts traditionally recognizes two bases for liability: fault and negligence. In discussing the fault requirement in certain defamation cases, the United States Supreme Court has used the phrase "actual malice", defining it in a way which virtually makes it a synonym for "intent". In other defamation cases, the Court has indicated that "actual malice" (*i.e.*, intent) is not required, but that liability without fault will not be imposed. In those cases, negligence may fulfill the fault requirement.

a. Actual malice: A defendant acts with "actual malice" when he makes a false statement either with ***knowledge*** that it is false or with a ***reckless disregard*** for the truth. A defendant makes a false statement with reckless disregard for the truth when he entertains serious doubts about its truth but makes it anyway.

i. Subjective standard: Actual malice involves a subjective state of mind. This means that in determining whether the defendant had actual malice, it is not relevant to consider what the reasonable person would have known or what doubts the defendant should have entertained.

Example: Although all evidence indicates that Plaintiff is not guilty of murder, Defendant, who has examined the evidence, actually believes that Plaintiff is guilty. After Defendant states that Plaintiff is guilty, Plaintiff asserts a claim for defamation, alleging that Defendant made the statement with actual malice.

Since Defendant actually believed that the statement was true when she made it, she did not have actual malice.

ii. Objective evidence: Since it is not usually possible to determine what a defendant actually knew or what doubts a defendant actually entertained, a conclusion about the defendant's state of mind may be based on consideration of what would have been in the mind of the ordinary person who acted as the defendant did.

Example: Defendant, the publisher of a weekly magazine, is told by Informer, a person with whom Defendant was previously unacquainted, that as the result of a telephone misconnection, Informer overheard a telephone conversation several weeks before. Informer states that the conversation was between Plaintiff, the coach of a college football team, and the coach of a rival team. Informer states that he heard Plaintiff and the other coach agreeing to "fix" a game which was played the day after the conversation. On the evening of its conversation with Informer, Defendant publishes an article containing the statements. The statements are false. Plaintiff asserts a claim for defamation, alleging that Defendant made the statements with actual malice.

Obviously, it is impossible to determine whether Defendant entertained doubts about the truth of the statements which it published. The following objective evidence may be considered: the incidents described by Informer occurred several weeks earlier and were no longer "hot news" (*i.e.*, there was no particular reason to publish the story so soon after the conversation with the informer); informer was a person previously unknown to Defendant, and had no background in journalism or investigation; plaintiff and the other coach were both professionals of long-standing and unblemished reputations. Defendant made no attempt to investigate the truth of the statements before printing them, although most journalists probably would have done so.

It may successfully be argued by Plaintiff that Defendant published the statements without making an investigation, because Defendant believed that the investigation would only reveal the falsity of the statements, and knew that discovery of their falsity would effectively prevent their publication. *Curtis Publishing v. Butts*, 388 U.S. 130 (1967).

b. **Negligence**: A defendant has acted negligently when, although she did not know that the statements she was making were false and did not entertain serious doubts about the truth when making them, the reasonable person in defendant's situation ***would have known*** that the statements were false or ***would have entertained doubts*** about their truth. A defendant may also have acted negligently in failing to make such investigation ***as the reasonable person in her situation would have made***.

4. **Kind of fault required**: The United States Supreme Court has made the kind of fault required depend upon the status of the plaintiff and/or the defendant.

a. **Public official**: If the plaintiff is a ***public official***, and the defendant is either a media or a non-media publisher, the plaintiff is required to show ***actual malice***.

b. **Public figure**: If the plaintiff is a ***public figure*** and the defendant is either a media or a non media-publisher, the plaintiff is required to show ***actual malice***.

c. **Private person v. media defendant**: If the plaintiff is a ***private person*** and the defendant is a media publisher, each state may set its own standard, so long as it ***does not impose liability without fault***. In effect, this means that the Constitution requires a showing of either actual malice or negligence in these cases.

d. **Private person v. non-media defendant**: The United States Supreme Court has not stated what fault is required if the plaintiff is a ***private person*** and the defendant is a non-media publisher. As a result, the states remain free to set their own standards. Some states have continued to apply strict liability to this class of defamation case. Other states have required either actual malice or negligence. A few states require actual malice in all defamation cases.

D. **Publication**: There is no liability for making a defamatory statement unless that statement is published.

1. **Definition**: Publication means ***communication of the statement to at least one person*** other than plaintiff.

Example: Defendant, a sales clerk in a department store, accuses Plaintiff of stealing a watch. No one but Plaintiff hears the statement. Plaintiff subsequently asserts a claim for defamation.

Since the statement was not communicated to a third person there has been no publication. Plaintiff's claim should therefore be dismissed. *Economopoulos v. A.G. Pollard Co.*, 105 N.E. 896 (Mass. 1914).

a. **Understanding**: No publication occurs unless the person to whom the statement is communicated understands it.

Example: Defendant, a sales clerk in a department store, accuses Plaintiff of stealing a watch. No one but Plaintiff hears the statement. Realizing that Plaintiff speaks only Greek, Defendant repeats the accusation in Greek. By now a crowd has gathered. All of the persons in the crowd hear the accusation made in Greek, but none of them understands Greek. Plaintiff subsequently asserts a claim for defamation.

When spoken in English, the statement was not communicated to a third person, and, therefore, was not published. When spoken in Greek, the statement was not communicated to a third person who understood it, and, therefore, was not published. Plaintiff's claim should, therefore, be dismissed. *Economopoulos v. A.G. Pollard Co., supra.*

b. **Foreign language periodicals**: A publication which is printed in a foreign language periodical is presumed to have at least one reader who understands it.

c. **Understanding of defamatory sense not required**: If the reasonable person would understand a statement to have a meaning which is defamatory, a publication may occur ***even though the person to whom it is communicated does not understand it in its defamatory sense***.

Example: The Koh-i-noor diamond is stolen at 3 PM. Defendant says to Listener, "Plaintiff had the Koh-i-noor diamond in his pocket at one second after 3 PM." Listener, who is unaware that the Koh-i-noor was stolen, does not understand that Defendant's statement accuses Plaintiff of being a thief. Plaintiff subsequently asserts a claim against Defendant for defamation. Defendant argues that there has been no publication of a defamation because Listener did not understand the statement in its defamatory sense.

Since the statement creates the innuendo that Plaintiff stole the diamond, it is defamatory. Since it was communicated to Listener, who understood it, it was published. The fact that Listener did not understand it in its defamatory sense may affect the element of damage, but does not prevent the communication from being a publication.

2. **Requirement of intent or negligence**: Communication does not satisfy the requirement of publication unless it results from some fault by the defendant. This means either that the defendant ***intended*** the communication or that it resulted from his ***negligence***.

   a. **Intentional publication**: A publication was intended if the defendant desired or knew to a substantial degree of certainty that it would occur.

   b. **Negligent publication**: A publication was negligent if the reasonable person in the defendant's situation would have known that it would occur.

Example 1: Plaintiff's secretary ordinarily opens all mail sent to Plaintiff's office, but Plaintiff ordinarily opens her own mail if it is sent to her home. Knowing this, Defendant addresses a letter to Plaintiff which says, "You are a thief," and sends the letter to Plaintiff's home. Because Plaintiff is ill on the day the letter arrives, Plaintiff's secretary comes to her home and, at Plaintiff's request, opens Plaintiff's mail and reads Defendant's letter and the statement which it contains. Plaintiff subsequently asserts a claim for defamation, alleging that Defendant published a defamatory statement to Plaintiff's secretary.

Since Defendant did not know that someone other than Plaintiff would see the statement, communication to Plaintiff's secretary was not intentional. Since the reasonable person probably would not have known that anyone but Plaintiff would see the statement, communication to Plaintiff's secretary was not the result of negligence. For these reasons, there has been no publication.

Example 2: Knowing that Plaintiff's secretary opens and reads all mail addressed to Plaintiff and sent to Plaintiff's office, Defendant sends a letter to Plaintiff at Plaintiff's office saying, "You are a thief." Plaintiff's secretary opens the letter and reads it. Plaintiff subsequently asserts a claim for defamation. Defendant argues that there has been no publication because the letter was addressed to Plaintiff only.

Since Defendant knew that the letter would be opened and read by Plaintiff's secretary, defendant intended the communication to the secretary. Therefore, there has been a publication.

Example 3: Defendant knows that all mail addressed to Plaintiff at Plaintiff's office is handled by several employees in the mail department before being delivered to Plaintiff. Defendant sends Plaintiff a postal card at Plaintiff's office which says, "You are a thief." The postal card is read by several mail department employees before being delivered to Plaintiff. Plaintiff subsequently asserts a claim for defamation.

The reasonable person in Defendant's situation probably would have known, human nature being what it is, that mail department employees would read postal cards before delivering them. If so, communication to the employees was the result of Defendant's negligence and a publication has occurred.

3. **Repetition and republication**: A publication may occur when a person repeats a defamatory statement which he heard from another.

a. **Publication by repeater**: ***One who communicates a defamatory statement to another publishes it***, no matter what the source of the statement.

b. **Publication by originator**: One who publishes a defamatory statement to another, ***when she knows or should know that the other will repeat it***, publishes it again when that repetition occurs.

Example: Knowing that John is employed as a reporter by Daily, a newspaper, Mary tells John that Plaintiff was fired for stealing from his employer. John writes an article repeating that statement about Plaintiff and delivers it to Daily, which prints the article in an edition which it sells to readers. Plaintiff asserts a claim for defamation against Daily, John, and Mary.

Since Daily knowingly communicated the statement to its readers, it has published the statement.

Since John knowingly communicated the statement to Daily, he has published it. Since he knew that Daily would print and distribute the article, he published it again when Daily did so.

Since Mary knowingly communicated the statement to John, she published it. Since she knew that he was employed by Daily as a reporter, it can be argued that the reasonable person in her situation would have known that John would repeat it by including it in an article, and that Daily would repeat it by printing and distributing the article. If so, Mary published it again when John delivered the article to Daily, and again when Daily sold newspapers containing the article to readers.

4. **Single publication rule**: A majority of jurisdictions in the United States hold that ***all copies of a single edition of a printed publication constitute a single publication***. A minority of jurisdictions regards each copy as a separate publication.

Example 1: On January 1, 1990, Defendant begins selling a hardcover book containing defamatory statements about Plaintiff. Defendant sells the last copy on June 1, 1990. On February 1, 1991, Plaintiff asserts a claim for defamation in a jurisdiction with a one year statute of limitations on defamation actions. Defendant demurs.

Under the single publication rule, all copies of a printed edition constitute a single publication. Since the first copy was sold on January 1, 1990, the publication took place on that date and the statute of limitations began to run on that date. Thus, in jurisdictions applying the single publication rule, Plaintiff's claim should be dismissed.

In jurisdictions which do not apply the single publication rule, every copy is a separate publication. Since the last copy was sold on June 1, 1990, the statute of limitations will not run out until June 1, 1991. Thus in jurisdictions which do not apply the single publication rule, Plaintiff's claim should not be dismissed.

Example 2: In the previous Example, assume that Defendant begins selling a paperback edition of the same book in July 1991, and that Plaintiff asserts a claim for defamation in August 1991.

Since the last sale of the hard cover book was made in June 1990 all jurisdictions would agree that a one-year statute of limitations bars a defamation claim based on publication of that book. edition. Since the paperback version was a new publication, however, a new period of limitations began in July 1991. For this reason, Plaintiff's claim is not barred, even in jurisdictions which apply the single publication rule. *Rinaldi v. Viking-Penguin*, 422 N.Y.S.2d 552 (1979).

5. **Form of publication**: The way in which a defamatory statement is published will determine whether it is libel or slander.

   a. **Written statements**: Defamatory statements which are published in ***written or printed form*** are ***classified as libel***.

   b. **Spoken statements**: Defamatory statements which are published in ***spoken form*** are ***classified as slander***.

   c. **Other statements**: Defamatory statements which are neither written nor spoken are classified as libel or slander depending on whether they are more like writing or more like speech.

   Example: Knowing that a red light in front of a house signifies that it is a house of prostitution, Defendant inserts a red bulb in Plaintiff's porch light fixture. Plaintiff subsequently asserts a claim for defamation.

   Since the statement made by the red light (*i.e.*, that Plaintiff was a prostitute) was published in a form which was perceived by the visual senses, it may be argued that it is like writing, and is therefore libel.

   On the other hand, since the red light left no permanent record of the statement which it communicated, it may be argued that it is like speech, and is therefore slander.

   d. **Broadcast statements**: Various points of view exist as to the classification of defamatory statements broadcast over radio or television.

i. **Scripted or spontaneous**: Some jurisdictions hold that if broadcast defamation is read from a written script, it is libel, but if it is spoken without a written script, it is slander.

ii. **Taped or live**: Some jurisdictions hold that if defamatory statements are broadcast live, they are slander, but if they are taped, they are libel.

iii. **Uniform Broadcast Defamation Act**: A majority of jurisdictions have adopted the ***Uniform Broadcast Defamation Act***, which provides that broadcast defamation is slander.

E. **Damage**: ***The element of damage is satisfied if the plaintiff's reputation has been injured*** as a result of the defamatory statement published by the defendant.

Example: Defendant publishes defamatory statements about Plaintiff. None of the people who hear the statements believe them, and so Plaintiff's reputation does not suffer. When Plaintiff hears what Defendant is saying about him, however, he becomes highly insulted and is so upset thinking about it that he has a heart attack. Plaintiff asserts a claim for defamation, seeking damages for his heart attack.

Since Plaintiff suffered no harm to his reputation, he cannot satisfy the damage element of the defamation cause of action, and his claim should be dismissed.

1. **Other damage**: Once the plaintiff establishes injury to his reputation, other damage which ***results proximately*** from the injury may also be recoverable.

Example: Defendant publishes defamatory statements about Plaintiff. Some of the people who hear the statements believe them, and so Plaintiff's reputation suffers. Plaintiff becomes so upset about the damage to his reputation that he has a heart attack. Plaintiff asserts a claim for defamation, seeking damages for injury to his reputation and for his heart attack.

Since Plaintiff suffered harm to his reputation, he can satisfy the damage element of the defamation cause of action, and if his claim is successful, he can recover damages not only for his injured reputation, but for the heart attack which resulted from it.

2. **Presumed damages**: In some defamation cases it has been traditional for courts to permit the plaintiff to rely on a presumption of damage. This means that in such cases the issue of how much the plaintiff should receive as compensatory damages may be submitted

to the jury even though the plaintiff has failed to prove any damage at all.

a. **Ordinary slander**: In cases of ordinary slander, the ***plaintiff may not rely on a presumption of damage***. This means that unless the plaintiff proves actual harm to her reputation, the case should be dismissed.

b. **Slander *per se***: However the plaintiff may rely on a presumption of damage ***if the slanderous statement accuses the plaintiff of*** one of the following. This kind of slander is called ***slander per se***.

   i. **Crime of moral turpitude**: If the defendant's statement attributes to the plaintiff a crime of inherent baseness, vileness, or dishonesty, (*i.e.*, a crime of moral turpitude) plaintiff may rely on a presumption of damage.

   Example: Defendant verbally accuses Plaintiff of possessing marijuana and of smuggling it into the United States. Plaintiff asserts a claim for defamation but is unable to establish damage to his reputation.

   Smuggling involves dishonesty and is a crime of moral turpitude. For this reason, Defendant's statement that Plaintiff engaged in smuggling is slander *per se*, and Plaintiff may make out a case without proving actual damage to his reputation.

   On the other hand, possession of marijuana is criminal only because statutes declare it to be so. It does not involve conduct which is generally recognized as base or vile or dishonest. For this reason, Defendant's statement to that effect probably should be classified as ordinary slander, which means that Plaintiff may not make out a case without proving that it resulted in actual damage to his reputation.

   ii. **Loathsome disease**: Since publication of a statement that the plaintiff suffers from a loathsome disease is likely to result in the plaintiff's being shunned by others, such a statement is classified as slander *per se*, permitting the plaintiff to rely on a presumption of damage.

      aa. Specific diseases: The only diseases which have ever been classified as "loathsome" are ***smallpox, leprosy***, and ***sexually transmitted diseases***.

      bb. Reference to present: This classification applies only when the defendant's statement asserts that the plaintiff ***presently*** suffers from the disease in question.

iii. **Unchastity in a female**: A statement that a female plaintiff is unchaste is classified as slander *per se*, permitting the plaintiff to rely on a presumption of damage. A statement imputes unchastity to a plaintiff if it says that she engages in sexual intercourse.

iv. **Unfitness for plaintiff's occupation**: A statement which attributes to the plaintiff behavior or conditions which make the plaintiff unfit for his occupation is slander *per se* and may result in a presumption of damage.

Example: Defendant says that Plaintiff suffers from a chronic illness which makes his hands shake. Plaintiff, a brain surgeon, asserts a claim for defamation, but is unable to prove actual damage to his reputation.

Since a brain surgeon must have steady hands, Defendant's statement asserts that Plaintiff is unfit for his occupation, and is, therefore, slander *per se*. Plaintiff may rely on a presumption of damage.

c. **Libel on its face**: If the defendant's statement is libelous on its face (sometimes called "libel per se"), the ***plaintiff may rely on a presumption of damage***.

Example: Defendant prints an article which states that Plaintiff is unfaithful to his wife. Plaintiff asserts a claim for defamation, but is unable to prove actual damage to his reputation.

Since the statement probably would expose Plaintiff to shame or disgrace before a substantial group of respectable people, it probably is defamatory. Since it was in writing, it is libel. Since no extrinsic facts are necessary to give it a defamatory meaning, it is libel on its face. For this reason, Plaintiff may rely on a presumption of damage.

d. **Libel by innuendo**: If a statement is libelous by innuendo, ***the rules which apply to slander are applied*** to it. This means that the plaintiff may not rely on a presumption of damage unless the statement fits into one of the four categories constituting slander *per se*, in which case damage may be presumed.

Example: Plaintiff is the author of a series of law school study aids on the law of torts. Defendant prints an article stating, "Plaintiff tried to read Prosser's hornbook, but did not understand what he was reading." Plaintiff asserts a claim for defamation, but is unable to establish actual damage to his reputation.

Since Prosser's hornbook is an important work on the law of torts, Defendant's statement means that Plaintiff does not know the subject in which he claims to be an expert. Since this probably would expose Plaintiff to disgrace before a substantial group of respectable people, it is defamatory. Since it is in writing, it is libel. Since the fact that Prosser's hornbook is an important work on the law of torts is not mentioned in the statement, and since this extrinsic fact is necessary to give the statement a defamatory meaning, the statement is libel by innuendo. For this reason, the slander rules should be applied. Ordinarily, this would mean that Plaintiff may not rely on a presumption of damage. Since this statement attributes to Plaintiff a condition which makes him unfit for his occupation, however, he may rely on a presumption of damage.

3. **Punitive damages**: As in any tort case, the plaintiff may recover punitive damages if he can show that the defendant was motivated by malice. For this purpose, malice means ill will or a desire to do harm. Do not confuse malice (required for punitive damage awards) with "actual malice" which is a term of art created by the United States Supreme Court and signifying that the defendant knew that the statement was false or entertained serious doubts about its truth (see *supra*, p. 262).

4. **Constitutional requirements**: Although a private person may make out a defamation case without establishing actual malice, the United States Supreme Court has held that ***damage cannot be presumed in the absence of a showing of actual malice***. So far, the Supreme Court has not indicated whether this requirement applies in cases brought by plaintiffs who are private persons against defendants who are non-media publishers.

Example: Plaintiff, a private person, asserts a claim for defamation against Defendant, a daily newspaper. Plaintiff proves that Defendant published defamatory statements about Plaintiff which were characterized as libel per se (*i.e.*, libel on its face), and that although Defendant did not know the statements were false, the reasonable person in Defendant's shoes would have known that the statements were false. Plaintiff is unable to prove actual damage to her reputation. Defendant moves to dismiss on the ground that Plaintiff has failed to make out a prima facie case. Plaintiff argues that she should be permitted to rely on a presumption of damage.

Although the common law of defamation permits presumption of damage in a case of libel *per se*, the United States Supreme Court has held that there can be no presumption of damage without a showing of actual malice. Since Plaintiff was unable to show that Defendant knew that the statements were false or doubted that they were true, she has failed to prove actual malice. For this reason, she cannot rely on a presumption of damage and her case should be dismissed.

CHAPTER 15

TORTS RELATED TO DEFAMATION

I. INJURIOUS FALSEHOOD

A. General concept: ***Injurious falsehood***, sometimes called ***business defamation***, is a tort committed by injuring the plaintiff's business reputation. Frequently, a statement which damages the plaintiff's personal reputation and is, therefore, defamatory, simultaneously damages the plaintiff's business reputation and is also, therefore, an injurious falsehood.

B. Distinguished from defamation: A statement is defamatory if it would tend to injure the plaintiff's personal reputation. A statement which would tend to damage the plaintiff's business reputation may be an injurious falsehood.

> **Example:** Plaintiff is the president of a bank. Defendant says, "Plaintiff cheats on his wife, employs accountants who can't add, and is dishonest." Plaintiff asserts claims for defamation and injurious falsehood.
>
> Since the statement that Plaintiff cheats on his wife would probably disgrace him in the eyes of a substantial group of respectable people, it probably is defamatory. Since it probably does not reflect on the quality of his bank, however, it probably is not an injurious falsehood.
>
> Since the statement that Plaintiff employs accountants who can't add reflects on the quality of his bank, it probably is an injurious falsehood. Since it would probably not tend to disgrace Plaintiff personally in the eyes of a substantial group of respectable people, however, it probably is not defamatory.
>
> Since people need to trust bankers with their money, the statement that Plaintiff is dishonest reflects on the quality of his bank, and probably is, therefore, an injurious falsehood. Since it would also tend to hold Plaintiff up to disgrace before a substantial group of respectable people, it probably is also defamatory.

C. Essential elements: The essential elements of injurious falsehood are substantially similar to the essential elements of defamation, and consist of: (1) ***a disparaging statement concerning the plaintiff's business interest***; (2) ***falsity***; (3) ***fault***; (4) ***publication***; and (5) ***damage***. We will discuss generally the ways in which these elements as applied resemble the elements of defamation and the ways in which they differ.

1. **Disparaging statement concerning plaintiff's business interests**: A statement is disparaging if it ***would lead a substantial group of respectable people not to do business with the plaintiff***. Since the tort of injurious falsehood does not involve damage to the plaintiff's personal reputation, it is not necessary that the statement involve shame or disgrace, but only that it would tend to discourage people from trading with the plaintiff.

   Example: Defendant says that equipment manufactured by Plaintiff is 40% less effective than equipment manufactured by Defendant. Plaintiff asserts a claim for injurious falsehood.

   Although there is no shame or disgrace in manufacturing equipment which is less effective than that made by another manufacturer, many people would rather purchase the better equipment. For this reason, Defendant's statement may be an injurious falsehood. *Testing Systems, Inc. v. Magnaflux Corp.*, 251 F.Supp. 286 (E.D. Pa. 1966).

2. **Falsity**: The Constitutional requirements which necessitate that the plaintiff prove falsity in a defamation action apply also to injurious falsehood claims. This means that if the plaintiff is a public figure, or a private person suing a media defendant, and the defendant's statement involves a matter of public concern, falsity is an essential element of the plaintiff's case.

   Example: Plaintiff, the manufacturer of stereo equipment, advertises that its equipment involves a new concept in speaker systems and that music played over the system sounds as though it is being performed live in the same room with the listener. Defendant publishes an article which says that music played on Plaintiff's system sounds as though it is being played by musicians who are wandering around the room and that the system makes the piano sound 50 feet long. Plaintiff asserts a claim for injurious falsehood.

   Since the way music sounds is a subjective matter, Defendant's statements probably are statements of opinion, and, therefore, cannot be false. For this reason, Plaintiff's claim probably should fail. *Bose Corp. v. Consumers Union of the United States, Inc.*, 466 U.S. 485 (1984).

3. **Fault**: The few cases which have been decided by the United States Supreme Court indicate that the ***fault requirement*** in injurious falsehood claims is ***substantially the same as in defamation claims.*** Thus, a plaintiff who can be classified as a public figure will be required to prove actual malice. A private person

plaintiff suing a media defendant will probably be required to prove either actual malice or negligence.

Example: In the previous Example, the fact that Plaintiff advertised that its system was based on a new concept could be regarded as a mounting of the rostrum, (*i.e.*, that Plaintiff injected itself into a public controversy for the purpose of influencing public opinion) on a matter of public concern. If so, Plaintiff is a public figure and will be required to establish that Defendant published with actual malice. *Bose v. Consumers Union, supra*.

4. **Publication**: The publication element of injurious falsehood is substantially identical to the publication element of defamation.

5. **Damage**: Injurious falsehood differs from defamation in that there is ***no presumption of damage***.

   a. **Special damage**: The majority of jurisdictions require proof of special damages to support an injurious falsehood claim. Special damages must be proven in terms of actual monetary loss. If a plaintiff is unable to do this, jurisdictions applying this rule will dismiss the case.

   b. **Minority rule**: A growing minority of jurisdictions holds that where it is not possible for the plaintiff to prove special damage, the question of damages may be submitted to a jury.

   Example: Defendant falsely states publicly that Plaintiff has gone out of business. Plaintiff asserts a claim for injurious falsehood, alleging that he has lost business as a result, but is unable to show how much business he would have received if Defendant had not made the disparaging statement.

   In the majority of jurisdictions, Plaintiff's case would be dismissed because of Plaintiff's failure to satisfy the damage element of the cause of action. Some jurisdictions, however, would permit Plaintiff to offer some evidence tending to indicate how much business he lost, and allow the jury to determine the amount of damages which would adequately compensate Plaintiff for that loss.

II. FALSE LIGHT

A. **General concept**: Casting the plaintiff in a false light in the public eye is an invasion of privacy tort which is closely related to defamation. Frequently, this tort is simply called "false light." It is committed by publishing false statements about the plaintiff which would embarrass the plaintiff and which would be offensive to the reasonable person in the plaintiff's situation. If the statements are embarrassing because they would tend to hold the plaintiff up to shame, disgrace, or ridicule, they may also be defamatory.

B. Distinguished from defamation: A defamatory statement is one which would hold the plaintiff up to shame, disgrace, or ridicule before a substantial group of respectable people. However, a statement may cast the plaintiff in a false light even if it is not defamatory. The essence of this tort is that plaintiff has been ***embarrassed*** by a false statement published by the defendant.

> **Example:** Defendant states publicly that Plaintiff died from a self-inflicted overdose of heroin. Plaintiff, who is not dead and does not use heroin, sues for defamation and false light.
>
> Since the use of heroin is criminal and is usually associated with unsavory people, the statement that Plaintiff took heroin would probably hold him up to shame before a substantial group of respectable people and, therefore, is defamatory. For the same reason, it probably is a false light privacy invasion.
>
> Since there is no shame or disgrace in being dead, however, the statement that Plaintiff died is not defamatory. It may, however, embarrass Plaintiff to have people think that he is dead. If so, the statement that Plaintiff died may, by itself, be a false light privacy invasion.

C. Essential elements: The essential elements of ***"false light invasion"*** are similar to those of defamation and are as follows: (1) ***embarrassing statement concerning plaintiff***; (2) ***falsity***; (3) ***fault***; (4) ***publication***; and (5) ***damage***. We will discuss generally the ways in which the elements as applied resemble those of defamation and the ways in which they differ.

1. **Embarrassing statement concerning plaintiff**: This requirement represents the greatest difference between false light and defamation.

   a. **Embarrassing statement**: Although a statement is ***not defamatory*** unless it would hold the plaintiff up to shame, disgrace or ridicule, a statement is sufficiently ***embarrassing*** to be the subject of a ***false light claim*** if the reasonable person in the plaintiff's situation would be offended by its publication.

   Example: Plaintiff's husband is killed in an accident. Several months later, an employee of Defendant newspaper attempts to interview Plaintiff. Unable to reach Plaintiff, the Defendant publishes a story stating that Plaintiff is grim-visaged, is wearing the same dress that she wore on the day of her husband's death, and is in financial difficulty. None of these statements is true. Plaintiff asserts a claim for false light.

Since there is probably no shame or disgrace associated with the statements made by Defendant, they are not defamatory. If a reasonable person in Plaintiff's shoes would find them offensive, however, they may be the subject of a claim for false light. Since they suggest that Plaintiff is in financial difficulty and since this is likely to make Plaintiff an object of pity, the reasonable person in Plaintiff's situation probably would find such publication offensive, and, therefore, it probably is a false light privacy invasion. *Cantrell v. Forest City Publishing*, 419 U.S. 245 (1974).

b. **Concerning plaintiff**: As in defamation cases, a statement concerns the plaintiff if the reasonable person who knows the plaintiff would recognize her from the statement.

2. **Falsity**: This requirement is substantially identical to its counterpart in a defamation action. Although the Supreme Court has not yet indicated whether the Constitution requires that the plaintiff prove falsity, it is clear that a statement cannot be the basis of liability for this tort if it is true. It is likely that all Constitutional requirements which have been applied to defamation will also be applied to false light.

3. **Fault**: Decisions of the Supreme Court indicate that in any false light privacy action against a media defendant, actual malice as defined in defamation cases is required.

4. **Publication**: This requirement is substantially identical to its counterpart in defamation actions.

5. **Damage**: Since false light is not based on damage to the reputation, it is not necessary for the plaintiff to show that her reputation has suffered. Some proof of damage is required, however, although this may consist entirely of a showing of mental suffering by the plaintiff.

III. INTENTIONAL INFLICTION OF MENTAL SUFFERING

A. **Relationship to defamation**: In an attempt to avoid the constitutional requirements in defamation cases, attempts have been made to assert claims for intentional infliction of mental suffering in cases involving the publication of insulting statements about the plaintiff.

B. Constitutional requirements: The United States Supreme Court has stated that if the claim of outrageous conduct is based upon the publication of statements about the plaintiff which are alleged to hold the plaintiff up to shame, disgrace, or ridicule, ***the same Constitutional requirements which apply to defamation liability apply to liability for intentional infliction of mental suffering***.

Example: Plaintiff is the leader of a nationally known pressure group and lobby, and, for this reason, is a public figure. Defendant, the publisher of a magazine, publishes a satire of a frequently seen advertisement. In the satire, Plaintiff is depicted describing a sexual experience with his mother in an outhouse. Plaintiff sues for defamation, but the case is dismissed on the ground that the publication did not contain any allegation of fact which might be false, and that, for this reason, Plaintiff could not satisfy the Constitutional requirement of actual malice. Plaintiff asserts a claim for intentional infliction of mental suffering on the ground that Defendant's publication was an outrageous act which resulted in severe mental suffering.

The Constitutional requirement of actual malice has been applied in defamation cases to protect the public's right to criticize public figures. For this reason, it should be applied similarly in any tort case in which the plaintiff is a public figure seeking to hold a defendant liable for publishing statements about him. Since the essence of this claim is that Defendant's publication about Plaintiff was tortious, Plaintiff should be required to prove falsity and actual malice, as in a defamation case. For this reason, Plaintiff's claim should be dismissed. *Hustler Magazine v. Falwell*, 485 U.S. 46 (1988).

IV. AFFIRMATIVE DEFENSES

A. Neutral reportage: A defendant which republishes a statement originally made by another may be liable for its tortious effects. In reporting the news, however, media may be required to quote statements made by others, without being able to determine whether those statements were true. For this reason, many jurisdictions recognize a privilege of neutral reportage. Where applicable, this privilege ***protects a media defendant which neutrally reports on newsworthy events***.

Example: Defendant, a newspaper, truthfully reports that it has received an anonymous letter accusing Plaintiff, the wife of the state's lieutenant governor, of misusing state credit cards. Plaintiff asserts a claim for defamation.

Since the fact that such an accusation was made, even

anonymously, probably is newsworthy, and since Defendant published the story in an accurate and neutral fashion, Defendant probably is privileged. *Burns v. Times Argus Ass. Inc.*, 430 A.2d 773 (Vt. 1981).

B. Justification: A defendant's publication of defamatory statements may be privileged ***if the publication was a reasonable way to protect a legitimate interest***.

1. **Legitimate interest**: It is legitimate to seek to protect one's own ***interest and the interests of another person to whom a moral obligation is owed, of society, or of persons with whom the defendant has a common interest***.

Example: Defendant, the owner of a sales company, believes Plaintiff, a former employee, to be a thief. Defendant writes letters stating this fact to the public prosecutor, to the sales company which is Plaintiff's present employer, to Defendant's cousin who is engaged to marry Plaintiff, and to Defendant's neighbor who is not acquainted with Plaintiff. Plaintiff subsequently asserts a claim against Defendant for defamation. Defendant argues that he was attempting to protect legitimate interests.

Since society's interest in suppressing crime can best be protected by the public prosecutor, and since society's best interest is a legitimate concern of all its members, Defendant's letter to the public prosecutor probably was an attempt to protect a legitimate interest. *Pecue v. West*, 233 N.Y. 316 (1922) (*infra*, 281).

Since persons in the same business have a common interest, and since that interest can best be protected by sharing information, Defendant's letter to Plaintiff's present employer probably was an attempt to protect a legitimate interest. *Jacron v. Sindorf*, 350 A.2d 688 (Md. 1976).

Since every person probably has a moral obligation to protect relatives against disastrous marriages, Defendant's letter to his cousin, who was Plaintiff's fiancee, probably was an attempt to protect a legitimate interest.

Since there is no reason to believe that Defendant's communication with his neighbor arose from an attempt to protect a legitimate interest, this communication was not privileged.

2. **Reasonable means**: The defendant's attempt to protect a legitimate interest must be by reasonable means.

a. **Method of publication**: The means used are not reasonable unless the method of publication is likely to accomplish the defendant's purpose without excessive disclosure to persons unconnected with that purpose.

Example: Defendant is the owner of a retail store with seven employees. Suspecting that Plaintiff is a shoplifter, Defendant purchases in a major city newspaper a full page advertisement containing a photograph of Plaintiff and the statement, "Notice to employees of Defendant. Beware of Plaintiff. She is a shoplifter." Plaintiff, who is not a shoplifter, sues for defamation.

Although Defendant's statement was false and defamatory, Defendant may have been privileged to make it because he was attempting to protect a legitimate interest (*i.e.*, his own business interest). However, Defendant was privileged only if his method of publication was reasonable under the circumstances. Since he had only seven employees, there were more effective ways of communicating the warning to them without communicating it to others at the same time. Since a full page advertisement in a major city newspaper is likely to be seen by many people who are not employees of Defendant, it was not a reasonable method of publication. For this reason, Defendant probably was not privileged.

b. **Reasonable belief**: Many cases hold that publishing a defamatory statement is not a reasonable means of protecting an interest unless the publisher has a reasonable belief in the truth of the statement published.

Example: Defendant receives a letter from a person whom he does not know, accusing Plaintiff of keeping a house of prostitution. Defendant does not know Plaintiff, and is not familiar with the area in which Plaintiff resides. Without making any investigation, Defendant notifies the public prosecutor that Plaintiff is the keeper of a house of prostitution. Plaintiff, who is not the keeper of a house of prostitution, asserts a defamation claim against Defendant.

Since Defendant did not know the person who had written to him, did not know Plaintiff, was not familiar with the Plaintiff's area, and did not conduct any investigation, Defendant's belief that Plaintiff was conducting a house of prostitution probably was not reasonable. For this reason, many jurisdictions would hold that Defendant's publication of a defamatory statement about Plaintiff was not a reasonable means of protecting society's interest. *Pecue v. West, supra.*

c. **Persons to whom publication is made**: Publication of a defamatory statement is not a reasonable means of protecting a legitimate interest unless the persons to whom the publication is made are in a position to help protect that interest.

Example: Defendant is the owner of a retail store with seven employees, six of whom are salespersons and one of whom is a janitor who works after the store is closed. Believing it to be true, Defendant personally notifies all seven of his employees that Plaintiff is a shoplifter. Plaintiff, who is not a shoplifter, asserts a claim for defamation. Defendant asserts that he was attempting to protect a legitimate interest by reasonable means.

Since the janitor only came to work after the store was closed, and since shoplifters could not operate after the store was closed, the janitor was not in a position to help protect Defendant's business interests. For this reason, publication of the defamatory statement to the janitor probably was not a reasonable means of protecting that interest. Therefore, Defendant probably was not privileged.

C. **Retraction**: In some jurisdictions, statutory or common law rules provide that a defendant may mitigate damages resulting from the publication of defamatory statements by retracting those statements. Some jurisdictions provide that a defendant who does so is liable only for actual damages.

V. ORGANIZATIONAL SUGGESTION

A. **Defamation, injurious falsehood, false light**: Since all of these torts involve publication of false statements about the plaintiff, and since the kind of statement which each requires is similar, they can effectively be discussed together. We recommend that the student write an essay discussing all of the elements of defamation. If the facts indicate the possibility of successful claims for injurious falsehood and false light, the discussion should be followed by a paragraph on each of these. The student should point out the difference between defamation and the tort being discussed — especially the nature of the statement involved — and relate that difference to the facts.

B. **Variation**: If success is most likely on an injurious falsehood theory or a false light theory, the main discussion should focus on this tort with a paragraph or two pointing out the differences between it and the other two torts.

C. **Intentional infliction of mental suffering**: Since the only similarity between this tort and the other three is the Constitutional fault requirement, it should be the subject of an entirely separate discussion. Reference should be made, however, to the question of fault and this reference should be incorporated into a discussion of intentional infliction of mental suffering.

Example: Defendant, a newspaper, publishes an article about Plaintiff, a banker, stating that Plaintiff is dishonest.

Since the statement is probably defamatory, write a full essay on defamation, discussing each of the essential elements of defamation. Among the issues to be discussed are: is the allegation of dishonesty an assertion of fact?; did Defendant have the necessary fault?; can Plaintiff rely on a presumption of damage?

Following the discussion of defamation, write a paragraph discussing the similarities between injurious falsehood and defamation, recognizing that most of the issues discussed in the defamation case would be resolved in the same way in the injurious falsehood case, but pointing out that the primary difference lies in the nature of the statement. Show how the facts satisfy this requirement. (*i.e.*, Since few people would want to do business with a dishonest banker, the statement was probably disparaging.)

Next, write a paragraph discussing the similarities between false light and defamation, recognizing that most of the issues discussed in the defamation case would be resolved the same way in the false light case, but pointing out that the primary difference lies in the nature of the statement. Show how the facts satisfy this requirement. (*i.e.*, since dishonesty is a reprehensible characteristic, the reasonable person in Plaintiff's situation probably would be offended by the publication.)

Next, consider the possibility of an action for intentional infliction of mental suffering. Since this tort is different from defamation, it should receive an entirely separate discussion, reviewing each of the elements. Among the issues to be discussed are: did Defendant have the necessary intent?; was Defendant's conduct in publishing the statement outrageous?; was Plaintiff's mental suffering sufficiently severe? Then discuss why the Constitutional fault requirements apply, and analyze them.

CHAPTER 16

INVASION OF PRIVACY

I. BACKGROUND AND GENERAL CONCEPT

A. History: Until about 1890, no cases in the United States officially recognized a right of privacy. The tort of invasion of privacy did not exist. Then, as a result of a famous law review article (Warren and Brandeis, *The Right To Privacy*, 4 Harv. L. Rev. 193, (1890)) and a series of statutes and decisions, the right of privacy sprang into existence.

B. Four torts: It is now generally recognized that there are four separate ways of committing a tort by invading privacy, each based on a different concept. One of these, *casting the plaintiff in a false light in the public eye (i.e.*, False Light), has already been discussed as a variation on defamation. (See *supra*, pp. 276-278.)

C. Personal right: It is generally understood that the ***right of privacy is*** personal and is ***not inherited*** by an individual's survivors following his death.

> **Example:** Decedent is an actor famous for the role of the Transylvanian vampire, Count Dracula. Following Decedent's death, Defendant sells posters containing a photograph of Decedent in the Count Dracula persona. Plaintiff, Decedent's heir, asserts a claim against Defendant for invasion of privacy.
>
> Since the privacy interest asserted is that of Decedent, and since Decedent is no longer alive, Defendant's conduct does not invade any existing right of privacy. *Lugosi v. Universal Pictures*, 160 Cal. Rptr. 323 (1979) (*infra*, p. 288-289).

D. Damage: In most cases, a ***plaintiff is not required to prove damage*** resulting from the invasion of her privacy. It is presumed that this invasion results at least in mental suffering.

II. APPROPRIATION OF PLAINTIFF'S IDENTITY

A. General concept: Appropriation of identity was the first invasion of privacy to be recognized as a tort. It is based on the principle that a plaintiff's identity is like an item of property, and that Plaintiff has a right to control its commercial use. Unauthorized use of a plaintiff's identity by a defendant who does so for purposes of personal gain is a violation of this right.

B. Essential elements: The essential elements of ***"invasion of privacy by appropriation of identity"*** are (1) ***unauthorized use***; (2) ***of the plaintiff's identity***; (3) ***for a commercial purpose***.

1. **Unauthorized use**: A defendant has made unauthorized use of the plaintiff's identity if he has used it without the permission of the person who has legal capacity to give such permission.

   Example: Plaintiff, who is seventeen years old, submits her photograph to Defendant's magazine for use in one of its features. Defendant uses the photograph. A statute in the jurisdiction provides that no person under the age of eighteen years is competent to consent to the commercial use of her likeness. Plaintiff subsequently asserts a claim against Defendant for appropriation of identity. Defendant argues that, by submitting her photograph, Plaintiff authorized its use.

   Since the statute declared that persons under the age of eighteen years were not competent to consent, Plaintiff did not have the legal capacity to give her consent. For this reason, her submission of the photograph was not consent, and Defendant's use of it was unauthorized. *Lopez v. Triangle*, 421 N.Y.S.2d 57 (1979).

2. **Plaintiff's identity:** Although privacy statutes in some jurisdictions make specific reference to use of the plaintiff's "likeness," it is generally understood that ***anything which serves to identify the plaintiff*** may be the subject of liability.

   a. **Identity**: Since the essence of this tort is that the defendant has gained commercial or other advantage from the use of the plaintiff's identity, it is necessary that the plaintiff be identified by the defendant's reference. Even the use of the plaintiff's name may not satisfy this requirement unless the reasonable person seeing or hearing the reference will identify the plaintiff with it.

   Example: Defendant, who operates a retail store, causes the publication of an advertisement containing the statement, "Our store was built with John Q. Public in mind." Plaintiff, whose name is John Quincy Public, asserts a claim for appropriation of identity.

   Although the name used by Defendant in its advertising is identical to Plaintiff's name, it is not an appropriation of Plaintiff's identity unless it identifies Plaintiff. This probably would be a question for a jury. Since "John Q. Public" is a common figure of speech meaning "everyperson", it is likely that a jury would find that its use did not identify Plaintiff. If a jury comes to that conclusion, no liability would be imposed on Defendant.

b. **Need not be name or likeness**: If the defendant's reference does identify the plaintiff, liability may be imposed regardless of how that identification was made. The use of the plaintiff's voice or a stylized drawing of the plaintiff's moustache might satisfy this requirement if the reasonable person would identify the plaintiff from it.

Example: Plaintiff is an actor who is known for a peculiar voice and speech pattern involving a distinctive and original combination of pitch, inflection, accent, and comic sounds. Defendant, a manufacturer of household cleaning products, uses a television commercial in which a cartoon duck speaks in a voice like Plaintiff's. Plaintiff subsequently asserts a claim for appropriation of identity. Defendant argues that it did not use Plaintiff's name or photograph and that the voice used in its commercial was not Plaintiff's, but that of another actor hired to perform.

If Plaintiff's voice and speech pattern are sufficiently distinctive so that the reasonable person would recognize him from them, and if the voice and speech pattern used by Defendant in its commercial were sufficiently like Plaintiff's so that a reasonable person hearing them would believe that they were Plaintiff's, the Defendant probably made use of Plaintiff's identity. *Lahr v. Adell Chemical Co.*, *supra*, p. 252.

3. **Commercial purpose**: Although not all the statutes and cases which define this tort use the phrase "commercial purpose," it is generally understood that the ***use of the plaintiff's identity is not tortious unless it does, or is likely to, enrich the defendant in some way***.

Example 1: Plaintiff is an author. Defendant publishes a novel in which it is mentioned that the main character is influenced by reading books written by Plaintiff. Plaintiff asserts a claim for appropriation of identity.

Since it is not likely that mention of Plaintiff's work in Defendant's novel would lead consumers to purchase Defendant's novel, Defendant's use of Plaintiff's name probably was not for a sufficiently commercial purpose to result in liability.

Example 2: Same facts as in previous Example, except that Defendant also causes Plaintiff's photograph to appear on the cover of the novel. Plaintiff asserts a claim for appropriation of identity.

Since it is likely that Plaintiff's photograph on the cover of Defendant's novel will induce consumers to purchase it, Defendant's use of Plaintiff's identity probably was for a sufficiently commercial purpose to result in liability.

a. **Newsworthy publications**: If the use of the plaintiff's identity is ***newsworthy***, it does not lead to liability for appropriation even though the defendant is in some way enriched by it.

Example: Plaintiff is a performer who as part of a circus act is shot out of a cannon into a net 200 feet away. His entire act takes 15 seconds. After a performance, Defendant, a television station, mentions, during a news program, that Plaintiff was shot out of a cannon at the circus, and shows a one second film clip depicting Plaintiff emerging from the mouth of the cannon. Plaintiff asserts a claim for appropriation.

Since the fact that Plaintiff was shot out of a cannon probably is of interest to the public, it is newsworthy. For this reason, mention of the incident and the airing of the one second clip showing Plaintiff emerging from the cannon probably will not result in liability. *Zacchini v. Scripps-Howard*, 433 U.S. 562 (1977).

b. **Exceeding the scope of newsworthy publication**: Since the cause of action for appropriation is designed to protect the plaintiff's right to profit from his own identity, a ***publication which goes beyond the scope of reporting the news may cause liability***, even if its subject is newsworthy.

Example: Some facts as in previous Example, except that Defendant shows a fifteen second film clip depicting Plaintiff's entire act. Plaintiff asserts a claim for appropriation.

Although Plaintiff's accomplishment probably is newsworthy, depiction of his entire act probably exceeds the scope of reporting the news and becomes a broadcast for entertainment. For this reason, the broadcast probably would result in liability.

Note: In commenting on this case, the United States Supreme Court compared the broadcast of Plaintiff's entire act to the unauthorized broadcast of an entire baseball game in the guise of making a newsworthy publication. *Zacchini v. Scripps-Howard, supra*.

4. **Strict liability**: Since the law of torts treats an appropriation of the plaintiff's identity in much the same way as an unauthorized use of a work in which the plaintiff has intellectual property (*e.g.*, a trademark), a ***plaintiff may recover without showing intent or negligence*** by the defendant.

Example: In composing a cooperative advertisement for a vaudeville show and a bakery, Defendant, a newspaper, erroneously uses a photograph of Plaintiff instead of a photograph of the vaudeville show's star. Plaintiff asserts a claim for appropriation of identity, but fails to prove that Defendant's use of Plaintiff's likeness was intentional or negligent.

Since Defendant derived commercial benefit from the unauthorized use of Plaintiff's likeness, Defendant should be required to pay damages without regard to fault. *Flake v. Greensboro News Co.*, 195 S.E. 55 (N.C. 1938).

C. Damage: Although damage, at least in the form of mental suffering, is usually presumed in cases of invasion of privacy, a plaintiff seeking damages for appropriation of identity may also be entitled to whatever profit the defendant derived from the unauthorized use of the plaintiff's identity.

Example: Without Plaintiff's permission, Defendant causes Plaintiff's picture to be printed on boxes of flour which Defendant markets. Plaintiff asserts a claim for appropriation, proving that without using Plaintiff's photo, Defendant would have sold ten thousand boxes of flour, but that because it used Plaintiff's photo, Defendant sold twenty thousand boxes of flour.

If Plaintiff is successful, Plaintiff should recover the profit which Defendant derived from the sale of the additional ten thousand boxes. *Roberson v. Rochester Folding Box*, 64 N.E. 442 (N.Y. 1902).

D. Right of publicity: Although it is generally held that the right of privacy dies with the person to whom it belongs, a person who profits from the commercial use of his or another's identity while he is alive, may thus convert it into ***an inheritable property right*** (sometimes called the right of publicity). This right may be the subject of an action by his heirs subsequent to his death.

Example 1: Decedent is an actor famous for the role of the Transylvanian vampire, Count Dracula. During his lifetime, Decedent does not sell or license the sale of any objects which capitalize on his identity. Following Decedent's death, Defendant sells posters containing a photograph of Decedent in the Count Dracula persona. Plaintiff, Decedent's heir, asserts a claim against Defendant for appropriation of Decedent's identity.

Since the privacy interest asserted is that of Decedent, and since Decedent is no longer alive, Defendant's conduct does not invade any existing right of privacy. Since Decedent did not capitalize on his identity during his lifetime, he did not convert his non-inheritable privacy interest to an inheritable right of publicity. For this reason, Plaintiff's claim probably will be dismissed. *Lugosi v. Universal, supra*, p. 284.

Example 2: Decedent is a popular singing star and actor who, during his lifetime, sells and licenses for sale numerous items bearing his likeness and other identifying marks. After Decedent's death, Defendant produces an entertainment program in which performers impersonate Decedent, and at which items bearing a likeness of Decedent are sold. Decedent's heirs assert a claim against Defendant, alleging that Defendant violated the right of publicity which they inherited from Decedent. Defendant argues that Decedent's privacy interest ceased to exist when Decedent died.

Since Decedent sold and otherwise made commercial use of his identity while alive, he converted the right of privacy into a right of publicity. Since this right of publicity is an inheritable property right, Decedent's heirs may maintain the claim for its violation. *Estate of Elvis Presley v. Russen*, 513 F.Supp. 1339 (D.N.J. 1981).

III. INTRUSION INTO SECLUSION

A. General concept: This tort is based on the principle that every person has a private space in which she is entitled to be let alone, and that an unreasonable intrusion into that space is a violation of that right.

B. Essential elements: The essential elements of this tort are (1) an ***intentional***; (2) ***intrusion***; (3) into ***plaintiff's private space***; (4) in an ***offensive manner***.

1. **Intent**: Although most of the cases do not deal with the issue of intent, it is unlikely that liability would be imposed for an intrusion which was not intended by the defendant. For this purpose, an intrusion is intended when the ***defendant desires or knows that his conduct will result in an invasion of the plaintiff's private space***.

Example: Believing it to be unoccupied, Defendant enters a lavatory on an airplane and sees Plaintiff, who is in the lavatory, in a state of undress. Plaintiff asserts a claim for intrusion.

Since Defendant believed the lavatory to be unoccupied, he didn't know that his entry would violate any person's private space. Since he lacked the intent to intrude, he probably will not be liable for intrusion.

2. **Intrusion**: When this tort was first recognized, the only intrusions which qualified as its targets were physical entries. In the past few decades, it has been held that intrusion can be by electronic devices as well. It is always necessary, however, that the defendant either make or cause the intrusion.

   Example 1: Defendant is the owner of a furnished apartment. While the apartment is unoccupied, Defendant places a microphone under the bed, wiring it to a tape recorder located in his own apartment. Defendant subsequently rents the apartment to Plaintiff and his wife and listens to their nuptial conversations by means of the hidden microphone. When Plaintiff learns of this, he asserts a claim against Defendant for intrusion. Defendant argues that he did not physically enter the apartment after renting it to Plaintiff, and therefore did not invade Plaintiff's private space.

   Since Defendant used an electronic device to eavesdrop on Plaintiff at a time when and in a place where Plaintiff obviously was entitled to privacy, Defendant has intruded into Plaintiff's solitude. *Hamberger v. Eastman*, 206 A.2d 239 (N.H. 1964).

   Example 2: Plaintiff is a United States Senator. Employees of Plaintiff remove secret documents from Plaintiff's private file cabinet, copy them, and sell them to Defendant, a newspaper columnist. After Defendant publishes the contents of the documents, Plaintiff asserts a claim against Defendant for intrusion. Plaintiff does not allege that Defendant hired or otherwise caused Plaintiff's employees to remove and copy the documents.

   Since Defendant did not physically invade Plaintiff's space and did not cause such an invasion to occur, Defendant is not liable for intrusion. *Pearson v. Dodd*, 410 F.2d 701 (D.C. Cir. 1969).

3. **Plaintiff's private space**: Since intrusion is an invasion of privacy, the incident must occur at a time when and in a place where the plaintiff is entitled to privacy. Ordinarily, a person has ***less right to seclusion in a public place than in a private place***.

   Example 1: While attending a fun-house, Plaintiff unwittingly steps over a device which expels a powerful blast of air causing her dress to be blown up over her head. Defendant looks at and photographs Plaintiff in this condition. Plaintiff subsequently asserts claims for intrusion. Defendant argues that since Plaintiff was in a public place, she had no right to privacy.

   Since Plaintiff was in a public place, her right to privacy was not as great as it would have been in a private place. For this reason, and since people are generally understood to have the right to look at each other, Defendant probably did not commit an intrusion by looking at Plaintiff when her dress was blown up over her head. Since Plaintiff did not voluntarily expose herself that way, however, and since even in a public place a person has some right to be let alone, Defendant may have committed an intrusion when he photographed Plaintiff in the exposed state. *Daily Times-Democrat v. Graham*, 162 So.2d 474 (Ala. 1964).

Example 2: Defendant, a freelance photographer, follows Plaintiff, the widow of a slain U.S. President, everywhere, harassing her and photographing her. While Plaintiff is attending a theater, Defendant harasses her in the lobby during an intermission, for the purpose of photographing her with an angry expression. Plaintiff asserts a claim for intrusion. Defendant argues that his observation and photographing of Plaintiff had always occurred in public places and that, therefore, he never invaded her seclusion.

Even in a public place, every person has some right to be let alone. Although Defendant probably was entitled to observe and photograph Plaintiff while she was in a public place, his constant harassment and annoyance of her may have been so excessive as to constitute an invasion of her right. *Galella v. Onassis*, 487 F.2d 986 (2d Cir. 1973).

4. **Offensive manner**: An intrusion is not tortious unless the method by which it is accomplished would be ***offensive to the reasonable person*** in the plaintiff's situation.

Example: After returning from a trip, Defendant discovers hair on her husband's pillow and suspects that it is Plaintiff's. Seeking to prove that her husband was having sexual relations with Plaintiff, Defendant seeks to obtain a sample of Plaintiff's hair. While Plaintiff is in a hospital, Defendant pays an orderly to obtain a sample of Plaintiff's hair. The orderly does this by entering Plaintiff's room and cleaning Plaintiff's hairbrush. Plaintiff subsequently asserts a claim for intrusion against Defendant.

Unless the intrusion occurred in a way which would be offensive to the reasonable person in Plaintiff's shoes, it will not result in liability. Since it is part of a hospital orderly's job to clean hospital rooms and provide for the comfort of patients, it probably would not offend the reasonable person for an orderly to clean his hairbrush while he is a patient in a hospital. For this reason, the intrusion procured by Defendant probably was not offensive, and liability probably will not be imposed. *Froelich v. Werbin*, 548 P.2d 482 (Kan. 1976).

IV. PUBLIC DISCLOSURE

A. General concept: This tort is committed by publicly revealing offensive secrets about the plaintiff. It is based on the belief that a person has a right to keep certain facts about herself from public knowledge.

B. Essential elements: The essential elements of this invasion of privacy are (1) ***public disclosure***; (2) of ***private facts about the plaintiff***; (3) the ***disclosure of which would be offensive to the reasonable person in the plaintiff's situation***.

1. **Public disclosure**: The essence of this tort is that secret information about the plaintiff has been made public, against her wishes. Unlike defamation or false light (which involve false statements about the plaintiff) publication to one or even a few persons is not sufficient to result in liability. In order for a disclosure to be sufficiently public, it must be ***made to the public in general, or to a large number of persons***.

   Example: Defendant, a physician, delivers Plaintiff's baby out of wedlock. Plaintiff thereupon gives the baby up for adoption. Subsequently, seeking to find her natural mother, the child consults Defendant who issues a document enabling her to do so. Plaintiff, who is married and has children of the marriage, does not want to see the child and asserts a claim against Defendant for public disclosure.

   Since Defendant communicated Plaintiff's secret to only one person, he did not publicly disclose it, and, therefore, is not liable for this tort. Defendant may be liable for another tort recognized in some jurisdictions and known as ***breach of confidence***. *Humphers v. First Interstate Bank*, 696 P.2d 527 (Or. 1985).

2. **Private fact**: The information disclosed must be something which was ***not formerly known*** to the general public.

   a. **Public record**: For this purpose, the United States Supreme Court has held that ***no fact which is a matter of public record may be regarded as a private fact***.

   Example: During the course of a trial for rape, the name of the victim is mentioned on the record. Defendant, a television station, in reporting an account of the trial, mentions the victim's name. The victim's family asserts a claim for public disclosure.

Since the name of the victim was mentioned on the record during the trial, it is a matter of public record and cannot be regarded as a private fact. For this reason, liability cannot be imposed on Defendant for mentioning it. *Cox Broadcasting Corp. v. Cohn*, 420 U.S. 469 (1975).

b. Persons in public eye: It is generally recognized that persons who have voluntarily placed themselves before the public, and persons who have involuntarily been involved in events which bring them to public attention, have less right than others to keep their private facts — at least as they relate to the matter which brought them to public interest — from public attention.

Example 1: Plaintiff, a well-known symphonic conductor, asserts a claim for public disclosure against Defendant, who published certain facts about Plaintiff's life.

Since Plaintiff has voluntarily pursued an occupation which has brought him to public attention, facts about him are less likely to be regarded as private. For this reason, Defendant probably will not be held liable. *Koussevitzky v. Allen, Towne, & Heath*, 69 N.Y.S.2d 432 (1947).

Example 2: Plaintiff's husband is murdered before her eyes. Defendant, a newspaper, publishes an account of the crime in which certain details are described. Plaintiff subsequently asserts a claim for public disclosure.

Although Plaintiff did nothing voluntarily to place herself in the public eye, her association with an event of interest to the public made her an involuntary public figure. For this reason, the facts published by Defendant probably are not sufficiently private to serve as the basis for the action, and liability probably will not be imposed on Defendant. *Jones v. Herald Post*, 18 S.W.2d 972 (Ky. 1929).

3. Offensive to reasonable person: Even if a defendant publicly discloses private facts about the plaintiff, no liability will attach unless the disclosure is one which the ***reasonable person in the plaintiff's situation would find offensive***.

Example 1: In his childhood, Plaintiff was a child prodigy, and appeared regularly on a radio program which featured bright children. As an adult, Plaintiff prefers that his neighbors and acquaintances not know about this aspect of his childhood. Defendant, a magazine, publishes an article identifying Plaintiff and describing his childhood and his appearances on the radio program. Plaintiff subsequently asserts a claim against Defendant for public disclosure.

Although Plaintiff preferred that his acquaintances not know about his childhood experiences, there was nothing about those experiences which would have embarrassed the ordinary person. For this reason, Defendant's disclosure probably would not have been offensive to the reasonable person in Plaintiff's situation, and, therefore, liability probably will not be imposed. *Sidis v. F-R Publishing Corp.*, 113 F.2d 806 (2d Cir. 1940).

Example 2: Plaintiff once was a prostitute and was implicated in a murder trial. Subsequently, Plaintiff changed her name, reformed, and led an exemplary life. Defendant makes a motion picture about Plaintiff's sordid past, identifying Plaintiff by the name she is now using. Plaintiff asserts a claim against Defendant for public disclosure.

Since the events of Plaintiff's past would embarrass most people, the reasonable person in Plaintiff's situation probably would find disclosure of those events highly offensive. For this reason, liability for public disclosure will be imposed on Defendant. *Melvin v. Reid*, 297 P.2d 92 (Cal. 1931).

CHAPTER 17

MISUSE OF JUDICIAL PROCEDURE

I. BACKGROUND

A. General concept: A system for resolving disputes without violence is a benchmark of civilized society. For this reason, our society seeks to encourage uninhibited access to the courts. On the other hand, judicial proceedings can take a heavy toll on the finances and peace of mind of the litigants. Recognizing both of these factors, the law of torts attempts to walk a delicate line in protecting the right to be free of unwarranted judicial proceedings.

B. A group of torts: We will discuss three distinct torts based on misuse of judicial procedure. The first two of these — malicious prosecution and malicious use of process — are so closely related that many jurisdictions and writers treat them as one. They involve the improper institution or continuation of a criminal or civil proceeding. The third — abuse of process — involves the use of a judicial proceeding for an improper purpose.

C. Nomenclature: The plaintiff in an action brought for misuse of judicial procedure is suing on the theory that he was victimized by a prior judicial proceeding in which he was the defendant. The defendant whom he is now suing may have been the plaintiff in that prior proceeding. Care should be taken to understand that reference in this section to parties as "plaintiff" or "defendant" is based on their status in a lawsuit brought on one of the theories discussed in this section.

> **Example:** Mary improperly sues John for breach of contract. After John wins in that breach of contract action, John sues Mary for malicious use of process.
>
> Although Mary was the plaintiff and John was the defendant in the breach of contract action, in discussing the action for malicious use of process John will be referred to as the plaintiff and Mary as the defendant.

II. MALICIOUS PROSECUTION

A. General concept: ***Malicious prosecution*** is a tort committed by improperly causing the plaintiff to be the subject of a ***criminal prosecution***.

B. Essential elements: The essential elements of malicious prosecution are (1) ***institution or continuation by defendant of a criminal***

proceeding against plaintiff; (2) ***termination of that proceeding in favor of plaintiff***; (3) ***lack of probable cause for the proceeding***; (4) ***malice***; and (5) ***damage.***

1. **Institution or continuation of a criminal proceeding against plaintiff:**

   a. **Institution**: Used in this sense, "institution" means the ***actual commencement*** of a proceeding. Ordinarily, a criminal proceeding begins with the issuance of a warrant, an arrest, or an indictment by a grand jury. This presents something of a paradox because ordinarily the persons empowered to issue the necessary process or to effect the necessary arrest are public officials who, in most jurisdictions, are immune from tort liability resulting from the performance of their official duties. However, most jurisdictions also recognize procedures by which a non-public official may make an arrest or otherwise commence a criminal proceeding. These are the cases which are most likely to lead to claims for malicious prosecution.

   Example 1: Defendant calls the police to complain about noise coming from a party at Plaintiff's house. Police officers come and listen outside Plaintiff's door. Deciding that the noise level is a violation, the police arrest Plaintiff. After being acquitted, Plaintiff asserts a claim against Defendant for malicious prosecution.

   Since the criminal proceeding against Plaintiff began with an arrest, and since Defendant did not arrest Plaintiff, Defendant did not institute the proceeding and will not be held liable for malicious prosecution.

   Example 2: Assume the same facts as in the previous Example, except that police come and arrest Plaintiff without first listening or making any other independent investigation of Defendant's complaint.

   Since the criminal proceeding against Plaintiff began with arrest, and since Defendant did not arrest Plaintiff, Defendant did not institute the proceeding against Plaintiff and cannot be liable for malicious prosecution.

   Example 3: Again, assume the same facts as in the previous Examples, except that when the police arrive, they refuse to arrest Plaintiff. Defendant places Plaintiff under citizen's arrest and demands that the police take Plaintiff into custody. Plaintiff is subsequently acquitted and sues Defendant for malicious prosecution.

   Since the criminal proceeding against Plaintiff began with an arrest which was made by Defendant, Defendant instituted the proceeding against Plaintiff and may be liable for malicious prosecution (if all other essential elements are satisfied).

b. **Continuation**: A defendant is said to have continued a criminal proceeding when she prevents it from terminating when it might, or fails to terminate it when she should.

Example: Plaintiff is prosecuted as the result of a complaint made by Defendant. At a court appearance, it becomes clear that there is no evidence against Plaintiff. Under a rule in that court, a prosecutor may not consent to a dismissal of a criminal proceeding without the approval of the complainant in that proceeding. The prosecutor asks Defendant if she will agree to a dismissal of the charge against Plaintiff. Defendant refuses. Plaintiff is subsequently acquitted and sues Defendant for malicious prosecution. Defendant argues that the proceeding was not instituted by her, but by the public prosecutor.

Since the proceeding would have terminated if Defendant had approved of the dismissal, and since Defendant prevented that termination by refusing to approve of the dismissal, Defendant continued the proceeding and may be held liable for malicious prosecution (if all other essential elements of the tort are satisfied).

c. **Criminal proceeding**: A proceeding is criminal if it could lead to the ***incarceration or execution*** of the person being prosecuted.

Example: Defendant, a police investigator, charges Plaintiff, a police officer, with corruption and institutes an internal affairs proceeding against Plaintiff before a police department disciplinary board, which has the power to discharge Plaintiff without pension or other benefits. After the board exonerates Plaintiff, Plaintiff asserts a claim for malicious prosecution against Defendant.

Since the proceeding could not have resulted in incarceration or execution of Plaintiff, it was not a criminal proceeding. *Groat v. Town*, 418 N.Y.S.2d 842 (1979).

i. **Quasi-criminal proceedings**: In some jurisdictions a quasi- criminal proceeding (*i.e.*, a proceeding which could result in the imposition of a fine or other punitive measure) may be the subject of an action for malicious prosecution.

Example: In the previous Example, some jurisdictions would regard the proceeding brought against Plaintiff as quasi-criminal, since it could result in the loss of job and benefits under ignominious circumstances, and is therefore, a proper basis to an action for malicious prosecution.

ii. **Civil proceedings**: Some jurisdictions hold that a civil proceeding can be the subject of an action for malicious prosecution. In effect, these jurisdictions recognize two varieties of malicious prosecution: malicious prosecution of a criminal proceeding, and malicious prosecution of a civil proceeding. For simplicity, this outline will regard these as two distinct torts. The name "***malicious prosecution***" will be used when discussing the improper institution of a criminal proceeding against the plaintiff, and the name "malicious use of process" will be used when discussing the improper institution of a civil proceeding against the plaintiff.

2. **Termination in favor of plaintiff**: To avoid inconsistent results and since the action for malicious prosecution can be used to intimidate the prosecution in a criminal proceeding, ***no action for malicious prosecution can be brought until the proceeding against the plaintiff which is the subject of that action has terminated***.

   a. **Final termination**: This requirement is not satisfied unless the criminal proceeding has terminated finally, ***in a way which prevents it from being re-instituted.***

      i. **Dismissal without prejudice**: Since a proceeding may be re-instituted after being dismissed without prejudice, such a dismissal is not a termination sufficient to justify a subsequent action for malicious prosecution.

      ii. **Appeals**: In the event of an appeal, termination is not final until the appellate process is complete.

      iii. **Discontinuance with leave to renew**: So long as the proceeding can be re-instituted, its termination is not final. For this reason, a voluntary discontinuance with leave to renew does not satisfy the requirement of a final termination.

   b. **In favor of plaintiff**: Since criminal proceedings may be terminated for a reason which does not establish the guilt or innocence of the person prosecuted, and since the law does not wish to permit a guilty person to sue his prosecutor for malicious prosecution, ***no action can be brought unless the termination was an indication that the person prosecuted was not guilty.***

i. **On the merits**: A termination on the merits is a termination which is adequate to fix guilt or innocence. For this purpose, a termination is on the merits if it occurs after a trial has begun.

ii. **Lack of evidence**: A dismissal for lack of evidence, even if it occurs prior to the commencement of trial, is an indication that the person prosecuted is innocent and satisfies the requirement of termination.

Example: Plaintiff is charged with possession of marijuana. After a court grants a motion to suppress the only evidence against Plaintiff, the prosecution is dismissed. Plaintiff subsequently sues for malicious prosecution. Defendant argues that Plaintiff's lawsuit should be dismissed because the criminal proceeding against Plaintiff was not determined on the merits.

Since the burden of establishing guilt is on the prosecution, a dismissal for lack of evidence indicates that the person prosecuted was not guilty and satisfies the requirement of a final termination in favor of plaintiff.

iii. **Abandonment and failure to prosecute**: Abandonment of the prosecution, or willful failure to prosecute, are regarded as indications that the prosecutor realizes that the person being prosecuted is not guilty, and are usually regarded as final terminations in favor of the person being prosecuted.

Example: After Defendant institutes a criminal proceeding against Plaintiff, the proceeding is postponed several times at the prosecutor's request. On one occasion, the court notifies the prosecutor that no further postponements will be permitted. The next time the matter appears on the court's calendar, the prosecutor requests a postponement on the ground that the arresting officer, whose testimony is required, is off duty that day. The court dismisses the prosecution for failure to prosecute, and Plaintiff subsequently asserts a claim for malicious prosecution. Defendant argues that the dismissal does not indicate that Plaintiff is innocent, and, therefore, is not a "final termination in favor of plaintiff."

Since the prosecutor had been advised that there would be no further postponements, and since a police officer, like any other witness, can be compelled to appear in court even when off duty, the prosecutor's failure to prosecute probably indicates that the prosecutor believes that the Plaintiff is innocent. For this reason, the dismissal probably qualifies as a termination in favor of Plaintiff. *Loeb v. Teitelbaum*, 432 N.Y.S.2d 487 (1980).

c. **Relitigation of Plaintiff's guilt**: For sound policy reasons, a person who was actually guilty of the crime for which she was prosecuted should not be permitted to recover damages for malicious prosecution against the person who prosecuted her. The requirement of termination in favor of the plaintiff is designed to prevent such an obviously bad result. The fact that a prosecution resulted in acquittal, however, does not establish that the person prosecuted was innocent. All it really establishes is that her guilt was not proven beyond a reasonable doubt in that criminal proceeding. In a tort case, however, proof does not have to be beyond a reasonable doubt, but rather by a fair preponderance of the credible evidence. For this reason, a ***defendant in a malicious prosecution action is permitted to prove affirmatively that the plaintiff really was guilty of the crime for which she was prosecuted.*** If the defendant is successful in doing so, the termination of the criminal proceeding does not satisfy the requirement of termination in favor of the plaintiff and plaintiff's action for malicious prosecution will fail.

Example: John institutes a criminal proceeding against Mary for the crime of armed robbery. After Mary is found "not guilty" by a jury, she asserts a claim against John for malicious prosecution. At the trial, John offers evidence tending to prove that Mary actually was guilty of the crime of armed robbery. Mary objects on the ground that her innocence has already been established and that therefore, John's action should be barred by *res judicata*.

Since the trial of the prosecution against Mary resulted only in the finding that her guilt had not been proven beyond a reasonable doubt, and since the burden of proof in a tort case is a fair preponderance of the evidence, John may attempt to prove by a preponderance of the evidence that Mary was guilty.

i. **Fair preponderance**: As with any other issue in a tort case, the defendant is required to establish the plaintiff's guilt only by a fair preponderance of the credible evidence.

ii. **Affirmative defense**: All jurisdictions place the burden of such proof on the defendant. Some jurisdictions treat a defendant's attempt to prove the plaintiff's guilt as an affirmative defense, requiring that it be pleaded as such. Other jurisdictions treat it as a response to the plaintiff's proof establishing the elements of her case and, therefore, do not require it to be pleaded by defendant.

iii. **No criminal consequences**: Proof offered in the malicious prosecution action which establishes by a preponderance of the evidence that the plaintiff was actually guilty can have no criminal consequences. This is for two reasons: first, the plaintiff has already been acquitted and the double jeopardy clause of the United States Constitution prevents another prosecution; and, second, a criminal conviction requires proof beyond a reasonable doubt.

3. **Lack of probable cause**: Our legal system requires a trial of a criminal issue when there is probable cause to believe that a person is guilty of a crime. For this reason, liability for malicious prosecution cannot be imposed on a person who instituted a criminal proceeding against another if he had probable cause to believe that the person prosecuted was guilty of a crime.

   a. **Definition**: ***Probable cause is defined as a sincere and reasonable belief that a crime has been committed and that the person prosecuted is the one who committed it.***

      i. **Sincere belief**: The sincere belief required is a subjective state of mind indicating that the person holding it is personally convinced that the person prosecuted has committed a crime. A belief that a conviction can be obtained does not satisfy this requirement unless the person holding that belief honestly believes that the person prosecuted is guilty.

      ii. **Reasonable belief**: A belief that the person being prosecuted is guilty is reasonable if it is supported by facts which would lead the reasonable person to so believe.

   b. **Exception for public prosecutor**: Since a public prosecutor is charged with the responsibility of representing the public in criminal prosecutions, his personal feelings or beliefs should not be a factor in determining who will be prosecuted. For this reason, in cases where a public prosecutor may be sued for malicious prosecution, he will avoid liability ***if he has a reasonable, but not necessarily sincere, belief*** in the guilt of the person being prosecuted.

   c. **Conviction**: The fact that the Plaintiff was convicted ***establishes a presumption that there was probable cause*** for the prosecution, even if that conviction is subsequently reversed on appeal. In many jurisdictions, this presumption is rebuttable only by proof that the conviction resulted from perjured testimony given by or procured by the defendant.

4. **Malice**: The requirement of malice exists to protect the notion of free and uninhibited access to the courts. Since probable cause

depends on the reasonableness of the defendant's belief in the guilt of the person prosecuted, and since fear of the liability which might result from acting unreasonably would inhibit resort to the courts, a defendant who prosecutes a plaintiff without probable cause to believe that he is guilty is not liable for malicious prosecution unless he acted with malice.

a. **Definition**: Although malice generally means ill will or a desire to do harm, in connection with this tort, malice specifically means a ***primary purpose other than to accomplish justice.***

Example 1: Defendant dislikes Plaintiff a great deal and sincerely believes Plaintiff to be guilty of crimes even though there is no evidence to support such a belief. Believing that Plaintiff should be incarcerated for his crimes, Defendant institutes a criminal proceeding against Plaintiff which terminates in Plaintiff's favor. Plaintiff subsequently sues Defendant for malicious prosecution.

Since Defendant believed that Plaintiff was guilty and instituted the proceeding for the purpose of punishing Plaintiff for his crimes, Defendant probably lacked malice and, therefore, probably is not liable for malicious prosecution.

Example 2: Defendant and Plaintiff are business competitors. Although she does not have reason to believe that Plaintiff is guilty of a crime, Defendant institutes a criminal proceeding against Plaintiff hoping that the notoriety which results will cause prospective customers to do business with Defendant instead of Plaintiff. After the proceeding terminates in Plaintiff's favor, Plaintiff asserts a claim against Defendant for malicious prosecution.

Since Defendant's primary purpose was not to do justice but to injure Plaintiff, Defendant acted with the necessary malice and will be held liable to Plaintiff for malicious prosecution.

b. **Inference of malice**: The fact that a defendant instituted a proceeding without probable cause raises an ***inference of malice*** which, although not conclusive, is sufficient to get the question of malice to the jury.

5. **Damage**: Since it is almost inevitable that a person prosecuted for a crime will suffer damage as a result, many jurisdictions recognize a presumption of damage. The following are some of the items of damage for which a plaintiff may recover:

a. **Attorney fees**: A plaintiff is entitled to recover reasonable attorney fees incurred in defending against the criminal prosecution. Note, however, that no recovery is permitted for attorney fees incurred in connection with maintaining the action for malicious prosecution.

Example: Defendant institutes a criminal proceeding against Plaintiff. In defending the proceeding, Plaintiff hires Attorney No. 1 and incurs a fee for his defense. After termination of the proceeding in his favor, Plaintiff hires Attorney No. 2 to sue Defendant for malicious prosecution and incurs a fee for the representation.

If Plaintiff is successful in his malicious prosecution action, he may recover the fee which he paid Attorney No. 1, since it was an expense caused by Defendant's institution of the criminal proceeding against him. Plaintiff may not recover the fee which he paid Attorney No. 2, however, because our system does not require the loser of a tort action to pay the winner's attorney fees.

b. **Reputation**: Since damage to reputation results frequently from criminal prosecution, a plaintiff who proves such damage may recover for it.

c. **Expenses and compensation for incarceration**: If the criminal prosecution resulted in any period of incarceration, the plaintiff is entitled to recover expenses connected therewith, and damages to compensate for the physical and mental suffering that resulted therefrom.

III. MALICIOUS USE OF PROCESS

A. **General concept**: ***Malicious use of process*** is a tort committed by improperly causing the plaintiff to be the subject of a civil proceeding. In some jurisdictions it is treated as a variation on malicious prosecution and is known as "***malicious prosecution of a civil proceeding***."

B. **Relationship to malicious prosecution**: Since malicious use of process is closely related to malicious prosecution, we will concentrate on the differences between them. To avoid redundancy, similarities will be indicated without repeating previous discussions.

C. **Essential elements**: The ***essential elements for the tort of malicious use of process*** are identical to the essential elements of malicious prosecution, and are as follows: (1) ***institution or continuation of a civil proceeding against plaintiff***; (2) ***termination in favor of plaintiff***; (3) ***lack of probable cause for the proceeding***; (4) ***malice***; and (5) ***damage***.

1. **Institution or continuation of civil proceeding**: Since anyone can maintain a civil proceeding, the problem resulting from the official immunity which exists in malicious prosecution cases does not ordinarily exist in malicious use of process cases.

   a. **Institution**: Ordinarily, ***a civil proceeding is instituted by the filing or service of process.***

   b. **Continuation**: The same definition applies to continuation of a civil proceeding as to continuation of a criminal proceeding, *supra*, p. 297.

   c. **Parties liable**: Most of the time, the person suing hires an attorney to represent her in instituting or maintaining a lawsuit. Since the client causes the proceeding to be instituted or maintained, and the attorney does the work of instituting and maintaining it, either or both of them may be held liable for malicious use of process.

2. **Termination in favor of plaintiff**: This requirement is subject to the same rules and principles as in malicious prosecution, *supra*, p. 298.

   a. **Must establish no liability**: As in cases of malicious prosecution, the plaintiff must show that the proceeding which was instituted against her terminated in a way which establishes that she was not liable.

   b. **No relitigation**: The termination of a civil proceeding in favor of the one against whom it was brought indicates a finding that liability was not established by a fair preponderance of the credible evidence. Since that is the same burden of proof which would be applied in the malicious use of process case there can be ***no relitigation of the issue whether the plaintiff was actually liable.*** In this sense, it is different from malicious prosecution, in which defendant can in effect retry the issue of plaintiff's guilt.

      Example: John sues Mary for breach of contract. After trial, the jury renders a verdict for Mary. Mary subsequently asserts a claim against John for malicious use of process. At the trial, John offers evidence which would tend to establish that Mary actually did breach a contract and should have been liable. Mary objects to the evidence on the ground that a jury has already found that she was not liable for breach of contract and that its finding should be barred by res judicata.

      The issue determined by the jury in John's action against Mary was whether Mary's liability was established by a fair preponderance of the credible evidence. Since that is identical to the issue which John is seeking to raise in Mary's action against John, the matter is barred by res judicata, and John's evidence will be excluded.

3. **Lack of probable cause**: This requirement is similar to its counterpart in malicious prosecution, except that it means a ***sincere and reasonable belief*** that the person being sued is liable.

   a. **Exception for attorney**: Since an attorney's job is to present her client's case and not to judge it, ***an attorney has probable cause to believe in the liability of the person being sued if such belief is reasonable, even though the attorney does not personally believe that her client will prevail.***

   b. **Judgment against plaintiff**: If the civil proceeding which is the basis for the malicious use of process resulted in a judgment against this plaintiff (*i.e.*, the defendant in that proceeding), there is a presumption that probable cause to sue him existed, even if the judgment was reversed by an appellate court.

4. **Malice**: The requirement of malice is similar to its counterpart in malicious prosecution in that it means a primary purpose other than to do justice, *supra*, p. 301-302.

   a. **Exception for attorney**: As with any other business person, an attorney's primary purpose in practicing law in general and in representing a specific client in particular, is usually to make a living. For this reason, ***an attorney does not act with malice in instituting or continuing a lawsuit on behalf of his client unless he does so with ill will or with a desire to harm*** his client's adversary.

   b. **No inference resulting from lack of probable cause**: Since there may be many reasons other than ill will why an attorney who lacks probable cause will institute or continue a proceeding, ***the fact that an attorney lacks probable cause ordinarily does not create the inference that he is acting with malice.***

5. **Damage**: Since the winner of a civil proceeding is usually awarded a judgment for statutory costs, a ***plaintiff suing for malicious use of process must prove damage in excess of the costs received in the proceeding***. The types of damage recoverable for malicious use of process are similar to the types of damage recoverable in cases of malicious prosecution, *supra*, p. 302-303.

IV. ABUSE OF PROCESS

A. General concept: Abuse of process is a tort committed by using a legitimate process of the court for an illegitimate purpose.

Example: After repairing Plaintiff's realty, Defendant, a plumber, offers to purchase it. Defendant is aware that Mary has made Plaintiff a better offer. Because Plaintiff has not yet paid Defendant for the plumbing repairs, Defendant files a mechanic's lien against the realty in hopes that it will make the property less attractive to Mary and cause her to withdraw her offer. After Mary withdraws her offer, Plaintiff asserts a claim against Defendant for abuse of process. Defendant argues that he was entitled to file the mechanic's lien because his bill had not been paid.

The purpose of a mechanic's lien is to assure that persons who perform repairs to real estate will be paid upon the sale of the real estate. Since Defendant had not yet been paid, he was entitled to file a mechanic's lien for this purpose. The lien was, thus, a legitimate process of the court. A mechanic's lien was not designed, however, to permit one party to secure an advantage over another in the purchase of realty. Therefore, if Defendant's purpose was to secure an advantage in the purchase of Plaintiff's realty, his use of the process was for an illegitimate purpose, and was therefore an abuse of process.

B. Essential elements: The essential elements of ***"abuse of process"*** are (1) ***use of legitimate process of the court***; (2) ***for an illegitimate purpose.***

1. **Legitimate process of the court**: If a defendant causes process to issue without probable cause, that process is not legitimate, and the appropriate cause of action against him would be malicious prosecution or malicious use of process. It is only when there is probable cause for the issuance of the process that the law of abuse of process comes into play.

Example: In the previous Example, assume that Defendant had received payment for the work before he filed the mechanic's lien against Plaintiff's property.

Since payment had already been received, Defendant could not have had probable cause to believe that he would succeed in any proceeding based on the mechanic's lien. From his lack of probable cause, malice can be inferred. For these reasons, Plaintiff may be entitled to sue for malicious prosecution. Since, however, the process which issued was not a legitimate one, Plaintiff is not entitled to sue for abuse of process.

2. **Illegitimate purpose**: Since abuse of process is based on the issuance of a process which was legitimate in the sense that defendant was entitled to use it and the court was entitled to issue it, it is necessary for the plaintiff to make a clear showing that defendant's purpose was an illegitimate one.

   Example: Defendant, a teachers' association, is involved in a labor dispute with Plaintiff, a school district. Under existing contracts, Plaintiff must pay teachers on days when they are absent for the purpose of attending a court hearing. Defendant serves subpoenas on all 120 teachers employed by Plaintiff requiring them to appear in court on the day of a judicial hearing connected with the dispute. Defendant knows that it will be impossible for more than two or three of them to testify on any single day, but serves the subpoenas so that Plaintiff will be required to hire temporary teachers for the day to replace those who are in court. Defendant's purpose is to apply economic pressure on Plaintiff to force Plaintiff to settle the labor dispute. Plaintiff asserts a claim for abuse of process. Defendant argues that it was entitled to subpoena witnesses on its behalf.

   Since all parties to a judicial proceeding are entitled to subpoena witnesses to testify on their behalf, the subpoenas issued by Defendant were legitimate process of the court. The purpose of a subpoena, however, is to secure testimony. Since Defendant knew that it would be impossible for all the subpoenaed teachers to testify on a single day, and since Defendant's intent was to apply economic pressure on Plaintiff to force a settlement, Defendant was using the process of the court for an illegitimate purpose and was therefore committing an abuse of process. *Board of Education v. Farmingdale Teachers*, 380 N.Y.S.2d 635 (1975).

   a. **Collateral coercion**: Process is being used for the purpose of ***collateral coercion*** when the defendant uses it to force a plaintiff to do something which the process was not designed to force the plaintiff to do. Although it is not necessary that the process be used for this purpose, this is frequently the basis for a defendant's abuse of process.

   b. **Legitimate coercion**: Since judicial process is designed to force people to do things which they are not otherwise willing to do, the use of process for coercive purposes is not an abuse, unless the process is being used to force conduct which the process was not designed to compel.

Example 1: Defendant obtains a judgment against Plaintiff. Although Plaintiff is employed and receives a weekly salary, Plaintiff refuses to make any payment to Defendant to liquidate the judgment. Defendant files a wage execution against Plaintiff with Plaintiff's employer to coerce Plaintiff into paying ten percent of her salary each week to Defendant. Plaintiff asserts a claim for abuse of process.

Since the purpose of wage execution is to force a judgment debtor to make payments to liquidate the judgment, Defendant's purpose was not illegitimate, and Defendant, therefore, has not committed an abuse of process.

Example 2: Defendant obtains a judgment against Plaintiff and is attempting to collect from Plaintiff. Plaintiff has a job and owns no property other than a car. Under existing statutes, Plaintiff's car is exempt from execution of judgments, and only ten percent of Plaintiff's salary can be taken under a wage execution. Plaintiff agrees to and does pay Defendant ten percent of her salary every week toward liquidation of the judgment. Defendant demands that Plaintiff sell her car to pay the judgment in full. When Plaintiff refuses, Defendant files a wage execution with Plaintiff's employer, knowing that the employer has a policy of firing employees against whom wage executions have been filed. Defendant's purpose is to coerce Plaintiff into selling her car to pay the judgment. When Plaintiff loses her job as a result, she asserts a claim against Defendant for abuse of process. Defendant argues that he was entitled to file a wage execution since he held a judgment against Plaintiff.

Since Plaintiff was a judgment debtor, Defendant was entitled to file a wage execution against her. However, the wage execution could not legitimately have resulted in Defendant's collecting any more from Plaintiff than she was already paying voluntarily. Since Defendant's purpose was to force Plaintiff to sell her car to pay the judgment in full, and since the statute made Plaintiff's car immune from execution, Defendant's purpose in using the process (*i.e.*, wage execution) did not comply with what the process was designed to do and, therefore, was illegitimate. For this reason, Defendant has committed an abuse of process.

c. **Termination in plaintiff's favor not required**: Even though the defendant's purpose in issuing it may be illegitimate, the process which is the subject of this tort must be a legitimate one and may be used to satisfy its legitimate purpose. For this reason, it is not necessary for the plaintiff to show that the proceeding which is the basis for her abuse of process claim terminated in her favor.

Example: Defendant and Plaintiff are involved in a legitimate dispute over the sum of $500. Defendant, an attorney, commences an action against Plaintiff for that sum. During the pendency of the action, Defendant demands every possible pre-trial discovery device. Defendant's purpose is not to obtain evidence for use at the trial (which is the legitimate purpose of pre-trial discovery), but to increase Plaintiff's attorney fees to the extent that Plaintiff will be forced to settle the case. Plaintiff asserts a claim for abuse of process while Defendant's lawsuit against him is still pending. Defendant argues that the proceeding has not yet terminated in Plaintiff's favor.

Since the dispute underlying the lawsuit is a legitimate one, Defendant has a right to institute the claim and to demand discovery. The proceeding which Defendant instituted may not terminate in Plaintiff's favor. Discovery process is designed to coerce disclosure, however, not to coerce payment.

Since Defendant used the discovery process for the purpose of coercing payment, he was using it for an illegitimate purpose. He has committed an abuse of process even though the proceedings which he instituted have not terminated, and may terminate adversely to the plaintiff.

CHAPTER 18

IMMUNITIES

I. GENERAL CONCEPT

A. **Definition**: Immunity is freedom from liability for conduct which would ordinarily be regarded as liability-forming. Rules of immunity usually exist for the purpose of protecting certain entities or persons because of their position in society.

B. **Modern trend**: In recent years, most traditional rules of immunity have either been abolished or severely restricted and modified.

II. GOVERNMENTAL IMMUNITY

A. **General concept**: Traditionally, governments are immune from tort liability to their subjects. In English law, the traditional reason given for this rule is that "the King can do no wrong." Since the English monarch's conduct could result in injury to a person deserving of compensation, however, it came to be understood that even though the king could do no wrong, he could give an injured subject permission to make a claim against him for damage. The result was a rule that the sovereign was immune from tort liability unless he gave permission for a claim to be brought. Although we have no monarch, the principle that the sovereign can do no wrong applies in American law as well. As in the English system, this rule of immunity has been softened by statutes which grant permission to sue the government on certain theories, as long as certain conditions are met.

B. **Federal immunity**: Until passage of the ***Federal Tort Claims Act*** (FTCA) in 1946 (28 U.S.C. §1346 (b)), a tort lawsuit against the United States of America could not be brought without being specifically authorized by an act of Congress. ***The FTCA waives the federal government's immunity in certain cases by stating that the government is liable "in the same manner and to the same extent as a private individual."*** This statutory authorization is subject to restrictions and qualifications.

1. **State law applies**: Although actions against the United States must be brought in Federal courts, the FTCA provides that state rules of tort law should be applied.

2. **No jury trials**: No claim against the United States brought under the FTCA may be tried before a jury. Instead, the judge sits as the trier of the facts as well as of the law

3. **Requirement of notice**: Under the FTCA, before a claim can be instituted against the United States, it is ***necessary that notice be given*** to the appropriate agency within two years after the claim arises. If the agency denies the claim, a lawsuit must be instituted within six months after such denial.

4. **No strict liability**: The United States Supreme Court has held that under the FTCA the ***federal government cannot be held liable under a strict liability theory.***

   Example: A federal agency directs blasting activities. Although the activities are conducted with reasonable care, Plaintiff is injured by a blast and asserts claims under the FTCA against the United States on theories of negligence and strict liability. The government moves to dismiss both claims.

   Since the activities were conducted with reasonable care, Plaintiff will be unable to establish negligence. Although blasting is generally considered to be an ultrahazardous activity for which strict liability may be imposed, the federal government remains immune from strict liability. For these reasons, both of Plaintiff's claims should be dismissed.

5. **War and postal service**: The ***FTCA does not waive the federal government's immunity from liability for damage resulting from military activities in wartime or from delivery of the mail.***

6. **Exercise of discretion**: The ***FTCA does not waive the federal government's immunity from liability for damage resulting from "discretionary functions or duties" of the government.***

   Example: The federal government adopts a plan to improve crop production in friendly nations by providing fertilizers. Because the fertilizers provided under the plan are made from explosive materials, a shipload of fertilizer explodes, causing damage to Plaintiff. Plaintiff asserts a negligence claim against the United States under the FTCA, alleging that the government acted unreasonably in selecting the fertilizers involved. The government moves to dismiss on the ground that the activity involved an exercise of governmental discretion.

   Since the choice of fertilizer occurred at the planning stage of policy implementation, it probably involved an exercise of governmental discretion for which immunity continues to exist. For this reason, the claim probably should be dismissed. *Dalehite v. United States*, 346 U.S. 15 (1953).

C. **State immunity**: The same common law principles which make the federal government immune from tort liability apply to state governments. In effect, this means that ***unless modified by statute, the law provides that a state government cannot be sued on a tort theory unless it gives specific permission for the suit to be brought***. Like the federal government, however, almost all of the state governments have enacted legislation granting blanket permission for tort claims to be made. Since these statutes vary from one state to another, it is always necessary to consult the appropriate statute in each jurisdiction.

D. **Municipal immunity**: ***Under common law, municipalities are immune from tort liability.*** Most states have enacted laws waiving this immunity, however. Since these statutes vary from one jurisdiction to another, it is always necessary to consult the appropriate statute in each jurisdiction.

III. PUBLIC OFFICIALS

A. **General concept**: To assure that public officials will be free to carry out their duties without the inhibitions likely to result from fear of tort liability, they all enjoy some form of immunity.

B. **Judicial officials**: So long as they are carrying out a judicial function, ***judges and other judicial officials are absolutely immune from tort liability.***

1. **No exceptions**: The immunity of judicial officials protects them ***even when they are acting with malice, in bad faith, or beyond the scope of their lawful authority.*** The reason usually given is that if liability were to attach to such acts, any litigant could maintain a lawsuit against a judicial officer simply by claiming that he acted in bad faith, with malice, or beyond the .scope of his authority. Since the litigation process is a traumatic one, such claims could have an inhibiting effect on judicial officials, even if actions against them were groundless.

   Example: In an ex-parte proceeding, petitioner seeks a court order directing that Plaintiff, her fifteen year old daughter, be sterilized. Defendant, the judge before whom the proceeding is brought, grants the request without investigating the veracity of the petitioner's allegations and without affording Plaintiff an opportunity to be heard. Plaintiff subsequently asserts a claim for damages against Defendant, alleging that state law does not give a judge the power to enter such an order under the circumstances. Defendant raises the defense of judicial immunity.

   Since Defendant was a judge carrying out a judicial function, he is absolutely immune from liability for damage resulting from his act. For this reason, Plaintiff's claim should be dismissed whether or not Defendant was acting beyond the scope of his authority. *Stump v. Sparkman*, 435 U.S. 349 (1978).

2. **Not applicable to non-judicial functions**: ***When a judge acts in a non-judicial capacity, the rule of judicial immunity does not apply***, although the judge may be protected by some other immunity (*e.g.*, executive immunity, *infra*). For this purpose, the United States Supreme Court has defined a judicial act as one normally performed by a judge and consistent with the parties' expectations. (*Stump v. Sparkman*, *supra*).

   Example: As presiding judge of the state court, Defendant has the power to hire and fire court employees. Plaintiff, a court clerk, is fired by Defendant, and subsequently asserts a tort claim for damages resulting from his firing. Defendant raises the defense of judicial immunity.

   Although the termination of employees was a power of the presiding judge, it was not a judicial power, and in exercising it Defendant was not performing a judicial function. For this reason, the rule of judicial immunity does not apply. It is possible, however, that, since she was acting in an executive capacity, Defendant will be protected by a rule of executive immunity. *Shore v. Howard*, 414 F.Supp. 379 (D.C. Tex. 1976).

C. **Legislators**: So long as they are carrying out a legislative function, ***legislators are absolutely immune from tort liability.***

1. **Not applicable to non-legislative functions**: When a legislator acts in a ***non-legislative*** capacity, however, the rule of absolute immunity does not apply.

2. **Definition**: While the legislature is in session, ***anything said by any of its members on the legislative floor*** is part of the legislative function.

   Example 1: During a session of the United States Senate, Defendant, a senator, states on the Senate floor that Plaintiff fleeced the government by obtaining a financial grant for a purpose which was not worthwhile. Plaintiff asserts a defamation claim, to which Defendant raises the defense of legislative privilege. Plaintiff argues that Defendant's remarks were not privileged because Defendant was not discussing pending legislation when he made them.

   Any issue which would require the court to interfere with the workings of a co-equal branch of government is a "non-justiciable political question" and will not be entertained by the court. Since the Plaintiff's argument would require the court to determine which discussions on the floor of the Senate are relevant to pending legislation and which are not, it probably raises a "non justiciable political question" and should be dismissed. *Hutchinson v. Proxmire*, 443 U.S. 111 (1979).

Example 2: In the previous Example, assume that later in the day, while the Senate is not in session, Defendant presents newspaper reporters with a transcript of the remarks which he made about Plaintiff. Plaintiff asserts a defamation claim to which Defendant raises the defense of legislative immunity.

Since the publication which Defendant made to newspaper reporters occurred outside the Senate chamber and when the legislature was not in session, it was not part of Defendant's legislative function and, therefore, was not privileged. *Hutchinson v. Proxmire, supra.*

D. **Executive immunity**: In most jurisdictions, the ***immunity afforded to executive officials depends on whether the acts they are performing are classified as discretionary or ministerial.***

1. **Discretionary acts**: An act is discretionary if the officer is required to use his judgment in deciding whether or not to perform it. For discretionary acts, most jurisdictions apply a rule of ***qualified immunity, protecting the official from liability only if his act was performed in good faith and without malice.***
2. **Ministerial acts**: Any act which is not discretionary is classified as ***ministerial***. In most jurisdictions, an executive official is ***not immune from liability for ministerial acts.***

TABLE OF CASES

SUBJECT MATTER INDEX

Products for 2000-2001 Academic Year

emanuel®

Emanuel Law Outlines

Steve Emanuel's Outlines have been the most popular in the country for years. Over twenty years of graduates swear by them. In the 1998–99 school year, law students bought an average of 3.0 Emanuels each – that's 130,000 Emanuels.

Civil Procedure ◆	$19.95
Constitutional Law	23.95
Contracts ◆	18.95
Corporations	19.95
Criminal Law ◆	16.95
Criminal Procedure	16.95
Evidence	18.95
Property ◆	18.95
Secured Transactions	15.95
Torts (General Ed.) ◆	18.95
Torts (Prosser Casebook Ed.) Keyed to '94 Ed. Prosser, Wade & Schwartz	18.95

***Special Offer...*First Year Set**
All outlines marked ◆ *plus* Steve Emanuel's 1st Year Q & A's *plus* Strategies & Tactics for the First Year Law Student. Everything you need to make it through your first year. $102.50

The Professor Series

All titles in these series are written by leading law professors. Each follows the Emanuel style and format. Each has big, easy-to-read type; extensive citations and notes; and clear, crisp writing. Most have capsule summaries and sample exam Q & A's.

Agency & Partnership	$16.95
Bankruptcy	16.95
Environmental Law	16.95
Family Law	16.95
Federal Income Taxation	16.95
Intellectual Property	18.95
International Law	17.95
Labor Law	16.95
Negotiable Instruments & Payment Systems	15.95
Professional Responsibility	18.95
Property	18.95
Torts	14.95
Wills & Trusts	16.95

Emanuel Law Tapes

Steve Emanuel's audio tapes on Constitutional Law.

11 tapes *$34.95*

Lazar Emanuel's *Latin for Lawyers*
A complete glossary and dictionary to help you wade through the complex terminology of the law.

New title *$15.95*

Question & Answer Collections

Siegel's Essay & Multiple–Choice Q & A's

Each book contains 20 to 25 essay questions with model answers, plus 90 to 110 Multistate-style multiple-choice Q & A's. The objective is to acquaint the student with the techniques needed to handle law school exams successfully. Titles are:

Civil Procedure ◆
Constitutional Law
Contracts ◆
Corporations
Criminal Law ◆
Criminal Procedure
Evidence
Professional Responsibility
Property ◆
Torts ◆
Wills & Trusts

Each title *$15.95*

Siegel's First Year Set - All titles marked ◆

$79.95 if purchased individually *$59.95*

The Finz Multistate Method

967 MBE (Multistate Bar Exam)–style multiple choice questions and answers for all six Multistate subjects, each with detailed answers – *plus* a complete 200 question practice exam modeled on the MBE. Perfect for law school and ***bar exam*** review.

$33.95

Steve Emanuel's First Year Q&A's

1,144 objective–style short-answer questions with detailed answers, in first year subjects. A single volume covers Civil Procedure, Contracts, Criminal Law, Criminal Procedure, Property, and Torts.

$19.95

For any titles not available at your local bookstore, call us at 1-800-EMANUEL or order on-line at **http://www.emanuel.com**.
Visa, MasterCard, American Express, and Discover accepted.